# CHINA

## Understanding Its Past

Eileen H. Tamura
Linda K. Menton
Noren W. Lush
Francis K. C. Tsui
with Warren Cohen

Curriculum Research & Development Group
University of Hawai'i
and
University of Hawai'i Press
Honolulu

© 1997 University of Hawai'i Press
and Curriculum Research & Development Group, University of Hawai'i
All rights reserved
Printed in the United States of America

10  09  08  07  06  05      7  6  5  4  3  2

**Library of Congress Cataloging-in-Publication Data**
China : understanding its past / Eileen Tamura ... [et al.].
    p. cm.
    Includes bibliographical references and index.
    ISBN 0–8248–1923–3
    1. China—Civilization.   2. China—History.   3. Communism—China.
I. Tamura, Eileen.
DS721.C4888   1997
951—dc21                                                        97–2545
                                                                  CIP

The contents of this book were developed partly under a grant from the U.S. Department of Education. However, these contents do not necessarily represent the policy of the Department of Education, and you should not assume endorsement by the Federal Government.

University of Hawai'i Press books are printed on acid-free paper and meet the guidelines for permanence and durability of the Council on Library Resources.

Send content inquiries to
Curriculum Research & Development Group
University of Hawai'i
1776 University Avenue
Honolulu, HI  96822

# *Authors*

*Eileen H. Tamura*, Ph.D., is the director of history and social studies projects at the Curriculum Research & Development Group, University of Hawai'i. She co-authored *A History of Hawai'i*, a standard textbook used in Hawai'i high schools. She is the author of *Americanization, Acculturation, and Ethnic Identity: The Nisei Generation in Hawaii*, University of Illinois Press, 1994, and of articles in *Social Education, The Social Studies, Pacific Historical Review, Journal of American Ethnic History*, and *History of Education Quarterly*.

*Linda K. Menton*, Ph.D., is an associate professor of education at the Curriculum Research & Development Group, University of Hawai'i. She is the co-director of the Curriculum on Asian and Pacific History Project that developed *China: Understanding Its Past*. She co-authored *A History of Hawai'i*, a standard textbook used in Hawai'i high schools. Dr. Menton's work has been published in *The History Teacher, Teaching History, History of Education Quarterly*, and *Pacific Educational Research Journal*.

*Noren W. Lush*, M.A., is a social studies teacher and curriculum developer at the Curriculum Research & Development Group, University of Hawai'i. His master's degree is in history, with a concentration in East Asia. Mr. Lush taught English to university students for five years at Yonsei University, Seoul, and served as on-air interpreter for a nationally broadcast television program, "Let's Learn Korean." He has taught history for many years at the secondary and college levels.

*Francis K. C. Tsui*, M.A., is a researcher and curriculum developer at the Curriculum Research & Development Group. He is a doctoral candidate in history at the University of Hawai'i, concentrating in ancient Chinese history and modern Chinese intellectual history. A graduate of the University of Hong Kong, Mr. Tsui reads and writes Chinese and speaks both Mandarin (Putonghua) and Cantonese.

*Warren Cohen*, M.A., is a social studies teacher and curriculum developer at the Curriculum Research & Development Group, University of Hawai'i. His master's degree is in philosophy. His book *Ethics in Thought and Action: Social and Professional Perspectives*, published by Ardsley House in 1995, includes selections from the *Dao de Jing* by Lao Zi.

*Curriculum Research & Development Group Production Team*
Director of the Curriculum Research & Development Group: Arthur R. King, Jr.
Manuscript Editor: Edith K. Kleinjans
Book Design: Wayne M. Shishido
Cover Design: Darrell T. Asato
Photo Collection: Simon Chiu, Haiyen Huang
Manuscript Production: Alice Santiago, Nora Seager, Jonathan Z. Wang, Byron Inouye, Kim Chang, Jen McKeon, Mary Monkoski–Takamure

*University of Hawai'i Press Production and Distribution Team*
Book Editor and Director of the University of Hawai'i Press: William H. Hamilton
Production Editor: Lucille C. Aono
Marketing Manager: Colins A. Kawai
Direct Mail Manager: Stephanie W. Y. Chun
Business Manager: Kay Y. Kimura

Cover: Dragon robe from the Qing Dynasty (1644–1911). Courtesy of Palace Museum, Beijing, People's Republic of China.

# *Consultants*

## *Content Specialists*

**Roger T. Ames,** Professor of Philosophy and Asian Studies, University of Hawai'i

**Paul A. Cohen,** Professor of History, Wellesley College

**Charlotte Furth,** Professor of Chinese History, University of Southern California

**Daniel W. Y. Kwok,** Professor of Chinese History, University of Hawai'i

**Michael Luk,** Senior Lecturer in History, Hong Kong Institute of Education

**William H. McNeill,** Emeritus Professor of History, University of Chicago

**Alvin Y. C. So,** Professor of Sociology, University of Hawai'i

**Wei-Ming Tu,** Professor of Chinese Philosophy, Harvard University

**Stephen Uhalley, Jr.,** Emeritus Professor of Chinese History, University of Hawai'i

**Gungwu Wang,** Historian and Vice Chancellor, University of Hong Kong

**William M. Zanella,** Professor of History, Hawaii Pacific University

## *Teacher Reviewers*

**Anne Bright,** The Friends' School, Hobart, Tasmania, Australia

**June Ching,** Aiea High School, Aiea, Hawai'i

**Kathy Ellwin,** Kailua High School, Kailua, Hawai'i

**Haunani Kauahi,** Kailua High School, Kailua, Hawai'i

**Ronald Kishimoto,** McKinley High School, Honolulu, Hawai'i

**Noren W. Lush,** University of Hawai'i Laboratory School, Honolulu, Hawai'i

**Rhonda Nagao,** Castle High School, Kaneohe, Hawai'i

**Robert Whiteley,** Campbell High School, Ewa Beach, Hawai'i

# *Contents*

# Maps

# Tables and Graphs

# *To the Reader*

What did it mean to be a daughter in imperial China? How did extraterritoriality affect China's ability to cope with foreigners in the nineteenth century? What was at stake as the Communists and the Guomingdang (Nationalists) fought a civil war to win the allegiance of China's people? This innovative textbook uses role-playing, simulations, debates, primary documents, first-person accounts, excerpts from literary works, and cooperative learning activities to explore these and other key aspects of China's history and culture. A glossary lists important words used throughout the text.

A **compact disc** entitled *China: Understanding Its Past, Musical Selections* is also available. It contains Chinese songs of different periods and locales. Liner notes include English translations of lyrics and other information about each selection.

# Chinese Names

In China, Japan, and Korea, surnames commonly come first in both speaking and writing. For example, in the name Sun Yat-sen, Sun is the surname, or family name, and Yat-sen is the given name. This book uses the Chinese method for Chinese names. Sun Yat-sen became provisional president of the Republic of China. His title then was President Sun. Mao Zedong as leader of the Communist Party was referred to as Chairman Mao.

# Romanization and Pronunciation of Chinese Words

The People's Republic of China adopted the *pinyin* romanization system in the 1950s. It has become the system commonly used in scholarship and journalism, largely replacing the older Wade–Giles system. For the most part, Western letters in the *pinyin* system indicate English sounds that are similar to Chinese sounds—with a few notable exceptions represented by the letters **q** and **x.**

| Pinyin | Pronunciation |
|---|---|
| **q** | ch |
| **x** | sh |

| *Pinyin* spelling | Pronunciation |
|---|---|
| Qin | chin |
| Xin | shin |

Another important rule applies to the letter **a**, always pronounced as ah.

| | |
|---|---|
| Tang | tahng |

For some names this book uses the Wade–Giles system because the older spelling is widely recognized in the West. For example, we use Chiang Kai-shek instead of Jiang Jieshi.

Although the book generally uses the *pinyin* system, students should also familiarize themselves with the Wade–Giles spellings of the names of important historical figures, places, and dynasties. Many important works on China use Wade–Giles, as does the government of Taiwan.

The following table shows *pinyin* spellings and pronunciations for Chinese words in this book. Words in excerpted materials are shown as they appear in their original source, spelled phonetically or in the Wade–Giles system.

| **Pinyin** | **Pronunciation** | **Wade–Giles or other** |
|---|---|---|
| Anhui | ahn hway | Anhwei |
| Aomen | ow mun | Macao |
| Beijing | beh jing | Peking |
| Beiping | beh ping | Peiping |
| Changan | chahng ahn | Ch'angan |
| Changsha | chahng sha | Changsha |
| Chengdu | chehng doo | Ch'engtu |
| Chongqing | chohng ching | Ch'ungking |
| Cixi | tz she | Tz'u-hsi |

| Pinyin | Pronunciation | Wade–Giles or other |
|---|---|---|
| dao | dao | tao |
| Daoguang | dao gwahng | Tao Kuang |
| Deng Xiaoping | duhng shou ping | Teng Hsiao-p'ing |
| Duan Qirui | doo-ahn cheeruey | Tuan Ch'i-jui |
| Feng Yang | fuhng yahng | Feng Yang |
| Feng Yuxiang | fuhng yu she-ahng | Feng Yu-hsiang |
| Fuzhou | foo jo | Fuchou (Fuchow) |
| Fuzi | foo zuh | Fu-tzu |
| Guang Xu | gwahng shoo | Kuang Hsu |
| Guangdong | gwahng dohng | Kwangtung |
| Guangzhou | gwahng jo | Canton |
| Guomindang (GMD) | guo min dahng | Kuomintang (KMT) |
| Han | hahn | Han |
| Hangzhou | hahng jo | Hangchou |
| Harebin | hahr bin | Harbin |
| Hong Xiuquan | hohng shiu chwan | Hung Hsiu-ch'uan |
| Hua Guofeng | hwa guo fuhng | Hua Kuo-feng |
| Huang he | hwahng huh | Huang Ho |
| Huang Xiang | hwahng she-ahng | |
| Huangpu | hwahng poo | Whampoa |
| Hubei | hoo bay | Hupeh |
| kang | kahng | k'ang |
| Jiang Jieshi | jee-ahng jehshur | Chiang Kai-shek |
| Jiang Qing | jee-ahng ching | Chiang Ch'ing |
| Jiangxi | jee-ahng she | Kiangsi |
| Kang Youwei | kahng yoo way | K'ang Yu-wei |
| Kong | kohng | K'ung |
| Kongfuzi (Confucius) | kohng foo zuh | K'ung Fu-tzu |
| Kongzi | kohng zuh | K'ungtzu |
| koutou | koh toh | k'ou t'ou |
| Lang Shining | lohng shur ning | Lang shih-ning |
| Laozi | lao zuh | Lao-tse |
| Li Matou | lee mah toh | Li Ma-t'ou |
| Li Mi | lee mee | |
| Lian Heng | lee-ehn huhng | Lian Heng |
| Liang Qichao | lee-ahng chee chow | Liang Ch'i-ch'ao |
| Lin Zexu | lin zeh shoo | Lin Tse-hsu |
| Liu Shaoqi | liu shao chee | Liu Shao-ch'i |
| Lun Yu | loon yoo | Lun Yu |
| manyi | mahn yee | man-i |
| Manchuguo | mahn joo guo | Manch'ukuo |
| Mao Zedong | mao zeh dohng | Mao Tse-tung |
| Miao | mee ow | Miao |
| Ming | ming | Ming |
| mou | moo | mou |
| Nanjing | nahn jing | Nanking |
| Nien | nee ehn | Nien |
| Ningbo | ning bo | Ningpo |
| Peng Dehuai | puhng duh why | P'eng Te-huai |
| Pu Songling | poo sohng ling | P'u Sung-ling |

| *Pinyin* | Pronunciation | Wade–Giles or other |
|---|---|---|
| putonghua | poo toong hwa | |
| Puyi | poo yee | P'u-i |
| Qianlong | chien lohng | Ch'ien-lung |
| Qin | chin | Ch'in |
| Qing | ching | Ch'ing |
| Qishan | chee shahn | Ch'i Shan |
| Qufu | choo foo | Ch'ufu |
| Sha'anxi | shahn shee | Shensi |
| Shandong | shahn dohng | Shantung |
| Shang | shahng | Shang |
| Shanghai | shahng high | Shanghai |
| Shenzhen | shen jehn | Shencheng |
| Shi Huangdi | suh hwahng dee | Shih huang-ti |
| Sichuan | sz-chuan | Szechwan |
| Song | soong | Sung |
| Sui | sway | Sui |
| Sun Yixian | shoon yee she-ahn | Sun Yat-sen |
| Taibei | tie bay | Taipei |
| Tang | tahng | T'ang |
| Tianjin | tien jin | Tientsin |
| Tongmenhui | tohng mun hway | T'ung-men-hui |
| Wangxia | wahng she-ah | Wanghsia |
| Wenhuibao | wun hway bao | Wen Wei P'o |
| Xi'an | she ahn | Sian |
| Xiamen | she-ah mun | Amoy |
| Xiao Jing | shiao jing | |
| Xin | shin | Hsin |
| Xinjiang | shin jahng | Sinkiang |
| Xiongnu | she-ong noo | Hsiung-nu |
| yamen | yah mun | yamen |
| Yan'an | yehn ahn | Yenan |
| Yang Menzhong | yahng mun johng | Yang Meng-chung |
| Yang Xiang | yahng she-ahng | |
| Yangzi | yahng zeh | Yangtse |
| Yannan | yahn ahn | Yannan |
| Yanti | yahn tee | Ch'efu (Chefoo) |
| Yuan | yu-ahn | Yuan |
| Yao | yah-oh | Yao |
| Yuan Shikai | yu-ahn shur kie | Yuan Shih-k'ai |
| Yunnan | yoon nahn | Yunnan |
| Zhao Ziyang | jao zuh yahng | Chao Tzu-yang |
| Zhang Zhoulin | chahng jo lin | Chang Tso-lin |
| Zheng He | chuhng huh | Cheng-ho |
| Zhengjiang | chuhng jee-ahng | Chinkiang |
| Zhongguo | zhong guo | Chungkuo |
| Zhou | jo | Cho |
| Zhou Enlai | jo ehn lie | Chou En-lai |
| Zhou Xun | jo shoon | Cho Hsun |

*Chapter*

# 1

# The Family, State, and Society in Imperial China

**600 B.C.E. to A.D. 1900**

This chapter introduces us to imperial China, a period of over two thousand years, when emperors ruled. During imperial times the family was a microcosm of Chinese society, where the patriarch—the male head of the household—ruled the family as the emperor ruled China. We examine the roles of sons and daughters in traditional Chinese society, learn what was expected of them, and consider their relationship to their parents. We then investigate what the great thinker Confucius said about family relationships and other relationships between people.

Although somewhat isolated during the imperial period, China did have contact with the outside world. Traders, invaders, and visitors all influenced the course of China's history. And so did the seafaring Chinese, who sailed their ships northward, southward, and westward to trade, explore, and establish ties between distant lands and their own country.

*The dragon was the symbol of imperial authority.*
*From Joseph D'Addetta,* Treasury of Chinese Design Motifs. New York: Dover Publications, 1945, *p. 35. Courtesy of Dover Publications.*

**Sections**
1. Daughters
2. Sons
3. Parents and Children
4. Foundations of Chinese Thinking
5. China and the Outside World

2

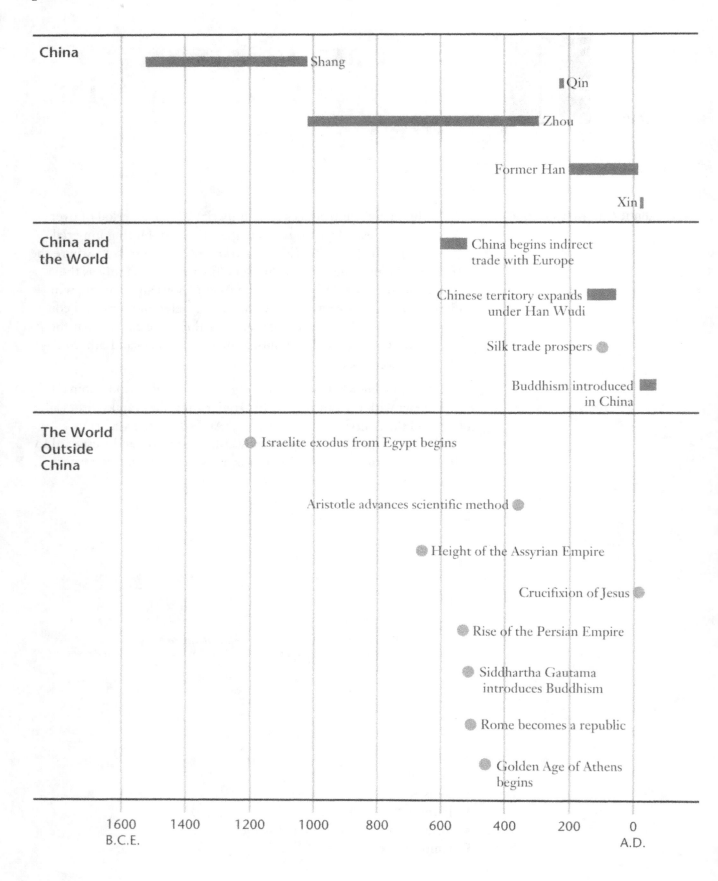

China

Shang

Qin

Zhou

Former Han

Xin

China and
the World

China begins indirect
trade with Europe

Chinese territory expands
under Han Wudi

Silk trade prospers

Buddhism introduced
in China

The World
Outside
China

Israelite exodus from Egypt begins

Aristotle advances scientific method

Height of the Assyrian Empire

Crucifixion of Jesus

Rise of the Persian Empire

Siddhartha Gautama
introduces Buddhism

Rome becomes a republic

Golden Age of Athens
begins

1600
B.C.E.

1400

1200

1000

800

600

400

200

0
A.D.

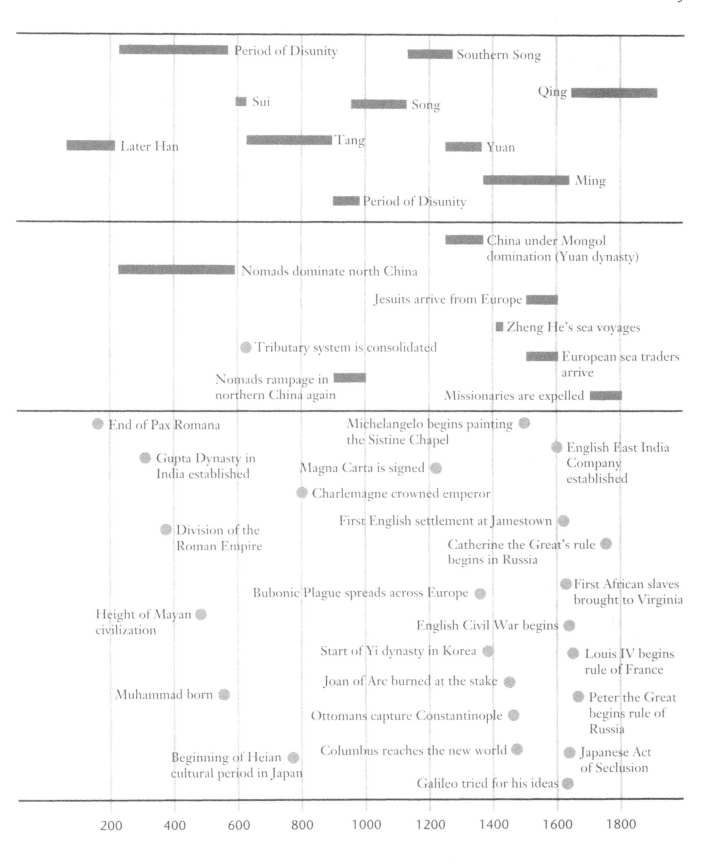

Period of Disunity

Southern Song

Sui

Song

Qing

Later Han

Tang

Yuan

Ming

Period of Disunity

China under Mongol domination (Yuan dynasty)

Nomads dominate north China

Jesuits arrive from Europe

Zheng He's sea voyages

Tributary system is consolidated

European sea traders arrive

Nomads rampage in northern China again

Missionaries are expelled

End of Pax Romana

Michelangelo begins painting the Sistine Chapel

English East India Company established

Gupta Dynasty in India established

Magna Carta is signed

Charlemagne crowned emperor

Division of the Roman Empire

First English settlement at Jamestown

Catherine the Great's rule begins in Russia

Bubonic Plague spreads across Europe

First African slaves brought to Virginia

Height of Mayan civilization

English Civil War begins

Start of Yi dynasty in Korea

Louis IV begins rule of France

Joan of Arc burned at the stake

Muhammad born

Peter the Great begins rule of Russia

Ottomans capture Constantinople

Beginning of Heian cultural period in Japan

Columbus reaches the new world

Japanese Act of Seclusion

Galileo tried for his ideas

200    400    600    800    1000    1200    1400    1600    1800

# 1 Daughters

*The stories in this section on daughters reveal ideas that Chinese families held for centuries about the place of girls and women in families and in society. Before you read the stories, you will share your own ideas of family life and the roles of family members.*

---

### Activity: Pairing Off

Consider the questions below and write your responses.

Your teacher will then divide the class into pairs. Discuss your responses with your partner. If you agree with a comment your partner makes, add it to your responses. If you disagree, tell your partner why. You may modify your responses after discussing them.

Share your responses with the class. Keep your responses; you will need them later.

1. What are the characteristics of an ideal daughter? Of an ideal son? Do you expect sons and daughters to behave differently and to receive different amounts of schooling? Explain.
2. Who will find you a marriage partner? Is that method a good one? Why or why not?
3. What qualities make a good husband? A good wife?
4. What should people do if they find they have a bad marriage? Why?
5. What are the characteristics of an ideal parent?
6. In issues of schooling, selecting a career, and choosing or divorcing a mate, are your own needs and desires or your family's more important? Explain.

---

### Reading: *The Story of Little Tiger*

This story—told to Ida Pruitt, an American who grew up in China—gives us a peephole into the life of a moderately well-off family in imperial China. Although Little Tiger was born in the 1860s, her story could almost be an account of life during the 1200s. As you read the story, compare Little Tiger's life with your own.

When I was three or four years old we moved to the Chou Wang Temple neighborhood. . . .

The house was convenient to the garden where my father worked part of the time. It was also convenient for my mother and my aunt to see the plays on the open stage across the street. My father was very strict and would not let them out to see the plays. My mother and my aunt took

benches and stood on them so they could look out the high north windows.

I was a difficult child to manage. I liked to play too much. I played with my brother and sister and the children of the neighbors. We played on the streets and in the garden next door.

I climbed trees, and hanging by the rope from the windlass I would let myself down into the well. I would put my toes into the cracks between the bricks that lined it. My mother didn't know this. She would have been frightened had she known. There was nothing that I did not dare to do. I was the baby and my parents favored me.

They did not begin to bind my feet until I was seven because I loved so much to run and play. Then I became very ill and they had to take the bindings off my feet again. I had the "heavenly blossoms"[1] and was ill for two years and my face is very pockmarked. In my childhood everyone had the illness and few escaped some marking.

When I was nine they started to bind my feet again and they had to draw the bindings tighter than usual. My feet hurt so much that for two years I had to crawl on my hands and knees. Sometimes at night they hurt so much I could not sleep. I stuck my feet under my mother and she lay on them so they hurt less and I could sleep. But by the time I was eleven my feet did not hurt and by the time I was thirteen they were finished. The toes were turned under so that I could see them on the inner and under side of the foot. They had come up around. Two fingers could be inserted in the cleft between the front of the boot and the heel. My feet were very small indeed.

A girl's beauty and desirability were counted more by the size of her feet than by the beauty of her face. Matchmakers were not asked "Is she beautiful?" but "How small are her feet?" A plain face is given by heaven but poorly bound feet is a sign of laziness.

My feet were very small indeed. Not like they are now. When I worked so hard and was on my feet all day I slept with the bandages off because my feet ached, and so they spread.

When I was eleven we moved into a house in the corner garden. The wall between the house and the rest of the garden was low. I was a very mischievous child. When I was naughty and my mother wanted to beat me I would run and jump over the wall and she could not catch me.

One day we wanted to go out to play, a neighbor's little girl and I. My mother said that we could go when I had finished grinding the corn. The neighbor's child said she would help me so that we would finish sooner. We ran round and round the mill, but to grind so much corn takes time. We were impatient, so while she ground I took handfuls of the corn and buried them under the refuse in the mill house, a handful here under some dust and a handful there under some donkey droppings. Then we told my mother that we were

through. She came and saw that the hopper was empty. But the chickens did not give us face.[2] They scratched here and a pile of corn showed. They scratched there and another pile showed. My mother scolded us. "You naughty, mischievous children." She started after us to beat me, but we ran and jumped over the wall and climbed into a pear tree in the garden. By this time there were several of us. My mother came to the foot of the tree and called but I would not come down. . . .

Seeing that my sister had so much trouble with a young husband, my father and mother said that I should be married to an older man who would cherish me. When the matchmaker told of such a one and that he had no mother—she was dead—my parents thought they had done well for me. I was to have an older husband to cherish me, but not too old, and no mother-in-law to scold and abuse me.

Our neighbor, the man who carted away the night soil,[3] made the match for me. He was a professional matchmaker. He did not care how a marriage turned out. He had used the money. As the old people say, "A matchmaker does not live a lifetime with the people he brings together." The matchmaker hid four years of my husband's age from us, saying that the man was only ten years older than I. But he was fourteen years older. I was twelve when the match was made, and I became engaged—a childhood match. I still had my hair in a plait [braid]. I did not know anything. I was fifteen when I was married.

They told me that I was to be a bride. I had seen weddings going down the street. I had seen brides sitting on the *k'angs* on the wedding days when all went in to see them. To be married was to wear pretty clothes and ornaments in the hair.

I sat on the *k'ang*, bathed and dressed, in my red underclothes and red stockings. The music sounded and they took me off the *k'ang*. I sat on the chair and the matrons combed my hair for me into the matron's knot at the nape of my neck. They dressed me in my red embroidered bridal robes and the red embroidered bridal shoes and put the ornaments in my hair. An old man whose parents and wife were still alive carried me out and

---

[1] "Heavenly blossoms" refers to smallpox. The Chinese referred to smallpox as *thien hua*, "flowers of heaven," because the erupting sores looked like flowering plants.

[2] give us face: an expression that means to make us look good. To lose face is to be shamed or embarrassed.

[3] night soil: human feces used as fertilizer.

*A bridal procession. Reproduction by permission of Urban Council Hong Kong from the collection of Hong Kong Museum of Art.*

put me in the wedding chair that was to carry me to my new home. I knew only that I must not touch the sides of the chair as he put me in, and that I was dressed in beautiful clothes. I was a child, only fifteen by our count, and my birthday was small—just before New Year. We count ourselves a year old when we are born and we all add a year at the New Year. I was counted two years old when I was a month old, for I was born near the end of the old year. I was a child. I had not yet passed my thirteenth birthday.

I was frightened. I was homesick. . . .

The musicians in their green uniforms and red tasseled hats sat by the table in the court. There were those who played on the bamboo reed flutes and those who played on wooden horns. At times the cymbals clashed. But during the ceremony of clothing the bride and while the groom, who had come to fetch the bride, drank in another room with the men of the bride's family, it was the flute that sounded. By the different motifs played those who passed by in the street or stopped to watch knew which part of the ceremony was in progress.

The table where the musicians sat and drank tea and played at intervals was next to the gate. It was time for the groom to take the bride home.

The musicians stood and played. The wooden horns joined the flutes. The cymbals clashed. The drums boomed. The groom came out of the house door. He was clothed in hired bridal robes, patterned like those of a mandarin's full dress. Once or twice at least in a lifetime every man and woman is equal to the highest in the land. When they are married and when they are buried they are clothed in the garments of nobility.

The father and the brother and the uncle of the bride escorted the groom. They bowed him to his chair. Then the red sedan chair of the bride was brought to the gate and placed against the gateway. The gateway was too small to allow the chair to enter the court as would be done in great households. All cracks between the chair and the gate were covered with pieces of red felt held by the chairmen to make sure that no evil spirit should enter. A long note of the horn was sounded and the bride was carried out kneeling on the arms of an old man. He was a neighbor, a carpenter who was no longer working but was spending the last years of his life in pleasant social pursuits. He was also a doctor—not the kind who had many honorary boards hanging outside his walls telling in poetic allusion of his healing powers, but a

*The bride and groom meet at the marriage ceremony of a couple of humble means. Watercolor. Reproduction by permission of Urban Council Hong Kong from the collection of Hong Kong Museum of Art.*

homely man who knew what to tell the mothers when their children's bellies ached, and how to keep their faces from scarring when the children broke out with smallpox, and how to break a fever when the inner fires got too hot. He was also a manager for weddings and funerals, and he was peacemaker for the neighborhood. Long days he would sit squatted on his heels in the lee of a sunny wall and listen to all sides of any quarrels. He was what was known as a whole man. Destiny had been kind to him. His father and mother still ate and slept in his house and not in the small brick vault he had prepared for them deep in the steepest slope of his wheat field. His wife, his old partner, was the one with whom he had started forty years ago as a boy of sixteen. He had sons and grandsons. Therefore at wedding ceremonies he was much sought after to bring good luck to the new

*A wealthy couple in a marriage ceremony in the 1800s. Compare the more ornate altar and richly embroidered silk clothes with those of the couple of humble means. Watercolor. Reproduction by permission of Urban Council Hong Kong from the collection of Hong Kong Museum of Art.*

couples. Dressed in his ceremonial black coat he carried the red-robed bride to the chair. She knelt on his arms and her head, heavy with ornaments, dropped over his shoulder. She was a bow of red arched over a bow of black. He sat her on the broad low seat of the sedan chair.

Matrons whose husbands were alive patted the bride's garments into place as she folded her arms and legs. They dropped the red curtain before her. The gong sounded and the bearers seized the chair. They ran the poles through the loops and lifted the chair to their shoulders. The procession started, and as both families were poor, it was not a long one. . . .

The bearers strutted as they walked, mincing in their gait, with one arm akimbo and the other swinging, for they carried a virgin bride and she was sitting in an official chair, wearing robes, though rented, patterned after the great. . . .

Outside the city the procession veered to the east and followed the cart track along the city wall. It crossed the wheat fields and went toward the sea and a village lying low and gray on the rocks of a small promontory.

It was a village of fishermen and the groom owned one of the fishing boats. He was also a farmer. He owned twenty *mou* of the wheatland that lay near the village. It was the family village of the Ning clan. All in the village were of this one clan. . . .

When I got to my new home and the wedding guests had left I found that there was a woman living in the house, a cousin's wife. She had lived there for many years and had borne a son to my husband. We all slept on one *k'ang,* the four of us. I was such a child that I told her I was glad she was there for I was frightened. Her husband had been gone many years and none knew whether he was alive or dead. She had an older son who had also gone to Manchuria. His name was Fulai, "May Fortune Come." This little boy's name was Fats'ai, "May Wealth Come." She lived with us for more than two years.

My husband's father was also with us. . . . When he was young he had been a servant in one of the yamen of the city.

I was but a child. We played games, the village children, Fats'ai, and I. We played knucklebones, hunting the tiger (hide and seek), kicking the shuttlecock, and coin throwing. . . .

*A bride and groom, circa 1870. Poorer couples like this one rented their bridal clothes. The bride's dress was usually red. Courtesy of Hong Kong Museum of History, Urban Council.*

As was the custom, I went home every month to see my mother. But because my husband smoked opium and did not bring home food, I stayed longer with my mother than was the custom. Half of every month I stayed with my husband and half of every month I went home to my mother. My brother came with our neighbor's white horse or a borrowed donkey and took me home.

When I left home to go back to my husband's village I would not let my mother see me cry. I went to the latrine and wiped my eyes. Then I waited until I had turned the corner of the street before I cried again. That was because my older sister always cried and screamed when she had to go back to her mother-in-law. And so my father would scold her.

"What can we do?" he would say. "What is done is done. What good to make such an ado?" So I was always careful not to let them see me weep. My sister's husband was good and brought them money, but her mother-in-law was cruel. I had no mother-in-law but my husband did not bring in money.

When I left my mother she always sat with her face set and her eyes wide open. She did not smile

## Rainfall, Crops, and Livestock

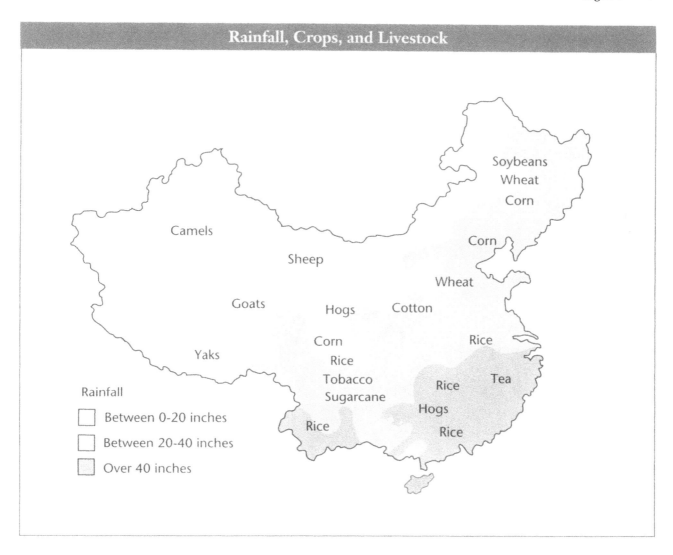

Camels

Sheep

Goats

Yaks

Hogs

Cotton

Corn
Rice
Tobacco
Sugarcane

Rice

Soybeans
Wheat
Corn

Corn

Wheat

Rice

Rice

Hogs

Tea

Rice

Rainfall

☐ Between 0-20 inches

☐ Between 20-40 inches

☐ Over 40 inches

but she did not weep. She held her eyes wide open and her face firm to keep from weeping.

I know now that there is no need to be angry with my parents for my marriage. They did the best they could for me. They thought they were getting a good home for me. Now I know that one's destiny is one's destiny. It was so decided for me. . . .

From Ida Pruitt, *A Daughter of Han: The Autobiography of a Chinese Working Woman.* New Haven, CT: Yale University Press, 1945, pp. 20–23, 32–39, 42.

Because marriage in ancient China was a family affair, not a personal one, parents traditionally chose marriage mates for their children. Marriage served several social functions. Sons born to a couple carried the husband's family name, thus continuing the family line, vitally important in Chinese society. A Chinese proverb states, "Rear a child for your old age; save up grain for a famine."[4] Raising children (especially sons) was a way of insuring comfort in old age, since sons, usually the eldest, were responsible for caring for elderly parents and providing proper rites upon their deaths. Another proverb says, "Bamboo door matches bamboo door; wooden door matches wooden door." Marriage united two families of similar economic and social status. Hence marriage tended to keep people at the same social and economic level they were born into.

[4] John T. S. Chen, *1001 Chinese Sayings.* Hong Kong: Chung Chi College, 1973, p. 138.

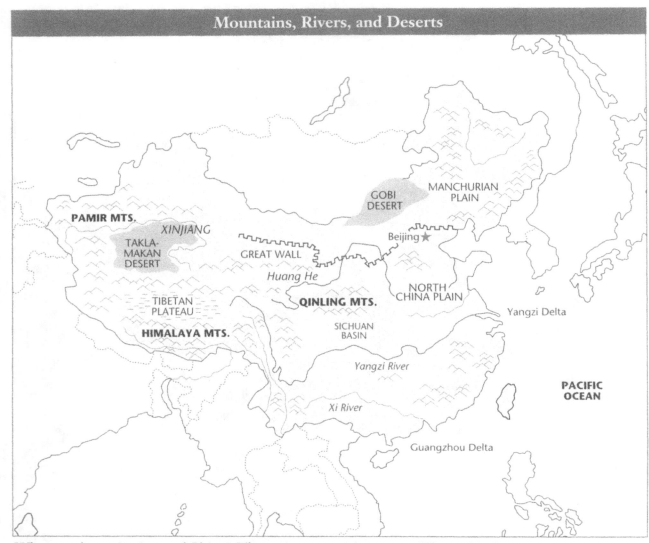

## Mountains, Rivers, and Deserts

What are the main rivers of China? The major mountain ranges? The major deserts?

## Questions

1. Little Tiger's family did not lead a lavish life as did wealthier families, and though she lived comfortably, Little Tiger had to help with household chores. How did she spend her days as a youngster?

2. What in the story tells you about the roles of husband and wife in a Chinese family?

3. How old was Little Tiger when she became engaged? When she was married? As a bride what was her feeling about marriage?

4. Was Little Tiger's husband a good provider? Explain. What was Little Tiger's way of coping with her unhappy marriage?

5. As with families in imperial China, patriarchs headed families in pre-modern Europe. Marriage decisions there, too, usually involved the consent of parents, who judged unions by economic, religious, and kinship criteria. Love had little or no place in such thinking; family interests were more important. Describe traditional Chinese marriages; then contrast modern Western marriages with traditional Chinese and European practices.

## China's Geography and Agriculture

China is the largest country in Asia. Its land mass is slightly bigger than that of the United States; of the nations, only Canada is larger than China.

Natural barriers surround China: tropical jungles to the south, the world's highest mountains to the southwest and west, vast deserts to the northwest, and the Pacific Ocean to the east. Only to the north is there an opening. Thus it was from the north that, over the centuries, invaders came. And it was through this opening that China extended its cultural and political domination thousands of miles beyond its border.

China's civilization began along the Huang He, or Yellow River, on the North China plain, an area of fertile soil but undependable rainfall. The Huang He begins on the Tibetan plateau, winds 3,000 miles toward the east, and drains into the Pacific. This silt-thickened river has been both a curse and a blessing to the people of North China. While its frequent floods often devastate the surrounding countryside, they leave behind fertile soil, enabling Chinese farmers to fill the plain with wheat and corn.

Unlike the north, the south of China is a land of hills and abundant rainfall. This region is bordered on the north by the 3,600-mile-long (5,792-kilometer) Yangzi River, China's longest and Asia's mightiest river. Just north of the Yangzi, paralleling its course, is the Qinling mountain range, which forms the climatic divide between north and south.

Every bit of level land in the south is intensively cultivated, and terraces creep up hillsides. Because of the abundant rainfall and sunlight, the area yields two to three crops each year. The region includes the Guangzhou (Canton) and Yangzi deltas and the Sichuan basin, the most productive areas in China. Rice has been the dominant crop there, but farmers have also cultivated tea, cotton, silk, sweet potatoes, tobacco, and sugarcane. Thick forests make lumbering another important industry. In addition, the many rivers and lakes in the south, as well as the irregular coastline of the southeast, have provided the Chinese with an abundance of fish. Because of these resources, South China has maintained a denser and better-nourished population than the north.

Together, North and South China make up China proper, the homeland of the Han people, the original Chinese. In the surrounding areas— the steppes and oases of Mongolia, the deserts of Xinjiang, and the high and rocky Tibetan plateau — minority groups with different lifestyles live alongside the Han. These regions support little or no farming. Where possible, the inhabitants raise livestock.

Except in these regions, China is densely populated. Today its population is four times that of the United States. Farmers have made up 80 percent of the people and continue as they have long ago tilling the soil with industry.

*Terraced rice fields in central China. Courtesy of Longman Group, Ltd., London.*

*Rice fields in the central Yangtze valley. Courtesy of Longman Group, Ltd., London.*

Planting the young rice

Raising water to the field

Preparing to transplant

Reaping

Threshing

Breaking the husks

*The process of cultivating rice. John June, of London, executed the original engravings circa 1760 from Chinese drawings. Courtesy of The Victoria and Albert Museum, London.*

## Peasant Life in China

The excerpt below was written by William Hinton, an American who in 1948 visited Long Bow Village in northern China. Hinton's depiction of peasant life there could well apply to other parts of China from 1200 to 1900.

The crops grew only on what was put into the soil each year; hence manure was the foundation of the whole economy. The chief source of supply was the family privy, and this became, in a sense, the center of the household. Long Bow privies were built in the form of a deep cistern, topped with timber, or stone, and provided with a single narrow slot at ground level for both deposition and extraction. . . .

Animal manure, together with any straw, stalks, or other waste matter, was composted in the yard. So highly was it valued that old people and children constantly combed the roads and cart tracks for droppings which they scooped up and carried home in baskets. This need to conserve every kind of waste and return it to the land was responsible for the tidy appearance of the streets and courtyards even though the walls were crumbling and the roofs falling in. Nothing, absolutely nothing, was left lying around. Even the dust of the streets was swept up and thrown on the compost heap or into the privy, for village dust was more fertile, by far, than the soil in the fields.

In cold weather everyone wore clothes padded with cotton. These made people look twice as big as they really were and provided warmth in two ways, first by the insulation of the thick layer of cotton and second by the lice which made themselves at home in the seams. Since the padded clothes could not be washed without taking the lining out—a major operation— it was almost impossible to get rid of lice from day to day.

Their constant biting and the interminable scratching that accompanied it generated a fair amount of heat. On any warm day in winter a large number of people could always be found sitting in various sunlit corners with their padded jackets across their knees. There they hunted the lice, picked them out, and crushed them expertly between their thumbnails.

Children under five were exposed from below in all weather because their padded clothes were not sewn together at the crotch. The slit, which ran upward from just above the knees to a point a little below the tip of the backbone, was very convenient when nature called but was drafty in winter. It must be said, however, that the children didn't seem to mind at all and ran about in the bitterest weather just as if they were all sewn in like their elders. . . .

The food eaten in Long Bow was very simple. Since maize was the major crop everyone ate corn dumplings, called *keta,* in the morning, and corn meal mush, or noodles made of corn at noon. At night they ate millet porridge with a few noodles in it. After the wheat harvest in July everyone ate noodles for several days, but this was considered quite a luxury and only the most fortunate carried the custom on into August. These same families were the only ones who ate three meals a day throughout the year. Most people cut down to two meals, or even one when winter set in. Thus undernourished they moved about as little as possible and tried to conserve their strength until spring.

In addition to the cereal grains people ate salt turnip all year round, cabbage when they had it, and other vegetables such as eggplant, scallions, chives, and wild herbs in season. But these were simply garnishment to the main dish which was always corn, millet, or wheat. The big problem facing the peasants over the years was not to obtain some variety in their diet, but to find anything to eat at all. . . . Each day that one survived was a day to be thankful for and so, throughout the region, in fat years and in lean, the common greeting came to be not "Hello" or "How are you?" but a simple, heartfelt "Have you eaten?"

From William Hinton, *Fanshen: A Documentary of Revolution in a Chinese Village.* New York: Vintage Books, 1966, pp. 23–25.

## Reading: *Footbinding*

Spread your thumb and forefinger three inches apart and compare the distance with the length of your foot. Three inches was the ideal size of a woman's foot during imperial China. If you recall, Little Tiger had her feet bound when she was nine. The practice of footbinding began in the tenth century and was officially sanctioned until 1902. In the following account a young woman recalls her experiences as a child.

I was inflicted with the pain of footbinding when I was seven years old. I was an active child who liked to jump about, but from then on my free and optimistic nature vanished. . . . Binding started in the second lunar month; mother consulted references in order to select an auspicious day for it. I wept and hid in a neighbor's home, but mother found me, scolded me, and dragged me home. She shut the bedroom door, boiled water, and from a box withdrew binding, shoes, knife, needle, and thread. I begged for a one-day postponement, but mother refused: "Today is a lucky day," she said. "If bound today, your feet will never hurt; if bound tomorrow, they will." She washed and placed alum on my feet and cut the toenails. She then bent my toes toward the [sole] with a binding cloth ten feet long and two inches

*Two women with bound feet sitting next to their maid with normal-sized feet, 19th century. Courtesy Hong Kong Museum of History.*

wide, doing the right foot first and then the left. She finished binding and ordered me to walk, but when I did the pain proved unbearable.

That night, mother wouldn't let me remove the shoes. My feet felt on fire and I couldn't sleep; mother struck me for crying. On the following days, I tried to hide but was forced to walk on my feet. Mother hit me on my hands and feet for resisting. Beatings and curses were my lot for covertly loosening the wrappings. The feet were washed and rebound after three or four days, with alum added. After several months, all toes but the big one were pressed against the inner surface. Whenever I ate fish or freshly killed meat, my feet would swell, and the pus would drip. Mother criticized me for placing pressure on the heel in walking, saying that my feet would never assume a pretty shape. Mother would remove the bindings and wipe the blood and pus which dripped from my feet. She told me that only with removal of the flesh could my feet become slender. If I mistakenly punctured a sore, the blood gushed like a stream.

*A pair of lotus shoes for women with bound feet. Courtesy of Hong Kong Museum of Art.*

My somewhat fleshy big toes were bound with small pieces of cloth and forced upwards, to assume a new moon shape.

Every two weeks, I changed to new shoes. Each new pair was one- to two-tenths of an inch smaller than the previous one. The shoes were unyielding, and it took pressure to get into them. Though I wanted to sit passively by the *k'ang,* Mother forced me to move around. After changing more than ten pairs of shoes, my feet were reduced to a little over four inches. I had been binding for a month when my younger sister started; when no one was around, we would weep together. In summer, my feet smelled offensively because of pus and blood; in winter, my feet felt cold because of lack of circulation and hurt if they got too near the *k'ang* and were struck by warm air currents. Four of the toes were curled in like so many dead caterpillars; no outsider would ever have believed that they belonged to a human being. It took two years to achieve the three-inch model. My toenails pressed against the flesh like thin paper. The heavily creased [sole] couldn't be scratched when it itched or soothed when it ached. . . .

From *Chinese Footbinding.* New York: Bell Publishing Co., 1967, pp. 26–28. Courtesy of Howard S. Levy and Walton Rawls.

Footbinding lasted for centuries in China. It is said to have originated when palace dancers began performing with bound feet on huge carved lotus flowers, from which bound feet came to be called "golden lotuses." The practice spread when the upper class imitated the fashion of the court dancers. As the practice slowly spread throughout China, the binding became so severe that girls and women with bound feet could only hobble about slowly and with difficulty.

In imperial China footbinding symbolized the lower status of women compared to men. Because women with bound feet could not move about easily, they remained at home most of the time. China was a man's society. Women were thought to be intellectually inferior, and staying at home kept them ignorant of the outside world. It also assured husbands that their wives were faithful to them. Female chastity was highly valued in Chinese society; women were

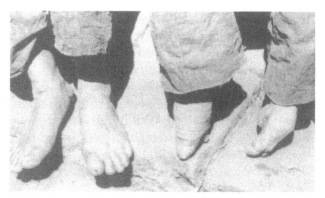

*In binding the foot, the large toe was left unbound while the other toes were forced inward toward the sole. The toes and heel were wrapped forcefully so that they came as close as possible together.*

expected to obey a strict moral code. But men—if they could afford the expense—could take concubines. Most Chinese men, who were peasants, artisans, and small shopkeepers, were too poor and remained monogamous.

Besides ensuring female chastity, "golden lotuses" marked family status. Bound feet showed that a woman belonged to a wealthy family that did not require her to work in the fields or the shop.

The Chinese poet Fü Hsuan noted, "How sad it is to be a woman! Nothing on earth is held so cheap. . . . No one is glad when a girl is born: By *her*, the family sets no store."[5] Parents generally greeted a boy's birth more joyfully than they did a girl's. Peasant families, especially the poorest, could not afford many children. Poor parents sometimes sold their daughters, and female infanticide was common. The birth of a girl caused little joy because she brought few benefits to the family. When a daughter married, usually in her teens, she moved to her husband's home and became part of his family. Sons, not daughters, carried on the family name and took care of aged parents.

After growing numbers of Chinese protested against footbinding, an imperial decree abolished it in 1902. During the last decades of imperial rule, age-old customs were constantly challenged by foreign ideas. Many young Chinese agreed that certain traditional ways should be rejected. The abolition of footbinding was one of the results of

[5] Arthur Waley, *Translations from the Chinese.* New York: Alfred A. Knopf, 1941, p. 72.

growing contact with the outside world. (Even though footbinding was officially abolished in 1902, some women continued to bind their feet well into the twentieth century.)

For more on footbinding and the place of women in China, see these books written for high school students: Marjorie Wall Bingham and Susan Hill Gross, *Women in Traditional China* and *Women in Modern China*, St. Louis Park, MN, Glenhurst Publications, 1980.

## Questions

1. If the mother in the story knew that footbinding was painful, having experienced it herself, why would she subject her daughter to it?
2. Behind each custom is a system of ideas. What beliefs about women does the tradition of footbinding illustrate?

3. Footbinding seems a strange custom, but people in modern societies also change their physical appearance to appear more attractive. What examples can you think of?
4. Many women all over the world today wear shoes with two- or three-inch heels. What similarities do you see between these shoes and the "lotus" shoes of women in imperial China? What differences? Why do women today wear high-heeled shoes? Have you ever worn them? How does walking in high heels differ from walking in jogging or walking shoes?

## Reading: *A Folktale of Love*

This folktale, still renowned in China, has been so popular that it was made into an opera and a movie; a violin concerto based on the story, called "The Butterfly Lovers," has become well known throughout China.

The village of the Liang family and that of the Chu family were close together. The inhabitants were well-to-do and content. Old excellency Liang and old excellency Chu were good friends. A son was born to the Liang family, who was given the name Hsienpo. Being an unusually quick and clever child, he was sent to the school in the town.

At the same time a daughter was born to the Chu family, who, besides being very clever, was particularly beautiful. As a child she loved to read and study, and only needed to glance at a book to know a whole sentence by heart. Old Chu simply doted on her. When she grew up, she wanted to go away and study. Her father tried in vain to dissuade her, but eventually he arranged for her to dress as a boy and study with Hsienpo.

The two lived together, worked together, argued together, and were the best of friends. The

eager and zealous Hsienpo did not notice that Yingt'ai was really a girl, and therefore he did not fall in love with her. Yingt'ai studied so hard and was so wrapped up in her work that her fellow students paid no attention to her. Being very modest, and never taking part in the children's jokes, she exercised a calming influence over even the most impudent. When she slept with Hsienpo, each lay on one side of the bed, and between them stood a bowl of water. They had arranged that whoever knocked over the bowl must pay a fine; but the serious little Hsienpo never touched it.

When Yingt'ai changed her clothes, she never stood about naked but pulled on her clean clothes under the old ones, which she then took off and finished dressing. Her fellow students could not understand why she did this, and asked her the reason. "Only peasants expose the body they have received from their parents," she said; "it should not be done." Then the boys began to copy her, not knowing her real reason was to prevent their noticing that she was a girl.

Then her father died, and her sister-in-law, who did not approve of Yingt'ai's studying, ordered her to come home and learn housework. But Yingt'ai refused and continued to study.

The sister-in-law, fearing that Yingt'ai had fallen in love with Hsienpo, used to send her from time to time babies' things, swaddling clothes, children's clothes and covers, and many other things. The students became curious when they saw the things, and Yingt'ai could tell them only that they were the things she herself had used as a child. . . .

The time passed quickly. Soon Yingt'ai and Hsienpo were grown up. Yingt'ai still dressed as a man, and being a well-brought-up girl, she did not dare to ask Hsienpo to marry her; but when she looked at him, her heart was filled with love. His delicate manner attracted her irresistibly, and she swore to marry him and none other.

She proposed the marriage to her sister-in-law, who did not consider it suitable, because after her father's death they had lost all their money. Against Yingt'ai's will the sister-in-law arranged a match with a Dr. Ma, of a newly rich family in the village. Yingt'ai objected strongly, but she could do nothing about it. Day after day she had to listen to complaints: she was without filial piety, she was a shameless, decadent girl, a disgrace to the family. Her sister-in-law still feared she might secretly marry Hsienpo, and she urged the Ma family to appoint a day for the wedding. Then she cut off Yingt'ai's school money, which forced her to return home.

Yingt'ai was obliged to hide her misery. Weeping bitterly, she said good-bye to Hsienpo, who accompanied her part of the way home. As they separated, Yingt'ai sang a song which revealed that she was a girl and that she wanted to marry him. But the good, dense Hsienpo did not understand her hints. . . . Yingt'ai saw that everything was hopeless, and went home in tears.

Hsienpo felt very lonely without his companion, with whom he had lived day and night for many years. He kept on writing letters to Yingt'ai, begging her to come back to school, but he never received a reply.

Finally he could bear it no longer, and went to visit her. "Is Mr. Yingt'ai at home?" he asked. "Please tell him his school friend, Hsienpo, has come and wants to see him."

The servant looked at him curiously, and then said curtly, "There is no Mr. Yingt'ai here—only a

Miss Yingt'ai. She is to be married soon, and naturally she can't leave her room. How could she speak to a man? Please go away, sir, for if the master discovers you, he will make a complaint against you for improper behavior."

Suddenly everything was clear to Hsienpo. In a state of collapse he crept home. There he found, under Yingt'ai's books, a bundle of letters and essays which showed him clearly how deeply Yingt'ai loved him and also that she did not want to marry any other man. Through his own stupidity, his lack of understanding, the dream had come to nought.

Overcome by remorse, he spent the days lost in tears. Yingt'ai was always before his eyes, and in his dreams he called her name, or cursed her sister-in-law and Dr. Ma, himself, and all the ways of society. Because he ceased to eat or drink, he fell ill and gradually sank into the grave.

Yingt'ai heard the sad news. Now she had nothing more to live for. If she had not been so carefully watched, she would have done herself some injury. In this state of despair the wedding day arrived. Listlessly she allowed herself to be pushed into the red bridal chair and set off for the house of her bridegroom, Dr. Ma. But when they passed the grave of Hsienpo, she begged her attendants to let her get out and visit it, to thank him for all his kindness. On the grave, overcome by grief, she flung herself down and sobbed. Her attendants urged her to return to her chair, but she refused. Finally, after great persuasion, she got up, dried her tears, and, bowing several times in front of the grave, she prayed as follows: "You are Hsienpo, and I am Yingt'ai. If we were really intended to be man and wife, open your grave three feet wide."

Scarcely had she spoken when there came a clap like thunder and the grave opened. Yingt'ai leaped into the opening, which closed again before the maids could catch hold of her, leaving only two bits of her dress in their hands. When they let these go, they changed into two butterflies which flew up into the air.

Dr. Ma was furious when he heard that his wife had jumped into the grave of Hsienpo. He had the grave opened, but the coffin was empty except for two white stones. No one knew where Hsienpo and Yingt'ai had gone. In a rage the grave violators flung the two stones onto the road, where immediately a bamboo with two stems shot up. They were shimmering green, and swayed in the wind. The grave robbers knew that this was the result of magic, and cut down the bamboo with a knife; but as soon as they had cut down one, another shot up, until finally several people cut down the two stems at the same time. Then these flew up to heaven and became rainbows.

Now the two lovers have become immortals. If they ever want to be together, undisturbed and unseen, so that no one on earth can see them or even talk about them, they wait until it is raining and the clouds are hiding the sky. The red in the rainbow is Hsienpo, and the blue is Yingt'ai.

From Wolfram Eberhard, ed., *Folktales of China.* New York: Washington Square Press, 1973 (1965), pp.15–18.

## Questions

1. Why, in your opinion, did Yingt'ai's sister-in-law want Yingt'ai to marry Dr. Ma?
2. Does this story imply criticism of arranged marriages?
3. Through contact with other societies, modern Chinese have come to question traditional practices. Yet even today some Chinese still accept arranged marriages. If such marriages could bring unhappiness, why has the practice lasted?
4. Why, in your opinion, has this story been so popular in China?
5. What does the story tell you about girls and schooling during imperial China?
6. Compare Little Tiger's story with Yingt'ai's. Which do you think was more typical of traditional China? Explain.
7. Describe the role of women in Western society today. How does it compare with their role in traditional China?

## Extension Activities

1. **Book review and presentation.** Read Arline and John Liggett's *The Tyranny of Beauty* (London: Victor Gollancz, 1989). Write a book review and make an oral presentation to the class. (Suggested by Anne Bright, teacher reviewer.)

2. **Videos.** *The Family*, based on Ba Jin's classic novel, focuses on a family in conflict over the selection of marriage partners and torn between old and new ways. *Raise the Red Lantern*, directed by Zhang Yimou, is a powerful film of a patriarch and his three wives. You might dramatize portions of either film for the class.
3. **Dramatization.** With some classmates, dramatize "A Folktale of Love" for the class. You might create props and costumes to enhance your presentation. (Suggested by Anne Bright, teacher reviewer.)
4. **Book review.** Although it was written for college students, Dorothy Ko's *Teachers of the Inner Chambers: Women and Culture in Seventeenth-Century China* (Stanford, CA: Stanford University Press, 1994) may interest you. The author criticizes the accepted view of women in imperial China as victims, arguing that practices differed with time, place, and social class.

## Further Reading

Feng, Jicai. *The Three-Inch Golden Lotus.* Translated by David Wakefield. Honolulu: University of Hawai'i Press, 1994.

Freedman, Maurice. *Lineage Organization in Southeastern China.* London: The Athlone Press, 1965.

Gernet, Jacques. *Daily Life in China on the Eve of the Mongol Invasion, 1250–1276.* Translated from the French by H. M. Wright. New York: Macmillan, 1962.

Lang, Olga. *Chinese Family and Society.* New Haven, CT: Yale University Press, 1946.

Spence, Jonathan D. *The Death of Woman Wang.* New York: Penguin Books, 1978.

# 2 Sons

*As you have seen, the Chinese traditionally valued their sons more than their daughters. Sons carried on the family name, took care of aging parents, and performed the necessary rites to honor family ancestors. Sons of well-to-do families could receive an education, and if they were bright enough, eventually compete in government examinations. If they succeeded, they brought honor to their families because they were recognized as scholars eligible to become government officials. The Chinese placed these scholar-officials at the top of their status-bound society.*

## Activity: Examination Rules

With a partner, list the rules you must obey when taking an examination at school. One way is to recall the procedure you must follow when you enter the room. Be ready to share your list with the class.

## Reading: *School Examinations*

In today's literate societies students must take a variety of examinations to show what they know. In many countries these examinations determine the type of schooling students receive, their chances of entering colleges and universities, and their future careers.

The Chinese were the first people to develop a complex examination system over a period of almost fourteen hundred years.[1] This system reached its greatest complexity about a hundred years ago during the Qing dynasty (1644–1911). Civil service examinations in imperial China determined which men would govern China's provinces and hold the most-honored positions in society. Although the Chinese valued educated men, most families were peasants too poor to let their sons attend school. If a boy showed promise of succeeding, his parents and family—if they could afford it—devoted time and attention to his education. Some young boys began learning to read and write as early as three.

Chinese is one of the hardest languages to read. To be functionally literate, a person must learn at least three to five thousand characters of a total of about fifty thousand.

Each day a boy would memorize a few characters, beginning with the most common ones. As he memorized each character, he practiced writing it with a brush made of rabbit hair. His ink came from an ink stick he rubbed onto an ink stone holding a little water. Grinding the ink stick over and over again made the ink thick and black. As he slowly became more polished in using the brush adeptly, he took pride in his writing, for calligraphy was a highly regarded art form, reflecting character and refinement.

From about the age of eight (seven in the Western method of counting age) until the age of fifteen, a boy attended private temple or village schools. If he came from a wealthy family, he was tutored at home. From the beginning of his schooling he studied the wisdom of Confucius, a great Chinese philosopher and teacher. He memorized *The Analects* and large sections of works edited by Confucius, along with works by scholars

[1] Selecting the talented was practiced during the second century B.C.E., but the testing system became well established about 700 years later.

who wrote about Confucius. The boy also learned Chinese history and poetry and composed essays and poems having classical and historical allusions. This rigor took mental discipline and perseverance. It was thought that such an education instilled in him the proper attitudes toward life and made him a wise person. According to Confucius, only the wise could govern well.

During the Ming and Qing dynasties, boys took entrance examinations that determined who could continue in school. The account below describes the final two-day school examination that determined who qualified to take the civil service examinations that decided who would govern China's provinces.

On the long-awaited morning of the first day, students from all over the province gathered in front of the examination compound. When the gates were finally opened, the candidates lined up to be inspected. Clerks searched them for books, notes, or money, which might be used to bribe clerks. If any such items were discovered, the inspecting clerk received a reward and the student was punished.

Once the inspection was over, the candidates entered a large examination room and went to their assigned seats. The first session lasted a full day, from early morning until evening. Two days after this session, the results were announced. The second session was held the next day. Those who passed both sessions passed the examination.

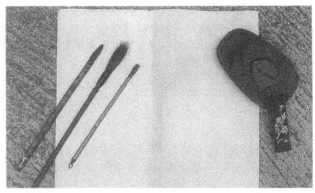

*The Four Treasures of the Chinese Study* **Paper.** *The Chinese use rice paper for it is rough-textured and absorbent.* **Ink brush.** *The handle is made from bamboo, the brush tip from rabbit and wolf hair.* **Ink stick and ink stone.** *Some ink sticks were beautifully decorated with characters written in gold. Courtesy of Simon Chiu.*

Since this was the last school . . . examination, it had to be conducted most strictly; and since so many candidates were gathered in one place, officials had to preserve silence and prevent irregularities. To this effect, the director of studies prepared ten different seals. When a clerk saw a candidate doing something improper he immediately went to his place and stamped the appropriate seal on his paper. The ten seals read:

1. *Leaving one's seat.* (A candidate was allowed to leave his seat only once, to drink tea or go to the toilet. When he did so he had to leave his answer sheet with a clerk and retrieve it when he

*Interior scene of an academy, watercolor on paper, circa 1840; artist unknown. Reproduction by permission of Urban Council Hong Kong from the collection of Hong Kong Museum of Art.*

returned to the hall. Because going to the toilet was a troublesome and time-consuming procedure, most candidates brought a pot, which they placed under their seat, and used that.)

2. *Exchanging papers.* (If students traded papers they were suspected of conspiring to have the better scholar write an answer for the other.)
3. *Dropping a paper.* (This was indiscreet because it aroused suspicion about exchanging papers.)
4. *Talking.*
5. *Gazing around and looking at others' papers.*
6. *Changing seats.* (Slipping into another's empty seat.)
7. *Disobeying.* (Failing to comply with clerks' instructions.)
8. *Violating regulations.*
9. *Humming.* (This often happened when candidates were preparing rhymes for poems, and was a great annoyance to others.)
10. *Incomplete.* (When a paper was not finished by sunset this seal was stamped upon it, lest someone add to it later.)

One such stamp upon a paper did not necessarily prove that something was wrong, but it seriously affected the judge's impression and meant certain failure, since many fine papers without a stamp were submitted. Another cause for instant failure was disorderly or illegible calligraphy, because the characters had to be written in the square style, with the brushstrokes correctly placed in the four corners. Otherwise, no matter how good the content of the paper was, it would be passed over, with the examiners barely glancing at it.

From Ichisada Miyazaki, *China's Examination Hell: The Civil Service Examinations of Imperial China,* translated by Conrad Schirokauer. New Haven, CN: Yale University Press, 1981 (1976), pp. 27–28.

## Question

How does each of the rules described in the reading compare with rules you must follow during examinations?

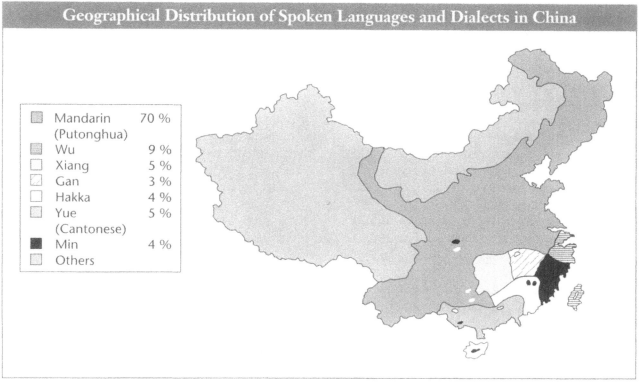

**Geographical Distribution of Spoken Languages and Dialects in China**

| | | |
|---|---|---|
| Mandarin (Putonghua) | 70 % | |
| Wu | 9 % | |
| Xiang | 5 % | |
| Gan | 3 % | |
| Hakka | 4 % | |
| Yue (Cantonese) | 5 % | |
| Min | 4 % | |
| Others | | |

*The Chinese speak a variety of dialects, but because their written language uses the same characters, people all over China can communicate with each other. A number of minority groups who have their own spoken and written languages, like the Tibetans and the Mongolians, live in the sparsely inhabited outer areas of China (see "others").*

## Chinese Language and Writing System

In 1899, some farmers on the North China Plain found bone fragments in their fields. Believing that these fragments were dragon bones that could cure illnesses, the farmers sold the bones to a pharmacist. Sometime later a scholar who was ill was offered some of these ground-up "dragon bones" as medicine. Curious, he inquired further, and discovered that these bones actually came from ancient tortoises and cattle. The lines scratched on them turned out to be the first known examples of Chinese writing, dating from 1300 to 1000 B.C.E., the time of the Shang dynasty, when China was still in the Stone Age.

No one knows exactly how writing began in China. It probably originated as a way for priests to communicate with spirits. On the bones the priests scratched pictographs that symbolized ideas and questions, then performed rituals to solicit answers. Chinese scholars called the bone fragments "oracle bones," bones that served to communicate with spirits for divine advice and predictions.

Since the invention of writing in ancient China, the Chinese have devised thousands of symbols that evolved into a sophisticated system enabling philosophers and poets to produce great Chinese classics.

In English we call these symbols "characters." They are basically a combination of pictographs (picture symbols) and ideographs (idea symbols). Simple examples of pictographs are 日 for sun, originally a circle with a line in it, 月 for moon, modeled after a crescent moon, and 木 for tree, the outline of branches and roots. Chinese pictographs originally did look something like the things they named, but over the years they changed until they looked much less like pictures. Simple examples of ideographs are 一 for one, 二 for two, and 三 for three.

Pictographs and ideographs combined to form other characters, such as forest 林, made up of two trees, and brightness 明, which places the sun and moon together. A woman beside a child 好 means "good" or "to like."

Many characters hold clues to meaning and sound. For example, a symbol for water 氵 combines with symbols that hint at sounds to produce words such as lake 湖, to swim 泳, and to fill 注 (with water).

Chinese writing requires years of time and effort to master. People must memorize about three to five thousand characters to be functionally literate. The complexity of the characters, together with their visual qualities, has elevated Chinese writing to an art form.

The use of Chinese characters has spread beyond China's borders—to Vietnam, Korea, and Japan. But because the Vietnamese, Koreans, and Japanese had their own oral languages before they began using Chinese characters, the same characters are pronounced differently by the different peoples.

A similar phenomenon arose within China. Chinese who speak mutually unintelligible dialects share the writing system, so those who don't understand each other's speech can still communicate in writing. Indeed, the Chinese writing system has been a prime unifying force in the civilization.

In the mid-twentieth century, leaders of the People's Republic of China mounted a threefold campaign to promote learning and literacy, which they believed would forge a stronger sense of national solidarity. First, they simplified the writing by reducing the number of strokes required for most characters to ease the learning process. Second, in 1956 they required all Chinese to learn putonghua, or common language, which derives from Mandarin. And finally, in the mid-1950s, leaders established the *pinyin* writing system, based on the Roman alphabet. Today pinyin is taught to illiterate adults and young children. Undoubtedly these measures have encouraged literacy, enhanced oral communication, and promoted national unity. But simplifying the characters and using *pinyin* have upset many Chinese who fear the loss of an important heritage of their culture—the traditional writing system.

# Development of Chinese Characters

| | Oracle Bone | Early Form | Modern Chinese | Simplified Chinese | Japanese Form | Korean Form |
|---|---|---|---|---|---|---|
| Sun | ⊙ | ⊖ | 日 | 日 | 日 | 日 |
| Door | 門 | 門 | 門 | 门 | 門 | 門 |
| Cart | 車 | 車 | 車 | 车 | 車 | 車 |

The Japanese and Koreans use Chinese characters in their writing systems.

*Chong-kit, a mythological figure, is said to have created the pictographs that later developed as Chinese characters. Note his four eyes, which represent his exceptional wisdom. This block print was created in 1498. From* A History of Chinese Block Prints. *Shanghai: Renmin Meishu, 1988, p. 104.*

*This Chinese character for "dragon" has a dragon's head where a dot would be in the character. From Tan Sri Lee Siow Mong,* Spectrum of Chinese Culture. *Petaling Jaya, Selagor, Malaysia: Pelanduk Publications, 1986, p. 97.*

**Reading:** *Civil Service Examinations*

The boys who passed the final school examination rejoiced, for now they were qualified to take the all-important civil service examination, which was given once every three years during the month of September in our modern calendar.

The following account of the examination setting and the examination itself will give you some idea of the importance of this event and of the seriousness with which it was taken.

In each provincial capital, there was a permanent examination compound. Like a honeycomb, it was an aggregation of thousands of single cells, each large enough to hold just one man. Cell adjoined cell to form a barnlike tenement, the whole maze occupying an extensive area. . . .

Within the Great Gate [the entrance to the examination compound] there was a large open area with a second gate on the north. Beyond that stretched a broad avenue, lined on both sides by the entrances to lanes. Each lane was about two meters wide and disproportionately deep, extending farther than the eye could see. Lining one side of each lane were countless small rooms or, more accurately, cells. These examination cells . . . had neither doors nor furniture and amounted to no more than spaces partitioned on three sides by brick walls and covered by a roof. The floors, naturally, were packed dirt. Each cell was equipped with only three long boards. When placed across the cell from wall to wall, the highest became a shelf, the middle one functioned as a desk, and the lowest served as a seat. There were no other facilities: it was really like a prison without bars. Here candidates taking the provincial examination had to spend three days and two nights in succession.

Because the building was used only once in three years, usually it was in poor condition even if occasional repairs were made. Shepherd's purse grew on the roof, the eaves were on the verge of collapse, moisture stained the walls. Since the lanes opened only at one end, a person walking in the

*A section of an examination compound having 7,500 cells. This compound differs slightly from the one described in the reading. Canton, circa 1873. Courtesy of Asian Collection, Prints and Photographs Division, Library of Congress.*

wrong direction would feel as though he were in a labyrinth. . . . But if he walked in the right direction, he would emerge on the broad avenue that led to the Great Gate. . . .

Subdivided within and isolated by a great wall from the outside world, the whole examination compound had only one entrance, the Great Gate, which was used by the staff and the candidates alike. . . . A large quantity of water was required for the candidates' inkstones as well as for cooking and drinking. To meet this need there was a "water platform" at the left and at the right of the Great Gate, where pure water was brought in from the outside. Before the examination, laborers drew water from there and filled large jars placed at the entrance to each lane. These they replenished as needed. After that it was the candidate's chore to fetch the water he needed in an earthenware pot. After the examination, the human waste deposited in the toilet tubs placed at the end of each lane was collected by laborers. . . .

On the . . . day before the beginning of the examination, the candidates entered the compound. . . . After the roll call, [they] passed through the Great Gate, one by one, each guided by a minor official. . . . Each candidate carried a large load, since he had to spend three days and two nights in the compound. He needed not only writing materials, such as an inkstone, ink brushes, and a water pitcher, but also an earthenware pot, foodstuffs, bedding, and a curtain to hang across the entrance to his cell.

As soon as the candidates . . . entered the compound through the Great Gate they were searched. Four soldiers at a time frisked one candidate from top to bottom and made him open his luggage for inspection. It goes without saying that books were forbidden, and so was any piece of paper with writing on it. Since a soldier who discovered such a paper was awarded three ounces of silver, the inspection was most stringent. It is said that the soldiers went so far as to cut open dumplings in order to examine their bean-jam fillings. . . .

After finding and entering his lane, each candidate located his own cell, identified by a number. Then he put up the three boards and arranged his things. Since at least ten thousand men—at times as many as twenty thousand—entered the compound and had to be searched, the procedure used up most

*Scholars waiting to enter the examination compound. Watercolor on paper. Reproduction by permission of Urban Council Hong Kong from the collection of Hong Kong Museum of Art.*

*Examination cells. From Ichisada Miyazaki,* China's Examination Hell: The Civil Service Examinations of Imperial China, *translated by Conrad Schirokauer. New Haven: Yale University Press, 1981 (1976).*

of a day. Those who got in during the early morning took a short, disturbed nap on their seats. . . .

When the day-long commotion of entering the compound came to an end, and all the candidates were settled in their cells, the superintendent latched the Great Gate and sealed it. Now the candidates had to pass the night all alone in their cells, with nothing to do. Despite the good weather of midautumn, the cold air of a night wind easily penetrated the curtains of the open cells, and the thin bedding on the hard seat did not entirely keep out the cold. Worst of all, the cells were so narrow that the candidates could not stretch their legs to the full, but dozed off while bent over like shrimp.

Yet a still more compelling reason why they could not have enjoyed a good long sleep that night was the fact that the examination began early in the morning of the next day, while it was still dark. . . .

After receiving the questions [on the morning of the first day] the candidates placed their heads between their hands and racked their brains, setting about to draw up their answers. Plenty of time was given: they had until the evening of the following day . . . to finish. After polishing their drafts on rough paper, they wrote out a clean copy when finally they had become sufficiently confident in their answers. While they suffered . . . time passed mercilessly. If they became hungry they ate the dumplings they had brought along, and those who had time to spare cooked rice in their earthenware pots. If rain fell during those two days, more than likely raindrops were blown by the wind into the doorless cells, and then the candidates desperately tried to shield their answer papers, more precious than life itself, making pathetic efforts to protect them although they themselves got wet. At night they were permitted to light a candle, but if it fell and burned a hole in the answer paper they were in trouble. Boys from good families, brought up carefully and never exposed even to a rough wind, had to fend for themselves, and for the only time in their pampered lives had to take care of everything by themselves alone. They were like raw recruits in an army.

When a candidate became tired at night, he could lay out his bedding again and take a rest. But a bright light in a neighboring cell would make him feel that he, too, should be hard at work, and so he would get up again to face his paper. Suffering from fatigue, and under heavy pressure, most candidates became a little strange in the head, and many were unable to work at their best. In the most severe cases, men became sick or insane. . . .

At about six o'clock [the next morning], the sound of cannon followed by some music signaled the end of the examination and indicated that it was time to hand in the answers. However, those who had not yet finished could remain behind and continue working until that evening. In this respect the system was relaxed and even generous.

Those who had finished writing handed in their papers at receiving counters arranged by district. Then the papers were thoroughly checked for violations of the formal regulations. Cutting out miswritten characters and pasting in a piece of paper, leaving blank spaces, skipping parts of a page, or handing in a completely white paper with no writing on it whatsoever were considered to be infractions of the rules. The name of anyone guilty of this kind of offense was posted outside the compound, and he was barred from taking future examinations. Those candidates whose papers were accepted received exit passes, packed their belongings, and left the compound through the Great Gate in large groups. That night they returned to their lodgings after an absence of two days, but they could not sleep there in comfort, for they had to get up in the middle of the night to enter the compound for the second time.

Early in the morning . . . while it was still dark, again they gathered in front of the Great Gate, went through the roll call, and entered the compound shouldering their baggage. The next morning the second round of problems was distributed, this time five questions on the Five Classics. After writing out clean copies of their answers, the candidates had to reproduce several sentences from the opening paragraphs of their answer to questions [from] the first session, or else add to the poem they had composed in the earlier test, in order to prove that the papers for the two examinations had been written by the same man. Forbidden to bring in or carry out any slips of paper, they had to rely on memory. For this reason, generally a discrepancy of up to ten characters was overlooked, but in a case of great discrepancy the man was presumed guilty of having used a substitute and was barred from examinations in the future.

The second session ended on the evening of the [following] day, and early the next morning the candidates entered the compound for the third session. . . .

Having handed in their papers at last the candidates could relax, but now the onerous duties began for the examination staff. . . . Since between ten and twenty thousand papers were submitted at each session they formed a mountainous pile that could be demolished only through a difficult and complex process.

Since the candidates' answers were written in black ink and absolutely no other color was permitted, they were called the "black versions." To guard against the possibility that the graders might show partiality to certain candidates whose writing they recognized, they were not shown the original papers. Instead, the black versions were copied by clerks in the outer section of the compound. Before that, however, the candidate's name, age, and other information about himself on the cover of the black version were concealed so that only the seat number remained visible. Then the black version was sent to the clerks to be copied on separate sheets of paper, this time using only vermilion ink, so that the copyists could not revise the original papers on their own initiative. Copying so many papers was hard work and required the services of several thousand clerks.

Next the vermilion copies, together with the black originals, were passed on to the proofreaders, of whom there were several hundred. They made their corrections in yellow ink. Both copyists and proofreaders noted their names on the papers, to make clear their responsibility; needless to say, if any wrongdoing was discovered, those responsible were punished.

When the proofreading was completed, both versions were sent to the custodian, who retained the original and delivered the copy to the examiners in the inner section. The transfer of the copies through the single narrow door that connected the two sections took place under strict supervision.

The vermilion papers first passed through the hands of the associate examiners, who had to do the grading in designated places and were forbidden to carry a paper somewhere else on their own initiative. They used blue ink for their remarks and, by carefully reading the vermilion copies, decided in general upon passes and failures. When they wrote "mediocre" on the cover, or "without merit," or other such critical comments, the paper failed. When the paper was considered to be "excellent in style and content," they wrote "recommended" on the cover and then the paper was delivered to the chief and deputy examiners, who usually read only these recommended papers. . . .

When the grading was completed, the results of the three examinations were averaged and the final decisions were reached about who should be passed. The number to be passed was fixed for each province, with more than ninety places allowed for a large province and forty for a small one. . . .

For the announcement of the results, the examination staff brought out a large placard on which, in full public view, they wrote the names of the successful candidates in sequence. Using a piece of white paper bearing a drawing of a dragon on the right and a tiger on the left, they left blank a small space at the beginning and wrote out the names from the sixth man on down. After writing the last name, they rested for a while. The candidates whose names had appeared were very happy; the others, even though most of them would be failures, still clung to a thin thread of hope, since it was not impossible that they might be among the top five names yet to be announced. At last the members of the staff returned, and as they wrote in the first five names, the crowd applauded. When the supervisor finished his inspection and affixed his great seal to the list, everything was over.

> From Ichisada Miyazaki, *China's Examination Hell: The Civil Service Examinations of Imperial China,* translated by Conrad Schirokauer. New Haven, CT: Yale University 1981 (1976), pp. 41–56.

## Questions

1. What procedures were used to minimize the possibility of bribery and cheating?
2. Describe the examination ordeal. Do you think you would have been able to undergo such an examination? Explain.

### Activity:  Creating a Title

Create an appropriate title for this reading. The title should be eye-catching and at the same time capture the essence of the reading. To create a title, summarize the reading in a few sentences.

Then think of a phrase that gets at the essence of the summary. Your teacher will divide the class into groups of four or five. Share your titles with your group and choose the best title.

The teacher will then call on someone in your group to share that title with the class.

*During imperial China, grand and crowded cities, vibrant with life, contained as many as a million people or more. Multistoried buildings, tea houses, taverns, restaurants, and shops carrying both common and luxury merchandise lined the busy streets. Courtesy of Palace Museum, Beijing.*

## Reading: *China's Civil Service System*

Those who passed the provincial civil service examination gained prestige. They could work as scholar-officials—government bureaucrats—in the provinces, and they were eligible to take another set of examinations given in the capital city, where the emperor resided. Candidates who passed these examinations became top officials.

Scholar-officials performed a myriad of tasks. Among other things, they advised the emperor, managed agricultural production, supervised the building and maintenance of roads, canals, and dams, settled legal disputes, recorded and maintained official records, and examined civil service candidates. They also embodied the highest level of ethical behavior.

Because being a scholar-official brought such great prestige, many men who failed the examinations took them again and again until they either passed or gave up.

The examination system originated in the Han dynasty (201 B.C.E.–A.D. 220). In 196 B.C.E. the emperor sought an alternative to the practice of giving aristocracy the right to govern merely by virtue of their birth. Seeking men of ability instead, the emperor decreed that virtuous men of excellent reputation be recommended from each province for government positions. He then had these aspirants examined on their knowledge of the Confucian classics. Those who did well were appointed to government posts. Thus began the link between Confucianism and the training and selection of government officials.

After the Han dynasty came a long period of disunity and local wars, during which the practice of examining candidates for government posts all but disappeared. But with reunification during the Sui dynasty (A.D. 587–618), the practice reappeared. The first Sui emperor held regular government examinations and asked those who did well to help him run the country. This practice gradually spread until it became firmly established centuries later, during the Song dynasty (A.D. 960–1279). So entrenched was this system that even when outsiders conquered and ruled China—the Mongols or the Yuan dynasty from 1279 to 1368, and the Manchu or Qing dynasty from 1644 to 1911—they chose to conform to this system to establish their rule in China. China's civil service examination system, refined over the centuries, lasted for well over a thousand years.

During the era of the examination system, officials went to great lengths to make it fair. But the system was not perfect. Those who graded the papers had to read long answers quickly; inevitably some sophisticated essays were passed over, and some intelligent literary men failed. Some critics asked whether memorizing the Confucian classics and writing poems and essays made one fit to run the government. Yet no other method of choosing leaders replaced the examination system during its thirteen hundred years.

In theory, examinations were open to any male. But not every male could take advantage of this opportunity. School was not free, and most families could not afford to send their sons to school because they needed the boys' help in the fields or outside the home to augment the family income.

Then, too, although no fees were charged, taking the examinations was costly. The candidate had to pay for travel and lodging, buy gifts for the examiners, and tip the staff.

For these reasons most scholars came from wealthy landowning families. Although government positions could not be inherited, sons from scholarly families often became scholars. These families could afford to have their sons study for many years before taking the examinations. An occasional peasant family suffered extreme hardship so that one son could go to school, perhaps pass the provincial examination, get a government position, and honor his family.

Although the system gave some commoners the opportunity to move up socially and economically, its original intent was to recruit able and intelligent civil servants indoctrinated in the teachings of Confucius —the foundation of Chinese government and society.

In the Chinese view the society had four classes of people: scholars, farmers, artisans, and merchants. Scholars had the highest status because they represented what was most highly valued—the Confucian virtues. They studied the classics and transmitted their knowledge to future generations. Farmers came second because they produced the food and clothed the people. Artisans, who made things people used, came next. Merchants were last because they did not produce anything; they just bought and sold the products of others' labors. Merchants were also thought to value profit-making to the neglect of Confucian virtues.

Yet the lines between classes were blurred. Although a rich merchant had less status than a great landlord-farmer, a shopkeeper was held about equal to a small landowning farmer and superior to a tenant farmer. Later, during the Song dynasty, merchants were regarded more highly because people saw that buying and selling were important to a society. Wealthy merchants could gain prestige by sending a son to school and seeing him pass the provincial examination or by marrying off a son or daughter to someone of the scholar class.

Below these four main classes were soldiers, whose job of destroying and killing was considered distasteful. Below the soldiers came a small group of actors, entertainers, brothel operators, prostitutes, and slaves. Members of this group and their children and grandchildren were excluded from taking the examinations.

The examinations were also closed to women —a fact that would offend most of us today.

One way of looking at imperial China's examination system is to compare it with what was happening elsewhere during the same period. It was the time of the Middle Ages and feudalism in Europe, where nobles, who had the power to govern, got their positions because of their status. The very idea that a common man could become a government official was almost unthinkable.

China's examination system ended during the reign of the last emperor of China. The onslaught of Westerners during the 1800s had shaken China, forcing the Chinese to question

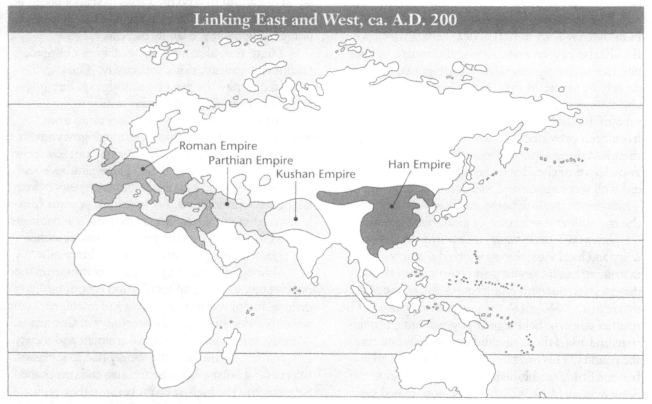

## Linking East and West, ca. A.D. 200

Roman Empire
Parthian Empire
Kushan Empire
Han Empire

*While the Han Dynasty led the Chinese Empire in the east, her silk trade counterpart in Europe, the Roman Empire, dominated the West. Bridging the two were the Kushan and Parthian Empires, who served as powerful middlemen for the trade and accompanying cultural exchanges. In the eyes of the Chinese, these trading partners, like all the people outside China, were barbarians who were inferior to the wealthy, prosperous, and civilized Chinese.*

## China's Changing Boundaries

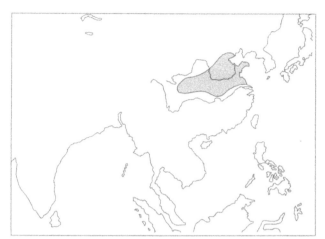

Shang Dynasty, around 1523–1027 B.C.E.

Han Dynasty, around 100 B.C.E.

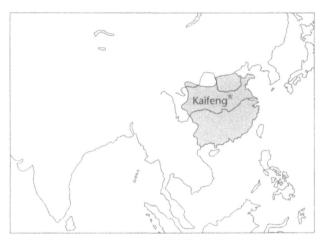

Song Dynasty, around 1050 B.C.E.

Qing Dynasty, 1644–1912

China's boundaries changed as its emperors won or lost control of certain territories. The maps on this page show how they varied at different times during a period of well over two thousand years.

As the maps indicate, Changan, Kaifeng, and Beijing served as capital cities for succeeding dynasties. (Not shown are Loyang, capital of the Southern Song Dynasty, and Nanjing, capital during part of the Ming Dynasty.)

The People's Republic of China

## Emperors and Dynasties

While scholar-bureaucrats ran the country, ultimate power and authority rested with the emperor. The first emperor, Qin Shi Huangdi, unified China in 221 B.C.E. He established the Qin dynasty, the first of many dynasties that ruled China until the twentieth century.

The emperor lived with his family in magnificent palaces surrounded by high walls and guarded by thousands of soldiers. When he died, he was buried in a mausoleum.

In later dynasties the Chinese called their emperor the Son of Heaven. They believed he had the Mandate of Heaven—authority to rule the people as he saw fit. The Chinese saw their history as one of successive dynasties that rose and fell at heaven's command. In this view, a challenger who overthrew a ruler showed by his success that Heaven had taken the Mandate from the deposed ruler and given it to the victor.

The Chinese looked at their past as a series of dynastic cycles in which dynasties followed a similar pattern: a heroic beginning, a period of stability and prosperity, a period of decline, and finally, total collapse. A dynasty began when a strong ruler won control of the country and passed leadership to his son. The throne continued to be handed down the family line, from father to son, generation after generation. With an ineffective emperor or succession of emperors, challenge from inside or outside China gradually weakened the authority of the central government until the dynasty collapsed. The Chinese saw their past as moving from unity to fragmentation, order to chaos, and centralization to decentralization, over and over again.

They also believed that their empire was the only civilized place on earth, a civilization surrounded by barbarians. Thus they called their land Zhongguo —the Middle Kingdom.

### The coat worn at court symbolized the universe.

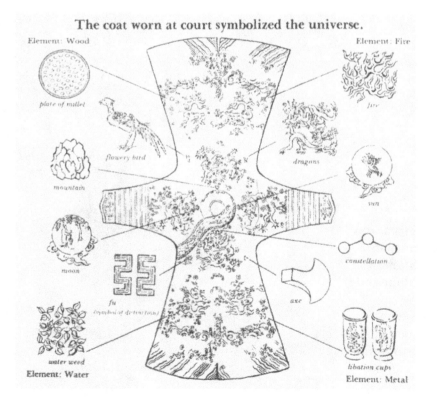

Element: Wood

plate of millet

flowery bird

mountain

moon

fu
(symbol of distinction)

water weed
**Element: Water**

Element: Fire

fire

dragons

sun

constellation

axe

libation cups
**Element: Metal**

*The twelve symbols embroidered on the emperor's robe reflect the belief that the "Son of Heaven" was the ultimate source of everything in the universe. Fire, sun, and dragon symbolize the element of fire, which stands for masculinity. Waterweed, moon, and fu (happiness) represent the element water, which stands for femininity. The millet, flowery bird, and mountain symbolize the element wood, while the ax, wine cups, and constellation represent the element metal. Both wood and metal represent other important aspects of the universe. From Tan Sri Lee Siow Mong,* Spectrum of Chinese Culture. *Petaling Jaya, Selangor, Malaysia: Pelanduk Publications, 1986, p. 199.*

*An emperor's dragon robe embroidered with symbols indicating good fortune. Courtesy of Hong Kong Museum of Art.*

their traditions and learn new knowledge and technology from the West. In 1901 the Qing government announced the establishment of a new school system for the entire country, abolishing the examination system. The last examinations were given in 1904.

## Questions

1. What were some of the shortcomings of China's civil service examination system? What were some of its strengths?
2. A popular saying in China was "If you care for a son, you don't go easy on his studies; if you care for a daughter, you don't go easy on her footbinding."[2] Explain this saying in light of what you have learned about traditional China.

[2] Howard S. Levy, *Chinese Footbinding*. New York: Bell Publishing Co., 1967, p. 49.

## Activity: Dynastic Timeline

1. Read the sidebar "Emperors and Dynasties." Then discuss the meaning of "dynastic cycles."
2. Your teacher will assign each student to a dynasty and its dates. On a sheet of looseleaf paper, write the name of your dynasty and its dates.
3. When your teacher gives the signal, find twelve other dynasties and line yourselves up in chronological order.
4. After sitting down, give your teacher the names of all thirteen dynasties in chronological order.
5. Examine the timeline at the beginning of this chapter and answer these questions: What European civilizations existed during the Qin dynasty? The United States was created during which dynasty?
6. Make a timeline showing all the dynasties. Next to the timeline, list some major European and American periods and events.

*The Forbidden City in Beijing, built during the Ming dynasty, housed the imperial court and included the emperor's residence. It was used until the end of the Qing dynasty. Today it serves as a museum. Courtesy of Palace Museum, Beijing.*

*Section from the painting "Wedding of the Emperor Guang Xu." This fabulously expensive imperial wedding took place in 1889 in the Forbidden City with intricate ceremonies that included presenting betrothal presents, conferring the title of empress on the bride, welcoming the bride to the palace, receiving congratulations from foreign representatives, and celebrating at a lavish feast. Notice the carpet laid for the emperor. Courtesy of Palace Museum, Beijing.*

## Extension Activities

1. **Research.** Research the Japanese examination system and compare it with the examination system of imperial China.
2. **Speakers.** Invite a Chinese to teach the class how to pronounce Chinese words and how to read *pinyin* and a few simple Chinese characters. The visitor might also demonstrate the use of the four treasures: rice paper, ink brush, ink stick, and ink stone.

## Further Reading

**The Examination and Civil Service Systems**
Miyazaki, Ichisada. *China's Examination Hell: The Civil Service Examinations of Imperial China.* Translated by Conrad Schirokauer. New Haven, CT: Yale University Press, 1981 (1976).
Wolfgang, Frank. *The Reform and Abolition of the Traditional Chinese Examination System.* Cambridge, MA: Harvard University Press, 1963.

**Dynasties and Emperors**
Hucker, Charles O. *China's Imperial Past: An Introduction to Chinese History and Culture.* Stanford, CA: Stanford University Press, 1975.
Hucker, Charles O. *China to 1850: A Short History.* Stanford, CA: Stanford University Press, 1975.

**Chinese Language and Writing**
Chang, Raymond, and Margaret Scrogin Chang. *Speaking of Chinese.* New York: W. W. Norton, 1978.
Karlgren, Bernhard. *The Chinese Language.* New York: The Ronald Press Company, 1949.
*Demystifying the Chinese Language.* Stanford, CA: Stanford University, Stanford Program on International and Cross-Cultural Education and the Bay Area Chinese Education Project, 1983. A set of engaging classroom activities that can be ordered from Stanford University.

# Parents and Children

**Section 3**

*The bonds between children and their parents were strong. Parents had obligations in raising their children, and children had obligations to their parents. In this section you will read about ideal parents and children. Although most Chinese fell short of the behaviors demonstrated by the people in these stories, accounts of their conduct served as models to which other Chinese could aspire.*

---

## Reading: *A Diligent Wife and Fine Mother*

The following story takes us back three centuries. It was written by a well-known writer, Pu Songling, who lived during the 1600s. Chinese storytellers often used stories to moralize. As you read about Hsi-liu, think of what the writer might have wanted to teach. What does the story tell us about the ideal wife and mother? What does it tell us about how the Chinese saw women?

Hsi-liu was the daughter of a scholar living in Chung-tu. She was given this name—which means "delicate willow"—because her waist was so incomparably slender.

She was an intelligent girl with a good grasp of literature and had a particular fondness for books on human physiognomy. Easygoing by nature, she was not one to criticize others; but whenever anyone came to make inquiries about possibly marrying her, she always insisted on taking a personal look at the suitor, and though she examined many men, she found them all wanting. By the time she was nineteen her parents had grown angry, and said to her, "How can there be no mate suitable for you on this earth? Do you want to keep your girlish braids until you're an old woman?"

Hsi-liu replied, "I had truly hoped that with my human forces I could overcome the divine forces, but I have not succeeded over these many years and can see that it is my fate. From this time on I will ask no more than to obey my parents' commands."

At this time it happened that there was a scholar named Kao, from a good family and known for his abilities, who asked for Hsi-liu's hand in marriage and sent over the bridal gifts. So the ceremonies were performed.

*A Chinese woman of some means wearing a traditional dress, circa 1890. Courtesy of Hong Kong Museum of History, Urban Council.*

Husband and wife got on well together. Kao had a son of five from a former marriage, named Ch'ang-fu, and Hsi-liu looked after the boy so lovingly that if she had to go off and visit her parents, he yelled and wept and tried to follow her, and no amount of scolding would make him stop. After a little over a year Hsi-liu gave birth to a son of her own, and named him Ch'ang-hu—"the reliable one." When her husband asked what the name signified, she answered, "Only that I hope he will remain long with his parents."

Hsi-liu was cursory over woman's work and seemed to take little interest in it; but she pored carefully over the records in which the acreage of their properties and the size of their tax assessment were listed, and worried if anything was not exactly accurate. After a time she said to Kao, "Would you be willing to give up attending to our family's business affairs and let me look after them?" Kao let her take over; for six months everything went well with the family's affairs, and Kao praised her.

One day Kao went off to a neighboring village to drink wine with friends, and while he was away one of the local tax collectors came, demanding payment. He banged on the door and cursed at Hsi-liu; she sent one of her maids to calm him down, but since he wouldn't go away, she had to send one of the menservants to go fetch her husband home. When Kao returned, the man left. Kao laughed and said, "Hsi-liu, do you now begin to see why an intelligent woman can never be the match for a stupid man?"

When Hsi-liu heard these words she lowered her head and began to cry; worried, Kao drew her to him and tried to encourage her, but for a long time she could not be comforted. He was unhappy that she was so caught up in running the household affairs, and suggested that he take them over again himself, but she wouldn't let him.

She rose at dawn, and retired late, and managed everything with the greatest diligence. She would put aside the money for each year's taxes a year in advance, and no more did the runners sent to press for payments come to her door; in the same way she calculated in advance for their food and clothing needs, and thus their expenditure was controlled. Kao was delighted, and playfully said to her, "How can my 'delicate willow' be so delicate? Your eyebrows are delicate, your waist is delicate, your little feet are delicate; but I am

*The interior of a wealthy family's home. Note the spacious interior with closets, furniture, and window decoration. Watercolor on paper. Reproduction by permission of Urban Council Hong Kong from the collection of Hong Kong Museum of Art.*

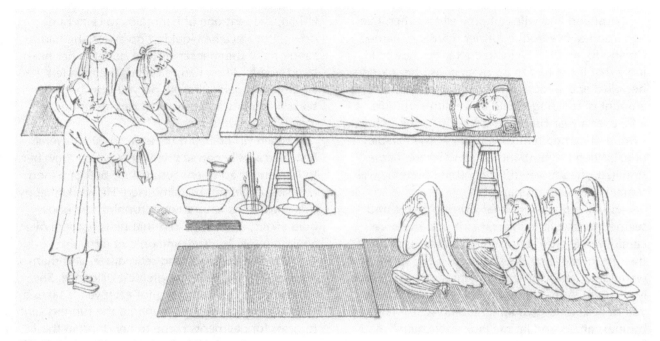

*Wailing ceremony at the death of a father. Pen and ink. Reproduction by permission of Urban Council Hong Kong from the collection of Hong Kong Museum of Art.*

delighted that your determination is even more delicate than those."

And Hsi-liu replied, "My husband's name means 'high,' and you are truly high: your character is high, your ambitions are high, your scholarship is high; but what I hope is that the number of your years will be even higher."

There was, in their village, a dealer who sold beautiful coffins, and Hsi-liu insisted on buying one regardless of the cost; since she didn't have enough money, she raised it by asking around among her relatives and neighbors. Kao did not see the urgency for the purchase and tried to stop her, but she paid him no heed. About a year later there was a death in a wealthy neighboring family, and they offered her double what the coffin had cost; the profit would have been so good that Kao urged his wife to accept the offer, but she wouldn't do it. He asked why not. She did not reply. He asked her again, and her eyes glistened with tears. Kao was surprised but did not want to contradict her directly, so he left the matter there.

Another year went by, and Kao was now twenty-five. Hsi-liu would not let him go away on long journeys, and if he was late coming back from some visit, she would send the servants over to ask him to return, and they would follow him back down the roads. Kao's friends all joked with him about this.

One day Kao was out drinking with some friends; he felt there was something wrong with him and started for home, but halfway back he fell from his horse and died. The weather at this time was damp and hot, but fortunately all his burial clothes had been made ready in advance. The villagers all praised Hsi-liu for her foresight.

Her stepson, Ch'ang-fu, was now ten years old and just beginning to learn essay writing, but after his father died he grew peevish and lazy and refused to study. He would run off and follow the herdsboys on their outings—scolding him had no effect, and even after beatings he continued his wanton behavior. Hsi-liu had no remedy left, so she called him to her and said, "You have shown that you don't want to study; how is there any way that we can force you? But in poor households there can be none without employment, so change your clothes and go and work alongside the servants. If you don't, I'll have you beaten, and it will be too late for regrets." So in ripped, wadded clothes Ch'ang-fu went to herd the pigs, and when he came home after work he took his pottery bowl and joined the other servants for a meal of gruel. After a few days he had suffered enough and, weeping, knelt outside the family courtyard, begging to be allowed to study again. Hsi-liu turned away from him toward the wall as if she hadn't even heard him, and there was nothing for Ch'ang-fu to do but pick up his whip, swallow his tears, and depart. As autumn came to an end Ch'ang-fu had no clothes for his body and no shoes for his feet; the freezing rain soaked into his body and he carried his head hunched into his shoulders like a beggar. The villagers all pitied him, and those who had children from a former marriage took Hsi-liu as a warning. They murmured angrily against her, and Hsi-liu gradually became aware of it, but ignored them as if it were nothing to do with her. Finally Ch'ang-fu could bear the hardship no more; he abandoned his pigs and ran away. Still Hsi-liu took no action, neither sending anyone to check on him nor even making inquiries about him. After a few more months there was nowhere left for Ch'ang-fu to beg for food, and deeply grieving, he returned home. Yet he dared not enter, and begged an old woman neighbor to go and tell his mother he was back. Hsi-liu said, "If he will accept a beating of one hundred blows he can come in and see me; if not, then let him be on his way again."

Ch'ang-fu heard this and ran in, weeping that he would gladly receive the blows. "Do you now understand how to change your ways and repent?" she asked.

"I repent," he said.

And his mother responded, "If you know how to repent, then there is no need to give you a beating. Go in peace and tend to your pigs; if you behave badly again, there will be no forgiveness."

Ch'ang-fu cried out, "I'd be happy to receive the hundred blows if you would let me study again."

Hsi-liu made no response, but when the old woman added her own pleas, she finally agreed. She gave him a bath and some clothes and sent him off to study with the same teacher as his younger brother. Ch'ang-fu worked diligently and well, far differently from the past, and after three years he passed the local district examinations. Governor Yang saw his essays and was impressed; he had Ch'ang-fu given a monthly stipend to help him along with the cost of his studies.

Ch'ang-hu, on the other hand, was incredibly stupid; after studying for several years he still could not remember the ideographs for his own name. Hsi-liu told him to put away his books and go out and work in the fields, but he preferred to fool around and showed himself unwilling to take the pains of hard work. His mother said angrily, "Each of the four classes has its occupation, but since you are incapable of study and unable to work in the fields, how are you going to avoid dying in some ditch?" She had him beaten, and from then on he went out with the hired hands to work in the fields. If he was late getting up, then she scolded him and followed after him, cursing. And secretly she began to give the best there was in clothing, food, and drink to his elder brother, Ch'ang-fu. Although Ch'ang-hu dared not complain, he could not avoid being deeply upset.

When the year's work in the fields was over, Hsi-liu took some money and gave it to Ch'ang-hu so that he could learn the ways of a traveling peddler; but Ch'ang-hu, who had a passion for gambling, lost all the money she gave him and then, in an attempt to deceive her, made up a story that he had been robbed. Hsi-liu found out and was having him beaten almost to death when his elder brother Ch'ang-fu knelt at her feet and begged for mercy, offering to substitute his own body in his brother's place; so her anger gradually abated, but from that time on whenever Ch'ang-hu left the house his mother had him watched. This made his conduct slightly better, but the change did not really come from within his heart.

One day Ch'ang-hu asked his mother if he could join a group of merchants who were traveling to Loyang. In fact, he wanted to use this chance of a distant journey to give full scope to his desires, and was deeply worried that his mother might not agree to his request. But when Hsi-liu heard it she seemed to have no suspicions at all, gave him thirty taels of silver, and packed his baggage for him. And as he was leaving she handed him an ingot of gold, saying, "This has been handed down from our ancestors and is not for ordinary spending; keep it as ballast in your baggage and use it only in an emergency. Besides, this is your first experience of life on the road, and I am not expecting you to make any profit; all I ask is that you not squander this thirty taels." She repeated this as Ch'ang-hu was leaving; he agreed completely and went on his way, elated and thoroughly pleased with himself.

When he reached Loyang he parted from his traveling companions with thanks and went to lodge in the house of a famous courtesan named Li; after passing ten nights or more with her, he had spent all his cash, but since he still had the gold ingot in his baggage, he didn't worry much about having run out of money. But when he took out the ingot and cut into it, he found it was fake gold; he was badly frightened and the color left his face. Li's mother, when she learned of the situation, cursed him sharply. Ch'ang-hu was deeply worried, for his purse was empty and there was nowhere for him to go; his only hope was that the girl would remember the happiness they had enjoyed together and would not cut him off right away. Suddenly two men came into his room with ropes which they fastened swiftly round his neck. Ch'ang-hu was terrified and had no idea what to do; when he piteously begged to know the reason for this treatment, he learned that the girl had taken the fake gold and lodged a complaint with the local prefect. Brought before the official, Ch'ang-hu was not allowed to testify but was put in fetters and beaten until he was nearly dead and then thrown into prison. Since he had no money for his expenses, he was badly mistreated by the jailers; by begging for food from his fellow prisoners he was just able to stay alive.

Now on the day that Ch'ang-hu had left home, his mother, Hsi-liu, had said to his elder brother, Ch'ang-fu, "Remember that when twenty days have passed I must send you off to Loyang. I have so many things to do that I'm afraid I might forget." Ch'ang-fu asked her what she meant, but she appeared overcome with grief and he withdrew, not daring to question her further. When the twenty days were up, he asked her again and she answered sadly, "Your younger brother is now leading a dissolute life, just as you did when you refused to study. If I had not acquired this terrible reputation, how would you ever have become what you are today? Everyone says that I am cruel, but none of them know of the tears that have flowed over my pillow." And the tears coursed down Hsi-liu's face while Ch'ang-fu stood respectfully waiting, not daring to inquire further. When she had finished weeping, Hsi-liu continued, "Since a

dissolute heart still beat in your brother's body, I gave him some fake gold so that he would be badly mistreated. By now he must already be locked in prison. The governor thinks well of you; go and ask him for clemency so that your brother will be spared from death and a true sense of remorse be born in him."

Ch'ang-fu departed immediately; by the time he reached Loyang it was three days since his younger brother had been arrested; when he visited him in prison, his brother was desperate, his face like a ghost's. Ch'ang-hu wept when he saw his elder brother and could not raise his head. Ch'ang-fu wept also. Now since Ch'ang-fu was especially admired by the governor of the province, his name was known to everyone around, and when the prefect learned that he was Ch'ang-hu's elder brother, he immediately ordered Ch'ang-hu released from prison.

When Ch'ang-hu reached home he was still afraid his mother would be angry with him, so he came up to her, crawling on his knees. "Have you satisfied your desires?" she asked. Ch'ang-hu's face was still tear-stained; he dared make no further sound. Ch'ang-fu knelt at his side, and the mother at last told them both to rise.

From this time on Ch'ang-hu was deeply repentant and handled all the business of the household with diligence; if it happened that he was remiss over something, his mother would ask him to correct it without getting angry. Yet several months went by and still she did not speak to him about his working in trade; he wanted to ask her but did not dare, so he told his elder brother of his wishes. Hsi-liu was happy when she heard about it; she pawned some of her possessions and gave the money to Ch'ang-hu; within six months he had doubled the capital. That same year, in the autumn, Ch'ang-fu passed the provincial exams; three years later he obtained the highest degree. By this time his younger brother had made tens of thousands in trade.

A local merchant, on his way to Loyang, managed to sneak a look at Hsi-liu. Though she was in her forties, she looked like a woman only a little over thirty; her clothes, her hair style were of the simplest. One would have thought she came from a poor family.

From *The Death of Woman Wang* by Jonathan D. Spence. © 1978 by Jonathan D. Spence. Used by permission of Viking Penguin, a division of Penguin Books USA Inc.

| Activity: Dramatizing the Story |
| --- |

Form groups of four. Decide who will take the role of each character in the story: Hsi-liu, Kao, Ch'ang-fu, Ch'ang-hu. Dramatize the story in your group while your classmates do the same in their groups. The teacher will call on volunteers to dramatize the story for the class.

## Questions
1. From evidence in the story, what personal qualities did Chinese society value? What in the story tells you this?
2. How does the story show that women came second to men?
3. A widow had greater authority over the household and over her children than a woman whose husband was still living. Yet even in marriage, a wife could have greater power than might have been expected. What in the story shows this?
4. This story illustrates the ideal Chinese woman, what the Chinese called "a diligent wife and fine mother." In what ways did Hsi-liu fit the ideal?

*A trial of an unfaithful wife. Reproduction by permission of Urban Council Hong Kong from the collection of the Hong Kong Museum of Art.*

5. Choose one of these Chinese proverbs.[1] Explain how the story illustrates it.
   Indulgent mothers spoil their children.
   He who leads an idle life will suffer from want and hunger.
   Better to teach your son a trade than to give him a thousand taels of gold.

| Reading: *Children and Filial Piety* |
| --- |

In the previous story Hsi-liu punished her sons severely until they obeyed her by mending their ways. Besides obedience, virtuous Chinese children showed reverence and devotion to their parents. The following account of events during the 1400s describes the actions of two sons who were later recognized by the emperor for their outstanding filial acts.

When Qin Xu was fifty-three years old, he developed a heart disease that troubled him every ten days or so. Medicine did not seem to have any effect, and [his sons Yongfu and Chongfu] could do nothing but pray. Their father recovered but had a more serious relapse the next year. His sons repeatedly struck themselves on the chest so that they could share his pain. Then Chongfu found out from ancient medical texts that rabbit's blood could be used to treat the ailment. He decided that human blood would be better. Perhaps he was influenced by the traditional Chinese belief that a serious sickness can be cured if the patient eats the flesh of someone who loves him deeply. . . .

The two brothers dug their long, sharp fingernails into their chests until the blood ran. They collected the blood in a vessel, mixed it with medicinal wine and gave the potion to their father. Qin Xu recovered and did not have another attack for many years.

[1] John T. S. Chen, *1001 Chinese Sayings.* Hong Kong: Chung Chi College, 1973, pp. 82, 144–45.

On another occasion their mother, the Lady Yan, fell while walking upstairs and injured her knee. She bled profusely and her sons called in the best physicians. In the summer heat, the injury became infected and oozed pus, causing such a stench no one was willing to go near her. The two brothers washed their mother's wound and changed the dressing regularly. At night, they sat beside her bed and fanned her, to relieve her from the heat and to chase away mosquitoes and flies. But the pus continued and the wound refused to heal. The two brothers then took turns licking the wound until all the pus was gone. When winter came, the knee finally healed.

From Frank *Ching, Ancestors, 900 Years in the Life of a Chinese Family.* New York: Ballantine Books, 1988, pp. 114–15.

The Chinese considered filial piety the source of all other virtues. The *Xiao Jing*, or *Classic of Filial Piety*, notes, "Our bodies, in every hair and bit of skin, are received by us from our parents, and we must not venture to injure or scar them. This is the beginning of filial piety. When we have established ourselves in the practice of the Way *(Dao)*, so as to make our name famous in future ages and thereby glorify our parents, this is the goal of filial piety. It commences with the service of parents; it proceeds to the service of the ruler. . . . Yes, filial piety is the way of Heaven, the principle of Earth, and the practical duty of man."[2] In other words, filial piety meant honoring parents by working hard and becoming successful, caring for them in illness and old age, and refraining from doing anything that would disgrace them.

A Chinese saying asserts, "Of all the teachings in the classics, filial piety comes first." Another advises, "Attend with care to the last rites (of your parents) and follow them (with sacrifices) though they are long departed."[3]

To instill proper attitudes and behavior, Chinese parents and other adults frequently recounted stories of filial children. One story

*Wu Meng's family was too poor to afford bed curtains. This caused much suffering, especially on summer nights when mosquitoes were plentiful. To lessen his father's discomfort, Wu Meng slept on his father's bed every night until his father retired so that the mosquitoes would have enough of Wu Meng's blood and leave his father alone. From* Twenty-four Filial Children. *Beijing: China Bookstore, 1993, p. 15.*

was of Huang Xiang, whose mother died when the boy was nine years old. To help his hard-working father, the boy did household chores after school. He tried to make life more comfortable for his father during the hot summer months by fanning the bed and pillow to cool them. During the cold winter months, because they were too poor to own a heating stove, Huang Xiang warmed his father's bed with his body before his father retired.

Li Mi was another filial child who chose to care for his aged grandmother instead of accepting an important government position as guardian to the prince. In his letter to the emperor, Li Mi explained that he could not leave his sick grandmother, who had raised him.

[2] Yu-Lan Fung, *A History of Chinese Philosophy*, vol. 1. Translated by Derk Bodde. Princeton, NJ: Princeton University Press, 1952, pp. 360–361.
[3] John T. S. Chen, *1001 Chinese Sayings.* Hong Kong: Chung Chi College, 1973, p. 138.

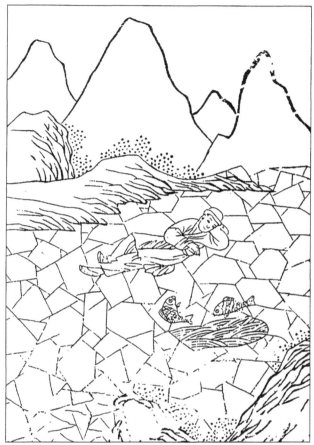

*When he was very young, Wang Xiang lost his mother. His stepmother treated him badly and made many demands on him. One winter, when the lake was frozen, she told him she wanted to eat some fish. To satisfy her, Wang lay on the ice to melt it. Then he made a hole in the ice and caught some fish. From* Twenty-four Filial Children. *Beijing: China Bookstore, 1993, p. 19.*

Impressed with Li Mi's devotion, the emperor granted the request.

Girls were often more devoted to their parents than were boys. Peikung Ying Erh, an only child, decided to sacrifice marriage and a family to care for her parents. Had she married, she would have had to live with her husband's family and would see her parents only on special occasions.[4]

Although Chinese moralists talked about devotion to both parents, the father, who was the head of the family, held the most power and received the

[4] These three stories are from Louis Fong Sui Hong, *Inspiring Deeds of Dutiful Children.* New York: Acme Press, 1965, pp. 24–25, 55–58, 60–61.

*When Yang Xiang and his father went to the fields, they were attacked by a tiger. To protect his father, Yang fought the beast with his bare hands and finally killed him. From* Twenty-four Filial Children. *Beijing: China Bookstore, 1993, p. 20.*

greatest respect. The family hierarchy was based on generation, age, and gender. The older generation was superior to the younger; within the same generation, the elder was superior to the younger; and men were superior to women.

The Chinese family was a microcosm of Chinese society. The entire country was thought of as a big family headed by the emperor. The filial piety shown to the father was like the respect and submission shown to the emperor. Confucius, of whom we will learn more later, taught the Chinese to observe Five Cardinal Relationships that became the foundation of Chinese society: emperor and official; father and son; husband and wife; elder brother and younger brother; male friend and male friend. These relationships were reciprocal in that each person had a responsibility that went with his role. The emperor was to be benevolent and his official to be loyal; the father was to be kind and the son to be filial; the husband was to be righteous, the wife to be submissive; the older brother was to be gentle, the younger brother to be obedient. Honesty and trustworthiness between friends were the only non-hierarchical obligations of the Five Cardinal Relationships.

## Questions

1. In your judgment, why do the Five Cardinal Relationships spell out no obligations for females except wives?
2. Filial piety has been a core Chinese value. What did filial piety mean for the Chinese during imperial times?
3. How do you compare with the ideal Chinese child? What have you done for your parents during the past week or past month?
4. How does the relationship of filial piety compare with the parent-child relationship in modern Western countries?
5. Discuss filial piety in "A Folktale of Love," which you read earlier.

## Extension Activities

1. **Book report.** You may want to read and tell the class about the stories in Louis Fong Sui Hung's *Inspiring Deeds of Dutiful Children* (New York: Acme Press, 1965).
2. **Interview.** Interview five adults. Ask them to agree or disagree with the following proverbs and explain why, giving specific examples when possible.

   Indulgent mothers spoil their children.
   He who leads an idle life will suffer from want and hunger.
   Better to teach your son a trade than to give him a thousand taels of gold.

## Further Reading

Fung, Yu-Lan. *A History of Chinese Philosophy*, Vol. 1. Translated by Derk Bodde. Princeton, NJ: Princeton University Press, 1952.

Hong, Louis Fong Sui. *Inspiring Deeds of Dutiful Children*. New York: Acme Press, 1965.

Lang, Olga. *Chinese Family and Society*. New Haven, CT: Yale University Press, 1946.

Pang, Loretta O. Q. "To Abide in Harmony: Family and the Individual in Confucian China," in *Chinese Social Relationships: The Ideal vs. the Real*. Honolulu: University of Hawai'i, School of Hawaiian, Asian, and Pacific Studies, 1988.

6. treat your parents well, follow their teachings, so they only worry about things they can't control — and be loyal/ respectful

7.) you have to respect and be loyal, not the bare minimum like taking care of a dog

19.) praise the good people not the bad and ppl will like you/ have respect for you

20.) show you follow same morals and they will respect that you're human as well

24.) do what is right even if it is hard or you are a coward

*Earlier sections in this chapter examined the roles of family members and discussed the importance of filial piety in Chinese families. This section discusses Confucius, the great scholar and* thinker *who articulated these ideas. His teachings became the foundation of Chinese thinking not only about the family, but also about the larger Chinese state and society.*

## Reading: *The Analects* of Confucius

Confucius believed that relationships between people were crucial, and he instructed his followers on the correct way for people to behave toward each other.[1] Confucius did not write down his thoughts. Most of what we know about his teachings was recorded by his students in twenty books called *The Analects*. The following are excerpts from these books. First read through the selections quickly to get a general idea of what Confucius said. Then do the activity that follows the reading.

**BOOK II**

*Political Philosophy*

3. The Master said, Govern the people by regulations, keep order among them by chastisements, and they will flee from you, and lose all self-respect. Govern them by moral force, keep order among them by ritual and they will keep their self-respect and come to you of their own accord.

6. Mêng Wu Po asked about the treatment of parents. The Master said, Behave in such a way that your father and mother have no anxiety about you, except concerning your health.

7. Tzu-yu asked about the treatment of parents. The Master said, 'Filial sons' nowadays are people who see to it that their parents get

enough to eat. But even dogs and horses are cared for to that extent. If there is no feeling of respect, wherein lies the difference?

19. Duke Ai asked, What can I do in order to get the support of the common people? Master K'ung replied, If you 'raise up the straight and set them on top of the crooked,' the commoners will support you. But if you raise the crooked and set them on top of the straight, the commoners will not support you.

20. Chi K'ang-tzu asked whether there were any forms of encouragement by which he could induce the common people to be respectful and loyal. The Master said, Approach them with dignity, and they will respect you. Show piety towards your parents and kindness towards your children, and they will be loyal to you. Promote those who are worthy, train those who are incompetent; that is the best form of encouragement.

24. The Master said, . . . to see what is right and not do it is cowardice.

**BOOK IV**

2. The Master said, Without Goodness a man
Cannot for long endure adversity,
Cannot for long enjoy prosperity.
The Good Man rests content with Goodness. . . .

5. Wealth and rank are what every man desires; but if they can only be retained to the detriment of the Way he professes [that is, the

[1] Confucius: China's great philosopher and teacher, who lived from 551 B.C.E. to 479 B.C.E. Confucius articulated ideas that became the foundation of Chinese thinking about the family, state, and society.

2.) better outlook with goodness

5.) follow the right path (teachings)/ and sometimes you have to take your medicine an accept

*[Handwritten top margin:]*
10.) Don't dwell on failure / respect your elders too and don't try to change it
21.) you can learn what's right and wrong moraly from ppl / what u wanna be and what you don't wanna be

*[Handwritten left margin, first:]*
11.) if you have money and flaunt it ppl will not like you rather than being humble

*[Handwritten left margin:]*
17.) look up to smth always keep your knowledge and learn

*[Handwritten left margin:]*
like a loved one I haven't be satisfied

*[Handwritten left margin:]*
7.) will of people will always remain while food an money come and go

*[Handwritten left margin:]*
17.) if you are a good leader and ppl like you they won't think twice

*[Handwritten left margin:]*
7.) there to help the ppl not hurt them

Rightful Path], he must relinquish them. Poverty and obscurity are what every man detests; but if they can only be avoided to the detriment of the Way he professes, he must accept them. The gentleman who ever parts company with Goodness does not fulfil that name. Never for a moment does a gentleman quit the way of Goodness. . . .

18. The Master said, In serving his father and mother a man may gently remonstrate with them. But if he sees that he has failed to change their opinion, he should resume an attitude of deference and not thwart them; may feel discouraged, but not resentful.

## Book VII

25. The Master said, Even when walking in a party of no more than three I can always be certain of learning from those I am with. There will be good qualities that I can select for imitation and bad ones that will teach me what requires correction in myself.

## Book VIII

11. The Master said, If a man has gifts as wonderful as those of the Duke of Chou, yet is arrogant and mean, all the rest is of no account. [The Duke of Chou was an enlightened ruler in ancient China. He was thought of as a model for other rulers.]

17. The Master said, Learn as if you were following someone whom you could not catch up, as though it were someone you were frightened of losing.

## Book XII

7. Tzu-kung asked about government. The Master said, Sufficient food, sufficient weapons, and the confidence of the common people. Tzu-kung said, Suppose you had no choice but to dispense with one of these three, which would you forgo? The Master said, Weapons. Tzu-kung said, Suppose you were forced to dispense with one of the two that were left, which would you forgo? The Master said, Food. For from of old death has been the lot of all men; but a people that no longer trusts its rulers is lost indeed.

17. Chi K'ang-tzu asked Master K'ung about the art of ruling. Master K'ung said, Ruling . . . is straightening. . . . If you lead along a straight way, who will dare go by a crooked one?

19. Chi K'ang-tzu asked Master K'ung about government, saying, Suppose I were to slay those who have not the Way in order to help on those who have the Way, what would you think of it? Master K'ung replied saying, You are there to rule, not to slay. If you desire what is good, the people will at once be good. The essence of the gentleman is that of wind; the essence of small people is that of grass. And when a wind passes over the grass, it cannot choose but bend.

20. Tzu-chang asked what a knight [that is, an aristocrat] must be like if he is to be called 'influential.' The Master said, That depends on what you mean by 'influential.' Tzu-chang replied saying, If employed by the State, certain to win fame, if employed by a Ruling Family, certain to win fame. The Master said, That describes being famous; it does not describe being influential. In order to be influential a man must be by nature straightforward and a lover of right. He must examine men's words and observe their expressions, and bear in mind the necessity of deferring to others. Such a one, whether employed by the State or by a Ruling Family, will certainly be 'influential'; whereas the man who wins fame may merely have obtained, by his outward airs, a reputation for Goodness which his conduct quite belies. Anyone who makes his claims with sufficient self-assurance is certain to win fame in a State, certain to win fame in a Family.

## Book XIII

6. The Master said, If the ruler himself is upright, all will go well even though he does not give orders. But if he himself is not upright, even though he gives orders, they will not be obeyed.

Reprinted with the permission of Simon & Schuster from *The Analects of Confucius*, translated and annotated by Arthur Waley. Copyright 1938 by George Allen & Unwin, Ltd.

*[Handwritten bottom margin:]*
20.) influencial can be physical, but it is best to be influencial because people like you and respect you
6.) if he does not have support he can give orders but if ppl like you they will obey happily and ppl don't care

*political/civic philosophy*     *Filial Piety*
*moral*

## Activity: Paraphrasing *The Analects*

A. Paraphrase each of the passages from *The Analects.*

1. Write the book and item number of the passage.
2. Next to the number, paraphrase the passage; that is, restate its meaning in your own words.
3. In the left margin next to each paraphrase; write FP if it gives advice on filial piety, G if it discusses how to govern, and OB if it advises on other behaviors.

B. To get started, the class could do the first two passages together. Then you can each paraphrase the rest of the passages from Book II on your own. Your teacher will then group you by threes to share your paraphrases of Book II. By this time you should be able to complete the rest of the passages on your own.

C. After you have paraphrased all the passages, summarize Confucius' thoughts on each of the three categories. What did Confucius teach about filial piety? About how rulers should govern? About other behaviors?

*Confucius and his followers. Confucius did not care whom he taught and where he taught.* A History of Chinese Block Prints. *Shanghai: Renmin Meishu, 1988, p. 100.*

## Reading: *Confucius and His Teachings*

*women have no power, no say*

"When she is young, she must submit to her parents. After her marriage, she must submit to her husband. When she is widowed, she must submit to her son."[2] Such were the "three submissions" Confucius taught and Chinese women followed.

Confucius also instructed the Chinese to act according to Five Cardinal Relationships that became the core of Chinese society. Thus in the relationship between emperor and official, father and son, husband and wife, and older brother

*He is very set on structure of power and rankings*

and younger brother, the superior was to behave responsibly and kindly toward his inferior, and the inferior was to be obedient and loyal to the superior. (The relationship between male friends was the only one that was not based on rank.)

The Chinese used Confucius' instructions as a way of life. They made Confucianism the state ideology, upon which they built their social and political institutions.

Knowledge of the Confucian classics became the only avenue to success. Aspiring young men preparing for the civil service examinations, the gateway to positions of honor and respect, studied the classics with uncompromising zeal.

[2] From "The Mother of Mencius." Translated by Nancy Gibbs, in *Chinese Civilization and Society: A Sourcebook*, edited by Patricia Buckley Ebrey. New York: The Free Press, 1981, pp. 33–34.

Confucianism justified the system of scholar-bureaucrats and legitimated the concentration of power in the emperor. No single person in the history of China has had such a penetrating and long-lasting impact on the country and its people as has Confucius.

The Chinese call him *Kongfuzi* or *Kongzi*, *Kong* being his family name and *fuzi* meaning "master." Confucius is the romanized form of *Kongfuzi*.

Born in 551 B.C.E. into a low-ranking aristocratic family, Confucius lived 2,500 years ago, during the Zhou dynasty, a period of turbulent change in Chinese life. Feudal lords battled to replace the Zhou court, and military power became the accepted way to gain dominance and rule.

Distressed with what he saw as the moral corruption of his society, Confucius decided to devote his life to cultivating virtuous leadership and restoring the country to an ideal social order. He traveled extensively, trying to persuade feudal lords to appoint him to office so that he could put his philosophy to work, but the lords rejected him.

Yet others flocked to him. By the time he died in 479 B.C.E., he had taught over three thousand students. The Six Arts of Confucius—a curriculum of ritual, music, mathematics, history, archery, and charioteering—were aimed at developing the character, intellect, and physique of his students, who he hoped would become well-rounded, moral gentlemen. His disciples continued his teachings after his death and wrote them down in what we now call *The Analects*, known in Chinese as *Lun Yu* (Record of Conversations).

Although Confucius failed to find a feudal lord who welcomed his principles, about 250 years after his death the rulers of the Han dynasty began to fill the bureaucracy with people said to practice virtues preached by Confucius. Later dynasties gradually developed a system of civil service examinations based on the Confucian classics. Like their great teacher, Chinese rulers came to believe that through proper education and the performance of rituals, learned men would be able to cultivate a moral society.

## The Spread of Confucianism

Confucius not only set a tradition that transcended his own time; his teachings also spread to Vietnam, Korea, and Japan.

Near the end of the third century B.C.E., during the Qin dynasty, the Chinese began to take control in Vietnam. The disunity of the Zhou period had ended, and China was ready to extend its influence beyond its borders. The Chinese then called their southern frontier *Nam-viet*, *nam* meaning "south" and *viet* meaning "to cross over." With Chinese in control of this southern territory over many centuries, Confucianism came to dominate Vietnam's political and intellectual life. The Vietnamese adopted China's examination practices and its writing system; they patterned their state structure and literature after China's. Vietnam's spoken language was strongly influenced by dialects spoken in southern China. Referring to themselves as "barbarians" according to the Confucian worldview, and calling their territory China's tributary state, the Vietnamese confirmed the acculturating power of Confucianism.

In the north, Chinese influence penetrated the Korean peninsula beginning in the Han dynasty. Confucian ideas slowly took root over the next six hundred years. In the fourth century A.D., Koreans in the northernmost state of Koguryo established a school devoted to the teachings of Confucius. Over the next several hundred years, Koreans developed a code of law and a system of government patterned after China's and followed Chinese methods in managing agricultural production and taxing harvests. Chinese influence continued even after the Korean peninsula was unified into a single state during the seventh century. Koreans used Chinese characters in their writing system and adopted the Chinese examination system to recruit government officials.

Korea not only adopted Confucianism but channeled it to Japan. Traveling Korean scholars near the end of the third century A.D. introduced *The Analects* to the Japanese court. Other visitors from the Asian continent during the next four centuries also helped to spread Confucianism.

Confucianism flourished in Japan during the seventh and eighth centuries. Court regent Prince Shotoku (573–621) used the teachings of

*[handwritten: Confucianism has helped China gain influence on surrounding countries]*

Confucius to justify both his assertion that the emperor was supreme and his actions in centralizing the Japanese government. Rulers after Prince Shotoku followed his lead in unifying the nation and in using Confucian principles to guide later reforms. Unlike Korea, Japan did not adopt China's examination system, but it did incorporate Chinese characters into its writing system and patterned its laws and government after the Chinese model. Thus Japan, too, was a willing student of Confucianism.

*[handwritten: How come?]*

## Neo-Confucianism

Confucianism proved potent in molding people's way of life and forming a foundation for social and political institutions both at home and abroad. In China, despite challenges from Buddhism and Daoism, and even during the long period of political disintegration after the Han dynasty, Confucianism continued to spread. During the eleventh and twelfth centuries it changed with the times, becoming what is known as Neo-Confucianism. This reinterpretation of Confucianism dominated Chinese thinking until the twentieth century.

*[handwritten: it does it still prevail]*

Neo-Confucianists of the eleventh and twelfth centuries incorporated Buddhist and Daoist concerns about the metaphysical world into their framework, hoping to capture the original vision of Confucius in ways compatible with other philosophies. Eventually they de-emphasized concerns that were not part of early Confucian thought and returned to the stress on mundane social and political matters.

*[handwritten: altering Confucianism]*

The Neo-Confucian movement reinvigorated China's commitment to Confucianism, and Confucian ideas became even more central in the examinations.

Neo-Confucianism spread to Korea during the late thirteenth century and to Japan during the sixteenth century, becoming incorporated into the social and political lives of the people living in the two countries.

## Confucianism Today

In 1949, after the victory of the Communists under Mao Zedong, the new government of the People's Republic of China decided to make a clean break with the past. Confucianism was officially replaced by Communism. Nevertheless, Confucian values survive in both the public and private arenas. In the public sector, Communists have replaced Confucianists in the state bureaucracy, yet state officials and party cadre are as privileged today as the scholar-gentry were in imperial times, and their duties are prescribed for them in as much detail. Moreover, government officials today, as in Confucian China, share a commitment to their ideologies, which justify their roles in directing and administering the government.

*[handwritten: why so quick?]*

*[handwritten: are they just covering up Confucianism]*

In the privacy of the home, sons continue to be favored over daughters, and the Chinese continue to stress interpersonal relationships in their daily lives.

Today, Confucian values are probably preserved more deliberately outside than inside China. Besides having established itself in Korea and Japan (in Vietnam, Buddhism and Communism have weakened earlier Confucian influence), Confucianism has taken root among Chinese living in such places as Taiwan, Hong Kong, and Singapore. Many scholars credit the economic successes of these countries to their people's adherence to Confucian values—hard work, dedication to schooling, and the primacy of the family.

*[handwritten: What countries still practice / follow it?]*

## Questions

1. What is an ideology? Give examples to show that Confucianism was the state ideology of China.
2. What was happening in China when Confucius lived? What did he care about, and what did he want to do?

---

### Activity: Spread of Confucianism

---

Draw a map of east Asia. Label the countries to which Confucianism spread. Draw arrows from China to these countries to show the direction of the spread of Confucianism.

## Activity: Letters to Confucius

### Part 1.

Put yourself in the place of a Chinese living in imperial China. You have a dilemma for which you need advice. Write a letter to Confucius explaining your situation and asking for his response.

First, decide whether you are a mother, a girl, a father, a boy, an emperor, or a government official.

Your letter should include the following:

1. who you are
2. your name

    Here are some names from which to choose. Note that in China the family name comes before the given name. Pronounce the letter *a* as "ah."

    **Family names:** Chen, Deng, Ding, Fang, Hu, Huang, Li, Lin, Ma, Ye, Zhang, Zhou
    **Female names:** Chunhua, Chunmei, Jiaying, Ling, Meiling, Yanyu, Yingping
    **Males names:** Changming, Dongfang, Huasong, Jiaming, Kaichang, Leiming, Lizhong, Ping, Yingming, Yingtang

3. your age
4. whether both parents are living, if it is relevant to your story
5. whether you have any sisters or brothers, and if so, how many of each, if it is relevant to your story

    Review all the readings in this chapter to generate some ideas. Remember, however, that your story should be original.

    Your letter should be believable. That is, you should describe a situation that could have happened in imperial China. Use your imagination!

### Part 2.

Your teacher will give your letter to another person in the class and give you a classmate's letter.

This time you are to take the role of Confucius. Although you have been dead for

*Laozi. From* A History of Chinese Block Prints. *Shanghai: Renmin Meishu, 1988, p. 105.*

many years, your teachings have had a profound impact on the Chinese, who have looked to you for guidance long after your death. Review the two readings in this section, "*The Analects* of Confucius" and "Confucianism." Write a response to the letter you have before you.

### Part 3.

Form groups of about five students. Each student should have a pair of letters. Take turns reading your letters to the others in your group. Have your group choose the best pair of letters. Then decide which two members of your group will read the letters before the class. If you are chosen, read with animation.

Afterward, discuss this question: How realistic and believable were the letters?

## Activity: Questions Posed Earlier

Turn to "Pairing Off," the first activity of this chapter. Now that you have learned something about life in imperial China, answer the questions as a Chinese of that period might have.

After you have answered the questions this second time around, compare your two sets of responses. In a paragraph or two, make some generalizations comparing traditional Chinese views with your modern views.

## Daoism

During the waning years of the Zhou dynasty, Daoism was one of the "Hundred Schools" of thought vying for attention in China. Its radical approach at a time of political and social turmoil offered an alternative to Confucianism. Confucianism suggested concrete solutions for improving social order; Daoism did not. Simply put, Confucianism emphasized socially approved activity, but Daoism recommended activity in accord with nature.

In Chinese, "Dao" means "the Way." To Daoists, "Dao" is the rhythm and regularity of the universe, the source of all things, and the natural way things happen. The teaching of Daoism has been passed down in the book of *Daodejing* (The Canon of the Way and of Virtue), a book of poetry supposedly written by an ancient sage, Laozi, the "Old Master." Based on the human being's relationship with nature, Daoism has presented an alternative to participating in the community. The philosophy centers on returning to nature rather than following the artificialities of culture. Furthermore, it teaches that government interference is a major cause of social troubles.

> *Govern the state with correctness.*
> *Operate the army with surprise tactics.*
> *Administer the empire by engaging in no activity.*
> *How do I know that this should be so?*
> *Through this:*
> > *The more taboos and prohibitions there are in*
> > > *the world,*
> > *The poorer the people will be.*
> > *The more sharp weapons the people have,*
> > *The more troubled the state will be.*
> > *The more cunning and skill man possesses,*
> > *The more vicious things will appear.*
> > *The more laws and orders are made prominent,*
> > *The more thieves and robbers there will be.*
> > *Therefore the sage says:*
> > *I take no action and the people of themselves are*
> > > *transformed.*

> *I love tranquility and the people of themselves*
> > *become correct.*
> *I engage in no activity and the people of themselves*
> > *become prosperous.*
> *I have no desires and the people of themselves*
> > *become simple.*[1]

Daoists believe that people's sufferings are of their own creation, and that achievement will arrive through *wuwei*—the action of inaction—or letting nature take its course.

True Daoists see no point in pursuing such artificial human ambitions as acquiring possessions or striving for honors.

> *He who stands on tiptoe is not steady.*
> *He who strides forward does not go.*
> *He who shows himself is not luminous.*
> *He who justifies himself is not prominent.*
> *He who boasts of himself is not given credit.*
> *He who brags does not endure for long.*

Although Daoism and Confucianism represent contrasting views of life, the two are compatible. Most scholar-officials combined the two philosophies into an interesting hybrid. In the public arena they taught Confucian values and adhered to Confucian mores; in their private lives most turned to Daoism, losing themselves in nature's beauty. Many famous romantic Chinese poets, landscape painters, and calligraphers drew their inspiration from Daoism.

Daoist influence has persisted over the centuries. Today it remains part of the Chinese tradition, even among overseas Chinese.

[1] This excerpt and the next are from *The Way of Lao Tzu*, by Wing-Tsit Chan. New York: Bobbs-Merrill, 1963, pp. 143 and 201.

*[handwritten top margin: Buddhism: letting go of everything/attachments of life, no material things, karma, learning the meaning of life, be reincarnated to help understand meaning of life]*

## Buddhism in China

Of all the foreign religions and ideas that entered China during the imperial age, Buddhism was the only one that met with much success; it has since become part of China's social and religious life.

Buddhism began about the time of Confucius, when Gautama, a prince born in the foothills of the Himalayas near the Nepal–India border, decided to give up his everyday life and his earthly possessions to go into the world to contemplate the reality of misery and suffering. For six years he traveled, fasted, meditated, and studied with different scholars, but he failed to find the answer to the meaning of life. Then one day, while meditating under a bodhi tree, he found the answer—and became the Buddha, the Enlightened One. *[handwritten: So it's all about life!]*

According to the Buddha, the reality of existence is unceasing suffering caused by desire—the clinging to life and material things. Central to Buddhism is the idea of karma, the belief that people exist in a cycle of reincarnation, reborn into a new status each time they die, the new status depending on how they lived their previous lives. To break this chain of reincarnation and reach nirvana—a state of blessedness and fulfillment beyond human comprehension—people must give up their selfish desires and practice good deeds and self-restraint.

Buddhism entered China sometime during the first century. Missionaries traveling in trading ships brought the religion from the south, while others traveling overland introduced it from the northwest. Between 400 and 700, Buddhist influence intensified. Chinese pilgrims traveled to India to visit sacred sites and collect scriptures and returned to spread the religion throughout China. Chinese forms of Buddhism developed, which later spread to areas beyond China's borders—to Korea in the fourth century and to Japan in the sixth. By the seventh century, Buddhists from Central Asia, India, and China had spread the religion to Tibet. *[handwritten left margin: was this forced or did korea and Japan accept it?]*

Apart from the few pilgrims who went to India, Chinese Buddhists had no firsthand knowledge of Indian Buddhism. Because the Chinese did not read Sanskrit, the ancient language of the Hindus in India, they had to rely on Chinese translations of Buddhist texts. These translated texts played a crucial role in sinicizing Buddhism—that is, transforming it to fit Chinese society. By the late sixth century, Chinese forms of Buddhism had spread to all parts of China, to all social levels, and northward beyond China's borders. Chan or Zen Buddhism, for example, commanded a significant following in China and then spread to Korea and Japan. *[handwritten right margin: were the religions slightly different?; spreading quick and vast]*

Although it threatened the dominance of Confucianism, Buddhism actually complemented and enriched Confucianism by offering a radically different world view. While Confucianism concerned itself primarily with everyday life, Buddhism concerned itself with metaphysical matters. *[handwritten right margin: unifying peoples beliefs even more]*

Today people throughout Southeast Asia and East Asia—in Burma, Thailand, Laos, Kampuchea, Vietnam, Hong Kong, Taiwan, Korea, and Japan, as well as China—have adapted Buddhism to make it compatible with their ways of life. *[handwritten: How many of these countries are still dominated Buddhist]*

*The Buddha and his followers. How did the artist show Buddha's compassionate nature? From* A History of Chinese Block Prints. *Shanghai: Renmin Meishu, 1988, p. 86.*

Confucious' words were put into the anolects. he came up with the "Golden Rule"
1.) he love ceramonies and sees it as very important 2.) treat parents with obedience and take for them when they are old, filial pietry. 3.) be obediand to people above yarself (superior and inferior/wind and grass) 4.) wisdom, benevolence and self reflection are important 5.)

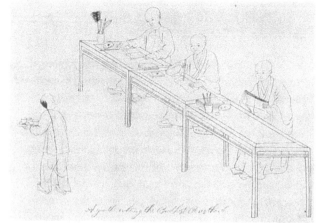

*An initiation ceremony of a Buddhist monk. Incense was used to burn his hair roots. Watercolor. Nineteenth century. Reproduction by permission of Urban Council Hong Kong from the collection of Hong Kong Museum of Art.*

*(top) These youths have not yet entered the Buddhist priesthood. Note the youth's pigtail. (middle) Buddhist priests collecting money for the temple. (bottom) Buddhist priests collecting rice. Pen and ink. Reproduction by permission of Urban Council Hong Kong from the collection of Hong Kong Museum of Art.*

*A Buddhist nun. Like the priest's, the roots of her hair were also burned. Like priests, nuns did not marry. Watercolor. Reproduction by permission of Urban Council Hong Kong from the collection of Hong Kong Museum of Art.*

Confucianism

*Daoism: How you live your life, be in nature, appreciate the worlds gifts, less about structure ~~rather than~~, more about inner peace, living in nature*

*Legalism: ~~laws and milit~~ laws are how you run/structure the world/society. Military is made to enforce law. Laws ensure consistency. Confucianism says no Leader sha~~be bound by law~~*

*Process of the Job Robe story*

*Confucists would reward the guy who gave the robe, legalist would punish him b/c he did a job that wasn't his Job*

## Legalism

The persistent turmoil in China in what is now called the Warring States Period during the last one hundred eighty years of the Zhou dynasty compelled the Chinese to think deeply about human nature and government. As the old order collapsed, newer ways of thinking competed for attention. It was during this politically turbulent time that Confucianism, Daoism, and Legalism spread among the Chinese.

Legalism was a school of thought that focused on ways to strengthen the state and its military. Legalists believed that the government should have a clear, strictly enforced code of laws; that is why they were called Legalists. Unlike other schools of thought, Legalism had no recognized founder. Most Legalists were government officials serving in the warring states. Among the best known was a nobleman named Han Feizi (circa 280–233 B.C.E.), who wrote a book that became a classic of Legalist thinking.

Han wrote that a ruler should control his ministers by means of "two handles . . . punishment and favor." "To inflict mutilation and death on men is called punishment," he said. "To bestow honor and reward is called favor."[1] A story in Han's book illustrates the use of one of the two handles:

Once in the past Marquis Chao of Han got drunk and fell asleep. The keeper of the royal hat, seeing that the marquis was cold, laid a robe over him. When the marquis awoke, he was pleased and asked his attendants, "Who covered me with a robe?" "The keeper of the hat," they replied. The marquis thereupon punished both the keeper of the royal hat and the keeper of the royal robe. He punished the keeper of the robe for failing to do his duty, and the keeper of the hat for overstepping his office. It was not that he did not dislike the cold, but he considered the trespass of one official on the duties of another to be a greater danger than cold.[2]

Legalists believed that rulers should use laws to control their subordinates. They held that people are basically evil and therefore need stern laws to keep them in line. Confucianists, on the other hand, believed in the primacy of moral persuasion and only reluctantly admitted the necessity of law.

Various lords of the warring states in the fourth and third centuries B.C.E. used Legalist ideas, but it was the Qin dynasty that applied Legalism most consistently and finally succeeded in unifying China. After the fall of the Qin dynasty, Legalism fell into disfavor, but its tendencies remained even among imperial governments claiming to follow Confucianism. The hybridization of the two systems of thinking has invited comments that Chinese imperial governments were Confucian on the outside but Legalist on the inside.

[1] Burton Watson, trans., *Han Fei Tzu: Basic Writings.* New York: Columbia University Press, 1964, p. 30, 32.

[2] Ibid, p. 32.

## Extension Activities

1. Video. See if your public library has the video *Taoism*, produced by the Hartley Film Foundation. This production is a good introduction to Daoism.
2. Mapping. Draw a map of Asia showing the countries to which Buddhism has spread.

## Further Reading

Welty, Paul Thomas. *The Asians: Their Evolving Heritage*, 6th ed. New York: Harper & Row, 1984. A good overview of aspects of Chinese history and culture, with chapters on Chinese Ideology, Confucianism, Taoism, Legalism, Buddhism in China, Chinese Social Life,

**Daoism:**
he became a hermit and his writings became the religion, people practice meditation and going in nature. He found whisper sweet because the world is sweet. Dao is the way of the world. ~~too late~~ make time for stillness and experience world, be open and ~~empty your mind from bad/negative thoughts~~

Gentry and Peasantry in China, The Clan in China, The Family in China, and Politics in China.

## Confucianism and the Spread of Confucianism

Balazs, Etienne. *Chinese Civilization and Bureaucracy.* Translated by H. M. Wright. New Haven and London: Yale University Press, 1964.

Fairbank, John King, ed. *The Chinese World Order.* Cambridge, MA: Harvard University Press, 1968.

Fairbank, John King, and Edwin O. Reischauer. *China: Tradition and Transformation.* Boston: Houghton Mifflin, 1989.

Hane, Mikiso. *Premodern Japan: A Historical Survey.* Boulder, CO: Westview Press, 1991.

Tu Weiming, Milan G. Hjetmanek, and Alan Wachman, eds. *The Confucian World Observed: A Contemporary Discussion of Confucian Humanism in East Asia.* Honolulu: East-West Center, Institute of Culture and Communication, 1991.

**Buddhism:**
meditate to let go of bad emotions
purify your soul
empty your mind from bad thoughts
because bad thoughts cause suffering

**Legalism:**
· binding framework
· law above everything

## Buddhism

Kitagawa, Joseph M., and Mark D. Cummings, eds. *Buddhism and Asian History: Selections from the Encyclopedia of Religion.* New York: Macmillan, 1989.

Creel, H. G. *Chinese Thought from Confucius to Mao Tse-tung.* Chicago: University of Chicago Press, 1953.

## Legalism

Ames, Roger T. *The Art of Rulership: A Study in Ancient Chinese Political Thought.* Albany, SUNY Press. 1994 [1983].

Creel, H. G. *Chinese Thought from Confucius to Mao Tse-tung.* Chicago: University of Chicago Press, 1953.

Watson, Burton, trans. *Han Fei Tzu: Basic Writings.* New York: Columbia University Press, 1964.

## Daoism

Chan, Wing-Tsit, trans. *The Way of Lao Tzu.* New York: Bobbs-Merrill, 1963.

Creel, H. G. *Chinese Thought from Confucius to Mao Tse-tung.* Chicago & London: University of Chicago Press, 1953.

Waley, Arthur. *Three Ways of Thought in Ancient China.* Garden City, NY: Doubleday & Co., Inc., 1939.

# 5 China and the Outside World

*T*his section looks at China's interactions with the outside world. These encounters, occurring over many centuries, did not fundamentally change China. Yet they did open Chinese eyes to the outside world.

Until the 1600s, the Chinese were advanced beyond other people, whom they considered barbarians. One group of so-called barbarians, the Mongols, eventually conquered China. Before reading about the Mongols, however, you should begin working on two activities, "Making a Timeline" and "Travel Guides to Imperial China," which you can do as you proceed through this last section of Chapter 1.

## Activity: Making a Timeline

Make a timeline showing the dynasties and events listed in this activity. Look at the timeline at the beginning of the book for ideas. Use colored pencils or pens to make your timeline attractive and easy to read. You may want to use a long roll of paper so that you can include every item listed.

Give each century the same amount of space. You might decide, for example, to have a hundred years equal to one inch. Be sure to indicate on your timeline the centuries "before the common era," or B.C.E., and the centuries Anno Domini (Latin words for "in the year of the Lord"), or A.D.

The readings sometimes refer to centuries instead of specific years. Note that the twelfth century B.C.E. means the years 1199 to 1100 B.C.E.; the third century B.C.E. means the years 299 to 200 B.C.E.; the fifth century A.D. means A.D. 400 to 499; and the thirteenth century A.D. means A.D. 1200 to 1299.

1. Place these dynasties on your timeline. The timeline in this book shows dates for each dynasty.

   Shang dynasty
   Zhou dynasty
   Qin dynasty
   Former Han dynasty
   Xin dynasty
   Later Han dynasty
   Period of Disunity
   Sui dynasty
   Tang dynasty
   Period of Disunity
   Song dynasty
   Southern Song dynasty
   Yuan dynasty (Mongol rule)
   Ming dynasty
   Qing dynasty (Manchurian rule)

2. Place these eras in the history of Western civilization on your timeline. They are listed on the timeline in this book.

   Classical Greek civilization
   Roman empire
   Middle Ages
   Renaissance
   Reformation

| 12th century B.C.E. | 3rd century B.C.E. | 5th century A.D. | 13th century A.D. |
|---|---|---|---|
| 1199 B.C.E.–1100 B.C.E. | 299 B.C.E.–200 B.C.E. | A.D. 400–A.D. 499 | A.D. 1200–A.D. 1299 |

3. Place these events on your timeline. Specific dates are in the readings in this chapter.

> Confucius is born.
> The Qin dynasty uses Legalistic ideas in ruling China.
> Daoism emerges as one of the "Hundred Schools" of thought.
> Buddhism enters China.
> The examination system becomes established for choosing government officials.
> Confucianism spreads to Korea; to Japan.
> Merchants travel the Silk Roads.
> China begins using paper money; Sweden begins using paper money.
> Marco Polo sets out for China with his father and uncle.
> Zheng He leads sea voyages during the Ming dynasty.
> Matteo Ricci, a Jesuit missionary, arrives in China.

## Activity:  Travel to Imperial China

What would it be like to travel back in time to the pre-modern period of Chinese history? Help the uninformed by creating a travel guide to imperial China. Include information from all of Chapter 1, including this last section, but remember to use your own words. Use atlases and other sources to help you. Draw pictures and use color to make your guide attractive. What follows are some suggestions. Think of other ideas.

- a description of the lives of the people
- a description of the emperor and his civil servants
- interesting places to visit
- a map of China
- great achievements during this period

## Reading:  *The Thirteenth-Century World of Marco Polo*

It is hard for us today, when foreign travel is undertaken so casually, to understand the extraordinary courage required to travel in the thirteenth century. Even rich and prominent people rarely traveled, for traveling was slow, difficult, and dangerous. In that world, cultures and languages developed in isolation.

The story of Marco Polo is fascinating for many reasons, not the least of which is that in a world of profound isolation, his story shows the clash of three cultures: Venetian, Mongolian, and Chinese. Marco Polo himself was from Venice, and he was an official of the Mongol court in China. To get perspective on his story, we must consider the place of the Chinese, the Mongolians, and the Venetians in the thirteenth-century world.

In many ways the story of the Mongolians is the most astonishing. Here was a group of about one million people who in twenty years changed from isolated tribes of illiterate nomads to a great unified power that eventually controlled the most

*Genghis Khan. Courtesy National Palace Museum, Taiwan.*

*Present-day Mongols on their short-legged ponies. Courtesy of Camera Press, Ltd., London.*

*A Mongol archer. By an anonymous fifteenth-century artist. Note the small size of the Mongol horse. The riding skills that made Mongols such effective warriors are still practiced today. Ink and color. Courtesy of Victoria and Albert Museum, London.*

far-reaching empire the world has ever seen. The story of that change is intimately connected to the life of Genghis Khan (circa 1160–1227).

The man who became known to the world as Genghis Khan (which could be translated as Universal Chief) was named Temujin at birth. Neither his family nor his tribe was particularly prominent. By ruthlessness and cunning, he was able to overthrow the overlord of his own tribe. He then set about conquering other Mongol tribes. By 1206 he was the chief of all the Mongols.

At this point the real adventure of Genghis Khan begins. Not content with control of the Mongols, he set about conquering other lands as well. Out of the small Mongol population he fashioned an extraordinary military operation that conquered most of North Asia, European Russia, and Europe itself as far as Hungary. Riding on horseback, the Mongols, in disciplined units of ten fighters, overwhelmed everyone they met, leaving a trail of destruction, massacring entire villages, raping and pillaging at will. For many years they were believed to be invincible in battle; the mere threat of a Mongol invasion led many people to surrender without a fight.

The vast scope of Mongol military operations made the conquest of China a protracted affair. Not until 1234, seven years after the death of the Great Khan, did all of northern China come under Mongol control. The conquest of southern China was not complete until 1279, during the reign of his grandson, Kublai Khan.

It would be hard to imagine a greater contrast than the one that separated the Chinese from their rulers. The Mongols knew how to endure the harsh weather of their homeland, a desertlike place where winters were long and bitterly cold, summers short and very hot. The land was suitable for pasture but not for farming. The Mongols lived in mobile tents called yurts and ate mostly milk and meat. Their prized possessions were their horses, and the most serious crime in Mongol society was stealing a horse. They had no luxuries. Even their clothes were rough and plain. Their effort went entirely to satisfy practical needs, with little of either science or art.

China, on the other hand, was largely agricultural but had a bustling urban and commer-

*The Great Wall of China is twenty-five feet high and over fourteen hundred miles long, about as long as the entire west coast of the United States. Today it is the only human construction visible from space. Qin Shi Huangdi, who was emperor of the Qin dynasty from 221 to 210 B.C.E., ordered thousands of men to build a continuous wall along China's northern border to protect the "civilized" Chinese from northern "barbarians." In creating this wall, Qin's workers joined shorter walls that had been built by local Chinese rulers. Because of inadequate food and shelter and the harsh climate—thousands of workers died and were buried inside the wall. Some emperors after Qin extended the wall even farther, even as late as the sixteenth century. Unfortunately for the Chinese, the Great Wall was unable to keep intruders out. Nomads invaded and dominated northern China from A.D. 220 to 590, and again from 900 to 100. Later, the Mongols occupied China and ruled as the Yuan dynasty, as did the Manchus, who ruled as the Qing dynasty. Courtesy of Francis Tsui.*

cial life as well. The Chinese had highly developed arts and literature, and their scientific accomplishments in such areas as astronomy and physics were well ahead of the work of contemporary Europeans. The south of China—the part under the control of the Sung dynasty until 1279—was the world's most sophisticated civilization in the thirteenth century. It is this area of China that most impressed Marco Polo when he saw it in the 1280s. The irony is that he did not recognize the greatness of Hangzhou and other southern cities as Chinese accomplishments. He assumed that Kublai Khan was responsible for their beauty and greatness.

The Mongols showed little interest in Chinese culture or civilization. Genghis Khan seriously

considered massacring the entire population of North China and turning it into pastureland. When he decided not to, it was because his advisors convinced him that he could gain more by encouraging agricultural production and imposing heavy taxes on the peasants. Genghis Khan viewed all his conquered land as personal property, to use for his own pleasure.

He showed remarkable talent as an administrator. He understood that running an empire required skills that Mongol tribesmen lacked, so he hired foreign advisors—Turks, Uighers, Persians, and even some Chinese—to help him control the vast area of the empire. He ordered that the Mongols formulate an alphabet so that written decrees could be sent throughout the

*Although it was painted after his death, this is considered the most realistic portrait of Marco Polo. Courtesy of The Hulton Deutsch Collection, London.*

*Kublai Khan, grandson of Genghis Khan. Marco Polo served as an official in Kublai Khan's court. From* A History of Chinese Block Prints. *Shanghai: Renmin Meishu, 1988, p. 109.*

empire. He instituted a rigid caste system to ensure that the Mongols were at the top, foreign advisors just below them, and conquered peoples at the bottom. In this way he assured that the Mongols would continue to dominate the empire.

The empire was, by medieval European standards, efficiently run. The roads were well policed and maintained, ensuring that travelers could move safely. Farmers who had feared taking crops to markets in the towns because of the threat of highwaymen now went freely. Couriers carried messages throughout the empire, and taxes were collected in a regular and orderly way. Such operations, which we now take for granted, were unique to the Mongol empire among European and Asian societies of the time.

The order that the Mongols imposed on conquered areas has been called the "Pax Mongolica," or Mongolian Peace, for in a world beset by petty conflicts and general lawlessness, internal order was a remarkable achievement.

One consequence flowing directly from the Pax Mongolica was that China became directly accessible to European travelers. Beginning in the 1240s, Franciscan monks eager to spread Christianity made their way to China, encouraged not only by the relative safety of the trip but also by the fact that the Mongols tolerated all religions as long as their adherents showed proper deference to the Khan. The monks' attempts to convert Chinese were not very successful, but some monks left vivid accounts of their travels. Merchants also traveled east from Europe to the newly opened empire, but few of them showed any literary inclination. It is surprising, then, that the most famous and lively of all European accounts of the Mongol empire comes from a merchant, the Venetian traveler Marco Polo.

Marco Polo's story, as told in his *Description of the World*, begins with the travels of his father and uncle, who arrived in the Mongol empire in 1260, after a journey of three and a half years. They met the Great Kublai Khan, leader of the entire Mongol empire and of China. He told the Polos to bring a hundred Christian scholars to his court. They returned to Europe in 1269, then set out for China in 1271 without the scholars but with the seventeen-year-old Marco Polo. The three men stayed in China for seventeen more years, during which they became officials of the Mongol court.

After their stay in China, the Polos spent another three years returning to Europe, arriving in Venice in 1295. Three years later Marco

## The Feudal System in Europe

When the Huns and Germanic tribes from the north invaded Italy and laid waste to the Roman empire (see Chapter 1 timeline), they left Europe in chaos. What followed in Europe was a period with no large governments. Travel became dangerous, and survival depended on maintaining isolated, secure, self-sufficient communities. During this period of a thousand years, known as the Middle Ages, most Europeans lived in such communities.

It was in this context that the feudal system evolved. Within the confines of a protected fortress, or castle, on an area of land varying from a few hundred acres to many square miles, self-sustaining communities formed. The area was presided over by a lord, who protected the inhabitants by maintaining a watch over the countryside and keeping robbers, armies, and other threatening forces from attacking. In return, a system of feudal obligations evolved in which peasants worked the land and gave a portion of their crops to the lord. The spiritual welfare of the inhabitants was handled by a priest living on the estate.

Craftsmen also helped maintain the independence of the feudal unit. There were fairs at which travelers, who must have led a risky life, came to entertain and sell things to those behind the walls. But for the most part, people had only sporadic contact with the outside world.

The system was far from uniform. Many feudal lords had obligations to kings who in their own way protected the feudal enclaves.

On maps of present-day Europe, we see remnants of Europe's feudal past. The tiny countries of Liechtenstein, Luxembourg, and San Marino are old feudal enclaves controlled by princes whose authority was at one time much like that of a feudal lord. Imagine an entire continent made up of small states the size of these principalities. This is what medieval Europe was like.

---

Polo was in jail, a victim of a war between Venice and Genoa. He dictated his story to a fellow prisoner, and it achieved a certain fame and notoriety for its author even in his own lifetime. The Venetians saw Marco Polo as a braggart and a liar; they refused to believe that China was so much more luxurious than Venice. Today most scholars believe that what Marco Polo wrote was substantially true, despite some glaring errors and omissions. There is no doubt that thirteenth-century Europe was a backwater compared to the China of the day.

Most Europeans in the thirteenth century lived on small feudal estates (see sidebar "The Feudal System in Europe"), protected and cut off from the outside world by moats and castles. They lived a life of primitive self-sufficiency. Peasants in such a society probably owned little more than the clothes on their backs. There was little learning; even the lord of the manor was probably illiterate and seldom saw anyone who lived outside the borders of the manor. Luxuries were unimag-inable, for even the most basic of spices—pepper—was outrageously expensive, affordable only to the richest lords. This life was a trial, and people believed that if they prayed and were faithful, they would be rewarded in the next life.

Marco Polo's life was far more exciting than theirs. Venice was a vibrant and exciting commercial center, an independent city overflowing with sinful luxuries, the most sophisticated and cosmopolitan place in Europe. But the glories of Hangzhou, with its one million inhabitants, extensive commercial life, beautiful architecture, and abundant literary, religious, and sporting associations, were too much for even the Venetians to imagine, and so they assumed that Marco Polo was a liar.

Marco Polo's view was severely biased by two facts: He was a privileged member of the Mongol court, and he never learned to speak or read Chinese, although he became well conversant with Mongol. Thus he saw China through the eyes of the privileged class, more Mongol

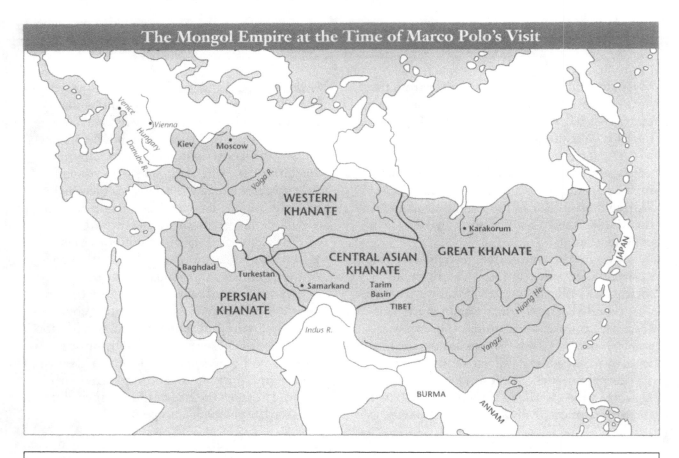

The Mongol Empire at the Time of Marco Polo's Visit

## Chronology of Mongol Conquests

| Name of Khan | Date | Event |
|---|---|---|
| Genghis Khan (1206–1227) | 1206 | Mongols united under Genghis Khan |
| | 1209 | Northern Tibet conquered |
| | 1211 | North China invaded |
| | 1217 | Tarim Basin (north of Tibet) conquered |
| | 1221 | West Turkestan (now Afghanistan) and part of Persia conquered |
| | 1223 | Russia invaded |
| Ogodei (1229–1241) | 1234 | North China conquered |
| | 1238 | Moscow conquered |
| | 1240 | Kiev conquered |
| | 1241 | Europe invaded; Mongolian cavalry reach Vienna |
| Möngke (1251–1259) | 1252 | Eastern Tibet conquered |
| | 1253 | All of Persia conquered |
| | 1258 | Baghdad conquered; Korea conquered |
| Kublai (1260–1294) | 1279 | Southern China conquered |

than Chinese. The China that he saw was not the China of peasants, whose lives would have had much in common with the simple life of European peasants. In both places peasants made up the vast majority of the population.

Marco Polo had little influence on his contemporaries. His book made him a minor celebrity in his lifetime; in the days before the printing press, the impact of the written word was not great. It was not until two hundred years after his death that his importance asserted itself. Then his story was read by Christopher Columbus. Inspired by the stories of Chinese wealth, Columbus determined to search for a faster route to the Orient. He tried to find China, found America instead, and the Age of Exploration began.

## Questions

1. Why did Genghis Khan embark on his conquering missions?
2. Contrast the lives of the Mongols and the Chinese.
3. In what ways did Genghis Khan show his skills as an administrator?
4. What were some of the consequences of the Pax Mongolica?
5. Why was Marco Polo's story not believed during his lifetime?
6. What colored Marco Polo's view of China?

### Activity: Enacting a Play

The play that follows imagines a miraculous encounter between Marco Polo, Kublai Khan, and two Europeans—a priest and a peasant. It illustrates the cultural clashes that would occur at such a meeting as each participant brings his own parochial perspective to the event. Such a meeting would, of course, have been logistically impossible in the real world.

1. Form groups of four students each. In your group, decide who will play which character. Then do a dramatic reading of the play. Read with feeling and follow the stage directions.

2. Now form groups of four or five students who have the same role. If there are more than twenty students in your class, you may need to form two groups of people for each role.
3. Have each person in your group read only the assigned character's part. Then choose the best performer in your group. If two groups are assigned to your character, the two groups should decide who will perform before the class.
4. The designated actors will perform the play for the class. They may want to wear costumes in keeping with their characters.

Marco Polo

Priest

Peasant

Kublai Khan

*The illustrations of Marco Polo, the Priest, and the Peasant are adapted from* Costume: An Illustrated Survey from Ancient Times to the Twentieth Century, *by Margot Lister. London: Herbert Jenkins, Ltd., 1967, pp. 124 and 129. That of Kublai Khan is adapted from* Le Costume Chinois, *Zhou Xun and Gao Chunming, eds. Hong Kong: The Commercial Press, Ltd., 1984, p. 248.*

## Reading: *A Play about Clashing Cultures*

CHARACTERS: Marco Polo (speaks Latin and Mongolian), Kublai Khan (speaks Mongolian), a Norman peasant (a peasant of northern France; speaks French), and a Norman priest (speaks Latin and French). Those who speak the same language can communicate with each other. Marco Polo, for example, can speak with Kublai Khan and the priest but not with the peasant.

SETTING: By some miraculous means of transport, the PEASANT and the PRIEST find themselves in a garden in China, where MARCO POLO, dressed in Venetian garb, is sitting. The priest is wearing a cassock. The peasant is in drab farmer's garb.

| | |
|---|---|
| Peasant: | Mother of God, it is the devil himself! What have I done! *(The PEASANT falls to his knees and starts to pray.)* |
| Marco Polo: | Excuse me? |
| Priest: | Ah, you speak Latin! Are you European? |
| Marco Polo: | Venetian. |
| Priest: | Are you one of those scoundrels who trade in money? Is that why you wear those fine clothes that frightened my poor parishioner? |
| Marco Polo: | This is how all Venetians dress. We are richer than you are. And yes, I am one of those scoundrels who trade in money. But my wealth is quite modest. |
| | *(The PRIEST laughs. Speaking in French, he explains the situation to the peasant, still kneeling in terrified prayer. As the priest explains, the peasant looks up at Marco Polo, puzzled and suspicious.)* |
| Peasant: | You are not the devil? |
| Priest: | No, he is not the devil, he is merely a sinner. *(To MARCO POLO, in Latin)* And do you really mean that your wealth is modest? The silk you wear would put the Pope to shame. No king or lord in our corner of the earth would wear such dazzling colors. Maybe all Venetians have made a pact with the devil himself. |
| Marco Polo: | What do you think of this garden? |
| Priest: | It is very strange. |
| Marco Polo: | Do you know where you are? |
| Priest: | No. And you have not answered my question about the Venetians and the Devil. |
| Marco Polo: | That is because you will consider the question very silly when you learn where we are. I am about to show you how modest my Venetian wealth is. Turn around and look at the fellow walking toward you. |
| | *(The PRIEST and the PEASANT turn around and utter a horrified shriek.)* |
| Priest and Peasant: | Mother of God, it is the Devil himself! What have I done! |
| | *(KUBLAI KHAN enters. He is dressed in his Chinese emperor robes, not his Mongolian conqueror clothes.)* |

| | |
|---|---|
| Marco Polo: | My lord, I would like you to meet some real Europeans. |
| Kublai Khan: | Are these two all that's left of the hundred priests your father promised to bring to me on his return journey? |
| Priest and Peasant: | Those whiskers! That beard! Those clothes! Those eyes! |
| Kublai Khan: | I gather that these friends of yours are less knowledgeable in the ways of the world than you are. Are they really going to try to convince me that their god will benefit me, when they themselves are so pathetic? |
| Marco Polo: | You must excuse their fears. They come from a part of the world that is poor and ignorant. Even Venice, which is poor compared to your vast kingdom, would seem to be unthinkably rich. *(To the PRIEST and PEASANT)* Do you really find my lord so frightening? |
| Priest: | What sort of person is he, if he is not the Devil? |
| Marco Polo: | He is Kublai Khan, the great Mongol leader, emperor of China, the most powerful ruler on this earth. |
| Priest: | A Mongol! I have heard that Mongols are devils! |
| Marco Polo: | Haven't you also heard that they defeated the Muslims in battle? And that they conquered a small piece of Christendom but left the rest of our lands in peace? |
| Priest: | Yes. I have heard that said as well. But I would not trust a person who looks as fierce as your great Khan. He certainly could be no Christian. |
| Marco Polo: | No, he is not a Christian. *(To KUBLAI KHAN)* My lord, would you like to address some questions to the priest and his poor friend? Perhaps he can convince you of the truth of Christianity. |
| Kublai Khan: | These sorry specimens could not convince me of anything. Besides, you know that I revere their god, just as I do the other gods. Let them know that. |
| Marco Polo: | I doubt that they will find that encouraging. *(To the PRIEST, in Latin)* The Great Khan would like you to know that he reveres our God, just as he does the other gods. |
| Priest: | Impossible! If he revered our God, he would never revere others. |
| Marco Polo: | I know. I have been trying to tell him that myself. He doesn't seem to understand the great truth of Christianity. |
| Priest: | But if he does not understand Christianity, why does he allow Christians like you to talk to him about religion? |
| Marco Polo: | He doesn't care what religion I practice. |
| Priest: | That is truly ridiculous. I thought the Great Khan was a strong ruler. How can he tolerate those who believe differently from himself? Would that not lead to chaos? |
| Marco Polo: | I assure you that the Great Khan is a wise ruler who presides over an area greater than all of Christendom, and that his religious tolerance has not led to chaos. I admit I do not understand it either. |
| Kublai Khan: | You two are boring me with your private conversation. What could I gain by adopting your religion? You said that even kings in Christendom can have only one wife at a time. Why, taking new wives is one of the great joys of a conqueror! If I became a Christian, would I too have only one wife? |
| Marco Polo: | Yes. |

| | |
|---|---|
| Kublai Khan: | My grandfather said that the greatest joy of the conqueror was to take the wives and daughters of the conquered people for himself. Why should I give that up? |
| Marco Polo: | The reward of Christianity is eternal life. |
| Kublai Khan: | I must say I am not convinced. You Christians have not the least spirit of true conquerors. Why do you feel it necessary to persecute those who do not practice Christianity? You know, Marco, that I would slaughter all the people of China if I felt they might rebel against my rule, but I do not care about their religions. Are the Christians so weak that they must have their subjects agree with them on everything? |
| Marco Polo: | But we believe that all people should be Christians. |
| Kublai Khan: | *(Pointing to the PEASANT)* Is he a Christian? |
| Marco Polo: | Yes. |
| Kublai Khan: | And you want me to share his religion? |
| Marco Polo: | Yes. I do. |

*(KUBLAI KHAN gives a prolonged laugh. The PEASANT recoils in horror and clings to the cassock of the PRIEST.)*

| | |
|---|---|
| Priest: | What is he laughing at? |
| Marco Polo: | He finds you two strange. |
| Priest: | Well, he is strange to us. Look how he's terrified this poor man. |
| Marco Polo: | Don't worry, he will not harm you. |
| Priest: | *(To the PEASANT)* Our Christian host assures me that the Great Khan will not harm you. |
| Peasant: | *(Pointing to MARCO POLO)* Are you sure he is Christian? |
| Priest: | Yes, I am sure, although he is more Mongol than he realizes. *(To MARCO POLO)* You are a servant of this great Khan of yours? |
| Marco Polo: | I am an official of this court. *(To KUBLAI KHAN)* I would like to show these people some of the glories of your kingdom, for they have never seen anything so beautiful. May I take them down to Hangzhou? |
| Kublai Khan: | Yes. Please report to me on the unrest that I hear rumors about. We must let the Chinese know their place. I am inclined to kill some people as an example to the rest of them. Well, I hope your little friends here enjoy being members of a higher class of society. Let me know if they think the riches they see are a vision from heaven or some temptation from hell. |
| Marco Polo: | I shall. |

## Questions

1. Why does the peasant find Marco Polo so frightening? Why does the priest suspect Marco Polo?

2. Why are the priest and the peasant terrified of Kublai Khan?

3. What does Kublai Khan think of the Europeans? Why does he think these things?

4. Why do the priest and Marco Polo think that religious tolerance is strange? Why is it easy for Kublai Khan to support religious tolerance? Why is he uninterested in Christianity?

## The Silk Roads

Silk. When Europeans first saw and touched this lustrous and delicate fabric in the second century B.C.E., they wanted more. Demand for this expensive cloth grew, so that by 100 B.C.E. a strong silk trade had developed with China.

The Chinese called it *si*. Europeans called it *sericum*, a Latin word. It was probably first introduced to Europe by the Parthians, traders who lived in the area we now call Iran (see map, "Linking East and West," in Section 2 of this chapter). The Parthians first encountered the fabric among the gifts they received from Chinese envoys. Finding it unlike any fabric they had ever seen, they began to buy more for themselves and then to trade it with Europeans. The fabric quickly became fashionable in the Roman empire, not only among women, who found it soft and enticing, but also among men, who loved to wear it as a status symbol. The demand for silk grew to such an extent that Rome's imports came to far exceed its exports, and in A.D. 14 the emperor Tiberius banned men from using the fabric. But the silk traffic continued, becoming the most far-reaching and large-scale commerce of antiquity.

Silk was carried to the Mediterranean primarily by an overland caravan on a route that spanned half the known world. The caravan started from Changan, today's Xi'an, traveled westward through deserts, steppes, and mountain passes, and after about one year, reached the Tigris River and then Antioch on the shore of the Mediterranean. At points along this main artery, paths branched off, forming a web of routes, some of which can still be used today. Ferdinand von Richthofen, a German geographer who lived in the nineteenth century, coined the term "Silk Roads" to refer to this vast network of routes.

Silk made up most of China's exports to Rome, but skins of snow leopards and Siberian sables, cast-iron objects and tools, and the popular cinnamon bark used in medicine, wines, and

incense also traveled westward. In addition, Roman demand for spices, perfumes, and gems from India was high. Although Europeans desired these Asian luxuries more than the Chinese and other Asians desired European products, Rome did export to the East such products as glass, rewoven silk, wool and other textiles, corals and pearls from the Red Sea, amber from the Baltic, and some drugs and perfumes.

Through these Pan-Eurasian trade routes, different ways of thinking spread. From the first century A.D., traders and Buddhist missionaries from the Indian subcontinent entered China on the Silk Roads, carrying with them sacred Buddhist scriptures. Later, Chinese converts to Buddhism made pilgrimages to Buddhist centers of learning in India. Other religions, such as Zoroastrianism and Manicheanism, and later Islam, all found their way to China via the Silk Roads.

Besides religious ideas, art forms spread via the Silk Roads. From the time of Alexander the Great, whose empire extended from Greece to parts of the Indian subcontinent, Grecian and Indian art forms had intermingled. With the expansion of the Silk Roads, Chinese artistic expressions combined with Grecian-influenced Indian art to create Buddhist sculptures and buildings along these routes.

Roman ships also transported silk from China to the Persian Gulf. Using the shifting winds of the monsoon, oceangoing vessels could cross the Indian Ocean from west to east in the spring and then return in winter with Asian goods when the winds reversed. These crisscrossing ships turned the Indian Ocean into a web of invisible sea lanes.

Traders continued to travel the silk routes until about the 1500s. Today, historians agree that these early routes diffused not only people, religions, and art forms but also foods, languages, and technologies.

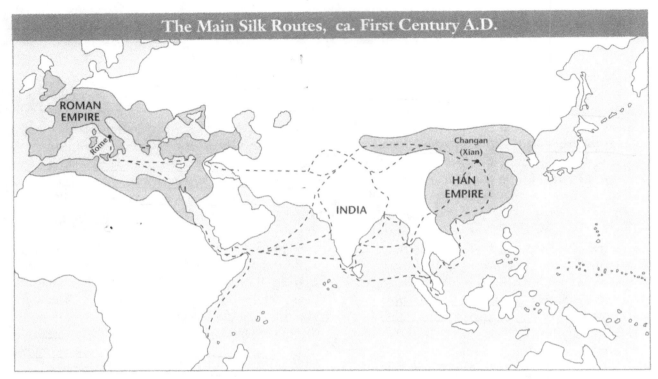

## The Main Silk Routes, ca. First Century A.D.

*Picking mulberry leaves to feed silkworms. Watercolor. Reproduction by permission of Urban Council Hong Kong from the collection of Hong Kong Museum of Art.*

*Collecting the cocoons. Courtesy of Asian Collection, Prints and Photographs, Library of Congress.*

*Sorting the cocoons. Courtesy of Asian Collection, Prints and Photographs, Library of Congress.*

*Twisting silk to make thread. Reproduction by permission of Urban Council Hong Kong from the collection of Hong Kong Museum of Art.*

## The Voyages of Zheng He

As early as the seventh century, Chinese trading ships sailed the seas surrounding China. Over the next eight hundred years, the Chinese made remarkable advances in shipbuilding and navigation and vastly expanded their knowledge of the ocean, which paved the way for the spectacular expeditions made between 1405 and 1433 by the Ming dynasty's grand eunuch Zheng He.

Zheng He sailed to Siam (now Thailand), Indonesia, India, Arabia, and East Africa. On his first voyage he led a fleet of 317 ships, some of which were 440 feet (134 meters) long and 180 feet (55 meters) wide, with masts the height of 9 stories and which housed up to 500 men. Sailing with Zheng were over 27,000 men. Subsequent voyages were of similar size.

His expeditions returned with information about the outside world and with curiosities previously unknown in China—ostriches, zebras, and giraffes. And he opened up avenues through which imports—horses, sulfur, timber, drugs, spices, copper ore, and precious stones favored by the court ladies—entered China.

Yet it seems that the primary mission of his voyages was diplomatic—to establish China's prestige in the known world and enroll tributary states. In this he succeeded. He exchanged gifts with the rulers he visited, often returning with envoys bearing tributes from distant lands.

Zheng's voyages made China a pioneer in seafaring. Chinese armadas sailed across the Indian Ocean almost a century before the Portuguese reached India by sailing around Africa. But China abruptly stopped the grand voyages in 1433, probably because scholar-officials opposed trade and foreign contact at the same time that they wanted to curb the power of the eunuchs. Many believe that ending Zheng's voyages delayed further technological and economic developments in China.

Zheng's explorations opened the outside world to the Chinese. Although Chinese traders had traveled overland and settled in Southeast Asia centuries before Zheng voyaged there, his voyages increased China's interactions with its southern neighbors. As a result, more and more Chinese traders visited and even settled in Southeast Asia.

## The Jesuits in China

With the discovery of a sea route connecting Europe and Asia during the sixteenth century, contacts between Europeans and Chinese multiplied. Europeans could now reach the East by sea as well as by land. Besides traders interested in the treasures of the East, Roman Catholic missionaries sailed on merchant ships bound for Asia. There they set out to spread the Gospel.

The Society of Jesus, founded in 1534, was the most successful of the Catholic missionary groups in East Asia. The Jesuits began by "sinicizing" themselves. They learned to speak, read, and write Chinese and studied Chinese customs. Some even gained the favor of high officials and won positions at the imperial court.

The most well-known Jesuit in China was Matteo Ricci (1552–1610), an Italian who came to China in 1582, during the Ming dynasty. Ricci adopted the Chinese name Li Matou, excelled in the Chinese language, studied Confucianism, wore the Confucian scholar's gown, and even rubbed ash on his face to make himself look less European. Instead of preaching, he conversed with Chinese scholars in Mandarin, arousing their curiosity with prisms, clocks, and European knowledge of the heavens and earth. In this way he succeeded in presenting Christianity as a system of wisdom and ethics compatible with Confucianism. He became known as a learned scholar of Chinese culture, a cartographer of world maps, a teacher of mathematics and astronomy, and only lastly, as a Christian missionary.

Other Catholic missionaries, the Dominicans and Franciscans, began going to China in the 1600s. Believing that all non-Christian cultures were the work of the devil, these priests were horrified that the Jesuits allowed Chinese converts to practice ancient Chinese rites. Because of their tolerant outlook, the Jesuits were most successful in converting Chinese to Christianity. By 1650, the Jesuits had converted 15,000 Chinese.

*Father Matteo Ricci (left) with his chief Chinese convert (right), rendered by a European artist. Courtesy of New York Public Library.*

From the 1600s until the early 1700s, about five hundred Jesuits went to China. They published Chinese translations of more than a hundred Western books—on cannon-casting, calendar-making, cartography, astronomy, algebra, geometry, geography, art, architecture, and music. At the same time, the Jesuits' writings about Chinese civilization found a wide audience in Europe, especially during the European Enlightenment in the 1700s, a time of discovery and new ideas. Europeans of this period used Chinese forms in architecture, porcelain, and furniture, a style called chinoiserie. (See Chapter 2 for more on chinoiserie.)

The Jesuits' organized efforts in China ended in 1724, when the Qing emperor decided that Christianity was a heterodox sect and banned Christian missionaries from his country. That ended an extraordinary period of cultural exchange between China and Europe.

## Inventions and Technological Wonders of Imperial China

When Jesuit missionaries in China presented the emperor with a mechanical clock in the seventeenth century, the Chinese marveled at the technological know-how of the Europeans. At that time, neither the Chinese nor the Europeans knew that China had once been at the forefront of inventions later adopted or re-invented in Europe.

One of the earliest Chinese discoveries, used as early as the fourth century B.C.E., was the compass. The Chinese used this instrument—a naturally magnetic piece of lodestone that pointed south—to communicate with the supernatural. They later discovered that the instrument helped them in navigating their ships, and their later use of steel needles to point north and south made the compass more accurate. Europeans learned of the instrument through contact with Chinese navigators some fifteen hundred years after it was first used in China.

Another early invention was the wheelbarrow, first used in China sometime during the first century B.C.E. Some of these "wooden oxen" or "gliding horses," as the Chinese called them, could carry as much as two tons. It took another thirteen hundred years before Europeans began using this tool.

In the ninth century, Chinese alchemists seeking immortality discovered gunpowder.

During the next century, the Chinese perfected the formula and then developed guns and cannons. Europeans learned of this powder in the 1300s, when Mongolian rule over a vast empire made travel between Europe and China safer than it had been before. Unfortunately for the Chinese, their invention was turned against them during the nineteenth century, when Western ships anchored off China aimed their cannons toward land and forced China to submit to Western demands.

Still another Chinese invention—paper money—is something we all take for granted today, but it was unheard of in Europe when Marco Polo visited China in the 1280s. Chinese merchants started using paper currency around A.D. 800. They called it "flying money," since a slight breeze could send it flying. It took at least another six hundred years before Westerners began using paper money.

The Chinese also invented the umbrella, fishing reel, printing press, and steam engine; and they made advances in agriculture, astronomy, navigation, and shipping well ahead of people in other parts of the world. But by the time of Europe's scientific revolution that began in the 1600s, the West had surpassed China in technological advances. You will learn of the repercussions in the next chapter.

*(left) An astronomical clock built circa 1088–92. Courtesy of Praeger Publishers at Greenwood Publishing Group, Inc. (right) Water-powered blowing engine for a blast furnace. One of the men is pouring molten metal into a mold. Woodcut, circa 1313. Courtesy of Weidenfeld and Nicolson Archive.*

*A farmer and a pig being carried to market on a Chinese wheelbarrow, circa 1865. Farmers often gave pigs alcohol to keep them tranquil. Courtesy of Peabody Essex Museum, Salem, MA.*

*Forging an anchor. From* A History of Chinese Block Prints. *Shanghai: Renmin Meishu, 1988, p. 268.*

## Extension Activities

1. **Research.** Although their fleets were not as large as Zheng He's, three earlier peoples navigated the seas in ancient times: the Phoencians, who sailed from 1200 to 200 B.C.E.; the Polynesians, who crisscrossed vast reaches of the Pacific from circa 500 to 1500; and the Vikings, who sailed across the Atlantic from 740 to 1050. Research one or more of these groups and report to the class. Along with other information, include the size of their vessels, the size of their expeditions, the distances they traveled by sea, and the distances they sailed from the sight of land. Draw maps to show where they sailed to.

   Find out about the religions of Zoroastrianism, Manicheanism, and Islam, and report to the class.

   Make a written and oral presentation on the process of silk production and its history.

2. **Mapping**. On a large map of Europe, locate three principalities—Liechtenstein, Luxembourg, and San Marino, which are remnants of feudalism (see sidebar "The Feudal System in Europe").

On a large map of Europe and Asia, mark the routes of the Silk Roads (see sidebar "The Silk Roads").

Draw a map of the Mongol empire. Then draw the boundaries of the countries now within this land area. Use an atlas to help you.

3. **Videos.** You may be interested in viewing Colin Thubron's *The Silk Road*, which takes its audience to remote northwest China.

Another video to see is *Rise of the Dragon: The Genius That Was China*, which shows China as the most technologically advanced civilization during the fourteenth century. The video was produced for NOVA by Film Australia and WGBH Boston.

## Further Readings

### Silk Roads
Hudson, Geoffrey F. *Europe and China*. London: Edward Arnold, Ltd., 1961.

### Mongols and Marco Polo
Boyle, John A., trans. *The History of the World Conqueror*, by 'Alā-al Dīn 'Ala-Malik Juvaini. Manchester: Manchester University Press, 1958.

Collins, Maurice. *Marco Polo*. London: Faber and Faber, 1950.

*Discovering Marco Polo: A Resource Guide for Teachers*. Stanford, CA: Stanford University, Stanford Program on International and Cross-Cultural Education, 1982.

Grousset, Rene. *Conquerer of the World*. New York: Orion, 1966.

Humble, Richard. *Marco Polo*. London: Weichenfeld and Nicholson, 1975.

Lamb, Harold. *Genghis Khan*. New York: Doubleday, 1927.

Lantham, Ronald E., trans. *The Travels of Marco Polo*. Baltimore: Penguin, 1958.

Power, Eileen. "Marco Polo: A Venetian Traveler of the Thirteenth Century," in *Medieval People*. New York: Harper & Row, 1963 [1924].

### Sea Voyages During Imperial China
Fairbank, John King. *China: A New History*. Cambridge, MA: The Belknap Press, 1992.

Hudson, Geoffrey F. *Europe and China*. London: Edward Arnold, Ltd., 1961.

Williams, Ralph T. "Admiral Cheng Ho, 15th Century Adventurer," in *Taipei American Chamber Topics* 1:5 (July–August 1971), pp. 16–23.

### Jesuits In China
Dunne, George H. *Generations of Giants: The Story of the Jesuits in China in the Last Decades of the Ming Dynasty*. South Bend, IN: University of Notre Dame Press, 1962.

Mungello, David E. *Leibniz and Confucianism: The Search for Accord*. Honolulu; University of Hawai'i Press, 1977.

Gernet, Jacques. *China and the Christian Impact*. New York: Cambridge University Press, 1982.

### Inventions of Imperial China
Needham, Joseph. *Science and Civilization in China*, Vols. 1–15. Cambridge, England: Cambridge University Press, 1954–1991.

Temple, Robert. *China: Land of Discovery*. Wellingborough, United Kingdom: Patrick Stephens, Ltd., 1986.

# Chapter 2

# Civilizations in Collision: China in Transition

**1750–1920**

*T*his chapter focuses on China during a time of extraordinary change. According to a prominent scholar, nineteenth-century China was marked by (1) foreigners invading, (2) Chinese rebelling, and (3) rulers trying to resist the invasions and quell the rebellions without losing their positions.[1]

We begin by looking at how China controlled its trade with Western countries for several centuries and what happened in 1793, when King George III of England sent an emissary to ask the Chinese emperor for more trade privileges. We then discuss the Opium War as an example of foreign invasion and see how the unequal treaties that China was forced to sign thereafter affected the country politically and economically.

Then we look at some internal conflicts, particularly the Taiping Rebellion. We also examine how China's rulers tried to control foreign invasion and how they responded to domestic rebellion. After considering the overthrow of China's final dynasty, the Qing (Ch'ing) dynasty, in 1911 and the establishment of the Republic of China, we conclude with a discussion of the May Fourth Movement and the beginning of Chinese nationalism.

**Sections**

---

[1] John King Fairbank, *China: A New History. Cambridge*, MA: Harvard University Press, 1992, p. 187.

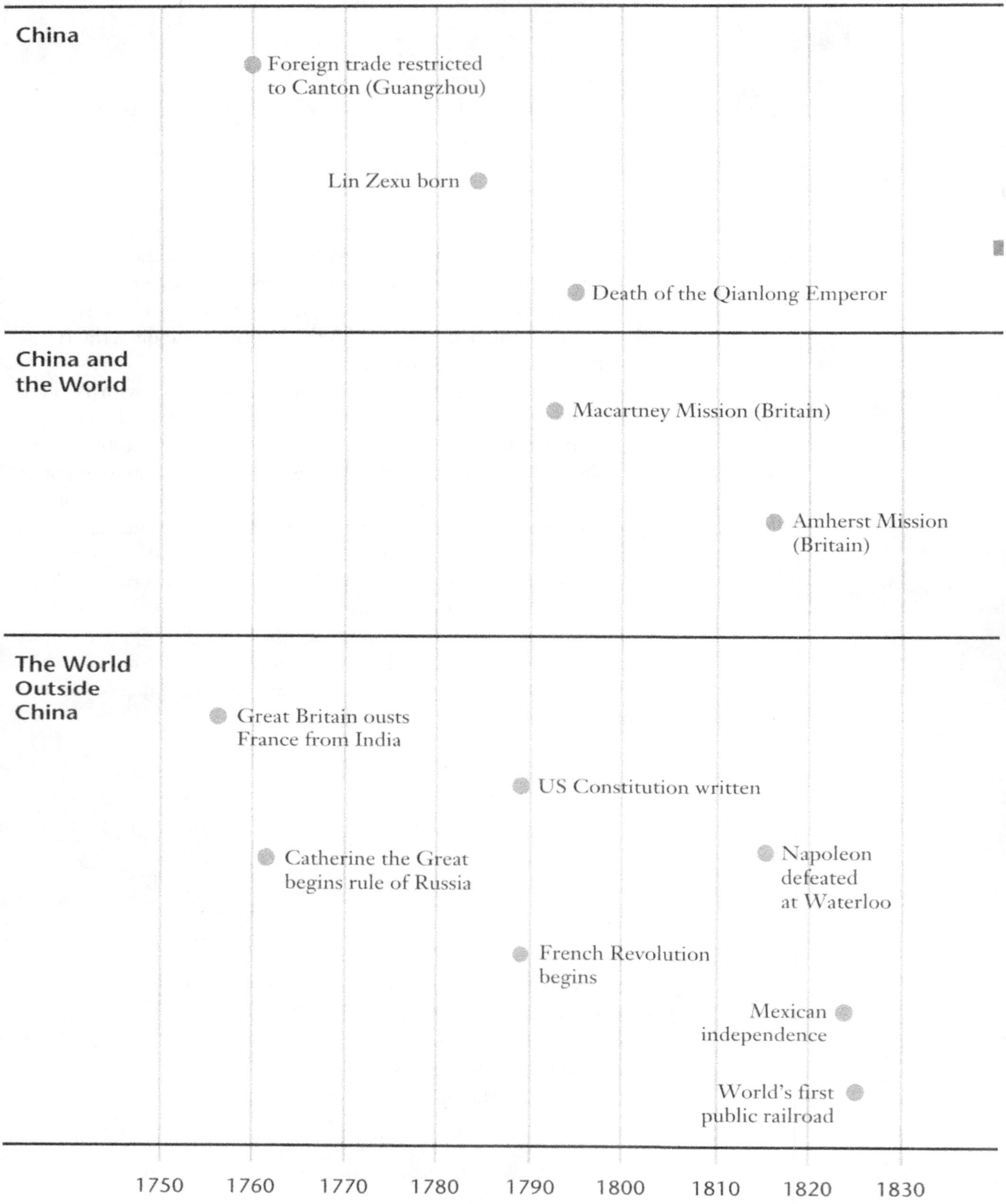

**China**

Foreign trade restricted to Canton (Guangzhou)

Lin Zexu born

Death of the Qianlong Emperor

**China and the World**

Macartney Mission (Britain)

Amherst Mission (Britain)

**The World Outside China**

Great Britain ousts France from India

US Constitution written

Catherine the Great begins rule of Russia

Napoleon defeated at Waterloo

French Revolution begins

Mexican independence

World's first public railroad

| 1750 | 1760 | 1770 | 1780 | 1790 | 1800 | 1810 | 1820 | 1830 |

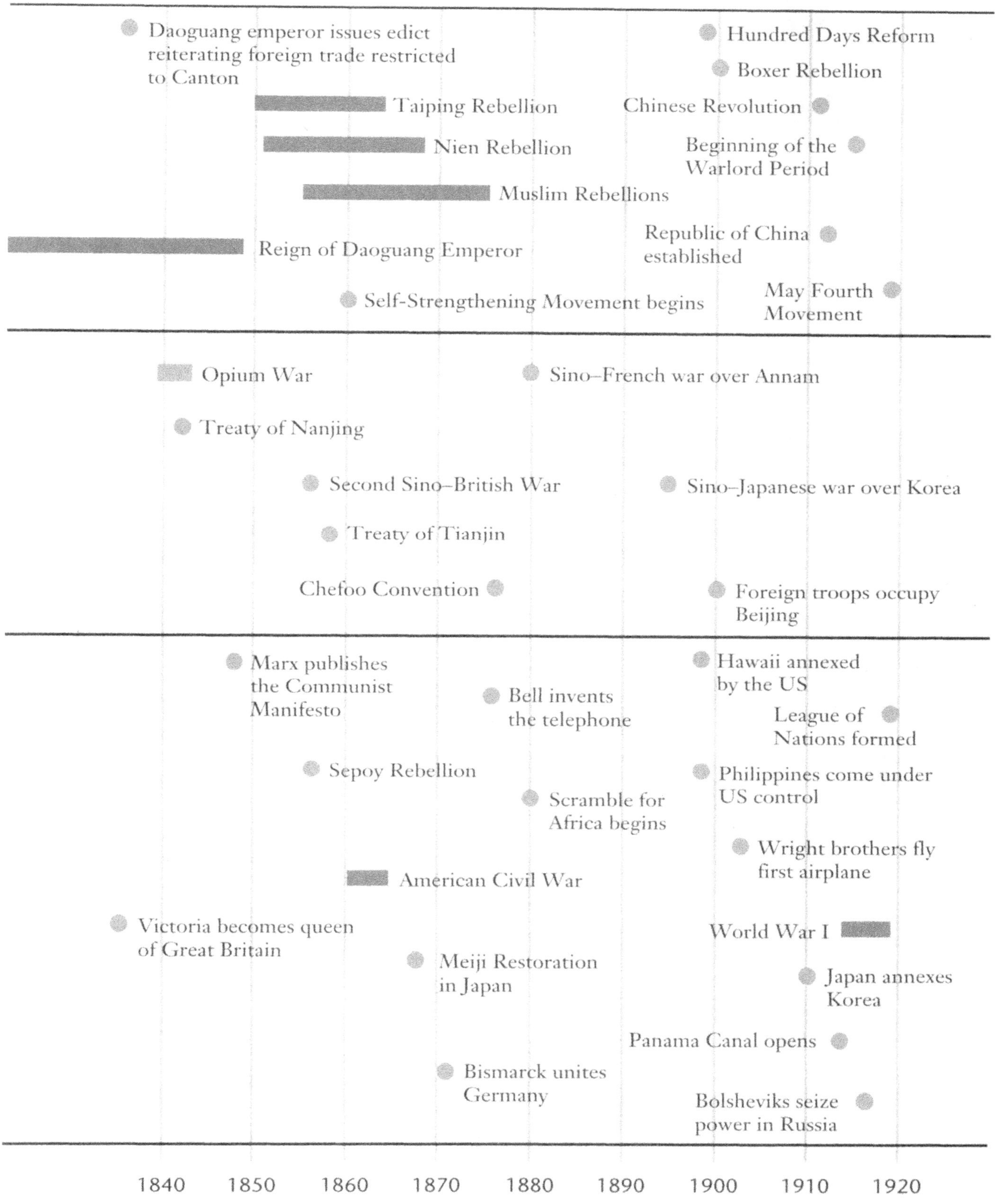

Daoguang emperor issues edict reiterating foreign trade restricted to Canton

Hundred Days Reform

Boxer Rebellion

Taiping Rebellion

Chinese Revolution

Nien Rebellion

Beginning of the Warlord Period

Muslim Rebellions

Reign of Daoguang Emperor

Republic of China established

Self-Strengthening Movement begins

May Fourth Movement

Opium War

Sino–French war over Annam

Treaty of Nanjing

Second Sino–British War

Sino–Japanese war over Korea

Treaty of Tianjin

Chefoo Convention

Foreign troops occupy Beijing

Marx publishes the Communist Manifesto

Bell invents the telephone

Hawaii annexed by the US

League of Nations formed

Sepoy Rebellion

Philippines come under US control

Scramble for Africa begins

Wright brothers fly first airplane

American Civil War

Victoria becomes queen of Great Britain

World War I

Meiji Restoration in Japan

Japan annexes Korea

Panama Canal opens

Bismarck unites Germany

Bolsheviks seize power in Russia

1840    1850    1860    1870    1880    1890    1900    1910    1920

# The Celestial Empire and the Outside World, 1750–1793

*Like many advanced civilizations, imperial China believed its culture surpassed all others. China believed itself the center of civilization, both culturally and geographically. Its rulers regulated foreigners' access to China and awarded trading rights to "tributary states"—ones that regularly sent extravagant gifts for the emperor.*

*Westerners from European nations, particularly the British, resented the restrictions China imposed on trade. In 1793 King George III of England sent a special ambassador, Lord Macartney, to the Chinese emperor asking him to grant England more trading privileges. This section includes the story of that meeting.*

## Reading: *The Middle Kingdom*

*[handwritten: like greek maps/thinking]*

### "All Under Heaven"

The map "A General Sketch of the Four Seas" was drawn in China circa 1730. The English words have been superimposed on it. By "the four seas" the Chinese meant the entire world, so this map gives us some idea of how they saw China in relation to the rest of the world in the eighteenth century. Although maps drawn by Jesuits in China in the late 1500s showed China as but one country in a world that included Europe and the Americas, during the Qing Dynasty (1644–1911) China still called itself

*[handwritten: did they just know of that continent?]*

"the Middle Kingdom," meaning it was the center of the earth, to which the rest of the world was insignificant. The Chinese sometimes called their vast, self-sufficient country "the Celestial Empire," at other times "All Under Heaven." The emperor, chosen by heaven, ruled under "the Mandate of Heaven" and was called "the Son of Heaven." Given this worldview, China had little interest in things foreign, believing it had nothing to learn from outsiders and little to gain from trading with them.

*[handwritten: like Egypt]*

### China's Tribute System

Traditional China had a formalized "tributary" relationship with nearby regions that shared much of its culture, including some form of its writing system and the practice of Confucianism and Buddhism. These regions included present-day Japan, Korea, Vietnam, Laos, Cambodia

*"A General Sketch of the Four Seas" by Chen Lun-chiung, from* Hai-kuo wen-chien lu, *or* A Record of Things Seen and Heard Concerning the Countries Across the Seas, *circa 1730, pp. 34–35. English labels reprinted from* China: Tradition & Transformation, *rev. ed., 1989, by John K. Fairbank and Edwin O. Reischauer. Used with the permission of Houghton Mifflin Company, Boston.*

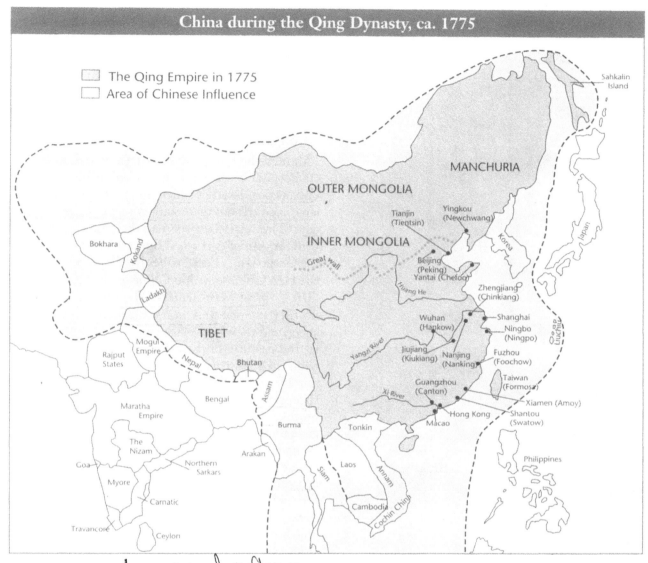

**China during the Qing Dynasty, ca. 1775**

☐ The Qing Empire in 1775
☐ Area of Chinese Influence

*[Handwritten annotation: huge area of influence]*

(Kampuchea), Thailand, Burma (Myanmar), and Tibet, as well as Nepal and Bhutan. Each of these "tributary states" paid tribute to China; that is, they offered gifts, respect, and reverence to the Son of Heaven. The tributary system accorded with the Confucian ideal of proper relationships between persons. Just as each person had a specific status in relation to other people, other *[handwritten: on different scales]* regions or states had a specific status in relation to China. It was not a status of equals; tributary states acknowledged China's cultural and political superiority. In return, they were allowed to conduct a strictly controlled trade with China.

During the Qing dynasty when tribute missions made their way to Peking (now Beijing),

they were allowed to meet with the emperor on an auspicious day. They offered him gifts and performed the requisite *koutou*, a ritual consisting of three kneelings and nine prostrations (bowing the head to the ground). The tribute mission was then allowed to stay in Beijing for three to five days selling goods, which they brought in duty-free.

The tribute system benefited both China and its tributary states. It protected the tributaries, especially in case of foreign invasion, and allowed them to trade with China. For China, it reinforced the idea that the emperor was lord of the universe, and it provided an outer line of defense against unruly nomadic tribes. It confirmed

*[Handwritten annotation: protection and money]*

to an elaborate guest ritual as a means of conducting foreign relations with other countries, a ritual that exhorted them to cherish these men who came from afar and to treat them with compassion and benevolence.

*[handwritten: image of unification and everybody is the same or similar]*

## The Barbarians

Although the Qing emperors treated tribute bearers hospitably, throughout most of its history China considered outsiders to be *man yi*, "barbarians," and treated them with condescension or disdain. They especially scorned the minority tribes who for centuries roamed the vast lands north of the Great Wall. These tribes lived differently from the Han Chinese within China itself. Most of the Han Chinese were farmers. The people of the *[handwritten: did this change?]* northern steppe were nomads dependent on their sheep and their horses for survival. Moving about to find pasture for their flocks, they could get from their animals everything they needed to sustain life. From their sheep they secured food, *[handwritten: very resourceful]* sheepskin for clothing, felt for their yurts (circular tentlike shelters), and dung for fuel. Their horses gave them mobility in a harsh and unpredictable climate. In some ways they were freer than the Chinese farmers because they were not tied to cropland. *[handwritten: they can't leave]* But because they were constantly on the move, they could not accumulate wealth from generation to generation. *[handwritten: pros and cons]* As skilled hunters and able horsemen, they were potentially fierce warriors whose nearness to the Chinese border affected China's military and political decisions throughout its imperial history.

The Chinese believed that *man yi* were greedy by nature and that greed made them aggressive. *[handwritten: don't like them already]* As early as the first century B.C.E., the Chinese recorded their opinion of the *man yi*. Statements such as "The Hsiung-nu people are against the Heavenly Way. [They] take robbing and stealing as their business" and "The reasons that they carry out robbing and looting is because their nature is so" exemplify traditional Chinese attitudes toward these northern barbarians. *[handwritten: they don't like them if they not tribe]*

Although this bias against the *man yi* persisted for centuries, the Chinese were willing to allow these "less civilized" people access to Chinese culture and to coveted items of trade, such as grain

*Chinese depictions of Japanese and Cambodian tribute bearers. From the scroll* Chi-kung T'u, *or* Portraits of Foreigners, *by the artist Hsieh Sui, Palace edition, 1761. Courtesy of the National Palace Museum, Taipei, Taiwan, Republic of China.*

China's superiority, security, and sense of being inviolable.

In practice, the tribute system was more complex than this brief description indicates. During the Qing dynasty, for example, the Chinese emperors graciously welcomed tribute bearers and sent lavish gifts to their rulers, who were powerful leaders in their own right. The emperors adhered

*The Spanish built the fort of San Domingo in present-day Taiwan in 1629. The Dutch expelled them and occupied it in 1642. The ruins are still called "Town of the Red-Haired People" because the Chinese term for the Dutch (and later other Europeans) was "Red-hair." Collection of the Historical Commission, Central Committee of the Kuomintang, Taipei, Taiwan, Republic of China.*

*The Dutch sent a successful tribute mission to Beijing in 1655 and complied with all the ceremonies required by the imperial court, including the* koutou. *From the book* Chi-kung T'u, *or* Portraits of Foreigners, *by the artist Hsieh Sui, Palace edition, 1761. Courtesy of the National Palace Museum, Taipei, Taiwan, Republic of China.*

and cloth, and luxury goods like silk, wine, and tea, under one condition: that the *man yi* acknowledge the superiority of the Chinese culture. Thus the Chinese placed their relationship with their northern neighbors into a hierarchy of superior to inferior.

The Chinese hoped that the *man yi* would give up their own way of life to adopt Chinese culture. But the "barbarians" of the northern steppe steadfastly refused. For centuries the nomads and the Chinese battled for dominance. Frontier conflicts became a way of life as the horsemen made forays into China proper. Twice, imperial Chinese dynasties were supplanted by the northern "barbarians." The first time was in the thirteenth century, when the Mongols actually conquered China, put it under virtual military occupation, and established the Yuan dynasty. Then in the seventeenth century, the Manchus (from Manchuria) usurped the Chinese throne and began the Qing dynasty. The Manchus, however, gradually became sinicized. That is, they adopted much of the Chinese

*The Dutch landed on Taiwan in 1623 and built this walled and moated town they called Zeelandia. Collection of the Historical Commission, Central Committee of the Kuomintang, Taipei, Taiwan, Republic of China.*

*China was lucky*

culture, so that by the time European merchants began to knock on China's door eager to trade, the Manchus had already acquired Chinese attitudes toward outsiders. They allowed these men from the western ocean to trade, but only under certain restrictions. *keeping exclusive to Chinese people*

## Early China Trade with the West

In traditional China, traders ranked at the bottom of the social order, below scholars, farmers, and artisans. Disdain for traders held for foreign traders as well. The first Western traders and explorers to arrive in China, during the time Western historians call the Age of Discovery, were the Portuguese, who landed off the coast of Guangzhou (Canton) in 1514. Like others to follow, they wanted to buy vast quantities of China's silks and teas. Although they made a very bad first impression on the Chinese, and indeed the Ming court issued orders to expel them, by 1557 the Portuguese had entrenched themselves in Macao, where they monopolized the China trade at Guangzhou. The Portuguese were followed by the Spanish in 1575. The Chinese allowed them to trade but not to establish a settlement like the

*or what were they trading?*

*so they were or weren't trading?*

one the Portuguese had in Macao. The Spaniards established a trade base on Taiwan, the island the Portuguese called Formosa, meaning "beautiful," until the Dutch expelled them in 1642.

During the seventeenth century the Dutch proved to be the most successful traders in Asia. Under the auspices of the Netherlands East India Company, the government of Holland dominated trade from India to Japan. Its center of trade was Java in present-day Indonesia, then called the Dutch East Indies. In China the Dutch soon established a thriving trade at Guangzhou. In time the Portuguese, the Spanish, and the Dutch would be followed by traders from Russia, Italy, Germany, and England, all subject to trade restrictions imposed by the Qing court.

*lots of trading now in China*

## The Canton System

One method China used to control foreign trade —and foreign traders—was what came to be called the Canton system. In the 1750s the Chinese imperial court decided to confine foreign trade to the port of Canton (Guangzhou) in southern China. Trade was run by Chinese merchants who banded together to form commercial

*The Canton factories after 1780, flying the flags of Denmark, Spain, the United States, Sweden, Britain, and Holland. Oil painting on glass by an unknown Chinese artist. Courtesy of Peabody Essex Museum, Salem, MA.*

companies. These *hong* merchants bought goods from inland China and had them ready when the foreign traders arrived once a year. Trading season lasted from October to March. When it was over, the foreigners had to close their warehouses and wait for favorable winds so they could sail home to Macao.

The Chinese emperor appointed an official, called the *hoppo*, to take charge of collecting taxes for goods traded and to see that all aspects of trade ran smoothly. The *hoppo* and the *hong* merchants were accountable to the Qing court for the good behavior of the ships' crews while they were berthed in Guangzhou. Foreign traders could not, of course, communicate directly with the emperor, or even with the *hoppo*, nor were they allowed to learn Chinese.

When in Guangzhou, traders were confined to "factories," foreigners' quarters outside the city walls. These were not places where goods were manufactured; they were places of business for foreign business agents, or "factors." The factories were confined to a riverbank area on a street called "Thirteen Factories Street." The Chinese sometimes called the factories "Barbarian Houses." Because women were not allowed in the factories, traders' families lived in Macao.

The Canton system soon began to grate on the foreigners, especially the British. They wanted specific Chinese goods—tea, silks, cotton fabric from Nanking (called nankeen in Europe), fine Chinese porcelains and lacquerware. But the imperial court was not much interested in what the British could trade in return—tin, copper, lead, and iron, or cloth made of wool, cotton, or linen—goods that the Chinese had little use for. In 1793, after several unsuccessful attempts to persuade the emperor, Qianlong, to grant them more privileges in trading, King George III sent his emissary, Lord George Macartney, to China to request that ports in northern China be opened to trade.

## Europe's View of China in the 1700s

For over a thousand years, Europeans took for granted a worldview dominated by the Bible. The Church was the final authority on most philosophical questions, and people's behavior was dominated by what they hoped would be a happy relationship with God in the next life. But in the eighteenth century a new type of thinking emerged, based on the ideas of human rights and responsibilities. Two centuries of religious bickering in Europe and exposure to other ways of thinking began to erode Europeans' serene certainty about the nature of reality. Leaders in this new way of thinking were a group of French thinkers known as *philosophes*. Among their ranks was the writer and philosopher Voltaire, known in his day as a rabble-rouser but remembered today for his writings, particularly the vivid social satire of his most famous book, *Candide*.

Voltaire was educated by Jesuits, who had many of their order serving in China. Their reports on this flourishing non-Christian society were greeted with great interest in Europe. The French, in particular, were fascinated with the impression that China was a well-ordered society with an advanced and disciplined civil service. For many, China became the ideal of the best type of government. Among the upper classes it was fashionable to own at least a few articles in what was considered Chinese style.

Voltaire retained an interest in all things Chinese throughout his life, constantly holding up the Chinese as models to follow in civil service and government. His great popularity did much to make Europeans aware of China, and his idealized picture of Chinese society was shared by many people. Other thinkers criticized Voltaire for idealizing China, and toward the end of his life he admitted that China was an imperfect society, even though he had a special affection for the Chinese way.

From a contemporary point of view, Voltaire's impression of China was strange. He thought, for example, that China was a benevolent despo-tism, that is, a government by a kindly dictator. In reality, many Chinese emperors were personally extravagant, and some were exceedingly cruel. The civil service did not always function fairly. At least Voltaire grasped that the Chinese did not really recognize individual rights. Other writers believed that China's government was somehow more democratic than the despotic governments of Europe. But the Chinese no more recognized the rights of citizens than the European monarchies did.

But there was one important way in which the Chinese allowed greater social mobility than their European counterparts. A boy of modest means could rise to prominence in the civil service through industry, persistence, and a capacity for memorization. The stories the Jesuits told of boys who had worked their way through the ranks impressed European intellectuals who were just starting to question whether a person's worth was set by the social class he was born into.

The Chinese fad in Europe lasted from about 1650 to 1750, reaching its height in the early eighteenth century. When the Jesuits were expelled from China in 1742, the fad quickly died, and by 1800 Europeans were again quite ignorant of and uninterested in China. By the time Macartney sailed to China in 1792, Europeans had abandoned any ideas of China as a model society. The few Britons who thought about it at all considered China a backward country, seriously deficient in its government, its scientific achievements, its technology, and the standard of living of its people.[1]

[1] P. J. Marshall, "Britain and China in the Late Eighteenth Century," in *Ritual and Diplomacy: The Macartney Mission to China 1792–1794.* London: The British Association for Chinese Studies, 1993, pp. 11–29.

## Chinoiserie

The height of interest in things Chinese coincided with a period in European history when the aesthetic taste inclined toward the highly ornamental. The elaborate Chinese style not only caught the eye of the Europeans but inspired them to coin a word, chinoiserie (sheen wah za ree), to describe things so ornate. Although the examples here are from England, chinoiserie was popular in France, Germany, Italy, Sweden, and later the United States. Motifs that were considered "oriental" were incorporated into buildings, gardens, furniture, wallpaper, vases, porcelains, and paintings.

*Chairs designed by English furniture-maker Thomas Chippendale, in the style still known as Chinese Chippendale. From his book* The Gentleman & Cabinet-Maker's Director. *London: 1762, Plate No. 28.*

*Engraving of the pagoda in Kew Gardens, London, 1763. From William Chambers,* Plans, Elevations, Sections, and Perspective Views of the Gardens and Buildings at Kew in Surry [sic]. *London: 1863.*

*Red and gilt bed probably designed by Thomas Chippendale, circa 1750–1752. Courtesy of the Board of Trustees of the Victoria and Albert Museum, London.*

## Questions

1. Why was the British monarch, King George III, who sent Lord Macartney to China in 1793, well known to the citizens of the young nation called the United States of America?

2. In December 1773 a group of men boarded ships in Boston Harbor and threw tea overboard. Explain the connection between the Boston Tea Party and China in the context of global trade at that time.

3. The Chinese word *koutou* literally means "knock the head." What does the Chinese word connote? The English version of the word is *kowtow*. What has the English word come to connote? If you do not know the English word, look it up in a dictionary.

4. Before he left for China, Lord Macartney read everything he could find, and talked with everyone who might be knowledgeable, to learn about China. Pretend you are either a British trader who lived in the British factory in Guangzhou before 1793 or a trader's wife or child who lived in Macao. Now you are at home in England. Because of your knowledge of China, you have been asked to talk with Lord Macartney and his assistants about your experiences there. What advice or information would you give him? How would you advise him to act if he were asked to *koutou?*

---

### Reading: *The Macartney Mission*

Macartney and his party arrived in northern China in September 1793. After a nine-month sea voyage, they traveled by boat and by road via Beijing to Jehol, near present-day Chengte. The emperor, Qianlong, was residing at his northern summer palace, beyond the Great Wall near Inner Mongolia, to escape the unbearable heat of Beijing.

During the long journey north, Macartney and his party were treated hospitably by Chinese. They brought a large stock of gifts for the emperor, some of which can be seen in Beijing to this day. But the journey was not without problems. Macartney knew, for example, that the flags on the boats bore the Chinese characters for "the English ambassador bringing tribute to the emperor of China" but decided, as he noted in his journal, to shut his eyes to it, complaining only if the proper opportunity arose.

However, Macartney made up his mind early on that he would never *koutou* to the emperor. Despite the advice, even the pleadings, of the Chinese officials responsible for the behavior of the Macartney party in the Celestial Empire, Macartney was implacable. He did not offer such homage even to his own monarch, George III, he declared, and he certainly would not do so for a

foreign one. Macartney finally said he would *koutou* to the emperor if a Chinese official of the same rank as his would *koutou* to a portrait of George III at the same time. When the Chinese rejected this offer, Macartney said he would go down on one knee and kiss the emperor's hand, as

*Lord George Macartney (1737–1806). Leader of the first formal British diplomatic mission to China, 1792–1794. This likeness is from an engraving done in 1806. Courtesy of the Historical Commission, Central Committee of the Kuomintang, Taipei, Taiwan, Republic of China.*

*[handwritten: f wouldn't he just do the kato]*

he would do for King George, but the Chinese refused this gesture as unsanitary. In the end, Macartney went down on one knee. The Chinese reluctantly allowed this, believing that the barbarians could not *koutou* because the garters holding up their stockings made it impossible for them to bend their knees properly. *[handwritten: well it worked out in the end]*

Despite Macartney's refusal to *koutou*, his meetings with the emperor went smoothly. At the first one Macartney delivered the king's letter with its requests; gifts and pleasantries were exchanged, and Emperor Qianlong presented Macartney with a cup of wine from his own hands. Macartney and his entourage were even invited to attend a play with the emperor. But even though he tried several times, Macartney was never able to negotiate business with the emperor or his representatives. Finally, just before he left (the Chinese were strongly hinting that he should do so—and quickly), Macartney sent a final note to China's chief minister, briefly repeating the requests he had been unable to discuss with the emperor. *[handwritten: which were what?]* Five hours after Macartney left the court, he was presented with two bamboo cylinders tied with

*[handwritten left margin: aking ood deals]*

ribbons of imperial yellow. The cylinders contained Emperor Qianlong's reply to King George's requests, along with a list of presents the emperor was sending to him. Macartney read the emperor's letter. *[handwritten: what did it say?]* Then he and his entourage continued homeward; the journey would again take them the better part of a year.

## Activity: Role-Playing

### Part 1. At Home

Your teacher will divide you into pairs. One person is to play the role of Emperor Qianlong, the other that of Lord Macartney. Here are the directions for each role. Part I can be done for homework.

#### Emperor Qianlong

You are the Son of Heaven, Emperor Quianlong. You have met with Lord Macartney several times and entertained him lavishly. You have ordered that gifts be sent to his king, George III. You have also sent gifts to the six hundred men Macartney left behind in Beijing. You know of the requests Macartney has made on behalf of his king, because Macartney has written and spoken to your officials. Now you write directly to King George, taking up his requests one by one and explaining why you will or will not grant them.

- a. Read the excerpts from Emperor Qianlong's edict given here. Read them several times so you will be comfortable reading them aloud later.
- b. Briefly list Macartney's five requests.
- c. Paraphrase the requests and the emperor's reply to each one, including the reason for his decisions.

#### Lord Macartney

You are King George's representative. You brought gifts to the emperor, including clocks, telescopes, and artillery pieces. You believe you have been respectful to the emperor, even though you refused to *koutou*. You have tried over and over to ask Emperor Qianlong, both

*Emperor Qianlong (1736–1795). This likeness of the emperor on horseback was painted on silk by the Jesuit artist Giuseppe Castiglione in 1744. Courtesy of the Historical Commission, Central Committee of the Kuomintang, Taipei, Taiwan, Republic of China.*

directly and through his officials, to grant certain requests to the British. Now, when you are miles from the court, you finally get the emperor's reply. You read his edict and decide you will write to him one more time and ask him to reconsider.

   a.  Read the excerpts from Emperor Qianlong's edict given here.
   b.  Briefly list your five requests.
   c.  Write the requests more fully in your own words.
   d.  Respond to the emperor, again in your own words, explaining how you will overcome each of his objections and asking him to reconsider his decisions.

## Part 2. At School

Sit facing your partner. Have your written work from Part I. The person playing the emperor begins by reading the introductory part of the excerpt aloud. Then begin a dialog. That is, Emperor Qianlong reads the paraphrase of Macartney's first request, and explains, again in paraphrase, why it cannot be granted. Macartney responds also in paraphrase, explaining to the emperor why he should reconsider. The pairs go back and forth for the remaining four requests. The emperor completes the dialog by dramatically reading the last paragraph of the edict aloud.

After each pair has completed its dialog, the teacher may ask different pairs to read the original excerpts aloud or to read their dialogs to the class.

## Part 3. Debriefing

1.  Could this dialog have really happened? Why or why not?
2.  What do you see as the main reason for the problem between the emperor and the ambassador?
3.  Give a current example of cultural conflict, either one you have experienced or one you have read about in the newspapers or seen on the news.
4.  Ethnocentrism is the belief that one's own ethnic group or culture is superior to others'. Would you characterize Emperor Qianlong as ethnocentric? What about Lord Macartney? Explain your responses.
5.  Some scholars contend that Macartney doomed his mission to failure by refusing to *koutou*. How would you respond to this statement?
6.  Speculate on how relations between China and Britain will progress. Will they improve or become worse? Give reasons for your speculations.
7.  Keep your list of Macartney's requests in a safe place. You will need it again in Section 2.

---

**Reading:** *Emperor Qianlong to King George III of England, 1793*

---

This edict, as letters from the emperor were called, was written in Chinese and translated into Latin and then into English. (Note the British spellings of words like *civilisation, favour,* and *centre* and the foreign spellings for Chinese proper nouns and place names.) These excerpts are from a much longer edict. Explanatory notes are in brackets.

    Yesterday your Ambassador [Macartney] petitioned my Ministers to memorialise me [write me a letter or memorial] regarding your trade with China, but his proposal is not consistent with our

dynastic usage and cannot be entertained. Hitherto [until now], all European nations, including your own country's barbarian merchants, have carried on their trade with Our Celestial Empire at Canton. Such has been the procedure for many years, although Our Celestial Empire possesses all things in prolific abundance and lacks no product within its own borders. There was therefore no need to import the manufactures of outside barbarians in exchange for our own produce. But as the tea, silk and porcelain which the Celestial Empire produces are absolute necessities to European nations and to yourselves, we have permitted, as a signal mark of favour, that foreign *hongs* should be established at Canton, so that your wants might be supplied and your country thus participate in our beneficence [goodness]. But your Ambassador has now put forward new requests which completely fail to recognise the Throne's principle to 'treat strangers from afar with indulgence,' and to exercise a pacifying [peace-making] control over barbarian tribes, the world over. Moreover, our dynasty, swaying [ruling] the myriad [many] races of the globe, extends the same benevolence towards all. Your England is not the only nation trading at Canton. If other nations, following your bad example, wrongfully importune [beseech] my ear with further impossible requests, how will it be possible for me to treat them with easy indulgence? Nevertheless, I do not forget the lonely remoteness of your island, cut off from the world by intervening wastes of sea, nor do I overlook your excusable ignorance of the usages of Our Celestial Empire. I have consequently commanded my Ministers to enlighten your Ambassador on the subject, and have ordered the departure of the mission. But I have doubts that, after your Envoy's [diplomatic agent's; in this case, Macartney's] return he may fail to acquaint you with my view in detail or that he may be lacking in lucidity [clear thinking] so that I shall now proceed to take your requests *seriatim* [one after the other] and to issue my mandate on each question separately. In this way you will, I trust, comprehend my meaning.

(1) Your Ambassador requests facilities for ships of your nation to call at Ningpo, Chusan, Tientsin and other places for purposes of trade. Until now trade with European nations has always been conducted at Aomen [Macao; however, when the emperor refers to Aomen in this letter he means Macao and Canton] where the foreign *hongs* are established to store and sell foreign merchandise. Your nation has obediently complied with this regulation for years past without raising any objection. In none of the other ports named have *hongs* been established, so that even if your vessels were to proceed thither, they would have no means of disposing of their cargoes. Furthermore, no interpreters are available, so you would have no means of explaining your wants, and nothing but general

inconvenience would result. For the future, as in the past, I decree that your request is refused and that the trade shall be limited to Aomen.

(2) The request that your merchants may establish a repository [warehouse] in the capital of my Empire for the storing and sale of your produce, in accordance with the precedent granted to Russia, is even more impracticable than the last. My capital [Peking] is the hub and center about which all quarters of the globe revolve. Its ordinances are most august [its laws are sacred] and its laws are strict in the extreme. The subjects of our dependencies [the tributary states] have never been allowed to open places of business in Peking. Foreign trade has hitherto been conducted at Aomen because it is conveniently near to the sea, and therefore an important gathering place for the ships of all nations sailing to and fro. If warehouses were established in Peking, the remoteness of your country lying far to the north-west of my capital, would render transport extremely difficult. [It is true that] before Kiakhta was opened, the Russians were permitted to trade at Peking, but the accommodation furnished to them was only temporary. As soon as Kiakhta was available, they were compelled to withdraw from Peking, which has been closed to their trade these many years. Their frontier trade at Kiakhta is on all fours with [equal to] your trade at Aomen.[2] Possessing facilities at the latter place [Aomen], you now ask for further privileges at Peking, although our dynasty observes the severest restrictions respecting the admission of foreigners within its boundaries, and has never permitted the subjects of dependencies [tribute states] to cross the Empire's barriers and settle at will amongst the Chinese people. This request is also refused.

(3) Your request for a small island near Chusan [an island off the port city of Ningbo], where your merchants may reside and goods be warehoused, arises from your desire to develop trade. As there are neither foreign *hongs* nor interpreters in or near Chusan, where none of your ships have ever called,

[2] The Russian–Chinese treaty of 1721 allowed the Russians to go to Beijing to trade every two to three years. This had stopped by Macartney's time, when the boundary between Outer Mongolia (China) and Siberia (Russia) had been agreed on and the Russians had acquired a trade site at Kiakhta on the Mongol–Siberian border.

such an island would be utterly useless for your purposes. Every inch of the territory of our Empire is marked on the map and the strictest vigilance is exercised over it all; even tiny islets and far-lying sandbanks are clearly defined as part of the provinces to which they belong. Consider, moreover, that England is not the only barbarian land which wishes to establish relations with our civilisation and trade with our Empire: supposing that other nations were all to imitate your evil example and beseech me to present them each and all with a site for trading purposes, how could I possibly comply? This also is a flagrant infringement [outrageous violation] of the use of my Empire and cannot possibly be entertained.

(4) The next request, for a small site in the vicinity of Canton city, where your barbarian merchants may lodge or, alternatively, that there be no longer any restrictions over their movements at Aomen has arisen from the following causes. Hitherto,[3] the barbarian merchants of Europe have had a definite locality assigned to them at Aomen for residence and trade, and have been forbidden to encroach an inch beyond the limits assigned to that locality. Barbarian merchants having business with the *hongs* have never been allowed to enter the city of Canton; by these measures, disputes between Chinese and barbarians are prevented, and a firm barrier is raised between my subjects and those of other nations. The present request is quite contrary to precedent; furthermore, European nations have been trading with Canton for a number of years and, as they make large profits, the number of traders is constantly increasing. How would it be possible to grant such a site to each country [a place for traders from each country to live permanently]? The merchants of the foreign *hongs* are responsible to the local officials for the proceedings of barbarian merchants and they carry out periodical inspections. If these restrictions were withdrawn, friction would inevitably occur between the Chinese and your barbarian subjects, and the results would militate against [go against] the benevolent regard that I feel towards you.

[3] The British had requested the emperor's permission to establish year-round permanent living quarters at Canton, so they would not have to leave for Macao, about 80 miles downriver, every year in March and then return for trading season in the fall.

From every point of view, therefore, it is best that the regulations now in force should continue unchanged.

(5) Regarding your nation's worship of the Lord of Heaven, it is the same religion [Christianity] as that of other European nations. Ever since the beginning of history, sage [wise] Emperors and wise rulers have bestowed on China a moral system and inculcated [taught] a code, which from time immemorial has been religiously observed by the myriads of my subjects. There has been no hankering after heterodox doctrines [ideas that depart from accepted beliefs]. Even the European officials [Jesuit officials at the Qing court] in my capital are forbidden to hold intercourse [talk to or associate] with Chinese subjects; they are restricted within the limits of their appointed residences, and may not go about propagating their religion. The distinction between Chinese and barbarian is most strict, and your Ambassador's request that barbarians shall be given full liberty to disseminate their religion is utterly unreasonable.

It may be, O King, that the above proposals have been wantonly [heedlessly] made by your Ambassador on his own responsibility, or peradventure [perhaps] you yourself are ignorant of our drastic regulations and had no intention of transgressing them when you expressed these wild ideas and hopes. I have ever shown the greatest condescension to the tribute missions of all states which sincerely yearn after the blessing of civilisation, so as to manifest my kindly indulgence. I have even gone out of my way to grant any requests which were in any way consistent with Chinese usage. Above all, upon you, who live in remote and inaccessible regions, far across the spaces of ocean, but who have shown your submissive loyalty by sending this tribute mission, I have heaped benefits far in excess of those accorded to other nations. But the demands presented by your Embassy are not only a contravention [contradiction] of dynastic tradition, but would be utterly unproductive of result to yourself, besides being quite impracticable. I have accordingly stated the facts to you in detail, and it is your bounden duty reverently to appreciate my feelings and obey these instructions henceforward for all time, so that you may enjoy the blessing of perpetual peace. If, after receipt of this explicit decree, you lightly give ear to the representations of your subordinates, and allow your barbarian merchants to proceed to Chekiang and Tientsin, with the object of landing and trading there, the ordinances [laws] of my Celestial Empire are strict in the extreme, and the local officials, both civil and military, are bound reverently to obey the law of the land. Should your vessels touch the shore, your merchants will assuredly never be permitted to land or to reside there, but will be subject to instant expulsion. In that event your barbarian merchants will have had a long journey for nothing. Do not say that you were not warned in due time. Tremblingly obey and show no negligence! A special mandate! [This is a special edict!]

> We express our gratitude to Far Eastern Publications of Yale University for permission to reprint certain passages from *China & the West: Cultural Collision*, edited by Richard L. Walker. New Haven: Yale University, Far Eastern Publications, ©1954, pp. 28–31. Additional translations by Francis K. C. Tsui.

## Extension Activities

1. Examine the painting of the factories before 1800 reproduced in this section. Note the flags of the nations represented there. When was the American factory established and why? The book *The China Trade: Export Paintings, Furniture, Silver, & Other Objects*, by Carl Crossman, Princeton, NJ, Pyne Press, 1972, has an excellent section called "Dating of the Views of Canton" that should help you.

2. Lord Macartney kept a journal of his embassy to China, as did several others in his party. Read at least one week's entries from Macartney's journal (the one edited by J. L. Cranmer-Byng listed below is probably the most accessible) and give an oral report on Macartney's account of that week.

3. Two artists accompanied the Macartney party. William Alexander painted watercolors of life in China. Both *The Immobile Empire* and *The Lion and the Dragon* (see list below) have excellent color reproductions of Alexander's work. Study at least ten of his paintings and decide what your image of

China would be if you were a British citizen in the late 1700s and the paintings were your only source of information about the Middle Kingdom. Report your findings to the class orally or in writing.

## Further Reading

Fairbank, John King. *China: A New History.* Cambridge, MA: Belknap Press of Harvard University, 1992.

Fairbank, John King, ed. *The Chinese World Order: Traditional China's Foreign Relations.* Cambridge, MA: Harvard University Press, 1968.

Fairbank, John King, and Edwin O. Reischauer. *China: Tradition and Transformation.* Revised ed. Boston: Houghton Mifflin, 1989.

Teng, Ssu-yü, and John King Fairbank. *China's Response to the West: A Documentary Survey, 1839–1923.* Cambridge, MA: Harvard University Press, 1954, 1961.

### The Macartney Mission

Bickers, Robert A., ed. *Ritual & Diplomacy: The Macartney Mission to China 1792–1794.* London: The British Association for Chinese Studies, 1993.

Cranmer-Byng, J. L. *An Embassy to China: Being the Journal Kept by Lord Macartney During his Embassy to the Emperor Ch'ien-lung 1793–1794.* Hamden, CT: Archon Books, 1963.

Hevia, James L. *Cherishing Men from Afar: Qing Guest Ritual and the Macartney Embassy of 1793.* Durham, NC: Duke University Press, 1994.

Peyrefitte, Alain. *The Immobile Empire,* New York: Alfred A. Knopf, 1992.

Singer, Aubrey. *The Lion and the Dragon: The Story of the First British Embassy to the Court of Emperor Qianlong in Peking, 1792–1794.* London: Barrie & Jenkins, 1992.

### Chinoiserie

Honour, Hugh. *Chinoiserie.* London: John Murray (Publishers), Ltd. 1961.

Impey, Oliver. *Chinoiserie: The Impact of Oriental Styles on Western Art and Decoration.* New York: Charles Scribner's Sons, 1977.

Jacobson, Dawn. *Chinoiserie.* London: Phaidon Press, 1993.

# 2 China, Britain, and Opium, 1839–1842

*This section focuses on opium and how the Opium War changed China. It includes a story about the effect of opium on an ordinary Chinese family, excerpts from a letter a Chinese official wrote to Queen Victoria asking for her help in suppressing the opium trade, portions of a diary written during the Opium War, and sections from the Treaty of Nanjing, the first of many unequal treaties China was forced to sign, first with Britain and then with other countries, including Japan.*

*Some place names in this section are in the foreign spellings used in the documents themselves, such as the Treaty of Nanjing and the excerpts from a diary kept by the Chinese poet Chushiyuan.*

---

**Activity: Life in Guangzhou**

---

The three images that follow were created between 1825 and 1840. Art works such as these can give us some idea of what life was like in Guangzhou at that time. Analyze each image using the steps listed below.

1. Look at the image carefully for two minutes to form an overall impression.
2. Divide the image into quadrants in your mind's eye and study each quadrant to see what new details become visible.
3. List the people, objects, and activities in the image.
4. Based on what you observed, list three things you might infer from the image.
5. What questions does the image raise in your mind?
6. Where might you find answers to those questions?
7. Write a caption for each image and share the captions with the class.

8. After you share your captions, your teacher will give you some information about each image. Compare what you wrote with this information and evaluate your response in light of it. Were you on the right track or did you misinterpret the image because you did not have enough information?

*Gouache (opaque watercolors), by unknown Chinese artists, circa 1825–1830. Courtesy of Peabody Essex Museum, Salem, MA.*

*Oil on canvas, by an unknown Chinese painter, circa 1825–1835. Courtesy of Peabody Essex Museum, Salem, MA.*

9. How can images such as these help us learn about a given place at a given time? What are the dangers of using images like these as historical documents? Do they really show what Guangzhou looked like from 1820 to about 1840? How do images such as these differ from photographs as historical documents? Which can be considered more accurate historically? Why?

*Procedure for image analysis adapted from an exercise created by the Education Branch, Office of Public Programs, National Archives.*

## Reading: *The Opium Trade*

Long after Lord Macartney's 1793 mission failed, foreigners still sent emissaries to China asking emperors to lift some of the restrictions on trade and to allow foreigners into ports besides Guangzhou. The response to all these requests was an unequivocal no. Foreign traders continued to be confined to the factories in Guangzhou from October to March, returning to their families in Macao when the winter shipping season was over. In 1836 the Daoguang emperor issued an edict reiterating the restrictions on foreigners: "As the port of Guangzhou is the only one at which the Outer Barbarians are permitted to trade, on no account can they be permitted to wander and visit other places in the Middle Kingdom."

Foreigners tolerated these limitations because they wanted China's goods—its silks and porcelains and, especially in the case of the British, its tea. By the late 1820s England had become a nation of tea drinkers, consuming thirty million pounds of tea every year—enough to supply every man, woman, and child in England with two pounds of tea. China, however, had no interest in trading its tea for Britain's woolen cloth or other manufactured goods. So Britain tried to balance its trade by trafficking in a substance long forbidden in China, yet smuggled in from India: opium.

Although opium had been forbidden in China as early as 1729, it flourished despite the severe punishments imposed on those found guilty of smoking it. In the early 1800s, for example, when the emperor discovered that even some of the officers in his bodyguard were opium smokers, he ordered that they be dismissed, flogged one hundred lashes, and made to wear the cangue for two months.

*prob no more trade*

Foreign traders were warned of dire consequences if they trafficked in opium, but for many of them, particularly the British, the trade was too lucrative to abandon. Besides, dealing in the drug *Har core* was not all that dangerous for foreigners. When the Chinese government cracked down on opium traders in the early 1820s, they simply retreated to Lintin, an island between Guangzhou and Macao. There clipper ships from India, a British colony, unloaded thousands of chests of opium onto smuggling boats called "scrambling dragons" or "fast crabs." The traders bribed Chinese officials and paid off the Chinese smugglers who rowed the boats, and the opium made its way east and north along China's long coastline, or into the country's interior.

*which is how much today*

Trading in opium was wildly profitable. A single chest of opium, usually 133 pounds of the drug, sold for as much as 700 to 1,000 silver dollars.[1] From 1838 to 1839 alone, the British East India Company illegally brought more than five *Jeez* million pounds of opium into China. There was ample demand for opium. Although no official count was ever taken, historians estimate that millions of Chinese smoked the substance they called "foreign mud."

In 1838 the Chinese government concluded that the opium trade was wreaking such havoc in China that it had to be stopped. Thousands of taels of silver were flowing out of China in exchange for opium.

*painkillers*

Besides economic problems, opium caused horrendous social problems as thousands became addicted to it. Opium is a powerful substance. Even today, some of its derivatives, such as morphine and codeine, are used to relieve severe pain. In nineteenth-century China, opium was usually smoked. As opium slowed the body, the smoker drifted off into hours of oblivion. Over time, addicts needed more and more of the drug to satisfy their craving. Those who tried to quit suffered from terrible physical symptoms, including sleeplessness, vomiting, diarrhea, excruciating pain in the head and limbs, chills and

*A person being punished in a cangue, Shanghai, circa 1870. The label usually listed the offender's name and address and the nature of the crime. The offender had to rely on passersby for food; offenders could not feed themselves or lie down. From* China, The Land and Its People: Early Photographs by John Thomson. *First published as* Illustrations of China and Its People *by Sampson Low, Marston, Low and Searle, London, 1873.*

*less effectiveness among the people*

fever, runny nose and sneezing; some even died. Giving it up caused psychological distress in the form of fear, anger, shame, uncontrollable weeping, and, if sleep came, in dreadful nightmares. Because opium was so addictive, and because withdrawal was so painful, users would do almost anything to get more of it. *not good*

Opium was not cheap. Common laborers earned about two tenths of a tael of silver a day; an opium habit cost at least half that amount. Families were destroyed as addicts spent days and nights smoking the drug in opium dens, squandering their families' resources until there was *more poverty* nothing left. Opium dealers armed themselves and banded together in secret societies; officials became more and more corrupt as they accepted bribes from dealers or became addicted to the drug themselves. Among soldiers, opium use became so common that non-smokers were the exception. *thats not good, like cigs*

[1] American, Mexican, Peruvian, and Spanish silver dollars were used in the opium trade. The Chinese thought Spanish silver dollars were the best, but Mexican silver dollars were commonly used. Silver dollars were weighed rather than counted.

## Questions

1. Why did the British persist in bringing opium to China even though it was illegal? Explain your response with reference to international trade.

2. Although the penalties for smoking opium were severe, they had little effect in curtailing use of the drug. Why?

3. Why did China finally decide to try to stop the opium trade?

## Reading: *"The Younger Child"*

This story is from Ida Pruitt's book *A Daughter of Han: The Autobiography of a Chinese Working Woman*. Pruitt was an American who grew up in China. Although the story is dated 1889, the account of a child sold to pay for opium could have been written fifty years earlier.

In the winter the rich of the city built mat sheds under which they gave out gruel[2] to the poor. We went every day for one meal of hot gruel. We met there, for he begged in one part of the city, carrying Chinya, and I begged in another, leading Mantze.

One day when my husband handed the baby over to me as usual, saying "Nurse her," one of the men in charge of the gruel station saw him do it.

"Is that your man?" said the man from the gruel station. I answered that he was.

"He is trying to sell the child. He tells people that her mother died last Seventh Month."

"Oh, that is the talk he uses for begging," I said. But in my heart I wondered if it was true that he was trying to sell our child and keep the knowledge from me.

One day when the ground was wet with melting snow, I found that even with three pairs of shoes my feet were not covered. The bare flesh showed through.

"You stay at home," he said, "and I will beg." He took the child in his arms as usual. "You wait at home," he said. "I will bring you food."

We waited, Mantze and I. The day passed; it got dark; and still he did not come. It was cold. I opened my clothes and took Mantze inside my garments to give her warmth and still he did not come. We lay in the dark. We had no lights that

winter; we had no money for oil. I heard the watchman beating the third watch and I knew the night was half over. Still he did not come.

Then I heard him push open the door and stumble as he crossed the threshold. He was opium sodden and uncertain in his movements. I waited for him to say as usual, "Here, take the child and nurse her." But there was no word. I heard him throwing something heavily on the bed.

"Now you have knocked the breath out of the child. Give her to me."

Still he said nothing.

"What is the matter? Give me the child." And he only grunted.

"Light the lamp and I will tell you," he said.

"It is not the custom to light lamps in this house. Do you not know me or do I not know you that we must have a light to talk by to each other? Tell me." Then he struck a match and I saw that there was no child, only a bundle, a bundle of sweet potatoes.

"I have sold her."

I jumped out of bed. I had no thought left for Mantze. I seized him by the queue. I wrapped it three times around my arm. I fought for my child. We rolled fighting on the ground.

The neighbors came and talked to pacify us.

"If the child has not left the city and we can keep hold of this one, we will find her," they said.

So we searched. The night through we searched. We went to the south city through the Drum Tower and back to the examination halls. We walked a great circle inside the city, and always I walked with my hands on his queue. He could not get away.

We found a house. The father of the child knocked. Some men came to the door. It was the house of dealers who buy up girls and send them

[2] *gruel:* in this instance gruel probably means a thick rice soup, *jook* or *congee.*

to brothels in other cities. Their trade is illegal, and if they are caught they are put in prison and punished. They dared not let me make a noise. So the dealer in little girls said soft words. My neighbors said, "What he says, he will do. Now that we have him we will find the child." But the child was not in that house.

"Take me to my child," I demanded. The man promised. So again we started out in the night, walking and stumbling though the streets. Then one of my neighbors who has more power to plan than the others said, "Why do you still hold on to him? He is now useless." I still had my arm twisted in my husband's queue. "Hold on to that one so he does not run away. He it is that knows where the child is."

So I let go of my husband's queue and in one jump was beside the man and seized him by the slack of his coat. "Why do you seize me?" he said.

"So that you will not run away and I lose my child again." My husband had gone into the night, and still we walked. We came to the entrance of a narrow street.

"You stay here," said the man, "I will go in and call them."

"No," said I. "Where you go, I go. What kind of a place is this that I cannot go with you?"

And when he said it was a residence, I said, "A residence! If you, a man, can go, surely I, a woman, can do so. If it was a bachelor's lair[3] I still would go in to find my child." I held onto him by the slack of his coat as we went down the narrow street to a gate. He knocked and still I held to him.

The man who opened it held the two parts of the gate together with his hands to prevent anyone going in. But I ducked under his arm before he could stop me and ran into the passage. I went through the courts, calling, "Chinya, Chinya." The child heard my voice and knew me and answered, and so I found her. The woman of the house tried to hide the child behind her wide sleeves, but I pushed her aside and took the child into my arms. The man barred the door and said that I could not leave.

"Then," I said, "I will stay here. My child is in my bosom. Mother and child, we will die here together." I sat on the floor with my child in my arms.

The neighbors gathered and talked. A child, they said, could not be sold without the mother's consent. He had, they said, got another five hundred cash from them by saying that I had not at first consented. They had first paid him three thousand. He had sold my child for a mere three thousand and five hundred cash.

They [the dealers] tried to frighten me. They said they would sell us both to get their money back. I was young then, and salable. But I said, "No. I have another child at home. I must go to that child also." The neighbors all began to talk and said that I had another child and that I must go home to her, and the dealers talked of their money that they must have back.

"You stay here until we go and get the money back," they [the dealers] said. But . . . we all started out together. I was carrying the child and they came along to get their money. They lighted a lantern and let it shine under my feet.

Then a neighbor who thought more quickly than others said, "It is cold tonight and the way is long. We have walked far. Let me carry the child."

I said that I was well and strong and could carry her myself.

But again she said, "My coat is bigger than yours. I can carry the child inside and protect her from the cold." So I gave the child to her. She walked ahead, and gradually disappeared into the night. When we got home she was there with the child, but my old opium sot was gone. She knew that he would have spent all the money and would have been unable to pay, and that when they had found this out they would have taken him out and beaten him. So she had gone ahead and warned him and he had slipped away into the night. And she also had the child safely at home.

So that passed over.

He promised not to sell her again and I believed him.

The old people tell us that her husband is more important to a woman than her parents. A woman is with her parents only a part of her life, they say, but she is with her husband forever. He also feels that he is the most important. If a wife is not good to her husband, there is retribution in heaven.

My husband would sit on the k'ang with his legs drawn up under his chin and his head hang-

---

[3] bachelor's lair: a place off-limits to women where unmarried men gathered to talk, drink, and gamble; it was not a brothel.

ing. He would raise his head suddenly and peer at me from under his lids.

"Ha! Why don't you make a plan? Why don't you think of a way for us to eat?"

I would answer, "What can I do? My family have no money. I know no one."

Then, at last, he would get up and go out to beg. People urged me to leave him and follow another man, to become a thief or a prostitute. But my parents had left me a good name, though they had left me nothing else. I could not spoil that for them.

In those years it was not as it is now. There was no freedom then for women. I stayed with him.

For another year we lived, begging and eating gruel from the public kitchen.

The father of my children was good for a while, and I thought he had learned his lesson. He promised never to sell the child again and I believed him. Then one day he sold her again and I could not get her back that time. . . .

> From Ida Pruitt, "The Younger Child," in *A Daughter of Han: The Autobiography of a Chinese Working Woman.* New Haven, CT: Yale University Press, ©1945, pp. 66–71.

## Questions

1. The teachings of Confucius, the great Chinese scholar and thinker, included instruction on how people in Chinese society were to relate to each other. In relationships between emperor and official, father and son, husband and wife, and older brother and younger brother, the superior was to behave responsibly and kindly toward his inferior; the inferior was to be obedient and loyal to the superior. Discuss the following statement in the context of the story:

> *Opium addiction was particularly disastrous for the old Chinese way of life because Confucianism set such great store by self-discipline and duty to family, whereas the opium addict had to satisfy his own craving first and sacrifice his family as well as himself.*[4]

(Refer to Chapter 1, Section 3, for more information on duty to family and to Section 4 for more information on Confucianism.)

2. In the story, the mother of the child sold for opium talks about her obligation to be loyal to her husband and to uphold her parents' good name. Discuss the values of loyalty to a spouse and respect for parents in modern Western societies. Do these values exist in modern Western societies? If so, how are they demonstrated today? If you think these values do not exist, tell what evidence supports your judgment.

## Reading: *Commissioner Lin and Opium*

*Harsh but necessary*

Perhaps as a result of hearing stories like "The Younger Child," along with the recognition that his country was being destroyed economically, the Daoguang emperor decided in the late 1830s that opium had to be stopped. He was said to have wept and demanded to know how he could face his ancestors while his people ruined themselves with opium. In 1839 the emperor sent one of his most trusted officials, Lin Zexu, to Guangzhou and charged him to suppress the opium trade in China permanently.

Commissioner Lin, as the foreigners called him, dealt harshly with Chinese opium handlers and users. Smugglers were punished, some were executed, and addicts were flogged or made to wear the cangue. Opium dens were raided, thousands of cakes of opium were burned, and thousands of pipes were confiscated. But all these measures, the commissioner knew, were ineffective if opium kept flowing into China. The only way to destroy it was to cut off the supply by persuading foreigners to stop trafficking in the drug.

At first the foreigners waited to see if the fuss about opium would blow over, as it had in

[4] John K. Fairbank, "The Motive Power of Opium," in *China Watch*. Boston: Harvard University Press, 1987, p.14.

*Commissioner Lin (1785–1850). By the time he was charged with suppressing the opium trade, he already had the nickname "Blue Sky"; he was considered so incorruptible that his reputation was comparable to the heavens. Courtesy of the Military Museum of China, Beijing, People's Republic of China.*

the past. But they underestimated the determination of Commissioner Lin. He gave the foreign suppliers two choices: They could leave China aboard their opium ships, or they could give up their opium to be destroyed. If they failed to do one or the other, the commissioner would close down all Chinese trade with foreigners. At this point many foreign traders left. The British, however, remained; for them, leaving China permanently was unthinkable. Then they began to haggle over how much opium they had to surrender. They hoped to give up a token number of chests, perhaps a thousand, to pacify the commissioner, and then resume business as usual. But Commissioner Lin declined to negotiate. Instead, he gave the *hong* merchants, the go-betweens in the opium trade (the commissioner called them traitors), three days to arrange for the surrender of all opium chests. If they failed, he would ask

*[margin notes: Black and white / so was there fighting? / They won't listen]*

the emperor's permission to execute one or two of them most active in the trade. Furthermore, he would confiscate their property, leaving their families destitute.

Despite the pleas of the *hong* merchants, the British continued to resist, explaining that they did not own the opium stored aboard their ships in Guangzhou's outer waterways. They insisted it belonged to the British East India Company or other companies in Calcutta or Bombay, and therefore they couldn't surrender it. All they could promise, they said, was that they would no longer buy or sell opium or bring it into China.

Commissioner Lin refused to be mollified. Instead, he repeated his threat to decapitate two of the *hong* merchants. Finally, when negotiations seemed to be going nowhere, the Commissioner instructed Chinese servants to withdraw from the foreigners' living quarters, the factories. Then he blockaded the factories with Chinese soldiers and citizens, isolating 350 foreigners for the next forty-seven days.

Finally the British gave in. They surrendered over twenty thousand chests of opium. Commissioner Lin himself supervised the destruction of the contents, three million pounds of raw opium. A bamboo fence was erected around the destruction site, and workers were searched daily to see that they did not take any opium off the premises. A man caught doing so was beheaded on the spot. The drug was thrown into water-filled trenches 7 feet deep and 150 feet long. Salt and lime were added to the water to dissolve the opium, and the entire mixture was washed down a creek and into the ocean. In a month millions of dollars' worth of opium had been swallowed by the sea.

In the summer of 1839, after the opium had been destroyed, Commissioner Lin wrote to Queen Victoria of England explaining China's position on opium and demanding that the British stop trafficking in the drug. After assuring her of China's beneficence, its willingness to let tea, silk, and other goods be shared everywhere "without begrudging it in the slightest," he described what would happen to barbarians who brought opium into China. Those who "beguile the Chinese people into a death trap" with opium, he promised, would be executed by

*[margin notes: Who owned it? / definately a lie / no way of getting to the people / jeez / damn / good for the fish / hurting society as well]*

## Excerpts from Lin Zexu's Letter to Queen Victoria

The kings of your honorable country by a tradition handed down from generation to generation have always been noted for their politeness and submissiveness. We have read your successive tributary memorials saying, "In general our countrymen who go to trade in China have always received His majesty the Emperor's gracious treatment and equal justice," and so on. Privately we are delighted with the way in which the honorable rulers of your country deeply understand the grand principles and are grateful for the Celestial grace. For this reason the Celestial Court in soothing those from afar has redoubled its polite and kind treatment. The profit from trade has been enjoyed by them continuously for two hundred years. This is the source from which your country has become known for its wealth.

But after a long period of commercial intercourse, there appear among the crowd of barbarians both good persons and bad, unevenly. Consequently there are those who smuggle opium to seduce the Chinese people and so cause the spread of the poison to all provinces. Such persons who only care to profit themselves, and disregard their harm to others, are not tolerated by the laws of heaven and are unanimously hated by human beings. His Majesty the Emperor, upon hearing of this, is in a towering rage. He has especially sent me, his commissioner, to come to Kwangtung [the province of which Guangzhou is the capital], and together with the governor-general and governor jointly to investigate and settle this matter.

All those people in China who sell opium or smoke opium should receive the death penalty. If we trace the crime of those barbarians who through the years have been selling opium, then the deep harm they have wrought and the great profit they have usurped should fundamentally justify their execution according to law. We take into consideration, however, the fact that the various barbarians have still known how to repent their crimes and return to their allegiance to us by taking the 20,183 chests of opium from their storeships. . . . It has been entirely destroyed and this has been faithfully reported to the Throne in several memorials by this commissioner and his colleagues. . . .

Now we have set up regulations governing the Chinese people. He who sells opium shall receive the death penalty and he who smokes it also the death penalty. Now consider this: if the barbarians do not bring opium, then how can the Chinese people resell it, and how can they smoke it? The fact is that the wicked barbarians beguile the Chinese people into a death trap. How then can we grant life only to these barbarians? He who takes the life of even one person still has to atone for it with his own life; yet is the harm done by opium limited to the taking of one life only? Therefore in the new regulations, in regard to those barbarians who bring opium to China, the penalty is fixed at decapitation or strangulation. This is what is called getting rid of a harmful thing on behalf of mankind. . . .

Yet the Emperor cannot bear to execute people without having first tried to reform them by instruction. Therefore he especially promulgates these fixed regulations. The barbarian merchants of your country, if they wish to do business for a prolonged period, are required to obey our statutes respectfully and to cut off permanently the source of opium. They must by no means try to test the effectiveness of the law with their lives. May you, O King [Queen Victoria], check your wicked and sift your vicious people before they come to China, in order to guarantee the peace of your nation, to show further the sincerity of your politeness and submissiveness, and to let the two countries enjoy together the blessings of peace. How fortunate, how fortunate indeed! After receiving this dispatch will you immediately give us a prompt reply regarding the details and circumstances of your cutting off the opium traffic. Be sure not to put this off.

Excerpted from Ssu-yü Teng and John K. Fairbank, *China's Response to the West: A Documentary Survey, 1839–1923*, pp. 24–27. Copyright ©1954, 1979 by the President and Fellows of Harvard College, © 1982 by Ssu-yü Teng and John K. Fairbank. Reprinted by permission of Harvard University Press.

*effective to cut off supply*

beheading or strangulation. The commissioner concluded his letter with these words: "After receiving this dispatch will you immediately give us a prompt reply regarding the details and circumstances of your cutting off the opium traffic. Be sure not to put this off."

*hmm*

Queen Victoria never received the commissioner's letter. When a British sea captain brought it to London, the Foreign Office refused to meet with him, and the letter was never delivered. It was printed in the *Times* but was the object of derision. The British clearly felt they had little to fear from the Celestial Empire.

## Questions

1. What do you think will happen next in the struggle between the foreign barbarians and Commissioner Lin? Who do you think will "win" the struggle? Give reasons for your opinion.

2. Can you think of any contemporary situations comparable to China's experiences with opium? What are they? How do governments today try to prevent illegal substances from entering their countries? How successful are their efforts? Compare Commissioner Lin's efforts to control the opium trade with the methods governments use today to control illegal drugs. How are they similar? How are they different?

## The Opium Struggle Continues

The British were furious about the destruction of their opium, a significant economic loss. Furthermore, they declined to sign a bond that Commissioner Lin demanded of all foreign traders as part of his campaign to destroy the opium supply. Traders were to file a statement, in English and Chinese, declaring that their ships would never again bring opium to China. Anyone breaking this pledge would be executed by strangulation or decapitation. Then the ship and its cargo would be confiscated by the Chinese government.

*so did they cut off the trade?*

For years the Chinese and foreigners had been at odds about whether the Chinese should

have any kind of legal jurisdiction over foreigners. By Western standards, Chinese justice was harsh and swift. Guilt was assumed, torture was used to exact confessions, and death was the penalty for many crimes. So when foreigners were accused of committing crimes on Chinese soil, their officials went to considerable trouble to protect them from facing Chinese justice. In some instances, the alleged criminal was sent back to his home country for trial and punishment. *because more law*

After the destruction of the opium, relations between foreigners and Commissioner Lin grew steadily worse. The British kept dunning the commissioner to pay for the loss of their opium. Commissioner Lin kept pressuring the British to sign his bond.

Then when it seemed impossible for things to get worse, a group of drunken British sailors were accused of killing a Chinese villager in Kowloon. The British refused to turn the men over to the Chinese authorities, saying they did not know which man was responsible. Commissioner Lin retaliated by pressuring the Portuguese to expel the British from Macao, where they had gone when they were released from the Guangzhou factories. The British then fled to Hong Kong, later described by one official as "a barren Island with hardly a House upon it."

The Chinese seemed not to understand why the British were so adamant about being paid for the destruction of their opium. They did not know they were no longer dealing with the English barbarians as private individuals doing business in China. In the late 1830s Britain had appointed a superintendent of foreign trade in China to represent the British government. Disagreements between Chinese and British were no longer simply disagreements with trading companies such as the British East India Company; they were disagreements with the British government, which had the military power to back up its complaining citizens, even when they were far from home.

As might be expected, the British in China did just that: They demanded that their home government back them up. To their way of thinking, their country had been insulted when the Chinese destroyed British property and refused to pay for it. Eventually the British parliament agreed and sent sixteen warships and 4,000 troops to recover the value of the destroyed opium and to make it clear to the Chinese that they were dealing with the mighty British Empire.

## The Opium War, 1839–1842

The Opium War started with skirmishes in the waterways of Guangzhou but quickly escalated. The British blockaded Guangzhou, then Ningbo. They then took the main town on the island of Chusan and sailed north to the city of Tinghai. Here it seemed that the war might end. In January 1841 the emperor's representative there, Qishan, agreed that China would pay the British $6 million and give them the island of Hong Kong. Furthermore, foreign merchants were to be allowed to return to trade at Guangzhou. Nothing in the agreement outlawed the opium trade.

The emperor, furious when he heard about this agreement, refused to accept any of the terms. Instead, he threatened to execute Qishan and confiscate his family's property; the sentence was later commuted to banishment. The British were also unhappy with the terms of the agree-

ment and with their representative, Charles Elliot. He was replaced.

The British quickly sent reinforcements, both men and ships, and hostilities resumed. In August 1841 the British occupied sections of Guangzhou. Then in the fall, under the command of Sir Henry Pottinger, they once again sailed north. Although the Chinese fought bravely, even fanatically, they were no match for the well-armed foreigners. Most of the Chinese were armed only with swords and spears or bows and arrows. Their guns and cannons were antiquated. Their rattan shields with devils' heads painted on them were useless against British muskets. Nor were Chinese war junks any match for the swift ships of the British navy. Pottinger moved quickly, capturing Xiamen, Ningbo, Shanghai, and Zhenjiang. British casualties were relatively light; Chinese died by the thousands. Although their officers made some attempts to stop them, British soldiers sacked and looted every city they captured. In some cases, defeated Manchu soldiers (the British called them Tartars) and their families killed themselves rather than submit to the enemy barbarians.

---

### Reading: *The Capture of Zhenjiang*

The following excerpts are from the diary of a poet, Chushiyuan, who lived outside the walls of the city of Chinkiang, spelled Zhenjiang in *pinyin*. Beginning in July 1842, rumors swept the city that foreign soldiers were moving up the Yangzi (Yangtze) River to attack the city. Chu sent his wife and family north of the city for safety before the four main gates to the city were closed. He and his younger brother stayed behind to guard the family home. Finally, on July 21, 1842, foreign troops disembarked from their ships. When the fighting began, the resistance in Zhenjiang was some of the toughest the British encountered. They lost over 1,500 men out of a force of 9,000. From his vantage point in the hills high above the city, Chu described the initial battle. In these excerpts, comments

added by the translator are in brackets; additional explanatory comments are in parentheses.

**July 21st (1842):** Today at the Hour of the Snake [9 a.m.] the foreigners disembarked. The Assistant Commissioner Ch'i-shen and the Commander-in-Chief Liu Yün-hsiao hastily marshaled the troops whom they had secluded in a fold of the hills, and directed operations sitting in carrying chairs. Our troops fired several rounds; but the foreigners continued to advance. The two generals then left their chairs and fled on horseback; whereupon all their men broke into a general stampede up hill and down dale, in the direction of the Tan-Yang high road [that is, to the south], to the great amusement of the foreigners.

I and my brother had our provisions ready and had decided that the time had come for flight. But my brother was not in favour of starting at once. However, he urged me to go and, reluctantly, I left by the back gate (of the family home) and went up the hill, to wait for him there. I looked toward the northern gate (of the city). Under the wall a fierce cross-fire of guns and rockets was in progress. Spurt after spurt of white smoke darted out in quick succession, till everything was covered in a thick coiling cloud; underneath which, I well knew, the dead must be piled corpse on corpse. I consoled myself by thinking that our men evidently still "had some wind in their sails" and hoped they might perhaps after all be victorious.

Suddenly the firing ceased, and at that moment flames shot up from the watch-tower at the northern gate. There was a fierce south-east wind blowing and the purple flames under the double eaves flounced out as though there were some demon in their midst. . . . Yet all the while a pall of blue smoke hung above, so dense that it did not budge. . . . My thoughts turned to the hundreds of thousands of souls, shut into this seething cauldron without chance of escape. What was happening at this moment to this or that life-long friend or near kinsman? I struggled in vain to keep back my tears.

When the fire at the north gate watch-tower was still only beginning, the rocket attack spread to the whole line of parapets[5] towards the east, and was replied to by our men. After a while there was an extremely concentrated attack by rockets on the part near the watch-tower on the eastern wall, and now when I cast my eye round the whole circuit of the walls I could not see a single defender, except at the point where the foreigners were actually trying to scale them; here twenty or thirty of our men were still crouching between the parapets.

Suddenly everyone pointed again at the watch-tower on the western wall. "It's ablaze again," they said. I was sure now that the city would not hold, and hastened to send someone to fetch my brother, while I myself rested for a time, in a small grotto at the foot of the hill. But soon the news became more and more desperate, and I hurried towards the southern hills. I reached a hill-top and

sat down on a rock. Looking round the walls I saw that the men between the parapets on the eastern wall were still firing guns and rockets, and knew that the city had not yet fallen. Suddenly three large cannon fired from the eastern wall, one after another. But they were a long way off from where the foreigners were making their assault, and may well not have reached them. In a moment I saw the foreigners spread out over the road and march straight through the southern gate.

**July 22nd**: I and my brother are at T'ang village [about a mile and a half south of Chinkiang]. We got up early and went for a walk in front of the village. Warmth was beginning to come into the morning light. Far villages and near villages showed dimly between the heavy green of the misty woods. The young women of the villages were busy drawing their morning supplies of water, or were going off to work in the fields. Chickens, dogs, mulberries, hemp—all the sights that speak of an untroubled life, and this only three or four leagues [a mile or so] from the city! Indeed no one here seemed to have any inkling that a deadly conflict was raging.

A villager came with a cart and I and my brother drove to another village, where the family of one of our servants lived. It was a mud hovel, cramped and tumbledown, entirely pervaded by the smell of manure. I spent the night in a small loft, where the heat was scorching, and could not get a wink of sleep. I kept on thinking of my wife and family whom I had sent far away to the north of the river. Having heard of the fall of the city they must be desperately anxious about what has happened to myself and my brother. I went on and on worrying about this.

**July 23rd**: A villager who has come back from the city told us: "They are letting people go in and out by the north gate. The foreign devils are going round from house to house, seizing gold and silver and women's headdresses.[6] The clothes they toss to the poor. Rogues from far and near got wind of this, and crowds of them have come to guide the foreigners to likely houses. When the foreigners have smashed in the gates and taken what they want, these scoundrels take advantage to make off with

---

[5] parapet: an embankment atop the city wall to protect soldiers from enemy fire.

[6] Chinese women's headdresses were family heirlooms used for ceremonies such as weddings. They were very valuable because they were often encrusted with jewels.

*The Treaty of Nanjing was signed aboard Her Majesty's Ship* Cornwallis *on August 29, 1842. Courtesy of the Historical Commission, Central Committee of the Kuomintang, Taipei, Taiwan, Republic of China.*

everything that is left, even loading onto carts what they cannot carry on their shoulders." Today my brother went back to our home to see how things are. The few relations whom we left behind are all right so far. This evening my brother came back.

**July 27th:** This evening someone came from north of the river and said that Yangchow has not been attacked, which made me feel easier about my wife and family. I also hear that large numbers of the foreign devils are embarking (leaving) on their ships, having impressed (forced) Chinese to carry their spare clothing and other goods. It looks as though they were detaching part of their forces to go to Nanking.

**July 28th:** The foreign devils, both inside and outside the city, are seizing people, cutting off their pigtails, and turning them into soldiers.[7] Early in the morning I went to various villages to visit friends. I was very tired when I got back, and my servant prepared a meat-dish for me. But my thoughts kept on going back to the old days and I was in such misery that I could not restrain my tears. In the evening I sat out in the open under some trees . . . . and wrote a letter to send north of the river.

**July 29th:** For days on end great numbers of women in the city have been raped or carried off. Their names are well known, but I forbear (refrain) to mention them. Two sons of well-to-do families have had their queues cut off and have been carried away; so it may well be imagined how others have fared. My servant has come back with a letter from my brother saying that south of the city the foreign devils' tents have all disappeared. They have also quitted the city itself and are now for the most part only stationed in the quarter outside the north gate; but there are still forty-five ships along the shore. He also said that black devils[8] came again yesterday to our house and took several things away.

*On July 31, Chu left Tang village and returned to his home.*

**August 4th:** There are now only about twenty foreign ships on the river. Someone came with a letter from my family north of the river. They are getting along fairly well.

**August 26th:** A Mr. P'an of Yangchow has given a sum of money to be spent on presents to the foreigners on their ships, asking them in return for this to allow ships laden with rice, for distribu-

[7] The diarist notes in another place that the British forced Chinese men into becoming soldiers. Perhaps the diarist was referring to the British practice of forcing Chinese men to do manual labor for them, such as carrying their supplies.

[8] black devils: perhaps the name the Chinese gave to the dark-skinned troops from India who fought with the British.

tion at reduced prices, to reach Chinkiang from Yangchow. The rice-ships have now arrived and two sheds have been put up to store the rice, one at the west gate and one at the south gate. At the same time a large stock of rough coffins has been brought, that people inside and outside the city may be able to bury the dead. But though the rice-ships have arrived there has been a hold-up of some kind, and after several days, they still have not yet been unloaded.

**August 28th:** The foreigners are selling clothes. These are clothes that they looted. They have put up stalls outside the north gate where they sell them very cheap, but will only take foreign dollars in payment.

**September 3rd:** The Governor has issued a proclamation saying he has received information from the Governor-General that peace has been concluded with the English foreigners. "The fighting being now over, I call upon all refugees to return to the city. There is to be no more looting."

**October 4th:** The foreign ships have all gone.

> Abridged from Arthur Waley, *The Opium War Through Chinese Eyes.* London: George Allen & Unwin, Ltd., 1958, pp. 197–221. Reprinted with permission of HarperCollins Publisher, London.

After the British captured Zhenjiang, their ships continued to move along the Yangzi River toward China's southern capital, Nanjing. The Chinese then accepted what had seemed unthinkable: Left unchecked, the foreigners might move all the way to Beijing. At that point the emperor agreed to sign a settlement with the barbarians. The Treaty of Nanjing was signed on August 29, 1842.

## Questions

1. In your opinion, why did Britain fight the Opium War? Was the destruction of the opium by Commissioner Lin the real reason or merely an excuse? Give reasons for your response.
2. What do you think was the most significant reason for China's defeat in the Opium War?
3. What is your reaction to the excerpts from Chushiyuan's diary? How would you characterize his experiences during the Opium War?

4. The Treaty of Nanjing was signed on August 29, 1842. Yet in his diary, Chu notes September 3 as the day when the governor in his province proclaimed that peace had been concluded with the English foreigners. Account for the discrepancy between these dates.

## Activity: Writing the Treaty of Nanjing

## Part 1. At Home

A treaty is a formal agreement between two or more nations. The Treaty of Nanjing ended the Opium War and listed the terms of peace between China and Great Britain.

1. For homework, review the list you made from the emperor's edict in Section 1. It contains five of Macartney's requests to the Qianlong emperor.
2. Look over your notes for Section 2. By the 1830s what else did foreigners want from the Chinese? Add these issues or concerns to your list.

## Part 2. At School

1. Bring your list to class. Your teacher will divide you into groups of four. Think of yourselves as a group of British citizens in China. Your forces having just won a war against the Chinese, you are in a position to get concessions from your former enemy. You know what requests the Chinese have refused to grant in the past. You think they were unreasonable about paying for the opium they destroyed. You feel justified in making them pay for all the problems you as foreigners have experienced in China. You have been asked to submit a list of the terms you want included in the Treaty of Nanjing.
2. In your group, share the lists you wrote at home. (There will be some repetition.) Then, as a group of British victors, decide what five terms you want included in the Treaty of Nanjing. Write your group's list on chart paper.

3. Post your group's list. Then take a few minutes to look at all the lists, noting similarities and differences.
4. Decide as a class which five terms must be included in the treaty. A class member should list these terms in rank order on chart paper.

## Part 3. Debriefing

1. Compare the group lists and the class list with the excerpts from the Treaty of Nanjing. Did you come close to the terms of the real treaty? What issue is conspicuously missing in the treaty? Why is this treaty referred to as an unequal treaty?
2. Discuss this question as a class: As a result of the Treaty of Nanjing, China was forced to open treaty ports, pay an indemnity of millions of dollars to Britain, and cede Hong Kong. Furthermore, the opium trade continued to flourish. Looking back from the perspective of well over 150 years, and knowing all this, do you think China should have made opium such an issue? For China, was the Opium War worth fighting? Was it worth it for Britain?

## Reading: *Excerpts from the Treaty of Nanjing*

### ARTICLE I

There shall henceforward be peace and friendship between Her Majesty the Queen of Great Britain and Ireland and His Majesty the Emperor of China, and between their respective subjects, who shall enjoy full security and protection for their persons and property within the dominions of the other.

### ARTICLE II

His Majesty the Emperor of China agrees, that British subjects, with their families and establishments, shall be allowed to reside, for the purpose of carrying on their mercantile pursuits, without molestation or restraint at the cities and towns of Canton [Guangzhou], Amoy [Xiamen], Foochowfoo [sic] [Fuzhou], Ningpo [Ningbo], and Shanghai.

### ARTICLE III

. . . His Majesty the Emperor of China cedes to Her Majesty the Queen of Great Britain, &c. [etc.], the Island of Hong Kong to be possessed in perpetuity by her Britannic Majesty, her heirs and successors, and to be governed by such laws and regulations as her majesty, the Queen of Great Britain, &c., shall see fit to direct.

### ARTICLE IV

The Emperor of China agrees to pay the sum of 6,000,000 dollars, as the value of the opium which was delivered up at Canton [Guangzhou] in the month of March 1839, as a ransom for the lives of Her Britannic Majesty's Superintendent and subjects, who had been imprisoned [in their factories] by the Chinese High Officers.

### ARTICLE VII

It is agreed, that the total amount of 21,000,000 dollars . . . shall be paid as follows [over the years from 1842 to 1845]:

| | |
|---|---|
| 6,000,000 | [for the opium] |
| 12,000,000 | [for the cost of the British military expedition] |
| 3,000,000 | [for the repayment of debts owned by the *hong* merchants to British traders] |

And it is further stipulated, that interest, at the rate of 5 percent, per annum [per year], shall be paid by the Government of China on any portion of the above sums that are not punctually discharged at the periods fixed.

We express our gratitude to Far Eastern Publications of Yale University Press for permission to reprint certain passages from *China and the West: Cultural Collision, Selected Documents*, ed. by Richard L. Walker. New Haven, CT: Yale University, Far Eastern Publications, 1956, pp. 107–109.

## Activity: Role-Playing

1. Your teacher will divide you into groups of four. Each person in the group will have one of these roles:

   - a mother whose husband sold their daughter for opium
   - Commissioner Lin
   - the poet Chushiyuan
   - a British trader who has made a fortune in the opium trade

2. When you have your role, review your notes and the parts of this section that have information about your character. The British trader should review information in Section 1 about the Canton system and information in this section about the Treaty of Nanjing. As you read and review, try to imagine how you would have thought and felt had you been that person living in China in the 1830s and 1840s.

3. After you review your notes and the readings, write your responses to these questions from the perspective of your character. Respond to each question as fully as you can. Write each response on a separate sheet of paper.

   a. Explain how you feel about the opium trade and why. Explain how the opium trade has affected you personally.
   b. Describe how you feel about foreigners in China. Has their presence, particularly the British presence, been helpful or harmful to you?
   c. Describe your reaction to the Treaty of Nanjing. How do you think it will affect you?

4. Meet in groups of three or four with other students who have the *same* role. Read your responses aloud and discuss them. As you listen, add to your responses on the proper sheet of paper. By the end of the discussion, you should have more ideas about how your character might have responded to the questions.

*Although Hong Kong was ceded to the British "in perpetuity" in the Treaty of Nanjing, it was returned to China on July 1, 1997. This photo, taken in June 1995 in front of the Museum of Revolutionary History in Beijing, shows a timer counting down the days and seconds until that return. Courtesy of photographer Hai-yen Huang.*

5. Take a few minutes to look over the questions again, along with your responses and those you added in the group. You will use this information (without reading it) in the next part of this activity.

6. Meet with your original group of four role-players. One person will read a "prompt," a statement to start conversation in your group. The other three people must respond to that prompt as their characters. Then another person reads the next prompt, and again everyone responds. Your group will have five minutes to respond to each prompt. Every person must respond to every prompt. Afterward, anyone one who wishes can respond to comments made by another character.

*Incorporation of "prompts" in this activity adapted from a teaching strategy developed by the Teachers' Curriculum Institute, Mountain View, CA.*

**Prompt A:** The speaker is the mother whose child was sold. "I think opium was very destructive to China and the Chinese people. It destroyed Chinese families and our Confucian values."

**Prompt B:** The speaker is Commissioner Lin. "Britain treated the Celestial Empire very badly. If it were not for China, Britain would not have any wealth at all."

**Prompt C:** The speaker is the poet Chushiyuan. "I think the Treaty of Nanjing is very unfair to the Chinese. We will regret that we signed it."

**Prompt D:** The speaker is a British trader who was held captive in the Guangzhou factories. "There is an old saying that applies to China, and you people will have to accept it: 'To the victor belong the spoils.'"

7. After everyone has responded to the last prompt, go around the group for one last comment from every group member.

## Activity: Writing an Essay

Look over the Treaty of Nanjing. Write an essay discussing this quotation as it applies to the Treaty of Nanjing: "To the victor belong the spoils." You can write from the perspective of any of the four characters in the role-play. Your notes from the previous activity should help you get started.

## Activity: Broadcasting the News

Add a fifth character, a news reporter, to the role-play activity. Working in groups of five, prepare a news report on the Treaty of Nanjing with the reporter acting as narrator and interviewing the four other characters about the impact of the treaty on their lives.

## Extension Activities

The following questions require library research. See the list of sources at the end of this section.

1. At a certain point in the struggle over the opium trade, Commissioner Lin disappeared from the scene. Prepare a report on Commissioner Lin and what happened to him after 1841.
2. Other countries besides Britain were active in the opium trade. Prepare a report discussing Americans who sold opium in China. Explain why the situations of the British traders and individual American traders differed significantly.
3. Opium became a controversial issue in Hawai'i in the late nineteenth century. In a report to the class, explain why. Tell how the Kingdom of Hawai'i regulated opium and how opium is regulated under state law today.
4. In 1843 the United States signed a treaty with China called the Treaty of Wanghia. Learn about this treaty and give an oral presentation on its terms.
5. Hong Kong was ceded to the British in the Treaty of Nanjing. What is its status today? Prepare a report about the history of Hong Kong after the British took it over in 1842. The sidebar in Chapter 3, Section 5, will help you get started.

## Further Reading

Chang, Hsin-pao. *Commissioner Lin and the Opium War.* Cambridge, MA: Harvard University Press, 1964.

Collis, Maurice. *Foreign Mud: Being an Account of the Opium Imbroglio at Canton in the 1830's & the Anglo-Chinese War that Followed.* New York: Knopf, 1947.

Fairbank, John K. "The Motive Power of Opium," in *China Watch.* Boston: Harvard University Press, 1987.

Fay, Peter Ward. *The Opium War, 1840–1842: Barbarians in the Celestial Empire in the Early Part of the Nineteenth Century and the War by*

*Which They Forced Her Gates Ajar*. Chapel Hill,
    NC: University of North Carolina Press, 1975.
Forbes, H. A. Crosby. *Shopping in China: The Artisan
    Community at Canton, 1825–1830*. n.p.:
    International Exhibitions Foundation, 1979.
Pruitt, Ida. *A Daughter of Han: The Autobiography of a
    Chinese Working Woman*. New Haven, CT: Yale
    University Press, 1945.
Spence, Jonathan D. *Chinese Roundabout: Essays in
    History and Culture*. New York: W. W. Norton,
    1992.
Teng, Ssu-yü, and John K. Fairbank. *China's Response
    to the West: A Documentary Survey, 1839–1923*.
    Cambridge, MA: Harvard University Press,
    © 1954, 1961 ed.
Walker, Richard L., ed. *China and the West: Cultural
    Collision: Selected Documents*. New Haven, CT:
    Yale University, Far Eastern Publications, 1956.
Waley, Arthur. *The Opium War Through Chinese Eyes*.
    London: George Allen & Unwin, Ltd., 1958.

# 3 Foreign Encroachment in China, 1842–1911

*I*n this section we consider the impact of foreign encroachments on China and some of the concessions made to foreigners during the late Qing dynasty. We also examine the most-favored-nation clause included in many of the treaties foreign powers made with China, along with the meaning of "spheres of influence" and "extraterritoriality."

## Reading: *Unequal Treaties*

*[handwritten margin note: don't have the reign anymore]*

For centuries before 1842, China traded successfully with foreigners, always on China's terms. But after the Treaty of Nanjing, foreign contacts increased and conditions of trade changed drastically because of a series of unequal treaties China was forced to sign with foreign powers. These treaties, drafted by foreigners to protect foreigners living and working in China, gave them rights and privileges never granted to Chinese living in other countries. The complex situation in China was unique in world history. Never before or since has a major country had living on its soil so many foreigners who were not subject to its laws. *[handwritten margin note: What laws? them]*

The first of the unequal treaties was the Treaty of Nanjing, which formally ended the Opium War. The British now had five cities where they could live and work unhindered. They had been granted Hong Kong "in perpetuity" and were able to establish uniform taxes on goods brought into these five "treaty port" cities. The most significant impact of this treaty was that it emboldened other nations to seek trading concessions from the Chinese. By 1844 both the French and the Americans had established similar treaties with China, including some important new concessions. The most significant was Article 21 of the agreement with the United States, which stipulated that Americans accused of committing crimes in China could be tried only by Americans and punished "according to the laws of the United States."

*[handwritten margin note: everybody wants China]*

## The Most-Favored-Nation Clause

On October 8, 1843, China and Britain signed a supplementary treaty to the Treaty of Nanjing. Known as the Treaty of the Bogue, it contained what has come to be called a most-favored-nation clause.[1] Article VIII read as follows:

The Emperor of China having been graciously pleased to grant to all foreign countries whose Subjects, or Citizens, have hitherto traded at Canton [Guangzhou] the privilege of resorting for purposes of Trade to the other four Ports of Fuchow [Fuzhou], Amoy [Xiamen], Ningpo [Ningbo], and Shanghai, on the same terms as the English, it is further agreed, that should the Emperor hereafter, from any course whatever, be pleased to grant additional privileges or immunities to any of the Subjects or Citizens of such Foreign Countries, the same privileges and immunities will be extended to and enjoyed by British Subjects; but it is to be understood that demands or requests are not, on this plea, to be unnecessarily brought forward.

From William F. Tung, *China and the Foreign Powers: The Impact of and Reaction to Unequal Treaties.* Dobbs Ferry, NY: Oceana Publications, Inc., 1970, p. 436.

[1] most-favored-nation clause: a clause written into a commercial treaty saying that if certain rights and privileges are later granted to a third country, they will automatically be given to the country making the treaty as well. In the instance cited here, the Treaty of the Bogue, Britain is the most favored nation, meaning that Britain will automatically get any privileges or immunities that China grants by treaty to other countries in the future.

## Questions

1. After reading Article VIII of the supplement to the Treaty of Nanjing, explain the meaning of "most-favored-nation clause." In this instance, which nation is the most favored?

2. Britain was only the first of many foreign nations to be granted a most-favored-nation clause. Why would other countries want such a clause in their treaties with China? What impact do you think the most-favored-nation clause had on China?

3. Note that the last sentence suggests that pleas for privileges and immunities should be reasonable. If you were a foreigner in China in 1843, what requests would you consider "reasonable"?

## Activity: Placard Posted in Guangzhou

1. Fold a piece of paper into four sections and label it as shown.

| content | context |
|---------|---------|
| insights | questions |

2. Read the placard reproduced below.

3. Read the placard a second time, jotting comments in the appropriate sections on your paper.

    a. Note the **content** of the placard. What does it say?

    b. Consider the **historical context** of the placard. When was it written? Why was it written? What was happening at the time? What is it all about?

    c. Write any **insights** or ideas that occur to you as you read the placard. (For example, you might want to note that the writers seem angry.)

    d. Write any **questions** you have that are not answered in the placard.

    e. Discuss your analysis of this historical document with the class.

    f. You may be asked to read the placard aloud in dramatic style.

Guangzhou has had a long history of commerce with foreigners. Until the Treaty of Nanjing, foreigners were not allowed to live in other Chinese cities, and in Guangzhou they had been restricted to areas called factories. In 1845, this poster or placard was posted there.

## Reading: *Placard Posted in Guangzhou*

We, the literati [scholars or learned people] and righteous people of Guangzhou, including those who live on the land and the water, those who live inside and outside the city, publish these instructions to let the barbarian merchants of all nations understand our intentions.

The injuries, deceits, cruel deeds, and evil acts of the English resident barbarians are as innumerable as the hairs of the head. Now they plot to coerce our high authorities. They have long wished to enter the city; and our superiors, from the depths of their virtue and greatness of their benevolence, have given in and issued a proclamation granting permission to enter the city. They have not considered that the English barbarians, born and raised in noxious regions beyond the bounds of civilization, having the hearts of wolves, the visage [face] of tigers, and the cunning of foxes, plan to take possession of our province and only desire to enter the walls so that they may spy out the land. Now having received a proclamation allowing their entrance, they will not only exercise violence and usurpation [illegal takeover] but will insult and injure the people to an unspeakable degree.

Therefore, we the literati and the people of Guangzhou, however small our strength, have prepared ourselves for the contest. We declare that sooner than obey the proclamation and suffer these wild barbarians, we will act in opposition and adhere to the old regulations of our government.

In public assembly, we decided to await the day they enter the city, then exterminate their odious race and burn their houses. With united hearts, we will destroy them in order to display celestial vengeance [revenge] and manifest public indignation [anger].

But we are aware that at the thirteen factories barbarian merchants of all nations are assembled together for commerce, the good and the bad mixed together. When the standard of righteousness is raised, the precious and the vile might be consumed together if they were not warned in advance. Therefore we give this special early announcement.

All the good barbarians who intend to remain in their places quietly and do not contemplate entering the city shall come to no harm if they promptly leave. As regards all the people who live in the vicinity of the factories, if they wish to guard themselves and their establishments, they should not go out of doors to protect or save the barbarians. Otherwise calamity will overtake them, and they will have no time for regrets. Be warned. Tremble. Be on your guard. These are special commands.

Posted in front of the thirteen factories on the 18th day of the twelfth month of 1845.

Reprinted with the permission of the Free Press, a division of Simon & Schuster, from *Chinese Civilization: A Sourcebook*, Second Edition, Revised and Expanded. Edited by Patricia Buckley Ebrey. Copyright © 1993 by Patricia Buckley Ebrey. Copyright © 1981 by the Free Press, pp. 311–312.

---

## Reading: *Unequal Treaties*, continued

Within a few years of the Treaty of Nanjing, many foreign countries entered into treaty relations with China. Trade privileges were granted to Belgium and the United Kingdom of Sweden and Norway. Further concessions were granted in treaties signed in 1858 with Russia and in the 1858 Treaty of Tientsin [Tianjin] signed with Britain, France, and the United States. This treaty allowed inland foreign travel and foreign shipping, opened ten more treaty ports, and allowed missionaries freedom of movement. In 1860 further treaties gave Kowloon, near Hong Kong island, to the British and ceded a huge area on the far side of the Amur and Ussuri rivers in Northern China to Russia. In 1876 the British were allowed to open frontier trade to Yunnan and to send an exploratory mission to China's former tributary state of Tibet. Between 1860 and 1885 many other nations entered treaty relations with China. Germany, Portugal, Denmark, the Netherlands, Spain, Italy, Austria–Hungary, Japan, Peru, and Brazil all signed unequal treaties with China and benefited from most-favored-nation clauses. In 1899 the American publication *Harper's Weekly* noted regarding the United States: "Our Treaty rights in the Celestial Empire . . . are all perfectly clear.

Under the 'most favored nation' clause we enjoy all the commercial privileges granted by China to any of our competitors."

## Why China Agreed to the Unequal Treaties

China and the Western powers had vastly different aims in agreeing to the unequal treaties. The Treaty of Nanjing had been forced on the Chinese, and they were unhappy with it and with later unequal treaties. Yet the evidence suggests that the Chinese regarded these arrangements as preferable to other possibilities, such as military confrontations with the Western powers. During much of this time, China was dealing with internal rebellions and widespread disenchantment with the Qing emperors. The Chinese government could not do battle on two fronts at once. It had enough trouble quelling internal rebels; it certainly did not need to fight foreigners at the same time. Ironically, the foreign presence within China caused further disarray because some of the rebellion was antiforeign. This was especially true of the Boxer Rebellion. (See Chapter 2, Section 4, for information on the Boxers.)

## Major Treaties Signed Between China and Foreign Powers, 1842–1901

| Year | Treaty | Signatories | Major Provisions |
|---|---|---|---|
| 1842 | Treaty of Nanjing | Britain | • China to pay indemnity to Britain<br>• Five ports opened for trade<br>• Hong Kong ceded to Britain<br>• *Hong* system abolished |
| 1843 | Treaty of the Bogue | Britain | • Import duties standardized<br>• Extraterritoriality granted<br>• Most-favored-nation clause included |
| 1844 | Treaty of Wanghia | United States | • Americans prohibited from trading opium<br>• Extraterritoriality granted<br>• Most-favored-nation clause included<br>• Foreign hospitals and churches allowed in treaty ports |
| 1844 | Treaty of Whampoa | France | • Extraterritoriality granted<br>• Most-favored-nation clause included<br>• Free propagation of Catholicism permitted |
| 1851 | Treaty of Ili | Russia | • Right to trade granted to Russia<br>• Right to build warehouses allowed<br>• Consulates established |
| 1858 | Treaty of Aigun | Russia | • Trade allowed to extend to interior China |
| 1858 | Treaty of Tianjin | Britain,<br>France,<br>United States | • Ten new ports opened to foreign trade<br>• Foreign travel allowed throughout China<br>• Inland transit dues standardized<br>• China to pay indemnity<br>• Freedom of movement for all missionaries permitted |
| 1860 | Beijing Convention | France,<br>Britain | • Diplomats allowed to reside in Beijing<br>• China to pay indemnity<br>• Kowloon Peninsula ceded to Britain |
| 1860 | Additional Treaty of Beijing | Russia | • Amur Province acquired by Russia<br>• Commercial concessions granted<br>• Most-favored-nation clause included |

Note: After 1860, more foreign countries entered into treaty relations with China for a final total of 17: Great Britain, the United States, France, Russia, Belgium, Norway, Sweden, Germany, Portugal, Denmark, the Netherlands, Spain, Italy, Austria-Hungary, Peru, Brazil, and Japan.

| Year | Treaty | Signatories | Major Provisions |
|---|---|---|---|
| 1876 | Treaty of Kanghwa | Japan | • Korea recognized as independent state<br>• Envoys exchanged<br>• Three more treaty ports opened<br>• Consular jurisdiction recognized |
| 1876 | Chefoo Agreement | Britain | • Yunnan frontier trade opened<br>• British officers allowed to station at Talifu or other suitable sites<br>• Expression of regret by China<br>• China to pay indemnity |

## Major Treaties Signed Between China and Foreign Powers, 1842–1901, *continued*

| Year | Treaty | Signatories | Major Provisions |
|------|--------|-------------|------------------|
| 1885 | Li-Fournier Agreement | France | • All treaties between France & Annam (Vietnam) recognized |
| 1895 | Treaty of Shimonoseki | Japan | • Korean independence recognized<br>• China to pay indemnity to Japan<br>• Taiwan and Liaodong Peninsula ceded to Japan<br>• More treaty ports opened<br>• Japan allowed to open factory in China |
| 1901 | Boxer Protocol | Allied Powers | • Chinese officials executed or punished<br>• Civil service examinations suspended in 45 cities<br>• Foreign Legation Quarter in Beijing expanded and protected<br>• 25 forts destroyed<br>• China to pay indemnity of $333 million |

*it is true*

The Chinese seemed to believe that foreigners wanted above everything else to make money. They thought the foreigners would stop bothering them if they just let them do business in China. In this context the most-favored-nation clause made sense to the Chinese. They thought that if they gave the same trading concessions to all countries that wanted them, these foreign nuisances would leave the Chinese alone. They

*it would cause more fighting*

did not grasp what Karl Marx, the great prophet of Communism, understood so well: business continually seeks new markets. The foreign traders, having gained some concessions, wanted more; the vast reaches of China held untold possibilities for those seeking new ways to get rich. To the Chinese the foreigners seemed insatiable; the foreigners thought they were merely making the most of their economic and political gains.

*china is prosperos*

---

### Reading: *Spheres of Influence*

*china has less control*

By late in the century, several foreign powers had carved China into spheres of influence, large areas where certain nations controlled natural resources, trade, and transportation. France, England, Russia, Japan, and Germany all claimed such spheres so as to benefit from Chinese resources without being hampered by the Chinese government. These spheres of influence seriously undermined the territorial integrity of China.

Look at the map entitled "Foreign Spheres of Influence in China, 1911," showing areas dominated by various world powers in 1911. Keep in mind that although a foreign power controlled transportation, mining, and trade in

specific areas, the area remained Chinese territory. Spheres of influence were not colonies. Chinese law still applied, at least to the Chinese who lived in the area, and foreign powers did not govern them. In fact, few foreigners, except for missionaries, even lived in these geographic spheres; most foreigners lived in enclaves, called concessions or settlements, in the treaty ports.

Nevertheless, control of trade, mining, and transportation was crucial for the foreigners. Can you imagine what it would be like, for example, to live in the United States but to have to send goods to another part of the country using a highway controlled by the French, with French officials telling you what you could and

*their own mines in China*

*yes they would*

could not send and forcing you to use French trucks and French personnel to send the items? Most Americans would be outraged if a foreign power had that much control over the movement of goods and people on their soil. Yet this is what China endured for many years.

*The American consulate and the residence of the United States consul general in the International Settlement in Shanghai. The electric streetlights and other wires indicate the photo was probably taken between 1885 and 1910. (Telegraph and local telephone service began in Shanghai in 1881, electricity a few years later.) Only the rickshas suggest that this was a street in China. Courtesy of Peabody Essex Museum, Salem, MA.*

### Activity: Spheres of Influence

Your teacher will divide you into pairs. Use the map "Foreign Spheres of Influence in China, 1911" on page 115 to discuss the following questions with your partner. Be ready to share your responses with the class.

1. Why would historians say that foreign powers "carved up China like a melon"?
2. How can you account for the fact that the British sphere of influence was so large?
3. Between 1863 and 1894 France gained control of the area that became known as French Indochina (Annam, Tonkin, Cambodia, and Laos). Where was France's sphere of influence in China? Why do you suppose it was there?
4. During 1894–95 China fought the Sino–Japanese War against its former tributary state, Japan, when both countries intervened in a rebellion in Korea. China lost the war. It was forced to recognize the independence

*Chinese money was printed by British, French, Russian, German, Japanese, and American banks circa 1900. Although the United States had no sphere of influence in China, American enterprises conducted business there. The five-dollar note pictured here was circulated by the American Merchant's Bank in Shanghai in 1905. Courtesy of Shanghai People's Press, Shanghai, People's Republic of China.*

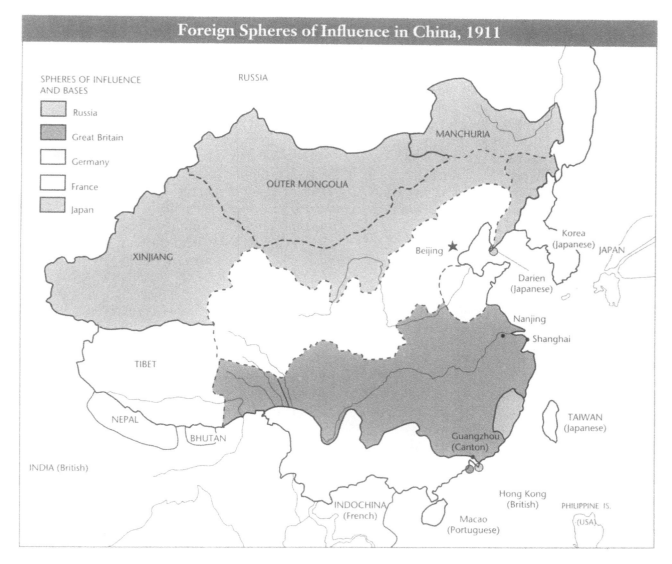

**Foreign Spheres of Influence in China, 1911**

SPHERES OF INFLUENCE
AND BASES

- Russia
- Great Britain
- Germany
- France
- Japan

of Korea and to cede Taiwan, the Pescadores Islands, and the Guangdong Peninsula to Japan. Shortly thereafter Germany and France forced Japan to give up the Guangdong Peninsula. Explain the most likely reason for the location of Japan's sphere of influence. Where was the German sphere of influence? Why?

---

**Reading:** *Extraterritoriality and Other Violations of Chinese Sovereignty*

Foreign powers violated Chinese sovereignty often during the late Qing Empire. Some nations acquired the right to station military personnel and warships in China (a right usually granted only with special permission or, these days, under the auspices of some international organization such as the United Nations). They were given the right to navigate freely in Chinese waters (a right usually granted only in return for reciprocal rights, which the Chinese did not get). Foreign nations even set up illegal post offices on Chinese soil, which the late Qing Empire was too weak to stop. In fact, the foreign post offices persisted well past the end of the empire in 1911.

## Imperialism

Imperialism is usually defined as one country's dominance over the economic or political affairs of a weaker country. It has a long history. From earliest times, countries sought to dominate other countries and to build empires. The Romans, for example, whose empire collapsed in the fifth century, had many colonies—outlying areas they controlled—in Europe, the Middle East, and Africa. In the thirteenth century Genghis Khan and his descendants established an empire that included China.

Modern imperialism dates from the fifteenth-century discovery of the "new world" by European explorers. It entailed the building of colonial empires, usually far from home, by European powers. By 1700 Spain had colonized much of Central America, and Spain and Portugal controlled large sections of South America. By the same time, France, Great Britain, and Spain had colonized North America. By the late 1800s parts of Africa, Southeast Asia, and Australia were either trading posts or colonies of European nations.

At first modern imperialistic countries were motivated by the desire for increased trade and for access to the natural resources of the Americas, India, Africa, and Asia. However, Western empire building expanded dramatically in the mid to late nineteenth century. Colonies served their mother countries as sources of raw materials and luxury goods, such as spices, diamonds, and gold; they also became markets for the excess manufactured goods the mother countries produced with their new technologies.

As a result of the explosive imperialism of the nineteenth century, "by 1900, one out of ten inhabitants of the entire world was governed by a European nation, and 20 percent of the earth's surface flew a European flag."[1] France was firmly established in Indochina, Indonesia was governed by the Dutch, and Portugal, Spain, Italy, and even tiny Belgium had colonies in Africa. And as the saying went, the sun never set on the British empire, which included countries as large as India and as small as Fiji. Even the United States had colonies, although they were seldom referred to as such, in the Philippines, Cuba, Puerto Rico, and the Pacific.

The Chinese government had resisted foreign economic encroachment for hundreds of years. Foreign traders were confined to Canton and restricted by the *hong* system. By the late 1890s, however, China had been carved into "spheres of influence" by Great Britain, Russia, Germany, and France. Later, even its former tributary state, Japan, would have a sphere of influence in China. Well into the twentieth century, each of these countries maintained a military presence and controlled trading rights in some part of China.

Today "imperialism" is a derogatory term. In Communist China the phrase "American imperialism" was often used scornfully after 1949. (See Chapter 3, Section 5.) But in the nineteenth century, imperialism was seen, on the part of the conquerors, as a means of building national prestige and of bringing Christianity and "civilization" to "pagans." Doing so, in the words of the British writer Rudyard Kipling, was the "white man's burden." This view, along with the economic exploitation and cultural destruction that colonialism wrought, would be increasingly challenged, particularly after World War II, as colonial states around the globe began to demand and win their independence.

---

[1] Philip F. Riley, Frank A. Gerome, Henry A. Myers, and Chong K. Yoon, *The Global Experience: Readings in World History Since 1500*, Vol. II. Englewood Cliffs, NJ: Prentice–Hall, 1987, p. 134.

*They can't even rule the people in their own country*

Another sensitive issue bearing on a nation's sovereignty is extraterritoriality, the right of foreign citizens to be judged by the laws of their country of citizenship rather than the country in which they live. The issue of extraterritoriality was an interesting one, for it showed perhaps most clearly how vast a gulf lay between China and other countries. Throughout most of history, extraterritoriality has been granted only under the most controlled and restricted conditions. Between the Treaty of Nanjing in 1842 and the 1920s, China granted (or was forced to grant) an extensive web of extraterritorial rights to people of many countries without receiving any such rights for its own citizens abroad. The initial justification for the insistence of the British and other foreigners for these rights was that the Chinese justice system was so vastly different from that of Western nations that no one could possibly expect Westerners to submit to it.

For Westerners, Chinese justice was fearsome because decisions were made by a person rather than according to law. To Westerners the Chinese system seemed capricious. A person was assumed guilty if accused; it was up to the accused to prove innocence, not up to the state to prove guilt. (Some European countries—France, for example—also demanded that the accused prove innocence). The rights of the person were subservient to the needs of the state, and it was thought right to sacrifice someone for the general good. Although cruelty and torture happened in Western justice systems, the tortures used by the Chinese, many of which scarred people for life, further terrified those who distrusted Chinese justice. It is easy to understand why Westerners were anxious to get extraterritorial rights for their citizens living in China. But the Chinese government undermined its own authority by extending such privileges so freely.

*well, it will keep foreigners from breaking the law*

---

### Reading: *Criminal Law in China and the West*

Chinese criminal law was written out as early as the eighteenth century B.C.E. By the middle of the sixth century B.C.E., details of penal law became public through bronze inscriptions. The essential purpose of laws and punishments was to prevent behavior the state considered unacceptable. As the Chinese put it, "Kill one, warn a hundred." To ensure that people were properly warned, punishment was brutal and public.

The social nature of law was further intensified by the fact that the courts were a part of the local administration, and the local court official was simultaneously judge, prosecutor, jury, and moral teacher. Before this official the accused had no rights.

In Chinese legal practice, it was considered worse to let a guilty person go free than to let an innocent person be punished. The explicit policy of the courts was "Rather wrong than let go." Traditional Chinese legal thinking included the idea of collective responsibility. Thus accused persons, by committing a crime, endangered not only themselves, but also those closest to them.

*Three women in a cangue, Shanghai, 1907. From* Imperial China: Photographs 1850–1912. *Courtesy of Pennwick Publishing, Inc., New York.*

Depending on the nature and seriousness of the offense, one's family, clan, or neighborhood could also be held accountable and, in some instances, be executed for the crime.

*Group of criminals condemned to execution, Guangzhou, 1890s. From* Imperial China: Photographs 1850–1912. *Courtesy of Pennwick Publishing, Inc., New York.*

When the Western nations opened treaty ports in China, they worried that Chinese justice would be applied to Westerners. Americans and Britons were most bothered about it, for their legal systems differed most strongly from the Chinese system. In American and British justice, law aims to make the punishment suit the crime, not to inflict a severe punishment as an example to others. In contrast to the Chinese "Rather wrong than let go" idea, the Anglo–Saxon tradition holds that no innocent person should be punished. The tradition also rejects the idea that one person can serve as judge, jury, and prosecutor, for it emphasizes the inequality of the relationship between the individual and the state. In the Anglo–Saxon legal tradition, the crime is clearly the individual's responsibility, and those close to the criminal are not punished unless they participated in the crime.

In short, Chinese legal tradition emphasizes the social nature of crime, its effect on society and the social order. Anglo–Saxon, and in fact most Western law, emphasizes individual responsibility. Because the needs of society are seen as more important than the rights of any individual, Chinese justice has often seemed cruel and unreasonable to Westerners.

## Questions

1. What is extraterritoriality?
2. Give some examples of special privileges granted to foreigners during the late Qing empire.
3. Why were Westerners fearful of Chinese justice?

*The cage punishment, Shanghai, circa 1870s. The prisoner either had to stand on his toes to relieve his neck or hang by his neck to relieve his toes, which just touched the bottom of the cage. The photographer, John Thomson, described the cage punishment and death of a man in Fuzhou who had murdered a little girl. Passersby were forbidden to give the criminal even a drop of water. He eventually went mad and strangled himself. From* China, The Land and Its People: Early Photographs by John Thomson. *Originally published as* Illustrations of China and Its People *by Sampson Low, Marston, Low and Searle, London, 1873.*

## Activity: Extraterritoriality

The extraterritorial privileges granted during the late Qing dynasty were extraordinary, but the idea that people living abroad need special consideration is well established. Here are some examples of people who have asked for or been granted special consideration in a foreign country.

### CASE 1

To be protected in a foreign country and to carry out their duties, members of the diplomatic community are generally exempt from the laws of the country where they are staying. They are protected from search, arrest, or prosecution. This status is called "diplomatic immunity." In general, diplomats are exempt from customs regulations as they move from country to country on a diplomatic passport. In practice this might mean that they can take gifts for friends and family into a foreign country without worrying about paying customs duties. Since diplomats are exempt from local laws, diplomatic immunity can mean that they or their families can park their cars without getting tickets. Should diplomats and their families have these privileges?

### CASE 2

American personnel on military bases abroad are generally tried for criminal acts by American military courts rather than the courts of the country. This practice has created resentment in those countries. In one instance, the Korean government insisted that an American serviceman accused of murdering a Korean citizen be tried by a Korean court and held in a Korean jail. Anti-American riots broke out when the American military did not immediately go along with this request. Do you think the accused serviceman should have been tried in a Korean court?

### CASE 3

Many Philippine citizens, mostly women, have gone abroad to work as domestic servants, especially in the Middle East. Some of these women have reported being raped or beaten by their employers. However, in these countries the employer often keeps a servant's passport until her contract is completed, so she cannot leave the country. On several occasions such women have shown up at American embassies, asking that Americans protect them from retaliation by their employers for trying to leave their jobs. An embassy is considered a place of refuge. An American embassy typically provides refuge for citizens of the United States and its allies. Should American embassies provide refuge for people in situations like the one described here?

### CASE 4

In Singapore in 1994 an American teenager, Michael Fay, was sentenced to six lashes with a bamboo stick for vandalism. The lashes are extremely painful and leave permanent scars. American officials, including President Clinton, protested the severity of the punishment because the boy vigorously protested his innocence, saying his confession was coerced, and because there was no way to appeal the sentence. Singaporean officials "conceded" by reducing the punishment to four lashes. Should Americans have protested by withdrawing trade privileges or support for Singaporean business ventures in the United States?

1. Your teacher will divide you into groups of four. Read each example and decide as a group how to answer the question at the end of each case. Answer yes or no and be ready to justify your responses.
2. The teacher will record each group's responses on a grid on the board or chart paper. You will then be able to see the other groups' views on the extent of extraterritorial rights that the class believes should be granted to foreigners.
3. Discuss the examples that show disagreement; be ready to justify your group's response. Listen to your classmates defend their positions. Are they convincing?
4. Meet in your groups again to discuss the cases on which there was disagreement. Decide if your group wants to hold to its original decision or reverse it.

| Group | Case 1 | Case 2 | Case 3 | Case 4 |
|-------|--------|--------|--------|--------|
| 1 | | | | |
| 2 | | | | |
| 3 | | | | |
| 4 | | | | |
| 5 | | | | |
| 6 | | | | |

5. The teacher will again record each group's responses on the grid, crossing out the original response if necessary. Is the class any closer to consensus? Star the cases where there is still disagreement. Agree to disagree.

6. Reread the cases of extraterritoriality again. Then answer these questions orally or in writing.

   a. Were the extraterritorial rights granted to foreigners in China during the late Qing dynasty excessive? Why or why not?

   b. Under the circumstances, what extraterritorial rights should China have granted to foreigners at that time?

   c. What extraterritorial rights do you think Americans should have in foreign countries today?

   d. What extraterritorial rights should Americans give to foreigners living in the United States?

---

## Reading: *The Influence of Foreigners on China in the Nineteenth Century*

As late as the end of the eighteenth century, foreigners respected Chinese institutions, culture, and art, even when they were frustrated by Chinese restrictions on trade. By the 1840s, however, foreigners felt they could live and work in China on their own terms. The Chinese, on their part, viewed the foreign intrusions with seething anger that they occasionally vented in anti-foreign riots, leading to the famous Boxer Rebellion. (See Chapter 2, Section 4.) They certainly never accepted the Westerners' attitude of superiority to the Chinese, and they often viewed with contempt the Chinese middlemen or compradors who worked for foreigners.

Chinese attitudes and life did change as a result of the vast foreign presence in China after 1843. While life among rural peasants continued much as it had for centuries, the explosive and exciting commercial life of the cities increased the wealth, influence, and power of the merchant class. The treaty-port cities became important cosmopolitan urban communities. China moved into the world of modern diplomatic and international trade relations and technological and commercial change.

### Question

How did the foreign presence in China differ from nineteenth- and twentieth-century waves of immigration to the United States from China and elsewhere?

## The Compradors

*Comprador, Guangzhou, circa 1861–64. From* Imperial China: Photographs 1850–1912. *Courtesy of Pennwick Publishing, Inc.*

Throughout the treaty-port period in China, foreign firms relied on the services of Chinese middlemen known as compradors. These men performed a wide variety of jobs that would have been difficult or impossible for foreigners to do. They bought and sold goods for foreign firms, contracted other Chinese to work for foreigners, and acted as bankers for foreign companies.

The compradors first came into being as agents for the lucrative tea trade in Guangzhou. Other foreign companies soon found their services useful, even essential. The number of compradors grew slowly at first; there were about 250 in 1854; by 1870 there were 700. From the 1870s to the early twentieth century their numbers grew rapidly, reaching 20,000 by 1910. This upsurge reflects both the vastly expanding trade between Chinese and foreigners and the increasing willingness of Chinese merchants to work for foreign companies.

Compradors were usually salaried employees of foreign firms, but they also made money from commissions on goods they sold, services they brokered, and financial transactions that passed through them. Many of them became very rich from these transactions; their lavish lifestyle was probably one reason that many Chinese resented them. Nor did it help their image that they often invested in foreign businesses to shield their money from Chinese officials. Because of their constant contact with foreigners, compradors developed some foreign habits of thinking and acquired a taste for foreign things. Some filled their luxurious homes with Western furniture and art. They all had to develop some proficiency in the language of the foreign bosses, and many went well beyond "pidgin English" (the mixture of English, Portuguese, and Chinese used in doing business with foreigners) to become fluent in foreign languages.

Some Chinese disdained the compradors because they were agents of foreign businesses; Chinese who resented foreigners thought of them as traitors. Nevertheless, they were not all that foreign. In the best Chinese fashion, they passed their positions on to sons and nephews, creating comprador families. Few compradors converted to Christianity; some were strong Chinese nationalists, participating in the reform movements that aimed to strengthen the Chinese government. The compradors straddled two worlds, Chinese and Western, learning from both but a part of neither.

In the early days of the comprador system, one duty of the comprador was to hire Chinese staff to work for foreigners as cooks, servants, and the like. In practice this meant that the comprador was personally responsible for the behavior of his staff. If one of them committed a crime, the comprador was punished. But once the compradors understood the Western idea that only the guilty person should be punished, they were no longer willing to guarantee the behavior of their countrymen. Once they became aware of Western ideas such as contracts and limited liability, the compradors helped the Chinese understand the foreigners and even helped the Chinese defend themselves against foreign incursions on their life and land.

## Extension Activities

1. By 1910 there were over a hundred treaty ports in China. Shanghai was the largest. Although Westerners were a minority in these cities, they often enjoyed a standard of living they could not have afforded at home. The first four chapters of Nicholas Clifford's *Spoilt Children of Empire: Westerners in Shanghai and the Chinese Revolution of the 1920's* (Hanover, NH: Middlebury College Press, 1991) have historical information about life in foreign Shanghai. Read the four chapters. Then focus on one aspect of life in Shanghai—government, the work of missionaries or businessmen or educators, or life in the foreign concessions. Devise a way to share the information with your classmates.

2. Prepare a report on the American Open Door policy in China. An article in an encyclopedia will get you started and refer you to other sources.

3. There was large-scale Chinese immigration to the United States after the middle of the nineteenth century. Then in 1882, the American Congress passed the Chinese Exclusion Act, which stopped Chinese immigration for ten years and barred Chinese from becoming naturalized citizens. Other exclusion acts in 1892 and 1902 extended the 1882 act. Prepare a report on these acts. Tell when they were repealed and why. Some of the readings in *Entry Denied: Exclusion and the Chinese Community in America, 1882–1943*, edited by Sucheng Chan (Philadelphia: Temple University Press, 1991), might help you get started.

## Further Reading

Beers, Burton F. *China in Old Photographs: 1860–1910*. New York: Charles Scribner's Sons, 1978.

Clifford, Nicholas R. *Spoilt Children of Empire: Westerners in Shanghai and the Chinese Revolution of the 1920's*. Hanover, NH: Middlebury College Press, 1991.

*Imperial China: Photographs 1850–1912*. Historical texts by Clark Worswick and Jonathan Spence.

Foreword by Harrison Salisbury. New York: Pennwick Publishing, Inc., 1978.

Thomson, John. *China and Its People in Early Photographs: An Unabridged Reprint of the Classic 1873/74 Work*. New York: Dover Publications, Inc., 1982. Originally published as *Illustrations of China and Its People*. London: Sampson Low, Marston, Low, and Searle, 1873–1874.

Tung, William F. *China and the Foreign Powers: The Impact and Reaction to Unequal Treaties*. Dobbs Ferry, NY: Oceana Publications Inc., 1970.

# Internal Factors

→ Silver Reserves depleting
  → can't pay armies
  → Peasants can't pay taxes
→ deflationary cycle → economy collapses under weight of British competition
→ Still has opium
→ Yellow River flooding
  → people mad about corruption
  → destroyed farmland, starving people
  → 44 million people dead by famine, disasters, economic downfall

→ People are pissed at the Gov for everything that has been going poorly in the country

→ Hong Xiuquan → "younger bro of Jesus"
  → unity
  → wants China to adjust
  → If you can't fight the enemy join them

*[handwritten annotation: Mercantilism;*
*• Gold · getting precious metals through trade*
*→ use gold to get land armies power]*

# 4 Domestic Strife, 1850–1873

*During the last years of the Qing dynasty, China was beset by problems from within and without, problems that historians have called "domestic strife and external threat." The preceding sections focused on how China dealt with the external threats of foreign invasion and Western imperialism. This section examines the domestic[1] or internal problems that plagued China, particularly*

*during the second half of the nineteenth century. Some of this "domestic strife" resulted from foreign incursion, some from problems that had existed in the Middle Kingdom for centuries. Whatever the cause, conditions in China at this time led to many peasant revolts. This section examines one of them, the Taiping Rebellion, in detail.*

---

### Reading: *After the Opium War*

*[handwritten annotation: no bueno]*

The years that followed the Opium War were tumultuous ones for China. Among the causes of this upheaval were the effects of treaties made with Western powers, a spate of natural disasters, a population explosion, famine, and internal rebellions. All these events coalesced to produce serious economic and social dislocation in the once self-sufficient Middle Kingdom.

The terms of China's treaties with foreign powers often proved disastrous to the country's economy. The opium trade, for example, which was allowed by the Treaty of Tianjin in 1858, *[handwritten: and]* continued unabated, and opium continued to *[handwritten: kill ppl]* drain China of its silver reserves. Peasants, who used strings of copper coins as currency for everyday transactions, had to pay their taxes in silver. As silver became scarcer, its price in copper coins went up and up. In this way, peasants *[handwritten: and]* were in effect forced to pay higher taxes, always *[handwritten: more poverty]* a reason for discontent and possible revolt. Opium, of course, kept exacting horrible social costs. Families were destroyed as addicts literally sold their ancestral lands and their children to get the drug.

*[handwritten annotation: sold kids?]*

The opening of the treaty ports also caused hardship. In Guangzhou, for instance, many boatmen and porters lost their jobs; they were no longer needed in such large numbers once other ports opened. In some cases, home industries, such as spinning and weaving, were destroyed as *[handwritten: economy is killed]* cheaper foreign goods flooded the market.

Natural disasters also disrupted China's economy, and with it the country's social order. In the 1850s, for example, the Huang He, the Yellow River, sometimes called "China's Sorrow," changed course, shifting its main stream from the south to the north of the Shandong peninsula.

*Strings of copper coins, called "cash," were used in China until the early twentieth century.*

[1] domestic: in this usage the word pertains to a country's internal affairs, as opposed to foreign affairs.

*no farming either*

One reason for the river's rampage was failure to maintain its dikes. The river overflowed, destroying crops and everything else in its path. There were indications that money for public works projects, such as repairing the dikes, had ended up in officials' pockets. Whatever the reason, flooding was widespread, countless lives were lost, and famine was the lot of those who survived.

## Activity: Reading a Graph

The possibility of famine was a constant in Chinese life, particularly for peasants. Most famines were caused by calamities like floods and droughts, but overpopulation during the Qing dynasty intensified the threat. The population figures here are probably low; Chinese historians and demographers believe that China's population may have been as much as 20 percent higher than the graph on the next page indicates.

*Foot-driven spinning machine, circa 1860s, Shanghai. Both mother and child are dressed in heavy winter clothing. From* China, The Land and Its People: Early Photographs *by* John Thomson. *Originally published as* Illustrations of China and Its People *by Sampson, Low, Marston, Low and Searle, London, 1873.*

## Questions

1. What was China's population estimated to be in 1741? In 1800? In 1850?
2. What happened to China's population between 1741 and 1800? Between 1779 and 1800? Between 1741 and 1850?
3. During the years that China's population increased so dramatically (1741–1850), China's arable land, land suitable for producing crops, increased only 8.5 percent. What is the likely result of such a discrepancy between a country's population and its amount of arable land?

4. Look over questions 1–3. What kind of questions can be answered with data in this graph? What kind of question cannot be answered with data from the graph?
5. Speculate on the Chinese government's response to disasters like flood and famine in the nineteenth century in the context of this statement:

*In the period between 1846 and 1878 it is estimated that human lives lost [in China] from famines and floods and from internal rebellions numbered over 44,000,000.*[2]

## Reading: *Famine in Shanxi Province, 1876–1879*

We can learn a great deal about the past by analyzing the kind of "hard data" in a graph. But hard data cannot give us a feel for how real people lived their lives. For this we need to look at other sources of information. Unfortunately, few firsthand accounts of nineteenth-century peasant life

in China exist. Most peasants were illiterate. They spent their lives trying to keep body and soul

[2] Ta Chen, *Chinese Migrations, with Special Reference to Labor Conditions* (Washington: Government Printing Office, 1923), p. 6; quoted in Tin-Yuke Char, *The Sandalwood Mountains: Readings and Stories of the Early Chinese in Hawaii.* Honolulu: The University Press of Hawaii, 1975, pp. 8–9.

## Population Growth in China, 1741–1850

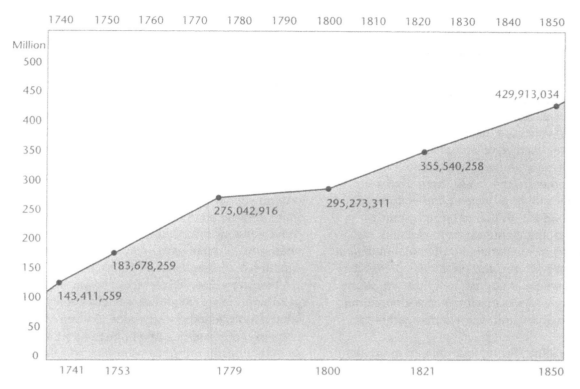

together, not writing their life stories. This account of famine in northern China's Shanxi Province was written by a Baptist minister, Timothy Richard. (Missionaries were allowed to work in China under the terms of treaties signed with Western countries after the Opium War.) This famine was caused by crop failure due to drought. Estimates of deaths range from 9.5 million to 20 million. Although this account tells of a famine in the 1870s, it could have been written at many other times during China's history.

On June 30th [1876] two scholars . . . between thirty and forty years of age . . . came to see me, but as I was too busy, they called the next day by appointment. On entering, they prostrated themselves and asked to be accepted as my disciples. After some talk I discovered they were a deputation from a number of people who desired me to head a rebellion as the authorities were not providing food for the perishing people. They had already rented a house, and a large number of men were ready to execute my commands. I told the deputa-

tion that I could not dream of any such action, as it would only increase the suffering of the people. Once begun, no one knew where such a revolt would end, but it would certainly entail great bloodshed. I advised them to devise constructive instead of destructive methods for improving the condition of the people. . . .

As the winter drew near, the distress became more acute. Reports came in from villages where previously there had been forty inhabitants reduced to ten survivors. The price of grain rose rapidly to three and four times its usual rate. Many people, hearing that grain was cheap in Manchuria, migrated across the Gulf of Pechihli. Those who could not afford to travel were forced to pull down their houses and sell every inch of woodwork in them, whether doors, windows, frames, or rafters, and so get money to buy millet chaff[3] to try and keep body and soul together.

---

[3] millet chaff: millet is a grass; its seeds or grains are used for food. Chaff is the husks of seeds or grains that are separated during threshing and discarded or used for animals. In this account, people were trying to survive on the chaff from millet.

In order to keep warm in the depth of winter the poor wretches dug deep pits underground, where twenty, thirty, and even fifty persons would live together. Here the vitiated [polluted] atmosphere, as well as the lack of food, caused a large number of deaths. At first the survivors could not afford to dig a separate grave for each, so they made two large holes, one for men, the other for women, into which the dead were thrown. Afterwards the dead were left where they fell, sometimes in their homes, sometimes in the villages, sometimes on the roads, there they were devoured by wild dogs, wolves, and vultures. . . .

**January 28th, 1878.** Started on a journey south through the centre of the province to discover the severity of the famine. I rode on a mule, and had a servant with me, also on a mule. Before leaving the city we could not go straight to the south gate, as there was a man lying in the street about to die of starvation, and a crowd had gathered round.

**January 29th.** Passed four dead men on the road and another moving on his hands and knees, having no strength to stand up. Met a funeral, consisting of a mother carrying on her shoulder a dead boy ten years old. She was the only bearer, priest, and mourner, and she laid him in the snow outside the city wall. . . .

**January 30th.** Saw fourteen dead on the roadside. One had only a stocking on. His corpse was being dragged by a dog, so light it was. Two of the dead were women. They had had a burial, but it had consisted only in turning the faces to the ground. The passers-by had dealt more kindly with one, for they had left her clothes. A third corpse was a feast to a score of screaming crows and magpies. There were fat pheasants, rabbits, foxes, and wolves, but men and women had no means of living. One old man beside whom I slowly climbed a hill said most pathetically: "Our mules and donkeys are all eaten up. Our labourers are dead. What crime have we committed, that God should punish us thus?"

**February 1st.** Saw six dead bodies in half a day, and four of them were women: one in an open shed, naked but for a string around her waist; another in a stream; one in the water, half exposed above the ice at the mercy of wild dogs; another

half clad in rags in one of the open caves at the roadside; another half eaten, torn by birds and beasts of prey. Met two youths of about eighteen years of age, tottering on their feet, and leaning on sticks as if ninety years of age. Met another young man carrying his mother on his shoulders as her strength had failed. Seeing me looking at them closely, the young man begged me for help. This is the only one who has begged since I left T'ai-yuan fu [the capital of Shanxi Province].

Saw some men grinding soft stones, somewhat like those from which stone pencils are made, into powder which was . . . to be mixed with any grain, or grass seed, or roots and made into cakes. I tried some of these cakes, and they tasted like what most of them were—clay. Many died of constipation in consequence of eating them.

**February 2nd.** At the next city was the most awful sight I ever saw. It was early in the morning when I approached the city gate. On one side of it was a pile of naked dead men, heaped on top of each other as though they were pigs in a slaughterhouse. On the other side of the gate was a similar heap of dead women, their clothing having been taken away to pawn for food. Carts were there to take the corpses away to two great pits, into one of which they threw the men and into the other the women. . . . For many miles in this district the trees were all white, stripped clean for ten or twenty feet high of their bark, which was being used for food. We passed many houses without doors and window frames, which had been sold as firewood. Inside were kitchen utensils left untouched only because they could not be turned into money. The owners had gone away and died.

**February 3rd.** Saw only seven persons today, but no woman among them. This was explained by meeting carts daily full of women being taken away for sale. There were travellers on foot also, all carrying weapons of defence, even children in their teens, some with spears, some with bright, gleaming swords, others with rusty knives, proofs of their terrible plight. We did not feel very safe in their midst. . . .

**February 4th.** Having gone so far, and seeing such terrible sights, I decided to return to T'ai-yuan fu, as I had sufficient proofs of the horrors of famine to move even hearts of stone.

*Dynastic Cycle*

Hero → prosperity → corruption → (back to Hero)

Even the wolves were becoming fearless. Seeing a wolf by the roadside one day, I yelled at him, expecting him to flee in terror. On the contrary, he stood and stared at me. . . .

Returning along the same road, we had a daily repetition of the same ghastly sights, until I sometimes wondered whether the scenes were not the imagination of a disordered mind.

From Timothy Richard, *Forty-five Years in China. Reminiscences by T. Richard.* London: T. Fisher Unwin, 1916. In Roger Pelissier, *The Awakening of China 1793–1949.* London: Secker & Warburg, English translation by Martin Kieffer, 1967, pp. 179–181. Reprinted by permission of Reed Books, London.

### Activity: Discussion

Discuss your response to the readings by discussing each of the following questions with a partner. Here is the procedure to follow:

- Compose your own response to the question asked.
- Tell your response to your partner.
- Listen to your partner's response.

- Write a new response together that incorporates both of your ideas and is of better quality than your individual responses.
- Share your new response with the class.

### Questions

1. Write five phrases that describe your initial reactions to "Famine in Shanxi Province."
2. Do you think the stories that Richard recorded were true? Do you think he exaggerated his experiences? Give reasons for your responses.
3. List some of the things people did to survive during the famine. Then list other survival actions they might have resorted to that are not mentioned in Richard's account.
4. Look at the last paragraph of the reading. How does the author respond to what he has seen about famine?
5. Speculate on how survivors of floods and famines might have reacted. What were their options? Give at least two alternatives that survivors might have pursued, if their circumstances allowed, as a means of improving their lives and their children's lives.

### Reading: *The Decline of the Dynastic Cycle*

*people on their own*     *thriving*     *only doing well for 200 years at a time*

The Chinese interpreted their long history as a series of dynastic cycles. Each dynasty began with a heroic leader who came to power by unseating a corrupt emperor. A period of prosperity followed, a time when even peasants had enough to eat. Then, after two or three hundred years, the dynasty would decline. Its later rulers were often weak and ineffective, unlike the dynasty's formidable founder. Official corruption became common. Peasants were taxed to the breaking point. Canals and dikes fell into disrepair. When floods or droughts ruined crops, there was no surplus in government granaries to feed the people. Then famine stalked the land and bandits preyed on the weak. Provincial officials and their armies defected from the emperor's ranks, and surviving peasants revolted. After

a period of warfare, the ruler would be vanquished, a new ruler would emerge, and the cycle would begin again.

Certainly for those who saw China's history as a succession of dynastic cycles, the nineteenth century was a period of extraordinary decline. Taxes went up and population increased, but arable land did not. Food production was inadequate, at best, for a population that grew every year despite an unimaginable death rate. Disasters, natural or manmade, decimated the population. Bandits roamed the land, and secret societies opposed to the government emerged, especially in southern China. There were sporadic uprisings and riots. The Qing government seemed unwilling or unable to correct any of these problems.

*did they ever do anything*

*did the Chinese government care*

Millions of people felt they had little choice but to leave China for a better life elsewhere. Most left in the hope of making a fortune and then returning home. Between 1840 and 1900, about 2.5 million people left China for Hawai'i, the United States, Canada, Australia, New Zealand, Southeast Asia, the West Indies, South America, and Africa.

Of those who stayed, millions died. Of those who survived, some joined secret societies and revolted, hoping that a new ruler would appear, a strong leader who would once again reverse dynastic decline and bring China back to peace and prosperity.

---

## Activity: Word Association

1. List words that you associate with the term "civil war."
2. Look up "civil war" in a dictionary or other reference source. Write the definition.
3. Compare your word associations with the definition. Cross out the words on your list that do not fit the official definition.
4. As you read the following information about the Taiping Rebellion, decide whether it was a civil war.

---

## Reading: *The Taiping Rebellion, 1850–1864*

China was ripe for revolt. The most devastating peasant uprising was the Taiping, which ironically means "Great Peace." The Taiping rebels were led by Hong Xiuquan, a schoolteacher from southern China who had repeatedly failed the civil service examinations. During a serious illness, Hong had a vision. He believed that he had seen God, that he was the younger brother of Jesus Christ, and that his mission was to save mankind. A charismatic leader, Hong put together his own religion, combining ideas from Confucianism, Buddhism, Daoism, and Christianity.

*not gonna end well*

Hong soon gathered thousands of people around him, including disaffected peasants and people who had lost their jobs and their livelihoods because of economic changes caused by the opening of the treaty ports. Tribespeople like the Miao and the Yao, along with the Hakka, Northern Chinese who had migrated to the south but had never been accepted by the dominant Han Chinese, also joined Hong. Hong, himself a Hakka, was proclaimed their "Heavenly King."

Hong's followers became a rebel army determined to overthrow the Manchus, whom they saw as responsible for China's plight. After cutting their queues, they unraveled the remaining hair and let it grow long; they became known as "the long-haired rebels."

*Hong Xiuquan, leader of the Taiping Rebellion, 1813–1864. Courtesy the Historical Commission, Central Committee of the Kuomintang, Taipei, Taiwan, Republic of China.*

In the early 1850s the Taiping rebels began to move northward through central China, gathering recruits along the way, routing the imperial troops, and taking city after city under their control. They were fanatical soldiers. On their

## Uprisings

After more than two hundred years of relative peace and prosperity, the Qing dynasty had, by the middle of the nineteenth century, entered into a period of decline and uncertainty. One of the most serious problems, and one that the inept Qing court did little to remedy, was the unequal distribution of land.

Even in the best of times the life of China's peasants, who toiled in their landlords' fields, was perilous. Any natural disaster, such as flood or drought, upset the precarious balance of their lives and pushed them into the abyss of starvation. While millions of peasants perished during famines and other millions struggled just to survive, some took part in revolts against a government that did little or nothing to resolve the food shortage or its causes. These revolts, although frequent, were small and short. Most rebels did not want to overthrow the dynasty, nor did they have any strategy to win and hold territory.

The largest and most devastating uprising in nineteenth-century China was, of course, the Taiping Rebellion. Three other major uprisings, the Nien Rebellion (1851–1868) and the Muslim Rebellions (1855–1873 and 1862–1875), occurred at about the same time. Unlike the Taiping rebels, however, none of these groups sought to overthrow the Qing dynasty.

The Nien Rebellion was not really a single cohesive revolt. *Nien*, which literally means "band," was the name for secret gangs active in the southern area of North China. A *nien* was usually a group of bandits who used guerrilla tactics to terrorize the countryside. They lived off looting and forced contributions. They pillaged deserted farms, hunted down wild animals, kidnapped rich families, and hijacked local trade convoys. After fifteen years the Qing government was finally able to suppress them.

While bandits were plundering one section of China, a Muslim revolt broke out in Yunnan in the southwest in 1855. The immediate cause was the heavy land taxes and other taxes the Qing government imposed on the country's Muslim minority. But this revolt was also rooted in old rivalries between Muslims and Han Chinese. By 1864 the whole southwest of China was in chaos. The Qing court was too preoccupied trying to suppress the Taiping Rebellion to spare troops to meet another revolt. Only after it suppressed the Nien revolt did the government deal with the Muslim problem, using military as well as economic and political force to get the area back under government control in 1873.

A second Muslim revolt broke out in the northwest in 1862. This one was triggered by a relatively minor incident—a quarrel between Muslims and a Chinese merchant over the price of some bamboo poles. Fights broke out and quickly grew into armed confrontations between the two ethnic communities. This rebellion too was finally put down in 1873—only after the Muslim leaders had been reduced to eating hides and grass, and finally the bodies of their dead. Thus in 1873, for the first time since 1850, with the suppression of the Nien, Muslim, and Taiping rebellions, the Qing court once again was able to assert its authority over all of China.

*were they people who opposed them?*

northward trek, they were supported by the local peasantry, whom they treated well; unlike the Qing army troops, they did not loot the districts they passed through. Nevertheless, thousands of people, perhaps as many as twenty thousand, died as the Taiping forces grew to half a million and forced their way north.

When the Qing dynasty was not able to suppress the rebellion with its regular military forces, it ordered that regional armies be formed. These armies were under the control of high provincial officials loyal to the emperor. Later, the formation of these regional armies would have serious consequences for China; they signified the breakdown of the central government's control.

Although it was unable to suppress the Taiping rebels militarily, the Qing government did

*How so?*

try to terrorize them into submission. "Long-haired rebels" who were unlucky enough to be caught by the authorities were executed. The following reading describes an execution that took place on the outskirts of Guangzhou in 1851, shortly after the rebellion began. It was witnessed by four foreigners, one of whom later described to French officials in Guangzhou what had happened.

*did the French fight with the Taiping rebels*

---

## Reading: *Execution in Guangzhou*

On the 1st of May [1851], I attended an execution with three of my friends on "Potter's Field" [official execution ground at the time]. . . . We arrived there at ten o'clock in the morning, and took our station in front of a shop belonging to a mender of old shoes. This was an excellent position, affording as it did a view over the whole ceremony. We remained there quietly until noon, at which time some soldiers and officers attached to the service of the Mandarins [government officials] arrived, to clear the street and thrust back the onlookers. As in Europe, those who came to see the spectacle were the vilest dregs of the populace—dirty, ragged people, with sinister faces, who wandered about this blood-drenched ground, where most likely they had already seen the execution of a number of their companions and perhaps of their accomplices.

In a short time, the roll of the gong announced the arrival of the whole procession. Mandarins of all ranks, with the red, white, blue or yellow button, riding on horseback or carried in palanquins[4] and followed by an escort of musicians, armed servants, and standard-bearers, alighted at a short distance from the place of execution. Contrary to their ceremonious habits, they took up their positions silently in the dismal enclosure.

Then came the condemned men. There were fifty-three of them, each locked in a basket, with his hands tied behind his back and his legs chained; from his neck hung a board on which his sentence was written.

You have often seen in Chinese streets a pair of coolies carrying a pig stretched out at full length in a bamboo case: well, just imagine a human being put in the place of the unclean animal, and you have a correct idea of the fifty-three unfortunate creatures in their cages. When the latter were set down, they were opened and emptied, just as when a pig is turned out in a butcher's shop.

I examined these poor wretches carefully: they belonged to the lower classes, and were worn out with hunger, looking much more like skeletons than living beings. It was obvious that they had suffered the most dreadful privations. They were clothed in loathsome tatters, wore long hair, and the disheveled tail attached to the crown of the head had been reduced to a third of its normal length. They had evidently belonged to the insurgent bands, which had adopted the fashion of the Mings, [the dynasty defeated by the Manchu in 1644] and allowed their hair to grow.

Many of these unfortunate fellows were quite young: some were under sixteen years of age, while others had gray hair. Scarcely had they been thrown on the ground, when they were compelled to kneel; but most of them were so weakened by suffering that they were unable to remain in this position, and rolled into the mud. An executioner's assistant then picked them up and lined them up in a row, while three executioners placed themselves behind them, waiting for the final moment. You certainly remember those horrible figures whom we have often seen together in the retinue of the criminal judge at Canton—dressed in a red blouse, wearing a copper crown adorned above the ears with two long pheasant's feathers. Well! These were the executioners, who were now waiting for the signal with a heavy cutlass in their hands. These enormous knives are about two feet long, and the back of the blade is two inches thick: altogether it is a ponderous weapon, shaped like a Chinese razor, with a crude handle of wood.

A Mandarin who closed the cortege now entered the enclosure. He wore a white button, and held in his hand a board showing the order of execution. As soon as this man appeared, the frightful task

---

[4] palanquin: sedan chair, a boxlike covered litter carried on poles on the shoulders of two or four men.

*Execution scene, Shanghai, circa 1870s, attributed to the photographer W. Saunders. Decapitation was one punishment for highway robbery. From* Imperial China: Photographs 1850–1912. *Courtesy of Pennwick Publishing, Inc., New York.*

began. The executioner's assistant, dressed in a long black robe . . . grabbed the victims from behind and, passing his arms under the latter's shoulders, gave them a swinging movement which made them stretch out their necks. The executioner, who now stood in front holding his cutlass in both hands, wielded the weapon with all his strength and, dividing the cervical vertebrae with incredible skill and speed, severed the head from the body at a single blow. The dreadful executioner never had to strike twice, for even if the flesh was not completely cut through, the weight was sufficient to tear it, and the head rolled on the ground. An assistant then floored the victim with a kick, as the corpse would otherwise have remained in a kneeling position. After three or four decapitations, the executioner changed his weapon: the edge of the blade seemed to be wrung, as if buckled. The execution of these fifty-three wretches lasted only a few minutes.

When the last head had fallen, the Mandarins withdrew silently from the scene, just as they had arrived. . . . After their departure, the executioner picked up all the heads, and threw them into a chest brought for that purpose. At the same time, the assistants took the chains off the victims as they lay in a pool of blood. The heads were carried away, but the bodies were left on the execution ground.

A very sad scene then began: a troop of women with disheveled hair approached with loud shrieks, and dashed wildly toward the fatal spot.

These unhappy beings were endeavoring to recognize their fathers, husbands, or children among the headless corpses. It was a frightful thing to see them hurrying about, pondering, and constantly mistaken in the midst of the mutilated remains. Their search continued all day, accompanied by a mournful noise, funeral dirges being mingled with loud cries and sobs.

From: Joseph Marie Callery et Melchior Yuan, *L'insurrection en Chine depuis son origine jusqu'à la prise de Nankin.* Paris: Librairie nouvelle, 1853, pp. 50–53. In Roger Pelissier. *The Awakening of China 1793–1949.* Translated by Martin Kieffer. London: Secker & Warburg, 1967, pp. 98–100. Reprinted by permission of Reed Books, London.

## Questions

1. In this account, who do you think the author sympathizes with, the Chinese government or the condemned Taiping rebels? Give reasons for your response.
2. The account mentions that some of those executed were young, under sixteen, while others had gray hair. Why do you suppose men of such differing ages were willing to risk death by joining the rebels?
3. How do you suppose the rebels responded to these executions? Do you think they were cowed or spurred into further action against the government? Justify your response.

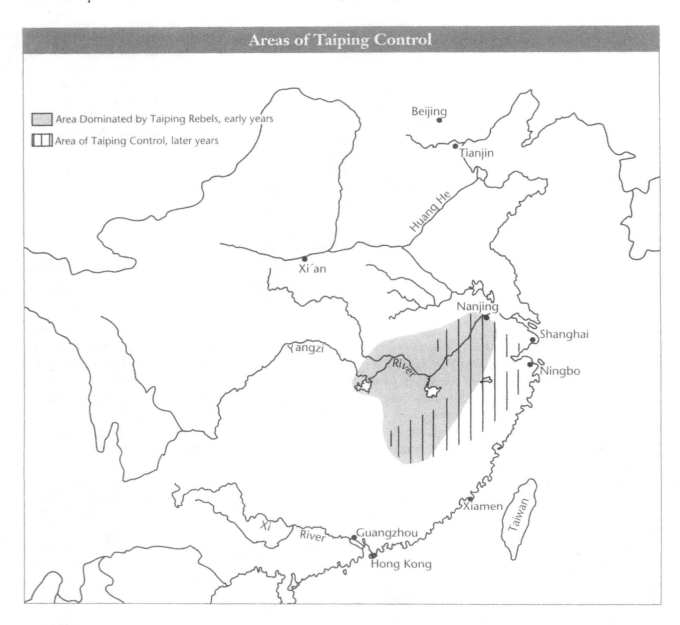

## Areas of Taiping Control

Area Dominated by Taiping Rebels, early years

Area of Taiping Control, later years

---

### Reading: *More on the Taiping*

Despite the efforts of the government and regional armies to contain them, the Taiping forces eventually controlled a third of China. In 1853 they captured Nanjing and set up their capital. They then began a program of land reform in areas under their control. Although it is not clear how much of this plan they carried out, they advocated dividing land on the basis of household size: larger families got more land. They also insisted that women be treated equally; women were to receive as much land as men, footbinding was abolished, and on at least one occasion, women were allowed to take the civil service examinations. But this civil service examination differed from the traditional one in that the questions dealt with the explanation and acceptance of Taiping beliefs. The Taiping believed in what we might call a primitive form of communism where land and its products were to be shared by all. One of their most important documents, "The Land System and the Heavenly Dynasty" stated:

*All lands in the empire must be cultivated by all the people in the empire as a common concern. If there is a deficiency of land in one place, the people must be removed to another; and if there is a deficiency of land in another place, the people must be removed to this place. The yields of all the land in the empire, whether the crops are good or bad, should be universally circulated. If there is a famine at one place, the [surplus food] of the place yielding good crops must be transported to relieve the famine-stricken place and vice versa. The purpose is to enable all the people in the empire to enjoy together the abundant happiness provided by the Heavenly Father, Lord on High, and Sovereign God. If there is land, it is to be shared by all to till; if there is any food, clothing, or money, these shall be shared by all. In this way all places will share the abundance equally and all will be equally well fed and clothed.[5]*

The Taiping imposed a rigid discipline on members. "Those who smoke opium or tobacco, drink wine, loot, or rape will be executed," one regulation stated. Another declared, "The punishment for those who smoke yellow tobacco [opium] is a hundred lashes and a week in the cangue for the first offense, a thousand lashes and three weeks in the cangue for the second offense, and execution for the third offense." They also forbade gambling: "At court [Nanjing] or in the army, all brothers who gamble will be executed."[6] Prostitution and concubinage were also forbidden.

The Taiping survived as a rebel state for eleven years. But as often happens, once the leaders had achieved some successes, they settled into complacency, corruption, and wanton destruction. Some of the leaders, called kings, lived in luxury. Some had large harems, even though they preached monogamy (marriage to one person at a time) and separated husbands and wives in military units. Inevitably, some Taiping

kings fought among themselves and killed each other; their followers did the same, killing thousands. The peasants, the heart of the Taiping movement, began to abandon it once they learned they would still have to pay heavy taxes, in some instances three times what they paid to the imperial government, to support what the Taiping called the Celestial Kingdom of Great Peace.

Foreigners, who had originally favored the Taiping rebels, decided in the end that it was in their best interest to support the Qing dynasty against them. England and France sent troops and arms to help suppress the rebellion. In some instances Westerners even trained Chinese soldiers. The Taiping forces were finally defeated in the summer of 1864, when their capital at Nanjing was retaken by troops loyal to the Manchus. Fire raged in the city for three days and nights. Thousands of civilians died in the battle. Hong and as many as 100,000 of his followers committed suicide. The victorious armies had no qualms about massacring every Taiping believer they hunted down, for their goal was to eradicate every trace of the rebels. Despite their efforts, however, some remnants of the Taiping rebels survived. Their ideas would surface again, in somewhat different but still recognizable form.

## Questions

1. Discuss the Taiping Rebellion in the context of the dynastic cycle. How did conditions in China in the nineteenth century fit the idea of the dynastic cycle? How might the followers of Hong Xiuquan have seen him in relation to the dynastic cycle?

2. Read your response to question 2 following the reading "The Execution" regarding why young and old men might have joined the Taiping forces, despite the risks. Then list any other reasons for their decision as noted in the text. Why did women join the Taiping?

3. Read your definition of "civil war." Do you think the Taiping Rebellion was a civil war? Why or why not?

[5] Vincent Y. C. Shih, *The Taiping Ideology: Its Sources, Interpretations, and Influences.* Seattle: University of Washington Press, 1967, p. 82.

[6] Ibid., p. 76.

## Reading: *The Weaver*

The following reading is a fictional account of one family's experiences after the opening of the treaty ports.

It was in the spring of the year 1876 that the weaver, Liu Mok, with the help of his first son, Chu, then nine years of age, loaded into his donkey cart the lengths of cotton cloth he and his wife had woven during the winter months.

Liu gazed proudly at the cloth. It was a good winter's work, and surely the merchant Chang would be pleased, for Liu was an excellent craftsman. Men such as he had made China famous for her textiles. They had learned their skills from their fathers and in turn passed them on to their sons, as Liu was doing for Chu.

"The dyes were not without distinction," Liu said, not looking at his wife. She cast her eyes down modestly, warmed by her husband's words, proud that he recognized her worth. She hesitated to think such thoughts, but felt no other woman in the village mixed dyes as vivid as hers.

Chu, his round face gleaming in the early morning sunlight, his eyes bright with anticipation of his

*Woman weaving in Shanghai, circa 1870s. This image, by photographer L. F. Fisler, was taken in a studio. Courtesy Peabody Essex Museum, Salem, MA.*

first journey to Ningpo, turned to his father. "Will I really be able to look upon the great sea, Father?"

"Perhaps," said Liu. "If you are a son who acts in a manner that gives pride to his father." He motioned the boy into the cart, and climbed aboard himself. "The journey is of one's day's duration in each direction," he told his wife as he did each time he made the trip. "And another to bargain properly with the merchant Chang. I will return then in three days."

The wife played her role in the ritual. "Chang is a thief," she called, as they drove away. "He is not to be trusted."

"Am I a child," Liu shouted over his shoulder, "to be tricked by a city merchant? We shall receive our due. Aiee, women," Liu ended with feigned annoyance.

"Aiee, women," Chu repeated.

Father and son looked at each other and burst into laughter.

It was already dark when the donkey cart reached the outskirts of Ningpo. Liu decided to enter the city in the morning. He built a small fire alongside the road and boiled water for tea. While they waited, he and Chu dined on cold rice.

"We will sleep in the cart," Liu announced. "The cotton will shield us from the chill of the night."

When the merchant Chang arrived the next morning to open his shop, Liu's donkey was already parked outside. The two men greeted each other formally, with short quick bows. Chu watched, smiling, until a sudden warning flicker in his father's eyes reminded him of the proper way to act. He bowed deeply, three times.

"A most unworthy son," Liu murmured.

"Enter my shop," Chang said. "Your presence honors me."

Chu trailed the men inside. The thick smell of incense tickled his nose. Chang opened the shutters, and sunlight streamed in like rungs of a ladder. Chu looked around in wonder. From floor to ceiling, shelves were crowded with bolts of fabric of such design and colors as he had never before seen. He noticed that his father's eyes roamed the shop, though Liu gave no indication of his thoughts.

Chang went behind the counter and clapped his hands together. "You have come to buy?" he began.

Liu could not keep his brows from rising in surprise. Chang knew full well that he had come to sell. He always came to sell. A weaver does not buy from a merchant. Ah! It was Chang's way of starting the bargaining. A worthy adversary. Each time Chang used a different approach. Liu smiled.

"I have decided to offer you the first opportunity," he replied, with studied matter-of-factness. "We have long dealt with each other, and I feel a bond between us. Before I offer my superior fabrics to other merchants, I allow you to select a few for yourself, if the price is suitable. My cotton is of supreme quality this year."

Chang waved his hands at the full shelves. "Look about you, man. Do I appear to be a person in need of fabric?"

Liu hesitated. He assured himself that this was merely another gambit of the wily Chang's. He made as if to move toward the door.

"I will go elsewhere. My work is not appreciated here."

"Yes," Chang said. "I wish to buy nothing. Only to sell."

Liu's heart began to thump in his chest. Fear thickened his throat. All at once he realized that Chang meant what he said: he did not intend to buy. Liu watched as Chang reached behind and took down a bolt of blue cotton with red and white flowers on it. The merchant spread a length of it on the counter.

"See what sort of goods I now sell. All are comparable to this one. See how fast the colors are, and how bright. Also, the fabric is strong and does not tear easily. The people who buy from me are pleased by such things."

"Who makes such fabrics?" Liu asked hoarsely.

Chang began to roll up the cotton. "I buy now from the English barbarians." He leaned toward the stunned Liu. "The cost of such goods is less than the cost of your work, Liu. And so the cost to those who buy from me is less." He put the bolt of material back on the shelf. "The barbarians own great machines with which to make such things. From now on I will buy only from them."

"But what of my cotton?"

Chang shrugged. "Offer them to the other merchants. But they will speak as I have spoken. No one will buy."

Liu gazed blankly at the other man. "What will I do? I have a family to feed."

Chang fixed his eyes on the far wall.

"All my life I have woven fabric. There is nothing else I can do."

Chang studied his shelves with rare intensity.

"My children will go hungry."

Chang busied himself straightening his stock. Liu shuffled slowly out of the shop. He lifted Chu back onto the cart. He would visit other merchants, but deep in his heart he knew that Chang had spoken the truth and that none of them would buy his cotton.

From: Burt Hirschfeld, *Fifty-Five Days of Terror: The Story of the Boxer Rebellion.* Great Britain: Bailey Brothers & Swinfen Ltd., 1971, pp. 33–36.

## Questions

Your teacher will divide the class into groups of three or four. Discuss the following questions in your group and be prepared to share your responses with the rest of the class.

1. Liu and his family lived near the treaty port of Ningbo. Explain what happened to Liu's ability to support his family, particularly as a result of the Treaty of Nanjing. (You will need to refer to Sections 2 and 3 to answer this question fully.)
2. Thirty-four years elapsed between 1842, when the Treaty of Nanjing was signed, and 1876, when the events in this story supposedly took place. Why do you suppose it took so long for people like Liu to be affected by the treaties China signed with the West?
3. Should Liu have been better prepared for what happened to him? Why do you suppose he failed to see that his way of earning a livelihood was becoming obsolete? What might he have done about the situation?
4. Speculate on what might have happened to the Liu family after it could no longer sell its cloth. What might have happened to Chu as he grew older?
5. Give at least three examples of jobs and skills that have become obsolete in the last

hundred years. Give three examples of jobs you think will become obsolete in the next twenty years. What should people do if they believe their job skills will no longer be needed? How can they prepare themselves for such a possibility?

6. Give two major reasons why Liu's means of making a livelihood became obsolete. How does the situation faced by Liu and Chu differ from that faced by people in contemporary American society who lose their jobs because their skills are no longer needed? How is it the same?

---

### Activity: Music Video

This activity will help you synthesize or put together what you have learned in this section about some of China's nineteenth-century domestic problems. You will do this by creating a storyboard and song lyrics for a music video. A storyboard is a series of panels. The panels are rough drawings that show the consecutive events or changes in scene for a planned video, film, advertisement, or television program.

1. Your teacher will divide you into teams of four. Decide what aspect of China's domestic history you want to make a music video about. Here are some titles to help you get started.

   "China's Sorrow and Mine"
   "We Survived the Famine Years"
   "China's Dynastic Cycle"
   "Life as a Taiping Rebel"
   "Hong Xiuquan, Taiping Leader"
   "A Day in Ningbo"

2. Be creative, but remember that your proposed video must be plausible. That is, there must be some possibility that what you describe could have happened.

3. Decide who is telling the story in your music video. Someone who experienced something that happened? Someone telling

a family story that has been passed on? A kind of all-seeing narrator?

4. After you have chosen a topic, decide how you will divide responsibilities. Perhaps two people can compose the song lyrics and two can create the storyboard.

5. The storyboard should have six panels. The panels need to be big enough for everyone in the class to see.

6. When your song and storyboard are complete, present them to the class. First, read the song lyrics that go with each panel, then sing them.

7. After all have completed their presentations, discuss this question as a class:
   What did you learn about writing or telling history by doing this activity?

8. If you have access to the equipment, use your storyboard and song lyrics to create a music video.

## Extension Activities

These questions require library research. Some of the sources at the end of this section may help you get started.

1. The Huang He, or Yellow River, is one of the world's most important rivers. Prepare a report or an exhibit on the Huang He explaining why it is often called "China's Sorrow."

2. The Qing dynasty developed a granary system to feed its population, especially during famine. Prepare a report on this granary system by reading one chapter from *Nourish the People: The State Civilian Granary System in China, 1650–1850,* by Pierre-Etienne Will and R. Bin Wong, University of Michigan, Center for Chinese Studies, 1991. Or read a chapter and prepare a report from *Bureaucracy and Famine in Eighteenth-Century China,* by Pierre-Etienne Will, Stanford, CA, Stanford University Press, 1990.

3. Many sources tell about Chinese immigration to the United States and other countries during the mid to late nineteenth cen-

tury. Read one of these sources and prepare an oral report. Include an explanation of why so many people who came to the United States were from southern China.

4. During the eighteenth and nineteenth centuries, China exported many textiles—silk, shantung, nankeen, and satin—to the West. Prepare an exhibit detailing the history of one or more of these textiles, telling where they came from and how they were made. If possible, include a sample of the textile(s) in your exhibit.

5. Pearl Buck wrote *The Good Earth* in 1931. It sold millions of copies and gave many Americans their first and only information about peasant life in China. Read *The Good Earth*. Then read the article "Pearl Buck—Popular Expert on China, 1931–1949" by Michael Hunt in *Modern China*, Vol. 3, January 1977, pp. 33–63. Prepare a written or oral review of *The Good Earth*. In your review summarize Hunt's article and tell what he says about Pearl Buck's role in shaping American public opinion about China.

6. Read *The Good Earth*. Then watch a video of the 1937 movie. Prepare a written or oral report comparing the two. In your opinion, which medium is more powerful, the written word or the film? Give reasons for your response. Why did Americans respond so positively to Buck's book? (It is estimated that the book had sold over 4 million copies by 1972 and that 23 million Americans saw the movie when it was released in 1937.) How well have the book and the movie held up over the years? What criticisms might be leveled at the book and the movie today?

## Further Reading

Cohen, Paul A. *Discovering History in China: American Historical Writing on the Recent Chinese Past*. New York: Columbia University Press, 1984.

Esherick, Joseph W. *The Origins of the Boxer Uprising*. Berkeley, CA: University of California Press, 1987.

Feuerwerker, Albert. *Rebellion in Nineteenth-Century China*. Ann Arbor: University of Michigan, Center for Chinese Studies, 1975.

Michael, Franz. *The Taiping Rebellion*, Vol. 1. Seattle: University of Washington Press, 1966.

Pelissier, Roger. *The Awakening of China, 1939–1949*. Translated by Martin Kieffer. London: Secker & Warburg, 1967.

Shih, Vincent Y. C. *The Taiping Ideology: Its Sources, Interpretations, and Influences*. Seattle: University of Washington Press, 1967.

Spence, Jonathan D. *God's Chinese Son: The Taiping Heavenly Kingdom of Hong Xiuquan*. New York: W. W. Norton, 1996.

Spence, Jonathan D. *The Search for Modern China*. New York: W. W. Norton, 1990.

Wills, John E. Jr. *Mountain of Fame: Portraits in Chinese History*. Princeton, NJ: Princeton University Press, 1994.

# 5 Reform and Revolution, 1890–1920

*B y the 1890s the failings of the Qing dynasty had become blatant. Some leaders, seeing that changes had to come, favored reform, even initiating some reforms in the late 1890s and the early 1900s. But others simply did not believe that reform could come from within; they advocated tearing down the old system and starting over.*

*This section focuses on these two kinds of change in China: reform and revolution. It examines the life and ideas of the man called "the father of the Chinese republic," Sun Yat-sen. We will study his short term as president of the Republic of China and look at the beginnings of Chinese nationalism as embodied in what came to be called the May Fourth Movement.*

## Reading: *Political Reform During the Late Qing Dynasty*

As foreign military strength exposed the weaknesses of the Middle Kingdom during the late nineteenth century, it became clear that the Chinese had to act or they would be forced to accede to every demand the foreigners made. The Chinese understood that change was needed, but they resisted change and disagreed about what needed changing and how much. What eventually happened was that change or reform came in stages, each of which failed. After each failure, there was a period of re-evaluation before further reforms were tried. Increasingly radical solutions to China's problems were proposed and eventually attempted, so stability did not come for a long time. In fact, some argue that China has still not really stabilized today, well over a hundred years after would-be reformers first grasped that it must adapt to the modern world.

### "Self-Strengthening"

At first, reformers thought it was most important to adapt to non-Chinese military ways. This was the easiest change to make because the Chinese had already seen the power of English gunboats during the Opium War. The Chinese also understood conquest by military might. The Qing emperors were, in fact, Manchurians who

had invaded and subjugated the Han Chinese.

The "self-strengthening movement" began in the 1860s. It was led by provincial officials who were loyal to the throne but had independent power bases and thought the key to the restoration of China was to adopt Western military technology. Over the next thirty years they made sporadic attempts to incorporate Western weapons into the Chinese military, and China started to manufacture its own materials for weapons, ships, and rail transport.

The self-strengthening movement was sharply criticized after military defeats by France in the 1880s. It was clear that China was still no match for European firepower. But the need for further reform was not really recognized until China suffered a far more humiliating defeat at the hands of its one-time tributary state, Japan, when China lost the Sino–Japanese War in 1895. This loss shook Chinese technical and intellectual society to the core. It was one thing to lose to a Western power with a long history of guns and firepower; it was another to lose to a former tributary state that had started its own modernization program only thirty years earlier. Japan quickly became a model for Chinese reformers. If we must reform, they said, perhaps the Japanese way can work for us. Into this atmos-

*[handwritten notes top margin]*
people have control of the government to prevent corruption

Sun Yat-sen
→ imperial system needs change
→ socialist republic

→ Government is there to provide for the people
→ Confucian paternalism

The Nanjing Arsenal was established in 1867 as one of China's many self-strengthening projects. Photo circa 1868 by John Thompson. Courtesy of the Military Museum of China, Beijing, People's Republic of China.

*[handwritten notes right margin]*
Cixi
100 days reform
- reform political, educational system
- modernizing - western approach
- self strengthening movement
- military-focused
- learn from outsiders

Boxer Rebel
- resistance against westerners
→ Boxer Protocol
300 mill to western powers

(far left) Kang Youwei (1858–1927), Confucian scholar and leader of the Reform Movement of 1898 and a constitutional reformist. He later became a fierce critic of Sun Yat-sen and advocated the restoration of the Manchus. (left) Liang Qichao (1873–1929), a student of Kang Youwei and a leader of the Reform Movement of 1898. He advocated that China become a constitutional monarchy. Courtesy of the Historical Commission, Central Committee of the Kuomintang, Taipei, Taiwan, Republic of China.

phere came several important reformers. The best known was Kang Youwei, who advocated not only military reform but also changes in the educational system, the adoption of modern techniques in agriculture, transportation, and communication, and the reform of the official system. Some of his ideas were original; some were based on Japanese reforms.

## The Hundred Days Reform

By 1898, three years after the defeat by Japan, the situation in China had deteriorated so badly that Kang Youwei was able to persuade the emperor to introduce a series of radical reforms. The

emperor had his own reason for advocating reform. He had long been under the control of the powerful Empress Dowager,[1] Cixi, and he saw the reforms as a way to assert his own will. There was enough agitation that Cixi initially felt she could not actively oppose the reforms, but she never gave them her blessing.

The "Hundred Days Reform" began in June of 1898 and lasted until September, ending in dismal failure and the restoration of the old order. But during that brief time the emperor initiated reforms that attempted to restructure Chinese

[1] dowager: in this context the widow of a king or emperor. The title Empress (or Queen) Dowager differentiates her from the wife of the reigning king or emperor.

society. The first reform established the Imperial University at Beijing, the first institution of its kind in China. The reformers then set about organizing an all-new educational system, including new schools and a thoroughly revamped curriculum. They revised the examination system, including "modern practical subjects" as a necessary part, and eliminated the grade given for calligraphy. They initiated a Chief Bureau of Agriculture, Arts, and Commerce to modernize agriculture and business practices. For the first time the government was to present an annual budget. The reformers also eliminated many useless official positions.

Eliminating those positions is probably what did in the Hundred Days Reform so quickly. The officials who held these positions did not give up their privileges easily, so the reformers decided to force them into submission. When the Empress Dowager saw this as an opportunity to regain authority, she sided with the officials. In this way they defeated the reformers, who rallied around the emperor. The Empress Dowager then imprisoned the emperor and controlled the throne until her death in 1908. By September 21 the Hundred Days Reform was crushed. A few of the reforms survived. The military, for example, was strengthened and reorganized, and Beijing University, which thrives to this day, was established.

What the Hundred Days Reform showed was that there was no great popular agitation for reform, that the emperor was not up to the task of spreading enthusiasm for reform among the officials, and that the forces of conservatism were still powerful. The reformers had seen foreigners ready to carve up China for their own use, and so they desperately rushed to equip China to defend itself. But they did this without trying to change the structure of the society. The emperor remained; the Empress Dowager remained; the court structure remained; the officials remained; the primacy of Confucian order and ethics remained. The failure of the Hundred Days Reform convinced some people that the problem was not simply to catch up to Western technology; the problem was that the structure of the imperial system itself needed changing. At

this point some reformers became revolutionaries. Other people concluded that the solution was to get rid of the foreigners. Some of these latter people joined the Boxers.

## Questions

1. Briefly explain the "self-strengthening movement."
2. Briefly list the reforms attempted during the Hundred Days Reform.
3. Was the Hundred Days Reform a failure? Explain your response.

## The Boxer Rebellion

The Boxer Rebellion began in North China in 1898 as a popular peasant protest movement. In the past it was believed to be both anti-dynastic and anti-foreign. However, recent scholarship indicates that it was a strictly anti-foreign movement, not a domestic rebellion. It ended in humiliating defeat for the Chinese empire in 1900, when military units from eight foreign countries, called an international expeditionary force, banded together to suppress it. At the height of the chaos the Boxers occupied Beijing. Hundreds of foreigners, including many missionaries, were killed, along with thousands of Chinese.

*A Boxer flag. The characters say "Support the Qing, Destroy the Foreigners." Courtesy of the Historical Commission, Central Committee of the Kuomintang, Taipei, Taiwan, Republic of China.*

*A member of the Boxers United in Righteousness, circa 1900. The flag says "Authorized Boxer Feeding Station." Courtesy of the National Archives, Washington, D. C.*

"The Boxers United in Righteousness," were dubbed "boxers" because they practiced the traditional Chinese martial arts. The Boxers believed that when they took part in certain rituals, spirits possessed them, making them impervious to foreigners' bullets. Hence they were extraordinarily brave in battle.

The Boxers hated foreigners and their increasing encroachment in China. They especially resented missionaries and called for an end to privileges enjoyed by Chinese converts to Christianity. Some converts, for example, got missionaries to intervene for them in disputes with local authorities. Some refused to take part in Chinese religious festivals. One of the Boxers' placards listed these accusations against one Chinese Christian: ". . . conspired with foreigners, destroyed Buddhist images, seized our people's graveyards. . . . This has angered Heaven."

The Manchu court decided to recognize the Boxers as a means of controlling the foreigners' demands for more concessions. The Boxers became more and more daring, destroying symbols of foreign encroachment, such as railroads and telegraphs. They roamed the countryside killing missionaries and Chinese Christians and

*Foreign powers sent troops to China to suppress the Boxers. Here black cavalrymen from the United States are shown in Tianjin, circa 1900. Courtesy of Peabody Essex Museum, Salem, MA.*

burning churches. They encouraged villagers to do the same and promised that anyone who hid converts would also be killed. In the cities they openly called for the killing of foreigners.

In June 1900 the Boxers occupied Beijing and Tianjin, where they burned foreign churches and residences and killed Chinese converts or buried them alive. They dug up the graves of early missionaries such as Matteo Ricci. On June 21 the Empress Dowager, Cixi, and the Manchu court declared war on all foreign powers. Government troops joined the Boxers and began to attack the foreign legations (embassies) in Beijing.

In response the foreign powers joined together and sent an expeditionary force to China. It consisted of 18,000 soldiers from Japan, Britain, Russia, the United States, France, Austria, and Italy. This force, with its superior firepower, occupied and then looted Beijing. The Manchu court fled the city in disguise and established a temporary capital in Xian. Meanwhile, Chinese authorities in China's southeastern provinces refused to recognize the Manchu government's declaration of war. They guaranteed peace in central and south China if the foreigners would keep their troops out of these areas. This suited the foreign powers because it left the treaty system intact. As a result, most of the turmoil caused by the Boxers and most of the killings occurred in North China.

The conflict ended in September 1901 with another "negotiated settlement" with eleven foreign powers. The Boxer Protocol, as it was called, was mainly punitive. Ten court officials were executed and a hundred others punished. The civil service examinations were suspended in forty-five cities. The foreign legations in Beijing were garrisoned by foreign troops. So were the railways. Twenty-five Chinese forts were destroyed, making it harder than ever for China to defend itself. The agreement also demanded that China pay an indemnity of 330 million dollars over a period of thirty-nine years—at interest rates that would more than double the amount.

The Boxer Rebellion and the war that followed it, called the War of 1900, was the largest

*The Empress Dowager, Cixi (1835–1908), in the palace at Beijing, circa 1900. Courtesy of the Historical Commission, Central Committee of the Kuomintang, Taipei, Taiwan, Republic of China.*

conflict the Qing government fought with the West during the nineteenth century. The humiliating terms of the Boxer Protocol, further infringements on China's sovereignty, especially in Manchuria, and more foreign interference in China's internal affairs sealed the fate of the Qing dynasty. Its days were clearly numbered. Still, there was one last effort at reform.

## The Late Qing Reforms

The defeat of the Boxers forced Cixi to accept the need for change. Between 1901 and her death in 1908, she instituted a series of reforms that closely paralleled many of the attempts of the Hundred Days movement. The Late Qing Reforms, as these changes are known, failed to save the Chinese empire, but they were more substantial than might have been expected, given how resistant the Qing court had been to reform in the previous half-century.

A modern school system, modeled on Japan's, was introduced in 1904. In 1905 the old

## Educational Reform in the Late Qing

Although reformers and revolutionaries alike devoted thought and action to the need for political change in China during the last years of the Qing Dynasty, they paid little attention to the need for social reform. However, between 1901 and 1911 the Chinese government did establish a national school system, first for boys and then for girls.

The new system included several kinds of schools. It began with kindergartens that admitted boys up to the age of seven free of charge, usually for two years. After kindergarten, a boy might go to a primary school, a five-year institution where parents paid a small tuition. Fortunate boys might then attend middle school, which lasted for four years. Middle schools emphasized learning foreign languages; English and Japanese were required. Students who passed the final examination in middle school might be admitted to a three-year course in a provincial college (comparable to high school today), taking arts or sciences. The brightest of the bright might then be accepted at the Imperial University at Beijing for a three-year course, which could conceivably be followed by four or five years of postgraduate work.

After 1906, girls fortunate enough to have parents willing to pay could go as far as middle school in this system. But many families considered education for girls a waste because girls were expected to marry young and to have no need for formal learning.

Despite this attitude, girls in fact did attend school in China several decades before government schools were established. After the Opium War (1840–1842) missionaries were allowed to work at converting Chinese to Christianity in the original treaty port cities, although they had little success in most of these cities. In 1858, however, with the Treaty of Tianjin, missionaries were allowed to move into the Chinese countryside for the first time. Here they were more successful in gaining converts. American Protestant missionary women, in particular,

devoted much effort to developing an educational system for Chinese girls. Girls whose families allowed it might attend a primary school in their village and then go to a boarding school at a mission station for middle school. Primary schools were usually taught by Chinese converts while middle schools were taught by missionaries themselves. Missionaries also founded institutions of higher learning for Chinese women, long before women were accepted at government-sponsored universities.

One custom that changed during the last years of the Qing dynasty was footbinding. The movement to do away with this painful practice originated in the treaty ports, where Chinese had been in contact with foreigners the longest. Western women and upperclass Chinese women alike were vocal in their arguments that the practice be stopped. In 1902 the Empress Dowager, Cixi, issued a decree recommending that footbinding be abolished. In fact, footbinding continued in parts of China well into the twentieth century, but at a diminishing rate. It was not completely abolished until after the Communists came to power in 1949.

*A missionary teacher listens as a student recites at North China Union Women's College, founded in 1905. The characters above the picture of Christ read, "Happy to obey the decree of God." By permission of the Houghton Library, Harvard University, Cambridge, MA.*

examination system, based on classical learning, was abandoned. A modern army was started under Yuan Shikai. This reform, ironically, worked against the throne because when the revolution finally came in 1911, the new army was not loyal to the throne but to Yuan Shikai personally. In 1906 opium-smoking was banned. Imperial decrees also promised to introduce constitutional government over a span of years. The emperor was to be retained, but the government would be a constitutional monarchy, like the governments of England and Japan. There was no serious attempt to introduce financial reform or to eliminate the colossal corruption in the administration. The imperial reformers were intent on finding ways to preserve the empire, not to end it.

## Activity: Word Usage

1. Cut out three advertisements or news articles that use the word "revolution" or derivations of it, such as "revolutionary,"
"revolutionize," or "revolutionaries," and circle the words in red.
2. Look up the definition of "revolution" in a dictionary.
3. Critique the use of the word "revolution" in each of your selections. That is, comment on how the word is used. Tell whether it is used appropriately and explain why or why not.
4. Paste your selections, comments, and explanations on chart paper to make a collage.
5. Bring your collage to class to display. Then look over your classmates' collages. What do they show you about how the word "revolution" is used today? Does any one sense predominate? Would you classify most of the usages as appropriate, inaccurate, or trivial?
6. Write a class list on chart paper, noting what you think an actual revolution in late nineteenth- and early twentieth-century China might entail. In making your conjectures, think of earlier Chinese attempts to overthrow the Qing dynasty, such as those of the Taiping. Keep the list for future reference.

## Reading: *Revolutionary Ideas*

At the same time that the late Qing reforms were being introduced, more and more people came to believe that the cause of China's problems was not a lack of guns, or inadequate communication between regions of the country, or archaic agricultural techniques and an outmoded educational system; China's problems, they believed, were caused by the imperial system itself. To them, just the very idea of an absolute monarchy was outdated, not only in China but throughout the world. Many Chinese believed that the Qing dynasty's days were numbered. China was being carved up by foreign powers and the government was powerless to stop it. Many concluded that nothing short of revolution, a forcible overthrow of the established government, could save the Middle Kingdom. China had to do away with emperors altogether and become a republic.

The leader of the revolutionaries was a Western-educated man, Sun Yat-sen. Sun and other revolutionaries thought that the imperial system was flawed and that China needed a thoroughly modern government. Sun's answer was to form a republic. A republic could achieve two purposes: it could control foreign encroachments, and it would oust the Manchus who controlled the throne. It would then be a Chinese government, run by Chinese for the sake of China. Nationalism, a strong strain in Sun's plan for China, was an idea shared by many who had far less radical plans for the country. Most reformers felt that the imperial system was not the problem. Sun and the other revolutionaries were sure that it was.

Sun was also attracted by such Western ideas as democracy and socialism. He was particularly keen to bring "socialism" (what he called "the People's livelihood") to China. It is important to understand that in this instance socialism implied that the government has a role in taking care of the people. Sun and other revolutionaries wanted to adapt Confucian paternalism, which taught that the emperor and officials had responsibility for the people's material welfare, to modern times, thereby broadening the idea of the government's social responsibility for the people.

## Activity: Reform or Revolution?

### Part 1. Preparation

1. Your teacher will divide the class into two teams, one that advocates reform and one that advocates revolution during the late 1890s and the first decade of the 1900s. If you must take a side you disagree with, do your best to defend it. Later you will have a chance to express your own point of view. Working on your own, do these two tasks:

   **Task A.** Identify at least three changes you believe need to be made in China immediately.

   **Task B.** Decide how to make those changes happen. (It is not enough merely to advocate change; you must explain, as reformers or as revolutionaries, *how* the changes will be made.)

   To complete tasks A and B, review Chapter 2, Sections 3 and 4, and what you have read thus far in this section.

2. Come together in groups of three or four reformers or revolutionaries. Discuss your responses to tasks A and B in your groups.

### Part 2. Mini-Debate

3. After all groups have discussed their responses to tasks A and B, your teacher will form pairs of one reformer and one revolutionary. Each person should wear a sign or tag with the label "reformer" or "revolutionary."

4. Each pair is to engage in a mini-debate, one person advocating reform as a solution to specific problems during the late Qing dynasty, the other advocating revolutionary solutions.

5. Use this format for your mini-debate. One person makes a statement about a change that needs to be made. For example, the revolutionary may say, "China should not tolerate foreigners on its soil; we should kick them all out immediately." The reformer might respond by saying, "We need the foreigners' money. If we kick them all out, their countries will stop trading with us. We must figure out ways to control them to our advantage. We need better weapons and better treaties." Then the reformer raises a new point. "I think we should ask the emperor to reform our judicial system; we need to think about a jury system." The revolutionary must respond, then raise a new point. This continues until neither person has any more points to raise.

6. Take notes as you debate; your opponent may have thought of points or ideas you missed.

7. Your teacher will select one or two pairs of students to repeat their mini-debate for the class. Again, you should take notes.

### Part 3. Debriefing

After this activity, discuss the following questions as a class.

1. In this debate, how did the revolutionaries and the reformers differ?
2. Did they differ in what they wanted or in how they wanted to achieve it?
3. Does the personality of an advocate make a difference in whether others follow that person? Do followers make their decisions on issues or on personality or on both?

### Part 4. Your Own Opinion

Write an essay of about 250 words explaining why you would have advocated reform or revolution during the final days of the Qing dynasty. You may choose either position. Because the essay is brief, you must give your reasons succinctly. Your notes should help you defend either position.

## The 1911 Revolution and the Collapse of the Qing

Two thousand years of almost unbroken imperial tradition ended on October 10, 1911. Double Ten, as the day is called, the tenth day of the tenth month, was not supposed to be the day the Chinese empire collapsed. The revolutionaries, inspired by Sun Yat-sen, had already failed ten times to stage successful uprisings in parts of China.

Then on October 9, 1911, a bomb accidentally exploded in the revolutionaries' headquarters in Wuhan, near the Yangzi River in central China. As the revolutionaries scrambled to get their injured members to hospitals, the Qing authorities, alerted by the destruction, raided their headquarters and promptly executed everyone they found hiding there. When the authorities found membership lists, the revolutionaries knew that unless they acted quickly to start an uprising, they would be destroyed by Qing authorities.

The revolutionaries were aided by rebellious army troops who sided with them against the imperial court. With their help, the revolutionaries quickly took Wuhan and two adjacent cities. The Qing court fought back vigorously, sending in troops to quell the revolt, but once the revolution started it couldn't be suppressed. In other provinces too, the army mutinied, siding with the revolutionaries. The revolution of 1911 produced far less bloodshed than the Taiping Rebellion and the massacres of the rebels in its aftermath. Within six weeks of Double Ten, all of China's southern and central provinces, along with some in the northwest, declared their independence of the Qing court. On January 1, 1912, Sun Yat-sen returned from the United States to become the provisional president of the new Republic of China.

But the Manchu court did not abdicate simply because a republic had been declared and Sun Yat-sen had been named its president. Before agreeing to step aside, the old order wanted specific guarantees, such as the promise of a yearly income and continued ownership of certain of China's treasures. The person who persuaded the Manchu court to abdicate was General Yuan Shikai. As a reward for using his influence with

*Puyi (1906–1967), the last emperor of China, ascended the throne at age three. He was six when he abdicated in February 1912. He is shown here on the right. His father, the Prince Regent, holds Puyi's younger brother. Courtesy of the Historical Commission, Central Committee of the Kuomintang, Taipei, Taiwan, Republic of China.*

the Manchus, General Yuan demanded that he be made China's president.

It seemed unbelievable, but in the end Yuan Shikai got what he wanted. On February 12, 1912, China's last emperor, a six-year-old boy named Puyi, was forced to abdicate. Sun Yat-sen, who had dedicated his life to establishing the new republic, agreed to resign in favor of General Yuan. In return, Yuan promised to support the new republic. And so it happened that the very general the Manchus had sent to suppress the revolution a few months earlier became China's president in March 1912.

Sun Yat-sen, excluded from the government of the fledgling republic, formed a new political party, the Nationalist Party or Guomindang. But Yuan Shikai and his followers had no intention of letting people like Sun establish a republic with political parties. They outlawed the Guomindang,

*[handwritten: Yuan Shikai becomes president because he had a lot of influence, even to make a republic, even though he fought against the rebellion in the first place]*

*Yuan Shikai (1859–1916), center, became president of the new Republic of China in 1912. After his death, warlords ruled China. Courtesy of the Military Museum of China, Beijing, People's Republic of China.*

*[handwritten: reform actually worked in the long run b/c Sun yet went to america and came back to China and got rid of the Qing dynasty]*

and Sun fled to Japan. Yuan promptly began to scheme to restore the empire with himself as the first leader of the new dynasty. Sun eventually moved to Guangzhou, where he continued to work for the establishment of the China he had envisioned. He did not live long enough to see all his ideas carried out, but his work was continued by his trusted lieutenant, Chiang Kai-shek, who became the leader of the Guomindang when Sun died in 1925.

When the revolutionaries took over in 1911, they were no more able to stabilize and strengthen China than the emperors had been, nor could they put into effect any consistent ideas on how to govern a country. China's problems were so deep-rooted that even a totally new government could not solve them. Within just a few years, Chinese would be agitating yet again for reform and revolution.

## Question

Retrieve the class chart where you predicted what "revolution" might entail in late nineteenth- and early twentieth-century China. Was the Manchu government overthrown in the way you thought it would be? Explain your response.

### Activity: Dramatic Reading

The following excerpts are from *The Three People's Principles*, written by Sun Yat-sen in 1924 as he sought to reorganize the Guomindang. Your teacher will divide you into groups of three. Each person in the group will read one excerpt aloud. These steps will help you understand your excerpt and read it with meaning.

1. Read your assigned excerpt to yourself at least twice to become familiar with its ideas. Look up words you do not understand so that you can convey the meaning of Sun's ideas when you read aloud.
2. Read your excerpt, in the order given here, to your group. You should be familiar enough with the reading that you can read confidently and dramatically, pausing when necessary and emphasizing the words and phrases you think are important. You should be able to glance up from time to time as you read.
3. Your teacher will choose members from different groups to read the excerpts to the entire class.

## Dr. Sun Yat-sen

Sun Yat-sen was born to a farming family in southern China, near Macao, in 1866. His birthplace, Guangdong (Canton) province, which had a long history of contact with foreigners, was also the birthplace of the Taiping, an area steeped in anti-Manchu sentiment. Most of the people who left China in search of a better life were from this province. At his father's urging, Sun left China at thirteen to join his older brother in Hawai'i. There Sun attended school, thus becoming one of China's earliest Western-trained intellectuals.

Sun began his foreign schooling in the islands at 'Iolani School. After graduating, he moved on to more advanced studies at Oahu College, a missionary-founded institution known today as Punahou School. Then his brother sent him home to keep him from being baptized a Christian. But Sun was a problem at home. He desecrated an idol in the village temple by breaking off its arm. His family urged him to flee to Hong Kong to avoid the repercussions sure to come down on them all. In Hong Kong he got further schooling and attended medical school. In 1884 he was baptized a Christian. Sun was inspired by the sights and sounds of Hong Kong. As he strolled the streets of the British Crown Colony, he wondered why the orderliness that prevailed there could not be achieved in his homeland.

Sun believed it was useless to try to reform China from within. He wanted to tear down the existing order and enlist the imperialists' help in creating a brand-new Chinese republic. In 1894 he formed a secret revolutionary organization, the Revive China Society. Its stated objectives were "the overthrow of the Manchus, the restoration of China to the Chinese, and the establishment of a republican government." Sun was forced into exile when his first attempt to overthrow the Manchus was discovered in 1895. He fled to Japan. The next year he was kidnapped in London by Manchu officials and sent back to China to be executed. He was rescued by friends from Hong Kong and became an international figure. He began writing in 1903 about his theory of revolution and his vision of what it could bring, advocating nationalism, democracy, and the people's livelihood in his "Three People's Principles." He also drew up a "five-power constitution" that supposedly improved on the checks and balances of Western democracies by adding censorship and examination branches to the government.

Sun toured overseas Chinese communities raising money to finance mutinies and uprisings in China. In 1905 he was elected by revolutionary-minded Chinese students in Japan to lead the Tongmenghui, or Revolutionary Alliance, an umbrella organization that coordinated revolutionary efforts. Because of his subversive activities, he was shunned by foreign governments. In 1907 he was banned from Japan, in 1908 from French Indochina. Sun's Revolutionary Alliance organized ten failed uprisings. When revolution finally came in 1911, the man who would come to be called the father of the Chinese republic was in the United States, raising more money for the cause.

Sun Yat-sen returned to China to become its provisional president, but his term of office was short-lived. In 1912 he agreed, for the sake of national unity, to step aside and allow Yuan Shikai, a Manchu general who had cut a deal with the revolutionaries, to become president of the Republic of China. Sun and his followers formed the Nationalist party, or Guomindang.

But Yuan Shikai never intended to let people like Sun establish a republic. Yuan began to scheme to restore the empire and set himself up as the first emperor of the new dynasty. The Guomindang was outlawed and Sun fled to Japan. After years in exile, Sun finally became president of the Nationalist government of China in Canton in 1923 as a result of an alliance he made with the Chinese Communist Party. He died in 1925.

## Reading: *The Three Principles of the People—Sun Yat-sen*

### On Nationalism

For the most part the four hundred million Chinese can be spoken of as completely Han Chinese. With common customs and habits, we are completely of one race. But in the world today, what position do we occupy? Compared to the other peoples of the world we have the greatest population and our civilization is four thousand years old; we should therefore be advancing in rank with the nations of Europe and America. But the Chinese people have only family and clan solidarity; they do not have national spirit. Therefore even though we have four hundred million people gathered together in China, in reality they are just a heap of loose sand.

Today we are the poorest and weakest nation in the world and occupy the lowest position in international affairs. Other men are carving knife and serving dish; we are fish and meat. Our position at this time is most perilous. If we do not earnestly espouse nationalism and weld together our four hundred million people into a strong nation, there is danger of China being lost and our people being destroyed. If we wish to avert this catastrophe, we must espouse nationalism and bring this national spirit to the salvation of the country.

### On Revolution

Revolutionary destruction and revolutionary reconstruction complement each other like two legs of a man or two wings of a bird. The republic after its inauguration weathered the storm of extraordinary destruction. This, however, was not followed by extraordinary reconstruction. A vicious cycle of civil wars has consequently arisen. Our nation is on the descendant like a stream flowing downward. The tyranny of the landlords together with the sinister maneuvers of the unscrupulous politicians is beyond control. . . .

As a schoolboy must have good teachers and helpful friends, so the Chinese people, being for the first time under republican rule, must have a far-sighted revolutionary government for their training. This calls for a period of political tutelage, which is a necessary transitional stage from monarchy to republicanism. Without this, disorder will be unavoidable.

*Sun Yat-sen (1866–1925) in Shanghai, 1916. Courtesy of the Historical Commission, Central Committee of the Kuomingtang, Taipei, Taiwan, Republic of China.*

We cannot decide whether an idea is good or not without seeing it in practice. If the idea is of practical value to us, it is good; if it is impractical, it is bad. If it is useful to the world, it is good; if it is not, it is no good.

### On the People's Livelihood

As soon as the landowners hear us talking about the land question and equalization of landownership, they are naturally alarmed as capitalists are alarmed when they hear people talking about socialism, and they want to rise up and fight it. If our landowners were like the great landowners of Europe and had developed tremendous power, it would be very difficult for us to solve the land problem. But China does not have such big landowners, and the power of the small landowners is still rather weak. If we attack the problem now, we can solve it; but if we lose the present opportunity, we will have much more difficulty in the future.

What is our policy? We propose that the government shall levy a tax proportionate to the price of the land and, if necessary, buy back the land according to its price. . . .

After the land values have been fixed we should have a regulation by law that from that year on, all increase in land value, which in other countries means heavier taxation, shall revert to the community. This is because the increase in land value is due to improvement made by society and to the progress of industry and commerce. China's industry and commerce have made little progress for thousands of years, so land values have scarcely changed throughout these generations. But as soon as progress and improvement set in, as in the modern cities of China, land prices change every day, sometimes increasing a thousandfold and even ten thousandfold. The credit for the progress and improvement belongs to the energy and enterprise of all the people. Land increment resulting from that progress and improvement should therefore revert to the community rather than to private individuals. . . .

If we do not use state power to build up these enterprises (railroads, waterways, mines, manufacturing) but leave them in the hands of private Chinese or of foreign businessmen, the result will be the expansion of private capital and the emergence of a great wealthy class with the consequent inequalities in society. . . .

> From William Theodore de Bary, *Sources of Chinese Tradition*, Vol. II. New York: © 1964 by Columbia University Press, pp. 105–121. Reprinted with permission of the publisher.

## Questions

After listening to Sun Yat-sen's ideas read aloud, rejoin your group of three and respond to the following questions. The person who read each excerpt must lead the group's discussion on that topic. Every person in the group is responsible for responding to all the questions.

1. **On Nationalism.** What does "nationalism" mean? What did the term mean to Sun Yat-sen? Why do you suppose Sun called his political party the Nationalist Party? Why did he believe that the Chinese people did not have what he called "national spirit"? Give at least one current example of a nationalist movement.

2. **On Revolution.** What does Sun say must happen in the wake of revolution? What failed to happen in China in the wake of revolution? Why does Sun think reconstruction failed to happen? What does he say must be done so that China can actually have republican rule? How does he believe that ideas should be evaluated?

3. **On the People's Livelihood.** How does Sun propose to end the inequity of land distribution and ownership in China? When land increases in value, who should receive the profits from that increase? Why? Why does Sun want the state, rather than private people, to build up enterprises like railroads and manufacturing? What does he say will happen if private individuals or foreign business people run these enterprises?

## The May Fourth Movement

Seven years after the 1911 revolution, China's domestic and political situation was as tumultuous and unstable as it had been earlier in the century. The death of Yuan Shikai in 1916 left a power vacuum that was fully exploited by rival regional military leaders, known as warlords, who reduced the Beijing government to helplessness. At the same time, the weakened government continued to suffer from foreign pressures. Japan became China's chief menace. In 1915, at the height of the first World War, when most European powers were preoccupied with fighting, the Japanese sent an ultimatum to Germany demanding that it transfer its leased territory in China's Shandong province to Japan. The next year Japan moved into the area and occupied Chinese soil.

When the first World War ended in 1918, the Chinese were jubilant. They expected that China, which had fought on the side of the Allied countries, would be treated favorably by other great powers and that territorial disputes, especially the one between China and Japan, would be equitably resolved. Some intellectual leaders went even further, believing that the Allied success

*Beijing students join a massive rally to protest the transfer of German interest in China's Shandong peninsula to Japan, May 4, 1919. Courtesy of the Historical Commission, Central Committee of the Kuomintang, Taipei, Taiwan, Republic of China.*

*May Fourth Movement student protest in 1919. Thousands of students were arrested by the police. Courtesy of Shanghai People's Press, Shanghai, People's Republic of China.*

was a victory of democracy over despotism, of the oppressed over their oppressors. Those who harbored such high hopes were in for a huge disappointment. The Paris Peace Conference did not redress China's grievances. In fact, it supported Japan's acquisition of Germany's interest in China.

Reaction in China was immediate and explosive. On May 4, 1919, thousands of students took to the streets in Beijing, assembling first at Tiananmen Square. Then, despite police orders, they marched to the foreign legations to protest Japan's actions, which they insisted violated China's territorial integrity, and to express their anger at the inept Chinese government officials who they believed had sold China out. The angry students beat up an official sympathetic to the Japanese. They torched the house of a Chinese cabinet member. The police moved in and arrested dozens of students; one was killed. But the arrests did not stop the uproar. Rather, over the next days and weeks, middle school and high school students joined college and university students in strikes and demonstrations in Beijing and other cities. Universities across the country closed down as students spilled into the streets. The public supported the students, and so did the press. Workers staged strikes and work stoppages. Traders boycotted Japanese goods. For once, China seemed united. The Chinese delegation in Paris refused to sign the peace treaty. In the face of this national solidarity, the Beijing government was forced to release the imprisoned demonstrators.

Some historians believe that the May Fourth Movement was the first popular mass movement in Chinese history, that it was the beginning of what Sun Yat-sen had so ardently preached, Chinese nationalism. Over the next turbulent decades, leaders from the Nationalist party, led by Chiang Kai-shek, and the Chinese Communist party, led by Mao Zedong, would become allies and then bitter enemies as the two men and their followers struggled for the soul of China.

---

## Activity: Images of China

1. Study the images that follow. Each one has a brief caption. Look at each one for at least a minute. Then mentally divide each one into quadrants and examine each quadrant; you may see something you missed earlier.

2. Arrange the images in chronological order by writing which one you think should come first, second, and so on in China's history. You may want to reorder your list several times. You can do this on a computer, or by renumbering, or by literally cutting and pasting your list.

3. When you are satisfied with the chronological order of the images, write a complete caption for each one.

4. Use the images, your chronological list, and your captions to write "China's story" as it was discussed in this chapter. The images should jog your memory and serve as a graphic outline to help you organize this essay.

*The Taiping rebels use a captured naval vessel to fight the Qing navies. Courtesy of the Military Museum of China, Beijing, People's Republic of China.*

*Emperor Qianlong hunting on horseback. Courtesy of the Historical Commission, Central Committee of the Kuomintang, Taipei, Taiwan, Republic of China.*

*Signing of the Treaty of Tianjin, 1858. Courtesy of the Historical Commission, Central Committee of the Kuomintang, Taipei, Taiwan, Republic of China.*

*Eight-nation expeditionary force at Beijing train station. Courtesy of the Historical Commission, Central Committee of the Kuomintang, Taipei, Taiwan, Republic of China.*

*May Fourth street protest. Courtesy of Shanghai People's Press, Shanghai, People's Republic of China.*

*Canton Factories, circa 1847–56. Courtesy of the Historical Commission, Central Committee of the Kuomintang, Taipei, Taiwan, Republic of China.*

*Medical doctor who became provisional president of the Republic of China. Courtesy of the Historical Commission, Central Committee of the Kuomintang, Taipei, Taiwan Republic of China.*

three major aspects of nineteenth-century Chinese history: (a) foreign invasions, (b) domestic rebellions, and (c) the rulers' attempts to manage these problems and maintain their own power.

3. Decide in your home group who will be responsible for gathering information about each of the three topics.
4. Form an expert group with two other people working on your topic. There will be several expert groups examining the same topic.
5. Work together in your expert group to collect information on your assigned topic. Review all of Chapter 2, take notes, and be ready to explain your topic to the members of your home group.
6. Here are some good sources of information.

John King Fairbank, *China: A New History*, Cambridge, MA: The Belknap Press of Harvard University Press, 1992.

John King Fairbank and Edwin O. Reischauer, *China: Tradition and Transformation*, rev. ed., Boston: Houghton Mifflin, 1989.

Brian Hook, ed., *The Cambridge Encyclopedia of China*, 2nd ed., New York: Cambridge University Press, 1991.

Immanuel C. Y. Hsü, *The Rise of Modern China*, 4th ed., New York: Oxford University Press, 1990.

Jonathan D. Spence, *The Search for Modern China*, New York: W. W. Norton, 1990.

## Activity: Summing Up the Past

1. Your teacher will divide you into groups of three. This group is your home group.
2. Each home group will use information in this chapter and other sources to explain

7. Return to your home group prepared to tell members of your home group what you have learned about your topic.

8. Decide how your home group will present its information coherently to the class. Be creative in the way you choose to do this. Your group could write a song, put on a role-play, make up journal entries, or write letters from someone who witnessed some aspect of China's history. You could create posters or some kind of display. However, there must be some kind of oral component in your presentation, and everyone in your home group must speak before the class in some way on the assigned topic.

## Extension Activities

1. The "self-strengthening" movement began in China in the early 1860s and continued through 1895. It encompassed a number of projects, including the establishment of shipyards and arsenals and sending Chinese students to the United States to study. Prepare a report on the self-strengthening movement, focusing on one of the many modernization projects China undertook. The article on self-strengthening in the second edition of the *Cambridge Encyclopedia of China* has good introductory information on this topic.

2. An interesting biography of Liang Qichao appears in John E. Wills, Jr.'s book *Mountain of Fame: Portraits in Chinese History*, Princeton, NJ, Princeton University Press, 1994. Read the biography and then devise a creative way to present what you have learned to your classmates.

3. Watch the film *The Last Emperor*, available on videotape. Read a review of the film to see whether you agree with it. Then write your own review, or give one orally. Did you notice any historical inaccuracies in the film? Would you recommend the film to others? Why or why not?

4. Read *The Last Manchu: The Autobiography of Henry Puyi, the Last Emperor of China*, or a biography of him. Compare what you have

read with the film. Which do you think is more historically accurate and why? How are the two similar? How are they different? How do you think history has judged or will judge the last emperor? Has it judged him favorably or unfavorably? How do you perceive him?

## Further Reading

Fairbank, John King. *China: A New History*, Cambridge, MA: The Belknap Press of Harvard University Press, 1992.

Fairbank, John King, and Edwin O. Reischauer. *China: Tradition and Transformation*, rev. ed. Boston: Houghton Mifflin, 1989.

Hook, Brian, ed. *The Cambridge Encyclopedia of China*. 2nd ed. New York: Cambridge University Press, 1991.

Hsü, Immanuel C. Y. *The Rise of Modern China*. 4th ed. New York: Oxford University Press, 1990.

Hunter, Jane. *The Gospel of Gentility: American Women Missionaries in Turn-of-the-Century China*. New Haven: Yale University Press, 1984.

Pelissier, Roger. *The Awakening of China, 1793–1949*. Edited and translated by Martin Secker. London: Secker & Warburg, 1967.

Spence, Jonathan D. *The Search for Modern China*. New York: W. W. Norton, 1990.

Wills, John E., Jr. *Mountain of Fame: Portraits in Chinese History*. Princeton, NJ: Princeton University Press, 1994.

# Chapter **3** Transforming Society: Chinese Communism

**From 1920**

*I*n this chapter we trace the beginnings of the Guomindang and the Communist Party, which in the 1920s emerged as the two dominant forces competing for control of China. We see the Guomindang, led by Chiang Kai-shek, use military might to end the constant battling among China's warlords, unite China under its rule, and attempt to destroy the Communists. We look at how Mao Zedong rose to Communist Party leadership and how he developed new theories on Marxism and revolution that won Communists the support of millions of poor peasants. We consider how the Japanese invasion and occupation of much of China during World War II eventually defeated the Guomindang army and took control of China.

We see how the Communists, once in power, tried to change Chinese society through sweeping mass mobilization campaigns, and how they attempted to control and manage the largest national population in the history of the world. Finally, we look at China's often volatile diplomatic relations with the United States and the Soviet Union.

**Sections**
1. Chaos, Confusion, and Civil War, 1920–1949
2. Winning Hearts and Minds
3. "Dare to Act": Restructuring Society and the Economy, from 1949
4. Marriage, Women, and the Family
5. China and Other Countries, from 1949

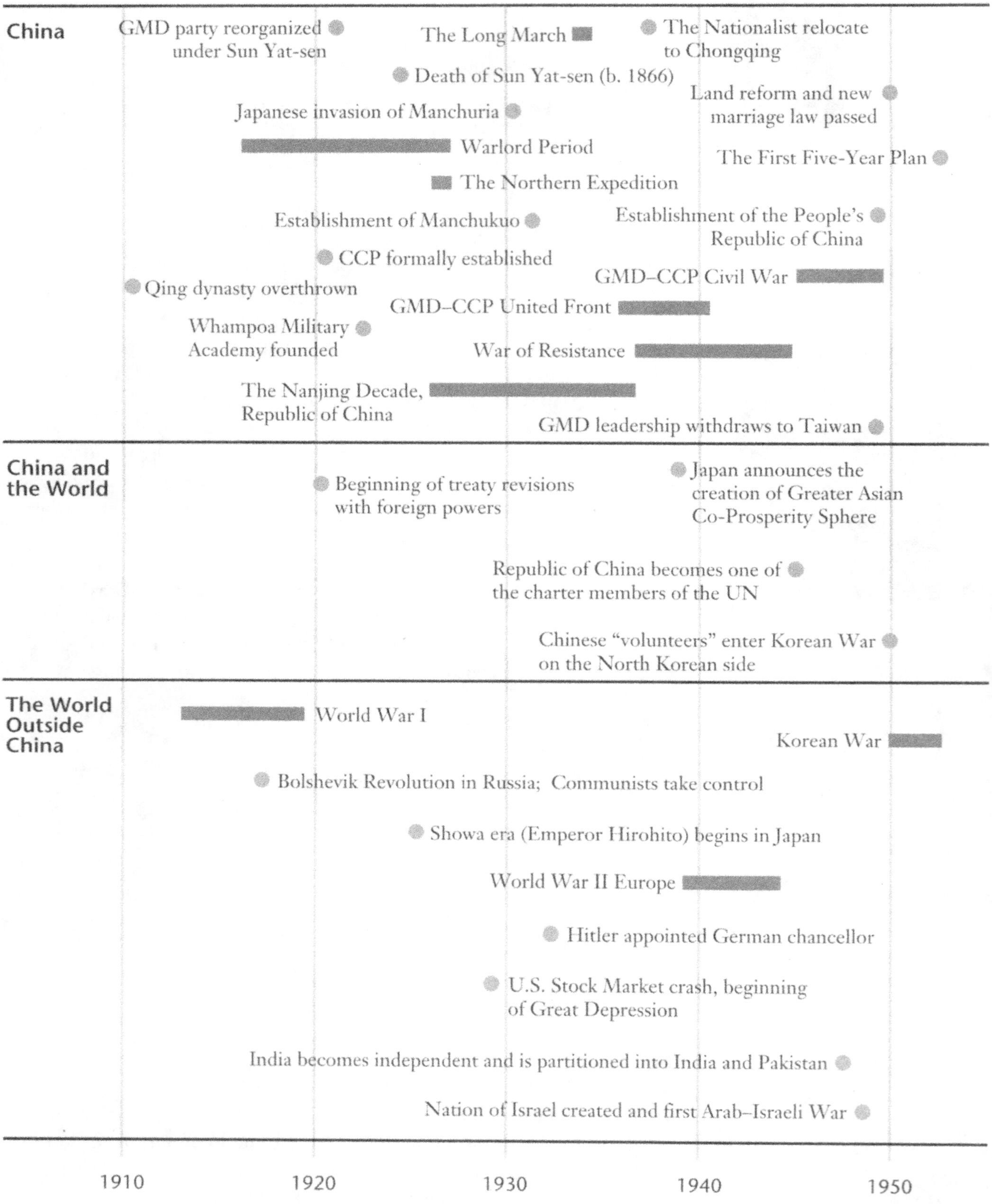

156

**China**

GMD party reorganized ● under Sun Yat-sen

The Long March ▬

● The Nationalist relocate to Chongqing

● Death of Sun Yat-sen (b. 1866)

Japanese invasion of Manchuria ●

Land reform and new ● marriage law passed

▬▬▬▬▬▬▬▬▬ Warlord Period

The First Five-Year Plan ●

▬ The Northern Expedition

Establishment of Manchukuo ●

Establishment of the People's ● Republic of China

● CCP formally established

GMD–CCP Civil War ▬▬▬▬

● Qing dynasty overthrown

GMD–CCP United Front ▬▬▬

Whampoa Military ● Academy founded

War of Resistance ▬▬▬▬▬▬

The Nanjing Decade, ▬▬▬▬▬▬▬ Republic of China

GMD leadership withdraws to Taiwan ●

**China and the World**

● Beginning of treaty revisions with foreign powers

● Japan announces the creation of Greater Asian Co-Prosperity Sphere

Republic of China becomes one of ● the charter members of the UN

Chinese "volunteers" enter Korean War ● on the North Korean side

**The World Outside China**

▬▬▬▬▬▬ World War I

Korean War ▬▬

● Bolshevik Revolution in Russia; Communists take control

● Showa era (Emperor Hirohito) begins in Japan

World War II Europe ▬▬▬▬

● Hitler appointed German chancellor

● U.S. Stock Market crash, beginning of Great Depression

India becomes independent and is partitioned into India and Pakistan ●

Nation of Israel created and first Arab–Israeli War ●

| 1910 | 1920 | 1930 | 1940 | 1950 |

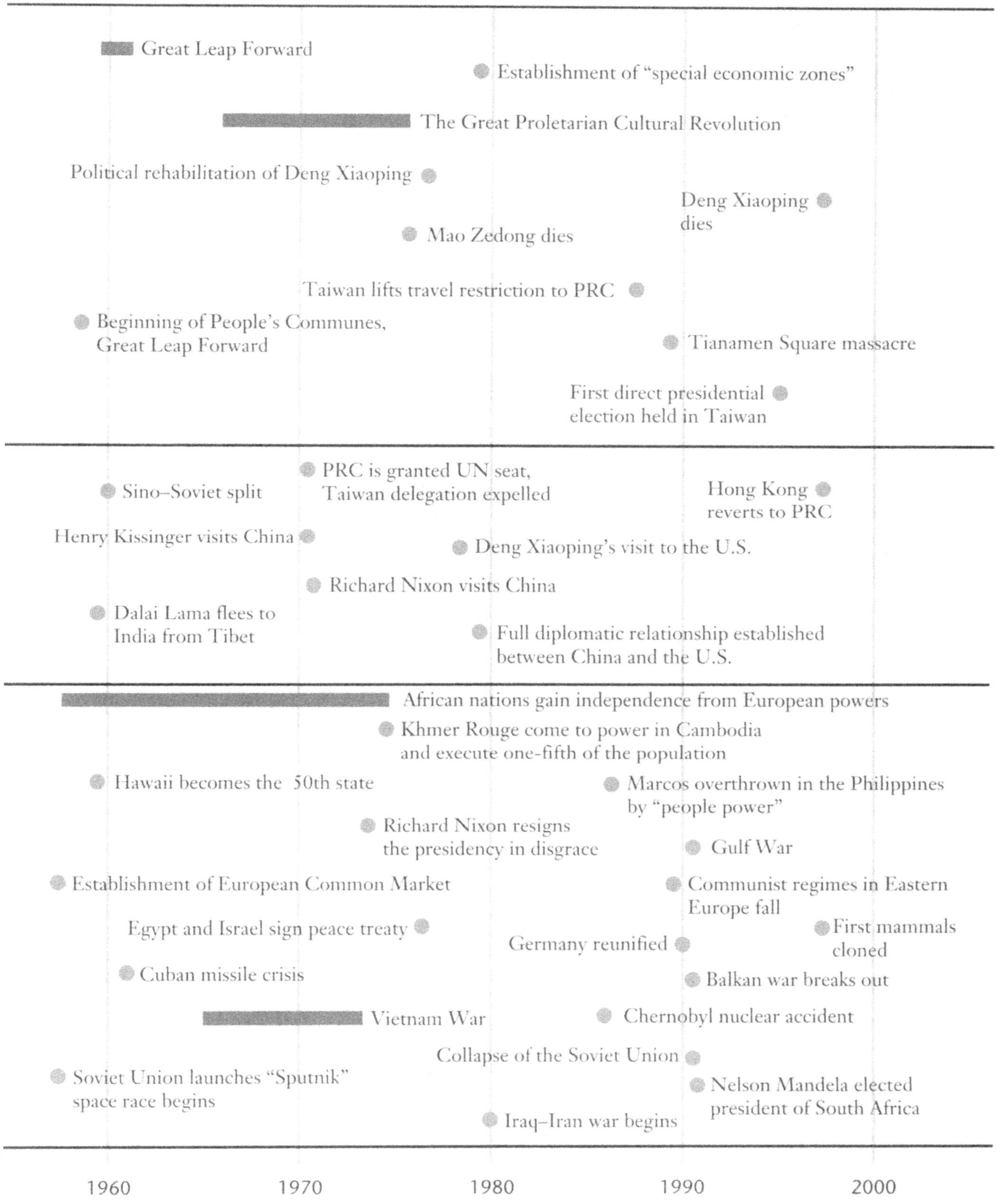

Great Leap Forward

Establishment of "special economic zones"

The Great Proletarian Cultural Revolution

Political rehabilitation of Deng Xiaoping

Deng Xiaoping dies

Mao Zedong dies

Taiwan lifts travel restriction to PRC

Beginning of People's Communes,
Great Leap Forward

Tianamen Square massacre

First direct presidential
election held in Taiwan

PRC is granted UN seat,
Taiwan delegation expelled

Sino–Soviet split

Hong Kong
reverts to PRC

Henry Kissinger visits China

Deng Xiaoping's visit to the U.S.

Richard Nixon visits China

Dalai Lama flees to
India from Tibet

Full diplomatic relationship established
between China and the U.S.

African nations gain independence from European powers

Khmer Rouge come to power in Cambodia
and execute one-fifth of the population

Hawaii becomes the 50th state

Marcos overthrown in the Philippines
by "people power"

Richard Nixon resigns
the presidency in disgrace

Gulf War

Establishment of European Common Market

Communist regimes in Eastern
Europe fall

Egypt and Israel sign peace treaty

First mammals
cloned

Germany reunified

Cuban missile crisis

Balkan war breaks out

Vietnam War

Chernobyl nuclear accident

Collapse of the Soviet Union

Soviet Union launches "Sputnik"
space race begins

Nelson Mandela elected
president of South Africa

Iraq–Iran war begins

1960  1970  1980  1990  2000

# Chaos, Confusion, and Civil War, 1920–1949

*Section* **1**

*B*etween the advent of the May Fourth Movement and the Communist takeover of the mainland in 1949, a multitude of conflicting social, political, and economic forces kept China in a precarious state of flux—trapped between its imperial past and an uncertain future. New political ideologies attacked time-honored Confucian traditions, and urban modernization and industrial growth created both unprecedented economic opportunity and social change. Meanwhile, civil war and foreign invasion ravaged the country, threatening the very existence of China as a sovereign nation.

Throughout this volatile period two political parties, the Guomindang and the Chinese Communist Party, locked horns in a life-or-death struggle to see who would win the hearts and minds of the Chinese people. To the victor would go the right to determine the future of China.

## Activity: A Chinese Village

It has been estimated that during the first half of the twentieth century, 90 percent of all Chinese lived in the countryside and 75 percent lived in small villages. To understand the conflict between the Guomindang and Communists, you must know something about life in the countryside.

This activity will give you a feeling for how people living in an imaginary farming village in northern China might have felt about their lives and place in society during the turbulent years 1936–1945. In this activity, four roles represent major socioeconomic groups in a typical Chinese village at this time.

After you complete this activity, read "Fragmentation to Unification," which briefly examines the people and events leading up to the period covered in the activity, as well as the four years following 1945.

In doing this activity, complete each numbered step before you do the next one.

1. Your teacher will assign you one of these four roles: Landlord, Peasant 1, Peasant 2, or Peasant 3. There should be an equal number of students in each role.
2. During the first part of this activity you will work alone, reading your roles and filling out a rating form that your teacher will give you. For each role there are three sections of readings, dated 1936, 1943, and 1945. For example, if you are assigned the role of Peasant 2, you will read the sections entitled Peasant 2, 1936; Peasant 2, 1943; and Peasant 2, 1945.
3. Your teacher will give you a rating form like this one:

Handout A

Name           Role

**RATING FORM**

Rate the following categories by marking an X on the rating scales. You may mark any point along the line.

**1936 Guomindang rule**

**Economic status**
How would you rate your financial condition?

extremely poor — poor — fair — good — very good

**Political power**
How would you rate the amount of political power you have in the village?

none — weak — fair — strong — very strong

**Future prospects**
What is your family's outlook for the future?

much worse — worse — same — better — much better

**1943 Japanese occupation**

**Economic status**
How would you rate your financial position in the village under Japanese occupation?

extremely poor — poor — fair — good — very good

**Political power**
How would you rate the amount of political power you have in the village under Japanese occupation?

none — weak — fair — strong — very strong

**Future prospects**
What is your outlook for the future under Japanese occupation?

much worse — worse — same — better — much better

**1945**

**Economic status**
What do you think your financial condition would be if the Communists controlled the village?

extremely poor — poor — fair — good — very good

**Political power**
How would you rate the amount of political power you would have if the village were under Communist control?

none — weak — fair — strong — very strong

**Future prospects**
What would be your outlook for the future if the Communists controlled the village?

much worse — worse — same — better — much better

4. When you fill out the rating form or work with others in small groups, you must act as if you were the person described in your role. You are no longer a student studying China; you are a Chinese landlord or peasant evaluating your living conditions and making decisions that will affect your family. (You will notice that all the roles are male, reflecting male-dominated Confucian society. Therefore all females in the class will be taking male roles.)

5. Read each section of your role, then rate your situation for the corresponding year on the rating form. For example, after finishing your 1936 reading, fill out the 1936 box on the form before you read about your 1943 situation. Keep your completed rating form for use later in this activity.

> **READ YOUR ASSIGNED ROLE IN "LANDLORD AND PEASANTS" AND FILL OUT YOUR RATING FORM NOW. DO NOT DO STEP 6 UNTIL YOUR TEACHER TELLS YOU TO.**

*Courtyard of a poor peasant family's home in 1936, about 160 miles north of Beijing. From Hedda Morrison,* Travels of a Photographer in China 1933–1946. *New York: Oxford University Press, 1987, p. 98.*

*(above) Japanese troops burning Chinese village houses, circa 1941. Courtesy of the Military Museum of China, Beijing.*
*(left) Peasants taking part in a public works project, 1941. Courtesy of the Collection of the Historical Commission, Central Committee of the Kuomintang.*

*Communists explaining their land reform policies to peasants during the War of Resistance, 1942. Courtesy of Shanghai People's Press.*

6. After you read the three sections of your role and fill out the rating form, you must make a decision. Here's the situation:

   *The Communist propaganda team that appeared in the village after the Japanese troops withdrew has abruptly left. Now rumors are flying that large contingents of both Nationalist and Red Army soldiers are nearby preparing to seize your village. Some villagers believe that all-out civil war between the Guomindang and the Communists is inevitable, and they worry that it might wreak more havoc on your village than the Japanese army did.*

7. **Choosing sides.** You must now choose the side you want to see take control of your village—the Communists or the Guomindang.

   a. At the top of a sheet of paper, write the title "Choosing Sides." Underneath the title write your role: Landlord, Peasant 1, Peasant 2, or Peasant 3.

   b. Beneath your role, write which side you would prefer to take control of your village: the Communists or the Guomindang. To help you decide, review your rating form and reading.

   c. In the middle of your paper draw a horizontal line at least five inches long. Along the line make eleven equally spaced markings. Number the markings from zero through 10 like this:

   0  1  2  3  4  5  6  7  8  9  10

   You have made a rating scale that you will use to show how strongly you support the side you choose.

   d. To show the level of support for your choice, circle one of the numbered markings along the line, from 1 to 10. The strongest level (10) means you would be willing to join your side's army and die for its cause. Respond as if you are the person whose role you have taken. Review your rating form to help you select your level of support.

   e. After you complete the rating scale, use the rest of your paper—front and back —to answer these questions:

      1. List and discuss the three main reasons you chose the side you did, Communists or Guomindang.

2. Explain how you decided on the level of your support for your choice.

3. List the following in order of their importance in deciding whom to support and how strongly. Write a 1 in front of the most important factor, a 2 in front of the second most important factor, and a 3 in front of the least important factor.

   _____ my family's security and well-being

   _____ maintaining traditional society

   _____ belief in the ideology of the side I chose

8. **Comparing results in groups of the same role.** Your teacher will assign you to work with three or four other students of the same role. For example, if you are Peasant 2, everyone in your group will also be a Peasant 2. Compare your rating forms and "Choosing Sides" scale with others in your group. Take turns explaining why you came up with your ratings for the different years. Next, take turns explaining your answers to the questions in step 7. Then, on clean paper, respond to the following:

   a. How similar are the responses on your rating form to those of the others in your group? Look primarily at your ratings for 1936 and 1945. Were the responses of the members of your group very similar, somewhat similar, or very different?

   b. Did everyone in your group support the same side?

   c. List the reasons people in your group gave for supporting the side they chose, Communists or Guomindang. If everyone chose to support the same side, you will need only one list. If some members chose the Communists and others chose the Guomindang, you will have to make two lists.

   d. Did everyone who picked the same side also choose about the same level of sup-

port? Consider numbers 1, 2, or 3 as weak support, numbers 4, 5, 6, and 7 as moderate support, and numbers 8, 9, and 10 as strong support.

   e. After listening to the other members' explanations of which side they chose to support and why, how do you now feel about the side you chose and your reasons? Do you now have more or fewer reasons for making your choice? Are you more certain of your decisions or less?

9. **Comparing results in groups of mixed roles.** Your teacher will now form mixed groups with at least one Landlord, one Peasant 1, one Peasant 2, and one Peasant 3.

   a. Because members of this group have different roles, introduce yourselves one at a time by showing your rating form for 1936 and explaining why you rated your financial condition, political power, and future prospects as you did. Use background information from the 1936 reading about your land, your family, your community activity, and so on.

   On clean paper, take notes on the others' roles and explanations. You will need this information later. Then repeat the process for the 1943 and 1945 rating sheets.

   b. Compare and explain your "Choosing Sides" responses. If you don't understand the reasons for someone's ratings or choice of the Communists or the Guomindang, ask questions. You must understand why people in each role chose as they did so that you can do the assignment at the end of this activity.

10. After you have the information you need about each role in your group, wait for the teacher to tell you to do the next part of the activity. When your teacher gives you the go-ahead, make your own copy of this chart. Entitle it "Support Analysis."

|  | Landlord | Peasant 1 | Peasant 2 | Peasant 3 |
|---|---|---|---|---|
| Guomindang (total) | a | b | c | d |
| strong support | e | f | g | h |
| Communist (total) | i | j | k | l |
| strong support | m | n | o | p |

11. Your teacher will ask the class, by role, who chose to support the Communists and who chose to support the Guomindang. For example, if your role is Peasant 2 and you chose to support the Communists, raise your hand when the teacher asks how many Peasant 2's chose to support the Communists. After the teacher counts the hands, write the number in box k. In the same way, fill in totals for boxes a–d and i–l.

12. Next the teacher will ask how many in each role chose to strongly support either the Communists or the Guomindang. Go back and look at your "Choosing Sides" support scale. If you circled 8, 9, or 10, your support is strong. As the teacher counts the raised hands, record the number in the corresponding box on your chart. Fill in the totals for boxes e–h and m–p.

13. **Analysis.** Now drop your assigned role and assume your student role. Using the information from your "Support Analysis" chart and what you learned about the roles from your work in small groups, write a short essay answering these questions:

   a. Which roles supported the Nationalists, or Guomindang? Which roles supported the Communists?
   b. Who were the strongest supporters of each side? Explain why.
   c. Which roles, if any, did not strongly support either side? Explain why.
      To explain why each role chose the side it did, make sure you use numbers from your "Support Analysis" chart and the notes you took on each role during your small-group session.

---

### Reading: *Landlords and Peasants*

---

## LANDLORD
### *1936*
### *The village during Guomindang rule*

The year is 1936. You are a wealthy landlord in a farming village several days' journey from the provincial capital. Your household has eight members: you, your wife, your mother, two daughters, a son, and two servant girls. Your living compound is one of the largest in your village. Inside the brick walls of your square compound is a central courtyard with a well and a small garden. Surrounding the courtyard on three sides are the living quarters. The servant girls sleep in the kitchen. Adjacent to one wall of

the compound is a thatch-roofed shed for oxen, carts, and farm equipment.

During a typical day your wife and daughters may spend their time keeping your elderly mother company or doing needlework. They need not concern themselves with doing any housework. The two servant girls run all the errands and do all the work in the compound. They are hardworking girls. One is the daughter of a poor peasant family from a nearby village who sold her to you as payment on a loan. The other is an orphan you took in after her parents died in a famine.

After he returns from the village school, your ten-year-old son spends the remainder of his day studying with a tutor. Unlike your studies, which focused on the Confucian classics, your son's modern curriculum includes science and math. You hope to send him to the provincial capital to attend middle school and high school. If he proves to be an exceptional student, you will put him through college as well. Your ancestors lived in this village for many generations and enjoyed a reputation as noted scholars, shrewd landlords, and village leaders. You hope that your son, too, will do honor to his family's legacy. Overall, your family leads a life of luxury compared with other inhabitants of the village, who have endured poverty and the insecurity of not knowing where their next meal is coming from.

Although you enjoy practicing calligraphy in your spare time, you spend most days tending to village matters and your business affairs. Your living compound borders part of the 210 *mou* of farmland you own. You rent most of your land to peasants and hire workers to farm the rest for you. You wouldn't dream of doing manual labor yourself. As landlord you make sure your tenants pay their rents and your farmhands work diligently on the farm. However, your most profitable business venture is moneylending. You lend money to people in your village and in neighboring villages at high interest rates. In fact, some of your clients will never be able to pay off their loans at the interest rates you charge. This does not make you popular among those indebted to you. You accept this because you know that peasants are ignorant of business matters and do not appreciate the risk you assume in lending them money.

As the largest resident landowner you are among the most influential people in the village. You, along with a handful of relatively educated and well-to-do men, run the village. Among other duties, your group settles disputes among villagers and pays for the upkeep of the Buddhist temple and the Confucian shrine. Your group also controls the village government, since it is composed of men your group has chosen. Besides setting and collecting taxes to pay for services like the local school and police, village officials sometimes carry out orders from the provincial and national governments, such as rounding up men to work on public works projects, like building

roads and bridges. The decisions of your leadership group are not always popular with the villagers, most of whom are peasants. However, you don't much care what anyone not of your social status thinks about the way you manage village matters. Peasants always complain that rents and taxes are too high or wages too low. You feel they just don't understand economics and government. It is not your fault if some are born into poverty and ignorance. It is their fate, just as it is your fate to lead a life of scholarship, wealth, and power. This is simply the way society and government have operated in your country for hundreds of years, and you see no good reason to change anything now.

---

**AFTER YOU FINISH THE 1936 READING, FILL OUT THE 1936 SECTION OF YOUR RATING FORM.**

---

## LANDLORD
### *1943*
#### *The village under Japanese occupation*

The year is 1943. In 1937 Japan launched an all-out invasion from Manchuria against the rest of China, and vast areas of Chinese territory have come under enemy control. Due to its remote location, your village escaped attack until early last year. Now Japanese soldiers occupy your village.

Before enemy troops arrived, you and other village leaders met and decided that armed resistance to the invaders would be futile. Villages that attempted to fight the enemy had paid dearly for their patriotism—often with razed homes, destroyed crops, and many casualties. Still, there was some talk of trying to arm as many men as possible. But you found the idea of giving poor peasants weapons unsettling. Granted, they might be able to defend the village for a short time, but letting uneducated men use weapons would be dangerous. Arming them could create a greater threat to the village's stability than foreign occupation. Giving weapons to men desperate to free themselves of debts to you might pose danger for you and your family. In the end, village leaders decided not to make a stand against the enemy in hopes that the village would be spared harm.

When the Japanese army finally took control, there was some looting by enemy soldiers and a few cases of violence against villagers, but for the most part the capture was calm and orderly.

You have lived under foreign occupation for over a year now and have tried to go about your daily life as though nothing has changed. However, you have had to adopt a strategy of reluctant cooperation with the Japanese commander in charge of the village. When the commander needs tax money, grain supplies, or workers to build fortifications for his troops, he turns to you and other former village leaders for advice and assistance. You don't like aiding the enemy, but in return for your cooperation the commander doesn't interfere with your business affairs, and he allows you to retain your property and wealth. This enables you to maintain your economic clout in the village, and it positions you to return to your leader status once the war is over and the troops leave. You feel your good relations with the enemy also benefit the peasants. For example, you can tell the Japanese commander when the demands he makes upon the peasants are unreasonable. Just last week you told him your tenants could not grow enough grain and cotton to pay both their rents to you and the new taxes he had ordered. You further pointed out that many peasants were barely getting by and could not bear the double burden of higher taxes and a small harvest. Already some poor peasants have run away to the city to look for work or to the mountains to join guerrilla bands fighting Japanese forces. Sometimes the commander heeds your advice, sometimes not.

You know that some villagers criticize you for working with the enemy. They call you a puppet and a collaborator. This doesn't bother you, for they are ignorant, unable to understand that you are really protecting the traditional way of life. You expect that when the Japanese leave, you will take up your rightful position once again as a village leader.

---

**AFTER YOU FINISH THE 1943 READING, FILL OUT THE 1943 SECTION OF YOUR RATING FORM.**

---

# LANDLORD
## *1945*

Last week, on August 15, 1945, Japanese forces surrendered to the Allies, bringing World War II to a close. Troops in your village had begun preparing to withdraw several days before the fifteenth and had left the village by the time the surrender was announced. But no sooner had the last enemy soldier left than a new group appeared in the village—a ten-member Communist propaganda team.

During the Japanese occupation, Communist guerrillas had slipped into the village to meet secretly with peasants. They not only tried to get peasants to join their ragtag army in fighting the Japanese, but they also claimed that you as a landlord were an enemy who had to be destroyed. These guerrillas promised the peasants that after Japan was defeated, the Communist Party would help them build a new society in which poor peasants and factory workers would rule. The Japanese commander had tried vigorously to capture or kill all suspected Communists when he was in charge, a policy you supported wholeheartedly.

With the Japanese soldiers gone and the Guomindang army nowhere in sight, there is no authority strong enough to silence this new group of troublemakers. They talk constantly of "class struggle" and tell the peasants that in "liberated areas"—areas under Communist control—land has been taken from the rich and divided among the poor. According to the Communists, you as a landlord are "an enemy of the people"—of poor peasants, factory workers, and anyone who supports the Communist party. The Communists also claim to have launched an anti-traitor campaign to punish those who cooperated with the Japanese during the war and occupation. They promise to do the same in your village.

One indication of how radical these Communists are is that they have several women soldiers in their group! They meet with woman peasants and lecture them on the equality of men and women. They talk about how the Communists will change the marriage laws so that women will have more say in selecting husbands and in choosing to divorce.

Fortunately, most peasants in your village, you believe, are too traditional to think men and women are equal or to believe this silly concept of class struggle that labels you their enemy. But you worry about your family's future. From your point of view, what the Communists are advocating is nothing short of turning traditional Chinese society on its head. Under Communist rule, your land and wealth would be taken away and distributed among the peasants, and you would probably have to answer for your friendly relations with the Japanese commander during the occupation.

---

**AFTER YOU FINISH THE 1945 READING, FILL OUT THE 1945 SECTION OF YOUR RATING FORM**

---

### PEASANT 1
### *1936*
#### *The village during Guomindang rule*

The year is 1936. You are a peasant in a farming village several days' journey from the provincial capital. Many in the village consider you rich because you own an ox, farm implements, and 90 *mou* of land. Your household has six members: you, your wife, a fourteen-year-old daughter, sons ten and eleven years old, and a servant girl. Your living compound, one of the largest in the village, is well maintained and envied by peasants less well-off than you. Inside the mud-brick walls of your compound are a small courtyard, living quarters, and a kitchen covered by a tiled roof. Behind the living quarters and within the compound is a stable for your ox, a storage area where you keep a cart and farm tools, and a heap of manure to use as fertilizer.

Your farm is too large to farm alone, so you hire poor peasants to help you. During planting and harvesting, your sons might also lend a hand with the farm work. However, you'd rather they focus on their studies at the village school. Your father, though uneducated, worked hard all his life to increase your family's land holdings. You hope that by the time you are ready to retire you will have an even larger inheritance to pass on to

your sons. Things have changed since your childhood, but you know that men who succeed are educated men. Your own education stopped after you graduated from the village school, which went only through the elementary grades. You push your sons to study hard so they can go further in school than you did. With a better education, you hope, they will have business opportunities and never have to work in the fields as you do.

Your wife and daughter spend their days sewing clothes and preparing meals. A servant girl, a gift from a hired worker in exchange for letting him use some of your farm equipment on his own small plot of land, washes clothes, cleans the compound, takes care of the ox, and does other chores. Your daughter is at the age when you will have to begin searching for a marriage partner. She is a shy, pretty girl with impeccable manners, and finding a husband from a respectable family—perhaps even the family of a wealthy landlord—is a possibility.

As one of the village's larger landowners, you are an influential person. Along with a handful of other relatively educated and well-to-do men, you make up an informal village leadership group. Your group settles disputes among villagers and pays for the upkeep of the Buddhist temple and the Confucian shrine. Your group also controls the village government, since it is composed of men your group chooses. Besides collecting local taxes to pay for services like the village school and police, village officials also carry out orders from the provincial and national governments, such as rounding up men to work on public projects, like building roads and bridges.

All in all you lead a good life. Your family is much better off than most of the village residents. Yours is not a luxurious life, yet your family has never gone without a meal or lacked warm clothes and heating fuel for the cold winter months. You believe that through hard work your sons will be able to improve your family's economic status and become respected landlords and village leaders.

---

**AFTER YOU FINISH THE 1936 READING, FILL OUT THE 1936 SECTION OF YOUR RATING FORM.**

---

## Peasant 1
### *1943*
#### *The village under Japanese occupation*

The year is 1943. In 1937 Japan launched an all-out invasion from Manchuria against the rest of China, and vast areas of Chinese territory have come under enemy control. Due to its remote location your village escaped attack until early last year. Now Japanese soldiers occupy your village.

Before enemy troops arrived, you and other village leaders decided that armed resistance to the invaders would be futile. Villages that attempted to fight the Japanese had often been punished and treated harshly after their capture. Still, there was some talk of trying to arm as many men as possible. But you found the idea of giving poor peasants weapons unsettling. If you gave poor peasants weapons, they might turn them on large landowners such as you. Land is wealth, and those with little or no land might be desperate enough to use their weapons to seize property rather than fight the Japanese. In the end your group decided that the best way to protect the village and preserve order was to offer no resistance to the advancing enemy army. When the Japanese soldiers eventually took control, they looted a few small shops, but for the most part the capture was calm and orderly.

Enemy troops have occupied and ruled your village for over a year now, and life has been difficult for most of the people. The enemy has demanded new taxes and more food to feed the troops. Now village tax collectors come accompanied by Japanese soldiers. Before, when you and other village leaders assessed taxes, you took into account how big a crop was or how much land a villager owned. Now the Japanese commander bases his demands only on how much he wants to collect. You have been forced to cut your workers' wages, and you have warned them that they must be more productive. In this way you will be able to pay the higher taxes without your own family having to suffer.

The Japanese commander has also forced villagers to build new military supply roads and fortifications. He often orders peasants to work on these projects during the height of the growing and harvesting seasons. This makes it almost impossible to meet the demand for producing larger crops. Several times you have had to pay a "fee" to the Japanese labor recruiter so your own sons would not be taken for this work. Fortunately, you have managed to befriend several of the higher-ranking Japanese officers in the village through small gifts and favors. In return, compared with most other families, yours has been spared many hardships. You hope the war will end soon and life will return to normal. You are not sure how much longer you can maintain your family's economic security under current conditions.

---

> **AFTER YOU FINISH THE 1943 READING, FILL OUT THE 1943 SECTION OF YOUR RATING FORM**

---

## Peasant 1
### *1945*

Last week, on August 15, 1945, Japanese forces surrendered to the Allies, bringing World War II to an end. Troops in your village had begun preparing to withdraw several days before the fifteenth and had left the village by the time the surrender was announced. However, no sooner had the last Japanese soldier left than a new group appeared in the village—a ten-member Communist propaganda team.

During the Japanese occupation, Red bandits—Communist guerrillas—had slipped into the village to meet with peasants. They tried to get peasants to join their ragtag army in fighting the Japanese and told the peasants that after Japan was defeated, the Communist Party would help them build a new society in which the poor would rule. The Japanese commander had tried vigorously to capture or kill all suspected Communists when he was in charge, a policy you supported.

With the Japanese soldiers gone and the Guomindang army nowhere in sight, there is no authority strong enough to silence this new group of troublemakers. They talk constantly of "class struggle" and tell the peasants that in "liberated areas"—areas under Communist control—land has been taken from the rich and divided among the poor. According to the Communists, you are a "rich" peasant and therefore a suspected "enemy of the people"—of poor peasants, factory workers, and anyone who supports the Communist party. The Communists also claim to have launched an anti-traitor campaign to punish those who cooperated with the Japanese during the war and occupation. They promise to do the same in your village.

One indication of how radical these Communists are is that they have several woman soldiers in their group! They meet with woman peasants and lecture them on the equality of men and women. They talk about how the Communists will change the marriage laws so women will have more say in selecting husbands and in choosing to divorce.

Fortunately, most peasants in your village, you believe, are too traditional to think men and women are equal or to believe this silly concept of class struggle that labels you their enemy. But you worry about your family's future. From your point of view, what the Communists are advocating is nothing short of turning traditional Chinese society on its head. Under Communist rule, most of your land would be taken away and distributed among the poor peasants. And you might have to answer for your cordial relations with the Japanese during the occupation.

---

**AFTER YOU FINISH THE 1945 READING, FILL OUT THE 1945 SECTION OF YOUR RATING FORM**

---

## PEASANT 2
### 1936
*The village under Guomindang rule*

The year is 1936. You are a peasant in a farming village several days' journey from the provincial capital. Besides your wife you have a seventeen-year-old son and a nine-year-old daughter. However, your son, along with a number of young men from the village, was forcibly taken away to fight in the Guomindang army.

Your one-room home, made of mud bricks and a thatched roof, is furnished with a *kang*, a

table, and chairs. You own 24 *mou* of land that during a good year produces enough food for your family. Your wife and young daughter help you work your own land, but you also hire yourself out to farm the land of rich peasants and landlords during the busy planting and harvesting seasons. Without your son's help in farming and without the income he brought in by hiring himself out, you, your wife, and daughter will face difficult times.

Your family's precarious existence depends on the whims of nature. When the weather is good, so too is the harvest, and you can feed your family and pay your taxes. But to make it through years when drought, flood, or storm destroys your crops, you must borrow from a rich landlord who charges exorbitant interest rates. In a poor harvest year, life is especially hard during the late winter and early spring as your food dwindles. During this time you have only two small meals a day, and sometimes you can not afford heating fuel to keep your family warm.

These days you have to work harder and harder just to keep what you have. In your father's day things were better. Back then you paid your taxes with a fixed percentage of your crop. If the harvest was small, you'd pay less than when the harvest was good. Now taxes are paid in cash at a fixed amount, so even if you have a bad harvest, you must pay as much as if you have a good harvest.

A handful of relatively educated and well-to-do men make up an informal leadership group in the village. They settle disputes among villagers and oversee the upkeep of the Buddhist temple and the Confucian shrine with "contributions" from you and other villagers. (You suspect much of what you "contribute" lines the pockets of this powerful group of men.) This group also controls the village government, since it is composed of men the group chooses. Besides setting and collecting local taxes to pay for services like the village school and police, village officials sometimes carry out orders from the provincial and national governments, such as rounding up men to work on public projects like building roads and bridges. Even during the most critical times of the growing and harvesting seasons, the village leaders might choose you for a public works gang. If you complain or try to resist, you only make your life more difficult. Village leaders could fine you, discriminate against you in settling disputes, or even alter your deeds to deprive you of land. Landlords and rich peasants have ways of keeping order in the village. It is useless to go against them.

---

**AFTER YOU HAVE FINISHED THE 1936 READING, FILL OUT THE 1936 SECTION OF YOUR RATING FORM**

---

### PEASANT 2
### *1943*
#### *The village under Japanese occupation*

The year is 1943. In 1937 Japan launched an all-out invasion from Manchuria against the rest of China, and vast areas of Chinese territory have come under enemy control. Due to its remote location, your village escaped attack until early last year. Now Japanese soldiers occupy your village.

Before enemy troops arrived, village leaders decided that armed resistance to the invaders would be futile. Villages that attempted to fight the Japanese had often been punished and treated harshly after their capture. Upon hearing the leaders' decision, a poor peasant neighbor half-jokingly commented that the real reason they did not want to arm village men was that they were more afraid of a peasant revolt than of the Japanese. When the Japanese soldiers took control, they looted some small shops, but for the most part, the actual capture was calm and orderly.

For over a year you have lived under foreign occupation, and your life has become even more difficult. Landlords and rich peasants still enjoy a life of privilege, and some don't seem to mind working with the enemy in running the village. Apparently they are allowed to keep their wealth and property in return for bilking even more rent from their tenants to pay the higher taxes the enemy is charging them. Before, when village leaders assessed taxes, they took into account how much your land could produce.

Now the tax collectors are accompanied by enemy soldiers, and the amount they demand is based only on how much the Japanese commander orders them to collect. Sometimes peasants who can't pay are severely beaten, or worse; if they own land, it is taken from them. The Japanese commander also orders villagers to do forced labor more often than the village leaders used to, and he makes you work much harder. You and other peasants—no landlord's son ever participates—build roads or fortifications and transport supplies, all for the benefit of the enemy army.

Many poor peasants have run away to avoid the forced labor and higher taxes. Some have run off to the cities to find work, while others flee to the mountains to join guerrilla bands fighting the Japanese. You hope the war will end soon and life will return to normal. Between the higher taxes you must pay and the reduced time you can spend farming, you are finding it harder and harder to make ends meet. The last thing you want to do is to sell part of your land to pay taxes that help the enemy, but you may have no choice.

---

**AFTER YOU HAVE FINISHED THE 1943 READING, FILL OUT THE 1943 SECTION OF YOUR RATING FORM**

---

### PEASANT 2
### *1945*

Last week, on August 15, 1945, Japanese forces surrendered to the Allies, bringing World War II to a close. Troops in your village had begun preparing to withdraw several days before the fifteenth and had left the village by the time the surrender was announced. But no sooner had the last foreign soldier left than a new group appeared in the village—a ten-member Communist propaganda team.

During the Japanese occupation, Communist guerrillas had slipped into the village to meet with peasants. Some of these guerrillas had left nearby villages to join the Communist forces fighting Japanese troops in the mountains. They told you that, besides the Japanese, rich peasants and landlords were also "enemies of the people"—

that is, enemies of poor peasants, of factory workers, and of anyone who supported the Communists. These guerrillas promised that after Japan was defeated, the Communist Party would build a new society in which you, the poor, would rule. The Japanese commander had tried vigorously to capture or kill all suspected Communists when he was in charge, a policy that rich peasants and landlords supported.

At first you and other poor peasants didn't take the guerrilla fighters seriously. They didn't look like soldiers, and no one really believed they could fight successfully against landlords and the Japanese. But when you saw how much effort the Japanese commander, with support from the landlords, put into hunting down and killing them, your opinion began to change.

With the enemy soldiers gone and the Guomindang army nowhere in sight, there is no authority strong enough to silence the propaganda team. They hold meetings to tell the villagers about their ideas for land reform. They talk constantly of "class struggle" and tell you that in "liberated areas"—areas under Communist control—land has been taken from rich peasants and landlords and divided among poor peasants. They are also trying to organize a peasants' association in your village to run your village after liberation. The association will also confiscate land from rich peasants and landlords and decide how to redistribute it among the poor. The Communists also say that all traitors who worked with the Japanese during the war will be severely punished.

You are not quite sure what to think of this group of agitators. Though not much, you already have land of your own, and you're not sure whether the Communists want to confiscate it, too. In some ways you feel the Communists are too radical. You are shocked that several woman soldiers are part of their group. They hold meetings with woman peasants where they talk about men and women being equal and about changing the marriage laws so women will have more say in selecting husbands and in asking for divorce.

On the other hand, if the Communists rid society of rich landlords, you and other villagers won't have to worry anymore about borrowing money from them at outrageous interest rates. You also wouldn't mind seeing those landlords and rich peasants who cooperated with the enemy for personal gain get their just rewards.

> **AFTER YOU FINISH THE 1945 READING, FILL OUT THE 1945 SECTION OF YOUR RATING FORM**

## PEASANT 3
### *1936*
### *The village under Guomindang rule*

The year is 1936. You are a poor peasant in a farming village several days' journey from the provincial capital. You moved to this village eight years ago to escape famine in your native province. You still remember fighting other villagers over tree leaves for your family to eat. But you could never scrape up enough food for your starving parents and siblings. Your parents and younger sister all died of malnourishment. Along with a younger brother, you ran away without paying debts you owed your family's landlord. You were able to move to this new village and buy a small plot of land with the money you got from selling your brother to a family who wanted him because they had no heirs. Selling your brother was the only good fortune either of you has ever had in life.

Now you own nine *mou* of land—not enough to support you, your wife, and your three-year-old daughter—so you must rent a small plot from a rich landlord and hire yourself out to work for others. You live in a hut made of mud, sticks, and thatch. Your only possessions are the clothes on your backs, tattered cloth shoes, an old quilt, and a small pot and a few dishes for meals, which usually consist of only gruel. Your life is a never-changing cycle. From late spring to autumn you work in the fields till you think you'll die from exhaustion; from winter until early spring you suffer from hunger and cold. Life is especially hard in the late winter and early spring as food from the last harvest begins to run out. During this time you have only two small meals a day. Sometimes you must forage in the mountainside for weeds and tree bark to eat. You have no padded winter clothes, and your only protection against the cold is your thin quilt. At this time of the year, every day is a battle for survival.

It seems you have to work harder and harder just to keep what you have. Your landlord keeps raising your rent, and on top of that, he charges hired field hands like you a fee to use his farm tools. To afford his fees, you have had to pawn all your land to the landlord. If you pay off your debt on time, the land becomes yours again. But if you cannot pay your debt, your land belongs to your landlord. Moneylending landlords keep peasants like you indebted for long periods. People say, "The debts of the poor begin at birth. When a boy is a month old the family wishes to celebrate; but they have to borrow money in order to make dumplings and so, before the child can sit up, he is already in debt to the landlord. As he grows the interest mounts until the burden is too great to bear."[1]

Rents and debt are not your only worry. Every year there are more taxes to pay. In your father's day things were not quite as bad. Back then you paid your taxes with a fixed percentage of your crop. If the harvest was small, you'd pay less than when the harvest was good. Now taxes are paid in cash at a fixed amount, so even if you have a bad harvest, you must pay as much as if you have a good harvest.

Village leaders—usually landlords and rich peasants—are in charge of conscripting men for public works projects such as building roads and bridges. Even during the most critical times of the growing and harvesting seasons, they might choose you for a public works gang. If you complain or try to resist, they just make your life more miserable. They could fine you, hire thugs to rough you up, discriminate against you in a dispute with another villager, or even alter your deed to take your land away.

Landlords have many ways of keeping poor peasants like you in line. They hold the power of life and death over you, and there's nothing you can do about it. It must be as they say—just a matter of fate. You were born under an unlucky

star and must live a life of misery with no hope of a better future.

> AFTER YOU FINISH THE 1936 READING, FILL OUT THE 1936 SECTION OF YOUR RATING FORM

## PEASANT 3
### *1943*
#### *The village under Japanese occupation*

The year is 1943. In 1937 Japan launched an all-out invasion from Manchuria against the rest of China, and vast areas of Chinese territory have come under enemy control. Due to its remote location, your village escaped attack until early last year. Now Japanese soldiers occupy your village.

Before enemy troops arrived, village leaders decided that armed resistance to the invaders would be futile. Villages that had attempted to fight the Japanese had often been punished and treated harshly after their capture. Upon hearing the leaders' decision, a peasant neighbor half-jokingly commented that the real reason they did not want to arm village men was that they were more afraid of a peasant revolt than of the Japanese. When the Japanese soldiers took control of the village, they looted some small shops, but for the most part the capture was calm and orderly.

For over a year you have lived under foreign occupation, and your life has become even more difficult. Landlords and well-to-do peasants still enjoy a life of privilege, and some don't seem to mind working with the enemy in running the village. Apparently they are allowed to keep their wealth and property in return for bilking even more rent from you and other tenants to pay the higher taxes the enemy is charging them. Now the tax collector is accompanied by Japanese soldiers. Before, when village leaders assessed taxes, they took into account how much your land could produce. Now the amount the Japanese commander demands is based only on how much he wants to collect. Sometimes peasants who cannot pay are severely beaten, or worse; if they own land, it is taken from them. The Japanese commander also orders villagers

---

[1] Hinton, William. *Fanshen: A Documentary of Revolution in a Chinese Village.* New York: Random House, 1966, pp. 44–45.

to do forced labor more often than the village leaders used to, and he makes you work much harder. You and other peasants—no landlord's son ever participates—build roads or fortifications and transport supplies, all for the benefit of the enemy army.

With the higher taxes you have to pay, your debt to the landlord, and the forced labor you have to perform, you do not know how your family will survive. You and your wife have talked about selling your daughter to pay part of what you owe. You love your daughter, but if you lose your land, you won't even be able to support your wife, and your chances of having more children will be poor. Many poor peasants have already lost their land and their families. Others have run to the cities to look for work. If the war does not end soon, you will be forced to give up your only child.

---

AFTER YOU FINISH THE 1943 READING, FILL OUT THE 1943 SECTION OF YOUR RATING FORM

---

### PEASANT 3
### *1945*

Last week, on August 15, 1945, Japanese forces surrendered to the Allies, bringing World War II to a close. Troops in your village had begun preparing to withdraw several days before the fifteenth and had left by the time the surrender was announced, but no sooner had the last Japanese soldier left than a new group appeared in the village—a ten-member Communist propaganda team.

During the Japanese occupation, Communist guerrillas had slipped into the village to meet secretly with peasants. Some of these guerrillas had left nearby villages to join the Communist forces fighting Japanese troops in the mountains. They told you that, besides the Japanese, rich peasants and landlords were also "enemies of the people"—that is, enemies of poor peasants, of factory workers, and of anyone who supported the Communists. These guerrillas promised that after Japan was defeated, the Communist Party would build a new society in which you, the

poor, would rule. The Japanese commander had tried vigorously to capture or kill all suspected Communists when he was in charge, a policy that rich peasants and landlords supported.

At first you and other peasants didn't take the Communist guerrillas seriously. They didn't look like soldiers, and no one really believed they could fight successfully against landlords and the Japanese. But when you saw how much effort the Japanese commander, with support from the landlords, put into hunting down and killing Communists, your opinion began to change.

With the enemy troops gone and the Guomindang army nowhere in sight, there is no authority strong enough to silence the propaganda team. They hold meetings with poor peasants like you to tell you their ideas for land reform. They talk constantly of "class struggle" and tell you that under a Communist government, land will be taken from the rich and divided among the poor. In fact, they claim to have already done this in "liberated areas"—areas under Communist control. They are also trying to organize a peasants' association to run your village after its liberation. The association will also confiscate land from rich peasants and landlords and decide how to redistribute it among the poor. The Communists also say they will launch an anti-traitor campaign in your village, once it is liberated, to punish those who cooperated with the Japanese army during the war and occupation.

However, you wonder if maybe the Communists are too radical. You are shocked that several woman soldiers are in their group. These women meet with peasant women and talk about how men and women are equal and how the Communists will change the marriage laws so that women will have more say in selecting husbands and asking for divorce. On the other hand, if the Communists come to power in your village, you would get your own land and your debt to the landlord would be canceled. You wouldn't mind seeing those landlords and rich peasants who prospered under Japanese rule get their just rewards.

---

AFTER YOU FINISH THE 1945 READING, FILL OUT THE 1945 SECTION OF YOUR RATING FORM

---

## Questions

1. In this activity, equal or nearly equal numbers of students played each of the four roles. In other words, 25 percent of the class had the same role. This does not reflect the reality of the Chinese countryside. It has been estimated that the rural population in the 1930s and 1940s broke down roughly as follows: landlords, 3 percent; rich peasants, 7 percent; middle peasants, 22 percent; and poor peasants, 68 percent.

    a. Using these percentages, calculate how many students in your class would be landlords, rich peasants, middle peasants, and poor peasants in a Chinese village of that time.

    b. From this information, what can you infer about which side, the Communists or the Guomindang, enjoyed the most support in the countryside?

2. The four roles in the activity (Landlord, Peasant 1, Peasant 2, and Peasant 3) represent four "class" designations the Communists used in deciding how to redistribute land. Mao labeled these classes landlord, rich peasant, middle peasant, and poor peasant. If we define a class as a group of people in a common economic situation, then the economic situations of landlord, rich peasant, middle peasant, and poor peasant must differ. Explain how the economic situations of these four classes differ. Look primarily at land ownership and work relations.

3. Landlords and peasants were not the only people living in the Chinese countryside. Can you think of other occupations in a rural village? Why does the activity use only four roles?

4. All the roles in this activity were males. Now imagine you are the wife of one of these men. Would your decision to support the Communists or the Guomindang differ from the men's? Why?

5. The activity forced you to choose between the Communists and the Guomindang. Would you have chosen neutrality if it had been an option? Explain.

---

**Reading:** *Fragmentation to Unification*

---

Nineteen twenty-one was a tumultuous year for China, fragmented and ruled by an assortment of regional military dictators, or warlords. With the fall of the decrepit Qing dynasty in 1911, and following the failure of the first Chinese Republic in 1916, a national government ceased to exist. Throughout China, warlords carved out autonomous districts with their own armies and tax systems. Intense competition over land erupted into open warfare. With warlords teaming against each other in a continual grab for more land, widespread fighting raged in China for years.

## Foreign Encroachment

Although Western powers had established treaty ports and staked out spheres of influence in China during the 1800s, it was Japan, a dynamic new national power, that posed the greatest threat to Chinese sovereignty in the twentieth century.

Japan had sought to extend its power to the Asian mainland as early as 1876, when the island nation forcibly "opened" the "hermit kingdom" of Korea against the strong protest of the Qing court. In 1894, after years of squabbling over which nation would have primary influence in Korea, Japan and China went to war. The modernized Japanese military handily defeated the ill-equipped and poorly trained Chinese forces in this first Sino–Japanese war.

Then in 1904 Japan and Russia went to war over economic rights in China's northeastern province of Manchuria, rich in natural resources. The world was stunned when Japanese forces easily routed the heavily favored Russians in

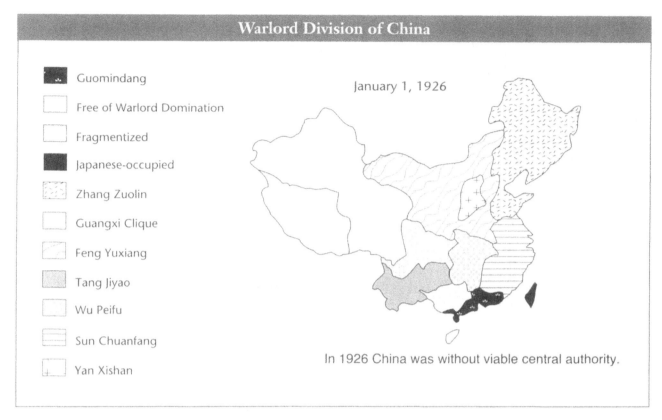

*Warlords pose together at the Japanese Concession in Shanghai, 1924. Zhang Zuolin (third from the left), Feng Yuxiang (second from the left), and Duan Qirui (fourth from the right). Courtesy of the Collection of the Historical Commission, Central Committee of the Kuomintang.*

*Sun Yat-sen (seated) and Chiang Kai-shek (center, standing) at the Whampoa Military Academy, June 16, 1924. Courtesy of the Collection of the Historical Commission, Central Committee of the Kuomintang.*

advocated a free and democratic society; the Communists wanted a government that would improve economic conditions for China's peasants and working class. Over the next thirty years these two parties and their armies battled warlords, Japanese invaders, and each other. Finally, in 1949, the Guomindang fled to Taiwan and the Communists victoriously united China under their rule.

## Guomindang (Nationalist Party)

Sun Yat-sen, considered the father of the Chinese revolution that overthrew the Qing dynasty and created the Republic of China, first organized the Guomindang, or Nationalist Party, in 1912. Initially Sun Yat-sen supported General Yuan Shikai as the first president of the fledgling republic. But within one year Yuan outlawed all political opposition, including the Guomindang, forcing Sun Yat-sen to flee to Japan. When Yuan died unexpectedly in 1916, Sun Yat-sen quickly returned to China and, in the early 1920s, reorganized the Guomindang[2].

After several setbacks in establishing a power base in southern China, Sun gained the backing of several local warlords and declared himself head of a military government in the southern port city of Canton. With assistance from the newly formed Soviet Union, Sun then set up the Whampoa Military Academy near Canton and appointed an ambitious young general, Chiang Kai-shek, as its superintendent. The Guomindang army grew rapidly in strength over the next few years. By 1925 it was strong enough for Sun Yat-sen to believe that the time was right to begin the Northern Expedition, a military campaign against warlords north to the capital of Beijing, uniting the nation under Nationalist rule.

But Sun Yat-sen never lived to see a united China. He died on March 12, 1925. Following Sun's death Chiang Kai-shek became Generalissimo, or commander-in-chief, of the Guomindang's 90,000-man National Revolutionary Army. On July 27, 1926, he set off with

mere months. Its confidence bolstered by these easy victories, Japan annexed Korea in 1910, thereby gaining a base for penetrating deeper into Manchuria and threatening northern China. In 1915, in return for Japanese financial support, the Chinese government accepted Japan's humiliating conditions.

During this period of foreign encroachment and domestic turmoil, the voice of Chinese nationalism began to make itself heard. Sparked by the May Fourth Movement, citizens throughout the country took to the streets in marches and demonstrations calling for an end to warlord rule and foreign imperialism in China. It was also at this time that two political parties formed—the reorganized Guomindang, or Nationalist Party, and the Chinese Communist Party. Both parties sought to create a new China by harnessing the nationalist sentiment sweeping the land. For both parties this meant eliminating foreign imperialism and establishing a unified government for the nation. The Guomindang, in its early years,

---

[2] For a discussion of Sun Yat-sen, see Chapter 2.

## Chiang Kai-shek (1887–1975)

Born in 1887 to a salt merchant family, Chiang Kai-shek rose from relative obscurity to become leader of the Guomindang—the Nationalist Party—and head of the Republic of China. As a youth, Chiang was fascinated by warfare. Reaching adulthood, he resolved to study military science in Japan.

For three years Chiang studied in Japanese military schools. He returned to China in 1911, just as revolution broke out, ending the Qing dynasty and overthrowing China's imperial system. During the next decade, he served the Guomindang revolutionary leader Sun Yat-sen ably and loyally. (Chapter 2 discusses Sun Yat-sen and the 1911 revolution.) In 1923 he persuaded Sun to send him to Moscow to study the Soviet military system. Upon his return, he became head of the new Whampoa Military Academy, established to train revolutionary officers. With this post, Chiang positioned himself to contend for leadership within the Guomindang.

Sun's death in 1925 provided the opportunity. By outmaneuvering his competitors and crushing the warlords, Chiang rose to the top of the Nationalist Party and reunified most of China under Guomindang rule. The world responded by accepting Chiang as China's sole leader.

Unfortunately for Chiang, during his ascendancy the Chinese Communists were also gaining military and popular strength. At the same time, Japan was challenging the independence of the young republic by seizing Manchuria in 1931 and threatening to move farther south. Before acting against the Japanese intrusion, Chiang decided to battle the Communists, almost destroying them in 1934. But Japan's expansion into China created a wave of public sentiment in the country to end the Guomindang–Communist conflict. During the 1937-to-1945 War of Resistance, the Guomindang and the Communists toned down their fighting, at times even cooperating to fight their common enemy.

But with the end of World War II, the two factions returned to all out warring. By then, ineffective administration together with rampant corruption among the Nationalists had turned many Chinese against them while enthusiasm for Communism had grown. On December 10, 1949, with the threat of fast-approaching Communist forces, Chiang boarded a military aircraft and escaped to Taiwan, where he relocated his government and named the island the Republic of China (ROC).

As head of the Nationalist government until his defeat in 1949, Chiang did not just represent China. To many in the world, he was China. Because he brought his country into the world's community of nations, Chiang is recognized as an important figure in twentieth-century Chinese history. He continued to rule Taiwan until his death in 1975.

*President Chiang Kai-shek reviewing troops during the Double Ten Celebrations in Taipei, Taiwan, 1954. Double Ten—October 10—is the anniversary of the beginning of the 1911 rebellion that overthrew the Qing dynasty. Courtesy of the Collection of the Historical Commission, Central Committee of the Kuomintang.*

his troops on the first leg of the Northern Expedition in a quest for national reunification.

## The Chinese Communist Party

After World War I, many Chinese no longer looked to Western nations as models of social, political, and economic reforms for their society. They questioned the morality of democracy and capitalism. After all, it was the capitalist nations of the West that had callously dissected China into spheres of influence for their own economic gain.

Disillusioned with the West, a number of Chinese students and intellectuals became fascinated with the writings of Karl Marx. Inspired by the successful revolution in Russia, they formed the Chinese Communist Party (CCP) in 1921. These idealists believed a Communist doctrine could improve the lives of poor urban workers and peasants in the countryside, two groups the warlords paid little attention to. With the support of these poorer classes—the masses, as Marx called them—Communists would drive out foreign imperialists and unite the country once and for all. Many young people were attracted to the new party because of its strong anti-warlord and anti-imperialist tenets. Soon

the Communists were organizing urban workers into labor unions and poor farmers into peasant associations.

Although they distrusted each other intensely, at the outset of the Northern Expedition the Communists and Nationalists decided to work together toward their common goal of defeating the warlords. To do this, Communists were allowed to join the Guomindang. But the alliance of these two parties was at best a tenuous marriage of convenience. Collaboration between Communists and Nationalists came to a sudden and violent end when, in 1927, during the Northern Expedition, Communist members of the Guomindang attempted to take over the Nationalist Party from within. Chiang Kai-shek, outraged, ordered all Communists purged from his party, hunted down, and killed. The Generalissimo never forgave the Communists for the takeover attempt.

## The Nationalist Government, 1928–1937

Despite the Nationalist–Communist split, the Northern Expedition succeeded in uniting most of China, if only superficially. By 1929 Chiang Kai-shek headed a central government vowing

Nationalist
unite china
capitalism
freedom
democracy

Communist
unite china
communist
state control
peasants interests

*Shanghai in the 1930s. Courtesy of the Collection of the Historical Commission, Central Committee of the Kuomintang.*

reform and the abolition of unequal treaties. The Nationalists moved the capital to Nanjing and changed the name of the Qing capital, Beijing, to Beiping, or northern peace.

Under the Guomindang government urban China modernized considerably. New factories sprang up, and new power stations supplied an ever-growing demand for electricity, not only for industry, but for small businesses and homes as well. New roads carried an increasing number of trucks and automobiles. Hundreds of miles of new tracks transported trains between China's booming cities. New hospitals cared for the sick, and new schools and universities offered educational opportunities for both boys and girls.

Social life in China's large cities was transformed in the 1920s and 1930s. Movie theaters became part of the bustling urban scene, radios and phonograph players were available to those who could afford them, and many young men and women began dressing in fashionable Western-style clothes. A large coastal city such as Shanghai assumed the trappings and cosmopolitan air of its European and American counterparts.

The countryside, however, was another world. While the cities were modernizing, life in rural China, where the vast majority of Chinese lived, remained largely unchanged. Village life centered on farming. Most Chinese were still illiterate peasants living in small villages untouched by the twentieth century. Health care was poor or nonexistent. Educational opportunities were scarce. Few peasants ever traveled to a city, rode a train, or saw an electric light or an automobile.

The Nationalists focused on developing the cities, where their strength was concentrated. Although the Guomindang government passed reform measures aimed at improving living conditions in the countryside, it lacked the power to carry out these measures. The authority of the central Nationalist government never reached deep enough to take root in the countryside. In many parts of the nation ultimate power still lay in the hands of local leaders, either "reformed" warlords or the scholar gentry, traditional leaders of rural China.

## Guomindang vs. Communists

After their disastrous attempt to seize the reins of the Guomindang in 1927, the Communists went underground. Some remained in the cities, organizing China's growing number of industrial workers. Others, including Mao Zedong, fled to the remote countryside to establish base camps from which to fight the Guomindang.

Chiang Kai-shek adamantly believed that the Communists and their Red Army had to be crushed before the Nationalists could focus on solving China's economic and social problems. Beginning in 1930, Chiang launched a series of "encirclement and extermination" campaigns against Communist-controlled districts in the countryside, decimating the Red Army. By 1934, it appeared the Nationalists would soon deal the Communists a final blow. But the trapped Communist army pulled off a daring escape and began a year-long 6,000-mile trek, known as the Long March. The survivors of this arduous journey established a base camp in Shaanxi, and under the leadership of Mao Zedong, the Communists were able to reorganize and challenge the Guomindang forces once again.

In 1931, while the Nationalists were preoccupied with setting up a new government and wiping out Communist forces, Japan seized Manchuria. A year later the Japanese created the puppet state of Manchukuo and installed the last Qing emperor, Puyi, as its figurehead.

The Chinese were appalled by Japan's seizure of their northeast province. Under intense public pressure to stop fighting each other in the face of foreign aggression, the Guomindang and the Communists agreed in 1936 to form a "united front" to oppose further Japanese seizure of Chinese territory. The test of their new alliance came almost immediately.

## The War of Resistance, 1937–1945

In July 1937 Japanese forces swarmed across the Manchurian border in an all-out invasion of China. Coordinating land and air attacks, they quickly captured large areas. Over the next eight years Japan seized all of northeast China, most of the coastal provinces, and every major sea-

## Long March, 1934–1935

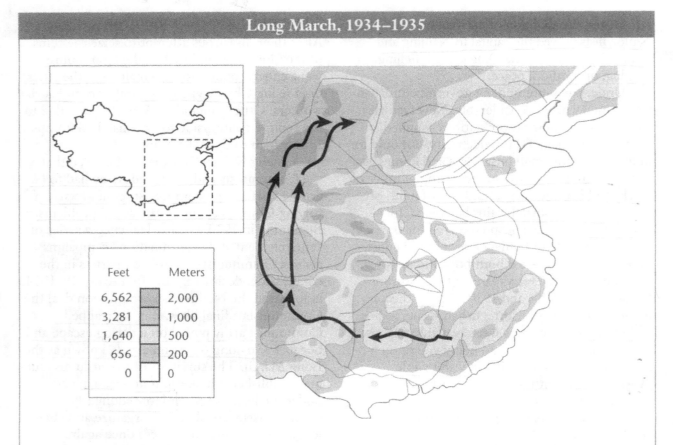

| Feet | | Meters |
|---|---|---|
| 6,562 | | 2,000 |
| 3,281 | | 1,000 |
| 1,640 | | 500 |
| 656 | | 200 |
| 0 | | 0 |

By 1934 the Nationalists controlled most of China, and it seemed that they would annihilate the Communists, who had retreated to Jiangxi, their base in southern China. There Chiang Kai-shek's forces surrounded them and threatened to destroy them. The Communists decided to break through the siege and flee to the northwest province of Shaanxi. Because the direct route would have taken them through land fully controlled by the Guomindang, the Communists took a roundabout route, often backtracking and zigzagging because of their enemies and the rough terrain. Finally reaching Shaanxi after 370 days, the Communists, under the leadership of Mao Zedong, established a firm base from which to fight the Guomindang.

Carrying heavy loads as well as their sick and wounded comrades through rain and snow, the marchers walked almost 6,000 miles up and down mountains and through marshy, desolate terrain, crossing large rivers and fighting off Guomindang forces along the way. This incredible achievement, which has inspired songs and stories and has become a legend in Chinese Communist party history, is called the Long March.

The exhausted marchers had saved their revolution, but the price was heavy. Of the original 100,000 people, only 8,000 reached Shaanxi. Those who completed the entire journey have been immortalized in the collective memories of the Chinese. The Long March became the central heroic saga in Chinese Communist history, and Mao Zedong emerged as the undisputed leader of the Chinese Communist movement.

Imagine walking eight to ten hours every day for over a year, under the same conditions as the Long Marchers. Could you survive?

*The last Qing emperor Puyi and Japanese military commanders. To win public support and international recognition for Manchukuo, Japan installed Puyi, a Manchu, as its emperor. But Puyi was a puppet ruler incapable of wielding real power, and only a few countries recognized Manchukuo as a legitimate nation. Courtesy of the Collection of the Historical Commission, Central Committee of the Kuomintang.*

*The Japanese bombing of Shanghai in 1937 concentrated on residential areas. Life magazine carried this picture of an unattended child crying amid the debris. Governments from around the world condemned the bombing of civilian targets. Courtesy of the Collection of the Historical Commission, Central Committee of the Kuomintang.*

port. The Nationalist government was forced to flee its capital at Nanjing to the city of Chongqing deep in the interior.

The united front could not contain the Japanese onslaught. Both Communists and Nationalists put up resistance against the invaders, but neither side threw everything it had into the effort. Neither the Communists nor the Nationalists could afford extensive losses of men and equipment because neither side trusted the other. Both were concerned not only with fighting the Japanese army but also with possibly fighting each other again.

During the War of Resistance, Mao Zedong, leader of the Communists since the Long March, rebuilt and reorganized the Communist Party in Shaanxi. It was here that Mao developed what he called the "mass line" strategy: The Communists would work to gain the support of millions of peasants in rural China who would use guerrilla

tactics to defeat the Guomindang and the Japanese.

In areas of the country under its control, the Communist Party and its Red Army began a radical and sweeping reform program. They confiscated land from large landowners, redistributed it to poor peasants, reduced their land

*In November 1944 Mao reviews Communist troops in Yenan, the Communist capital from 1936 to 1947. Courtesy of the Military Museum of China, Beijing.*

*Chiang Kai-shek and members of the Guomindang govern-ment in Chongqing during the War of Resistance. After 1941, American financial aid and military equipment began pouring into the Guomindang via India and Burma. Despite the strong urging of the United States, Chiang was reluctant to use his new supplies against the Japanese. He was waiting instead for the final showdown with the Communists. Courtesy of the Collection of the Historical Commission, Central Committee of the Kuomintang.*

*Japanese occupation troops in Nanjing after the Nanjing Massacre, December 1937. Chinese historians claim Japanese troops executed over 200,000 Nanjing citizens in an attempt to intimidate the Guomindang government into surrendering.Courtesy of the Military Museum of China, Beijing.*

rents, and encouraged them to participate in making political, economic, and military deci-sions in their communities. By addressing the needs of poor peasants, Mao and the Communists were able to enlist widespread sup-port among a large but ignored segment of Chinese society. While the Communists fought hard against the Japanese invasion, they focused their energies and resources on devising policies aimed at garnering the support of China's rural poor for a showdown with the Guomindang. By the end of the war in 1945, a fifth of the Chinese population was living under Communist rule in "liberated" areas.

### Civil War, 1945–1949

Soon after the United States dropped atom bombs on the Japanese cities of Hiroshima and Nagasaki in early August 1945, Japan surren-dered to the Allied forces, bringing World War II and the War of Resistance to an abrupt end.

Suddenly Communists and Nationalists were scrambling to seize formerly Japanese-occupied territory. Communists quickly established their main area of military strength in Manchuria and northern China, while the Guomindang took control of major urban centers and coastal and southern regions. Despite attempts to mediate a peaceful settlement over who would govern China, full-scale fighting soon erupted as neither side would compromise with its archenemy.

Early in the civil war it looked as though the Nationalists might prevail. They controlled key cities, their well-equipped troops far outnum-bered Communist troops, and they had support from the United States. But soon after the first year of fighting, their military might began to crumble. Eight years of war with Japan had drained the strength and morale of the Nationalist forces, and widespread corruption in the military led many soldiers to desert.

Public support for the Guomindang deterio-rated badly. Poor decisions by Chiang's govern-ment, such as printing vast amounts of new money to finance its war against the Communists, led to runaway inflation that brought economic hard-

Communists get more support from the people

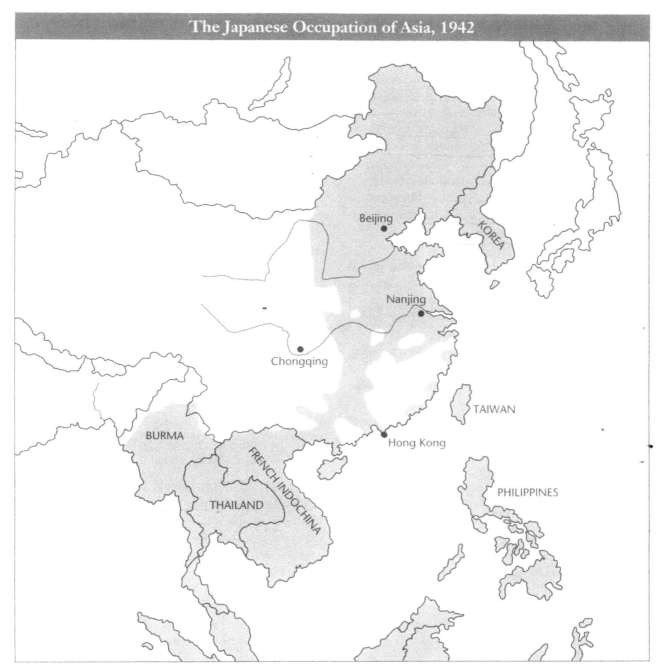

**The Japanese Occupation of Asia, 1942**

*Adapted from* The Rise of Modern China, *by Immanuel Hsu. Hong Kong: Oxford University Press, 1978, p. 706.*
*Attempting to establish the "Greater East Asia Co-Prosperity Sphere," Japan advanced into East and Southeast Asia and stayed until the end of World War II.*

ship for most Chinese and drove millions into abject poverty. Rampant corruption in government further undermined support for the Guomindang throughout the country.

On the other hand, the War of Resistance had revitalized the Communists. They had used this time to perfect guerrilla tactics against Japanese troops and to develop their sweeping social and land reform programs in remote "liberated areas." After Japan's surrender, the Communists moved swiftly to capture new territory, where they quickly seized land from rich landlords and

## Peasants as Vanguards of the Revolution

During Mao Zedong's lifetime, most Chinese lived in the countryside, as they had for centuries. Understanding that the peasants were crucial to the success of the revolution, Mao cultivated their loyalty, and they became his devoted followers. Even after the Communist victory in 1949, Mao knew how important it was for him to remain popular among the peasants. In the following passages, Mao discusses his belief that the peasants were vanguards of the revolution.

In a very short time . . . several hundred million peasants will rise like a mighty storm, like a hurricane, a force so swift and violent that no power, however great, will be able to hold it back. They will smash all the trammels [restraints] that bind them and rush forward along the road to liberation. They will sweep all the imperialists, warlords, corrupt officials, local tyrants and evil gentry into their graves. . . .

[A] revolution is not a dinner party, or writing an essay, or painting a picture, or doing embroidery; it cannot be so refined, so leisurely and gentle, so temperate, kind, courteous, restrained and magnanimous. A revolution is an insurrection, an act of violence by which one class overthrows another. . . .

According to the survey of Changsha County, the poor peasants comprise 70 percent, the middle peasants 20 percent, and the landlords and the rich peasants 10 percent of the population in the rural areas. . . . This great mass of poor peasants . . . are . . . the vanguard in the overthrow of the feudal forces. . . . Without the poor peasants there would be no revolution. To deny their role is to deny the revolution. To attack them is to attack the revolution. . . .

From "Report on an Investigation of the Peasant Movement in Hunan" (March 1927), in *Selected Works*, Vol. 1 (Peking: Foreign Language Press, 1965), pp. 23–24, 28, 32–33.

If our comrades . . . understand that the revolution must at all costs be spread throughout the country, then they should in no way neglect or underestimate the question of the immediate interests, the well-being, of the broad masses. For the revolutionary war is a war of the masses; it can be waged only by mobilizing the masses and relying on them. . . .

[A]ll the practical problems in the masses' everyday life should claim our attention. If we attend to these problems, solve them and satisfy the needs of the masses . . . they will truly rally round us and give us their warm support. . . .

I earnestly suggest . . . that we pay close attention to . . . the problems of land and labour to those of fuel, rice, cooking oil and salt. . . .

What is a true bastion [something that is used as a defense against attack] of iron? It is the masses, the millions upon millions of people who genuinely and sincerely support the revolution. That is the real iron bastion which no force can smash, no force whatsoever. . . .

From "Be Concerned with the Well-Being of the Masses, Pay Attention to Methods of Work" (January 27, 1934), in *Selected Works*, Vol. 1 (Peking: Foreign Language Press, 1965), pp. 147–50.

We Communists are like seeds and the people are like the soil. Whenever we go, we must unite with the people, take root and blossom among them. Wherever our comrades go, they must build good relations with the masses, be concerned for them and help them overcome their difficulties. We must unite with the masses; the more of the masses we unite with, the better. We must go all out to mobilize the masses, expand the people's forces and, under the leadership of our Party, defeat the aggressor and build a new China. . . .

From "On the Chungking Negotiations" (October 17, 1945), in *Selected Works*, Vol. 4 (Peking: Foreign Language Press, 1961), pp. 58–59.

*Peasant conscripts roped together and led off for induction into the Guomindang army during the Chinese Civil War. The Guomindang forced many peasants to join its army and fight the Communists. These unwilling recruits often ran away at the first opportunity. Courtesy of the Library of Congress.*

*Under the Guomindang government in the 1940s inflation soared. People had to carry bundles of paper money to buy daily necessities. Courtesy of the Military Museum of China, Beijing.*

the *paper majority is happy* redistributed it to poor peasants. Communists also publicly tried and punished those accused of collaborating with the Japanese during the occupation. The Communist land reform and anti-traitor campaigns succeeded in gaining the support of many poor peasants, some of whom enthusiastically joined the Communist army.

Communist military strength started to snowball. More and more peasant recruits joined the Communist ranks so that by the end of the civil war the Communists' troop strength surpassed the Nationalists'. As the People's Liberation Army (PLA) began winning large-scale battles in northern China, Communists started picking up strong support in urban areas. More and more city dwellers, fed up with the deepening economic crisis and Guomindang corruption, turned to the Communists as China's only hope of reuniting the country and solving its pressing problems.

The Nationalist collapse was swift, and by May 1948, a Communist victory seemed in the cards. In January 1949 the PLA, having seized control of all of North China, marched victoriously into Beijing. On October 1, 1949, confi-

*Mao Zedong declaring the establishment of the People's Republic of China from atop Tiananmen (Gate of Heavenly Peace), Beijing, October 1, 1949. Courtesy of the Collection of the Historical Commission, Central Committee of the Kuomintang.*

dent of final victory, Mao Zedong stood atop the main gate to the Qing imperial palace and formally declared the founding of the People's Republic of China.

Chiang Kai-shek and the Guomindang government fled in defeat to the island of Taiwan on December 8. <u>The Communist conquest and reunification of mainland China was complete.</u>

## Questions

1. Define "revolution." Would you describe the Communist revolution in China as a political revolution where the form of government changes, a social revolution where power shifts among classes, or both? Explain.

2. In your opinion, why did Mao Zedong and the Communists choose to focus on gaining the support of the peasants?

3. What were some of the weaknesses of the Guomindang that led to its defeat in 1949?

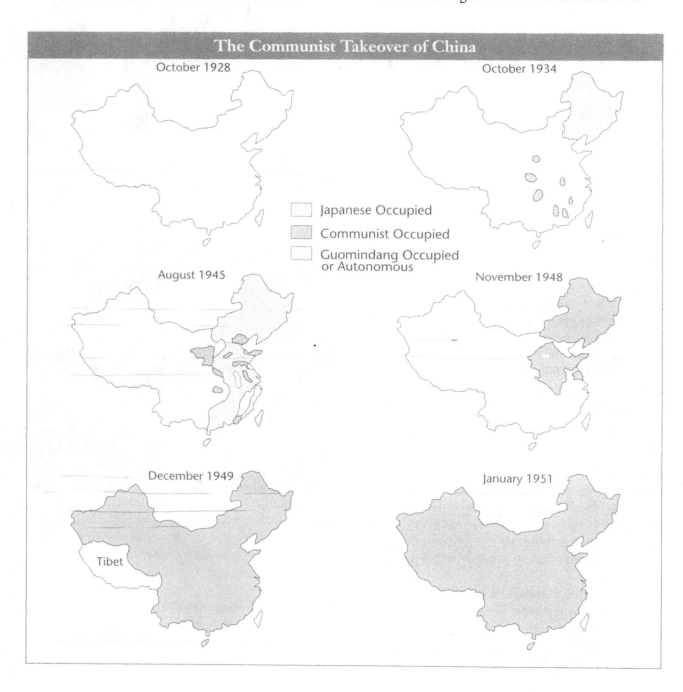

**The Communist Takeover of China**

October 1928

October 1934

Japanese Occupied
Communist Occupied
Guomindang Occupied or Autonomous

August 1945

November 1948

December 1949

Tibet

January 1951

## Reading: *From Marxism to Marxism—Leninism to Maoism*

When Mao Zedong became leader of his country in 1949, he renamed it the People's Republic of China (PRC). He vowed that this Communist nation would be true to the principles of "Marxist–Leninist thought." The PRC, he said, would weed out the "bourgeois element" and move with vigor and confidence to eliminate all "class antagonisms" in order to achieve the "Communist Utopia." At that point, the "Great Proletariat Class," together with the peasants, would rule through the Communist Party.

Mao spoke in stark contrast to Confucianism, which had guided China for so long. Mao did not refer to the Five Cardinal Relationships or to filial piety. Where did Mao's ideas come from? In this reading we look at the roots of his thinking. We discuss the Marxist tradition that he followed, focusing first on the development of Marxism, then on Marxism–Leninism, and finally on Maoism.

*Karl Marx (1818–1883). Courtesy of the Library of Congress.*

## Marxism

Karl Marx was a great intellectual who inspired revolution in half the globe and whose thoughts still exert a tremendous influence. Born in Germany to a prosperous family, Marx early on showed an intellectual bent. In college he became fascinated with the thinking of the philosopher G. W. F. Hegel. Marx was particularly interested in what Hegel called a dialectical process. According to Hegel, every idea produces an opposite idea. Eventually the two opposites merge or synthesize into a new idea, which in turn creates its own opposition. Hegel thought of history as an ongoing dialectical process.

Marx used the idea of the dialectic in thinking about the economy, that is, about how wealth in a community is produced and how people's needs and wants are met. For Marx, the important dialectic was the struggle between the ruling class and the class being ruled. He believed that class struggle was the process that moved history. "The history of all hitherto existing society," he wrote in *The Communist Manifesto*, "is the history of class struggles. Freeman and slave, patrician and plebeian, lord and serf . . . in a word, oppressor and oppressed, stood in constant opposition to one another, carried on an uninterrupted, now hidden, now open fight, a fight that each time ended, either in a revolutionary reconstitution of society at large, or in the common ruin of the contending classes."

Marx lived during the Industrial Revolution, when factory workers and other wage earners, whom Marx called the proletariat, lived and worked in poverty and misery. The proletariat labored for the wealthy and powerful capitalists that Marx called the bourgeoisie, who owned the factories and other means of production. According to Marx, the important class struggle in the nineteenth century was between the bourgeoisie and the oppressed proletariat. Eventually, Marx believed, the proletariat would wrest control from the bourgeoisie and set up a "dictatorship of the proletariat." What fascinated Marx about the proletariat taking over was that for the first time in history the ruling class would be the majority of the population. In time, all remnants of the bourgeois class would disappear, and there would be only one class. The cycle of class antagonism would end; in this Communist Utopia all would work to the best of their ability and receive all they needed for a comfortable life. This idea was reflected in the Marxist saying "From each according to his abilities, to each according to his needs."

## Marxism–Leninism

The second great person in the history of Communism was Vladimir Ilyich Ulyanov, a Russian revolutionary who went by the name of Lenin. Marx theorized about revolution; Lenin lived a revolutionary's life. He believed that Marx's analysis of history was correct, but he thought he needed to revise and elaborate on certain points. Lenin faced practical problems in applying Marx's ideas to Russia. Marx had said little about how to seize power, and Lenin wanted to overthrow the system of tsars that he hated. He also needed to justify a Communist revolution in Russia, a land of peasants, not an industrial state that Marx believed was ripe for revolution.

Lenin thought the only way a Communist movement had any hope of taking over a country was if the party itself was a tightly controlled group of revolutionaries bound to secrecy and agreed on actions and tactics. This group would lead and act for the proletariat but would not necessarily include members of the proletariat. (Indeed, Lenin and his close associates were of the middle class, not the proletariat.) Lenin believed that only a small group of disciplined revolutionaries could seize power. Any larger group could be too easily infiltrated by government agents, and any disagreement in the ranks would weaken the revolutionary will.

In Lenin's judgment, any action that would lead to the establishment of a Communist state was good, no matter how treacherous, deceitful, or cruel. Slogans need not be truthful, he claimed, if only they incite people to action. This kind of thinking was summed up in the statement "The end justifies the means," repeated often within Communist circles.

*Vladimir Ilyich Lenin (1870–1924). Courtesy of the Library of Congress.*

How could revolution occur in Russia, a land of peasants? Unlike Marx, who said that revolution would come to industrialized countries where the proletariat was large, Lenin said that revolution could occur where industrialization was just beginning. And unlike Marx, who dismissed the role of the peasantry in revolution, Lenin argued that peasants could become a revolutionary force and an ally of the proletariat.

Lenin expanded on the idea of the dictatorship of the proletariat, an idea that Marx mentioned only briefly. For Lenin, the dictatorship of the proletariat entailed seizing all property owned by the bourgeoisie and having the state control and distribute all property and goods. The state would become landlord and boss, and in so doing, act in the people's interest. In Russia, where the proletariat was small, Lenin saw state control as a way to industrialize the country rapidly and create a proletariat class. At the same time, the state would ensure that no bourgeois class formed to exploit the workers. (Lenin was practical enough not to hold to this view rigidly. He later allowed for some private ownership of property.) In 1917 Lenin led a group of revolutionaries called the Bolsheviks to power and established the Soviet Union.

## Maoism

The best-known figure in twentieth-century China, Mao Zedong, was born to a peasant family in 1893. When he was eighteen, he witnessed the collapse of the Qing dynasty. He cut off his queue and for a short time served as a private in the army of his home province, Hunan. Soon after, he left his family's farm and rebelled against his parents by rejecting the marriage they had arranged for him.

Although Mao had only a modest education, he was eager to learn. On his own he studied the writings of a wide range of important Western and Chinese thinkers. In 1919 he moved to Beijing, where he landed a clerical job at the Beijing University library. There he read many books, including *The Communist Manifesto* and other Marxist books that had just been translated into Chinese. He became active in literary and political groups, and in July 1921 he became a Hunan delegate to the first meeting of the Chinese Communist Party (CCP), held in Shanghai.

In the early years of the Chinese Communist movement, the Soviet Union's influence was strong. CCP members were well acquainted with Lenin's thinking and that of his successor, Joseph Stalin. Mao accepted Lenin's idea of a disciplined revolutionary elite working on behalf of the masses, and he elaborated on Lenin's belief that peasants could join forces with the proletariat. Mao argued that China could have a revolution based on an alliance among peasants, factory workers, and soldiers and that the revolution should begin in the countryside and then move to the cities. At this time most CCP members dismissed the role of peasants in the revolution. But Mao's thinking eventually held sway because China was a rural country with a huge population of poor peasants. And as their living conditions worsened, these peasants became increasingly attracted to Communism.

The Long March of 1934–1935 made Mao the undisputed leader of the Communist movement. (See the map of the Long March and its legend.) Soon after, during the struggle against the Japanese occupation, Mao skillfully brought the peasants into the fighting, at the same time

*Mao Zedong (1893–1976) in 1921, the year the Chinese Communist Party was founded. Courtesy of the Military Museum of China, Beijing.*

gaining their support for the Communist Party. The CCP became a well-disciplined guerrilla fighting unit, more or less along the Leninist model. Finally, in 1949, Mao led the CCP to victory over the Guomindang. (See the reading "Chiang Kai-shek.")

One reason Mao could win the support of the peasantry was that he harmonized the old with the new. He was well read in both traditional Chinese thinking and the revolutionary ideas of Communism, and he combined the two effectively in speeches and writings. In fact, before the 1949 CCP victory, he quoted Confucius even more than he did Marx and Lenin. But once Mao came to power, he distanced himself from China's past, and at the height of the Cultural Revolution (see Section 4 of this chapter), he denounced Confucianism as one of the evils passed on from old China.

When Mao's power within the Communist Party was threatened, he created a personality cult that gave him tremendous popular support and enabled him to prevail over his political opponents. From 1949 until his death in 1976, he remained China's foremost leader.

## Questions

1. Explain the saying "From each according to his abilities, to each according to his needs." Do you agree with this idea?
2. What did Lenin mean by "the dictatorship of the proletariat"? How does it compare with the economic system in which you live?
3. Trace the development of Communist thinking, from Marxism through Marxism–Leninism to Maoism.

## Extension Activities

1. **Videos.** Suggested videos on the period covered by this section: *The Threat That Was Japan: The Genius That Was China*, produced by Film Australia for NOVA; *China in Revolution, 1911–1949*, produced by Ambrica Productions; and *The Family*, based on Mao Dun's classic novel of life during the Japanese invasion.
2. **Research.** Look into the Tibetan independence movement. What does it aim to achieve? Who supports it? Do Tibetans and the Chinese government agree on when Tibet became a part of China? Find a map that shows Tibet as an independent nation.

## Further Reading

### Peasant Life in China
Hinton, William. *Fanshen: A Documentary of Revolution in a Chinese Village*. New York: Vintage Books, 1966.
Huang, Philip C. C. *The Peasant Economy and Social Change in North China*. Stanford: Stanford University Press, 1985.
Myrdal, Jan. *Report From a Chinese Village*. New York: Random House, 1965.

### Warlords
Chi, Hsi-Sheng. *Warlord Politics in China, 1916–1928*. Stanford: Stanford University Press, 1976.

### The Chinese Communist Revolution
Bianco, Lucien. *Origins of the Chinese Revolution, 1915–1949*. Stanford and London: Stanford University Press and Oxford University Press, 1971.

Chalmers, Charles A. *Peasant Nationalism and Communist Power: The Emergence of Revolutionary China, 1937–1945*. Stanford: Stanford University Press, 1962.
Ch'en, Jerome. *Mao and the Chinese Revolution*. London: Oxford University Press, 1965.
Skocpol, Theda. *States and Social Revolution: A Comparative Analysis of France, Russia, and China*. Cambridge: Cambridge University Press, 1979.
Snow, Edgar. *Red Star over China*. New York: Grove Press, 1968.

### Chiang Kai-shek and the Guomindang
Eastman, Lloyd E. *Seeds of Destruction: Nationalist China in War and Revolution, 1937–1949*. Stanford: Stanford University Press, 1984.
Eastman, Lloyd E., Jerome Ch'en, Suzanne Pepper, and Lyman P. Van Slyke. *The Nationalist Era in China, 1927–1949*. New York: Cambridge University Press, 1991.
Sheridan, James E. *China in Disintegration: The Republican Era in Chinese History, 1912–1949*. New York: The Free Press, 1975.

### Marxism
Heilbroner, Robert L. *The Worldly Philosophers: The Lives, Times, and Ideas of the Great Economic Thinkers*. 5th ed. New York: Simon and Schuster, 1980, pp. 133–167.
Heilbroner, Robert L. *Marxism: For and Against*. New York: Norton, 1980.
Marx, Karl, and Friedrich Engels. *The Communist Manifesto, with an Introduction by A. J. P. Taylor*. New York: Penguin Books, 1967.

### Marxism–Leninism
Appignanesi, Richard. *Lenin for Beginners*. New York: Pantheon Books, 1980.
Draper, Hal. *The Dictatorship of the Proletariat from Marx to Lenin*. New York: Monthly Review Press, 1987.
Service, Robert. *Lenin, A Political Life: The Strengths of Contradiction*. Vol. 1. London: Macmillan, 1985.
Service, Robert. *Lenin: A Political Life: Worlds in Collision*. Vol. 2. Bloomington and Indianapolis: Indiana University Press, 1991.
Shub, David. *Lenin, A Biography*. London: Harmondsworth Penguin Books, 1966.
Williams, Robert Charles. *The Other Bolsheviks: Lenin and His Critics*. Bloomington: Indiana University Press, 1986.

## Maoism

Lawrence, Alan. *Mao Zedong: a Bibliography.* New York: Greenwood Press, 1991.

Meisner, Maurice. *Mao's China and After.* New York: Free Press, 1986.

Schram, Stuart R., ed. *Quotations from Chairman Mao Tse-Tung.* New York: Bantam Books, 1967.

Schram, Stuart R. *The Thought of Mao Tse-tung.* New York: Cambridge University Press, 1989.

Schwartz, Benjamin. *Chinese Communism and the Rise of Mao.* Cambridge, MA.: Harvard University Press, 1966.

Selden, Mark. *The Yenan Way in Revolutionary China.* Cambridge, MA.: Harvard University Press, 1971.

## Twentieth-Century China

Hsu, Immanuel C. Y. *The Rise of Modern China.* 4th ed. New York and Oxford: Oxford University Press, 1990.

Spence, Jonathan D. *The Search for Modern China.* New York and London: W. W. Norton & Company, Inc., 1990.

# Winning Hearts and Minds

*Section* **2**

*C*ommunists used forms of propaganda to win the trust and support of poor peasants throughout China. Propaganda taught peasants about Communist programs and helped convince them that their lives would improve under Communist rule. As a result, millions of poor peasants joined the Communist ranks and played a pivotal role in defeating the Guomindang.

Since 1949, Communist leaders have ordered a number of mass mobilizations in which the government tried to engage all citizens in carrying out its directives designed to radically change Chinese society. Large-scale propaganda campaigns, aimed at reaching every man, woman, and child in the People's Republic of China, played an important part in these mobilizations. This section looks at how Communists have used a popular form of entertainment—drama —for propaganda purposes.

## Activity: Enacting the Play

During the civil war with the Guomindang, theater troupes served as the most powerful Communist propaganda weapon in the countryside. Along with every Communist army, they traveled from town to town staging melodramas or "living newspapers," in which performers acted out the Communist version of the latest news events. In rural areas these popular productions drew crowds starved for information and entertainment. Propaganda theater proved an effective way for Communists to indoctrinate their largely illiterate peasant audiences with Communist ideology, to explain their reforms, and to portray themselves as strong nationalists.

Even after defeating the Guomindang, Chinese Communists relied on theatrical performances to propagandize. This section includes

*The China Peking Opera Troupe gives a performance of* The Red Lantern *for poor peasants in the countryside. Courtesy of* China Pictorial, *February 1969.*

an excerpt from a well-known Chinese revolutionary opera, *The Red Lantern*. This opera, which takes place during the War of Resistance, was written in 1964. As you read the excerpt, think about what values and behavior the opera condemns and what values and behaviors it promotes.

1. The teacher will assign you to a group with three other students. Take turns reading aloud the excerpt from *The Red Lantern*, which follows these directions. Do not take roles yet.

2. After your group has read the excerpt, answer the following questions. You should work together, with each person recording the group's responses.

    a. What does the opera say about class loyalty and the poor?
    b. Give four adjectives that could describe the heroes and heroines in this opera. Why are they unafraid of death?
    c. What do you think the red lantern in the story symbolizes?
    d. What does *The Red Lantern* say about women's role in fighting for their country and the Communist cause?
    e. What is the propaganda message of the opera; in other words, what does it try to teach its audience?

3. Share your group's responses with the class. As you listen to what the other groups say, take notes to improve your own responses.
4. Your group is now a propaganda theater troupe that will perform Scene 8 of the revolutionary opera *The Red Lantern*. Although it is an opera, you will present this excerpt as a radio play. Actors need not memorize their lines but should be familiar enough with them to give a dramatic reading. To prepare for the performance, do the following.

    a. Decide who will take the following roles or role combinations.

        1. **Reader 1.** Because you will perform *The Red Lantern* as a radio drama, the Readers will read scene introductions and stage directions to help the audience visualize the scenes.
        **Sergeant,** aide to Hatoyama.
        **Sound-effects person,** responsible for creating sound effects that will help your performance come alive for the listening audience.
        2. **Hatoyama,** chief of the Japanese police.
        **Hou,** Hatoyama's Chinese assistant.
        **Reader 2.**

        3. **Li Yu-ho,** railroad switchman, member of the CCP and son of Granny.
        **Aunt Liu,** Tieh-mei's neighbor.
        4. **Li Tieh-mei,** daughter of Li Yu-ho.
        **Granny,** Tieh-mei's grandmother.

    b. Choose a director who will help the members perform better.
    c. Rehearse by reading your lines. Those playing more than one role should use different voices to denote different characters. The director should pay special attention to the stage directions to get a feel for the dramatic mood of the opera. The sound-effects person should decide which scenes need what type of sound effects. The director should coach the actors and sound effects person to perform effectively. The director may stop the reading at any point to improve the performance. Remember, the purpose of this opera is to propagandize, to teach a lesson about proper behavior. The more forceful the acting, the clearer the lesson.

5. Review the main ideas of the opera by rereading your responses to the questions in step 2.
6. After all the troupes have rehearsed, the teacher will ask for volunteers to perform the radio play for the class. You may volunteer to perform your role, or your entire group may ask to perform. The teacher might assign roles instead of soliciting volunteers.
7. If you are not performing, you will be in the radio audience. Position yourself so that you cannot see the performers. As you listen to the performance, consider its effectiveness at propagandizing. Write three things you like about it and three suggestions for improving it.
8. After you share your evaluations with the class, respond to these questions:

    a. What makes propaganda effective?
    b. How do students today differ from the Chinese audience that revolutionary theater was aimed at?

## Reading: *The Red Lantern*

(Scenes 8, 9, 10, and 11, with minor adaptations, are from Walter J. Meserve and Ruth I. Meserve, eds., *Modern Drama from Communist China*. New York: New York University Press, 1970, pp. 359–367. The summary of Scenes 1–7 is from Edward Gunn, *Twentieth-Century Chinese Drama: An Anthology*. Bloomington: Indiana University Press, 1983, pp. 400–401.)

| | |
|---|---|
| Reader 1: | **SETTING** |
| | *North China, during the War of Resistance to Japan (1937–1945)* |

(Scenes 1 through 7 and Scenes 9 through 11 are summarized. Scene 8 and part of Scene 9 are reprinted.)

| | |
|---|---|
| Reader 2: | **SCENES 1–7 (SUMMARY)** |

Li Yu-ho, a railroad switchman, lives with his adoptive mother, Granny Li, and his adopted daughter, Tieh-mei. Each of the three is the sole survivor of worker families wiped out by warlords, and each has become a firm supporter of the Communist Party in its underground guerrilla warfare against the Japanese during the War of Resistance to Japan, 1937–45.

Li Yu-ho has been assigned the task of delivering a secret code to a guerrilla unit in the Cypress Mountains; he is to identify himself by carrying a red lantern. However, Wang Lien-chu, a former member of the underground, informs Hatoyama, chief of the Japanese gendarmerie (military police), of Li's mission. Arrested and tortured, Li will not reveal the location of the code. Hatoyama now arrests Granny Li and Tieh-mei, hoping to use them to extract information from Li, who earlier did inform them of the code's location. Just before their arrest, Granny Li has told Tieh-mei for the first time that no blood relationship exists among the members of their little family.

| | |
|---|---|
| Reader 2: | **SCENE 8** |
| | *(Night. The Japanese police headquarters outside the prison. Enter* Hatoyama, Hou Hsien–pu *and the* Sergeant.*)* |
| Hatoyama: | It doesn't look as if we shall get anywhere with our interrogation. Hurry up and get the tape recorder ready. We'll hear what the old woman says when she meets her son. We may find out something. |
| Hou and Sergeant: | Yes, sir. |
| Hatoyama: | Bring the old woman in. |
| Hou: | Yes, sir. Fetch the old woman. |
| Reader 1: | *(Two Japanese gendarmes bring* Granny *in.)* |
| Hatoyama: | Do you know this place, madam? |

Granny:    It's the police headquarters.

Hatoyama *(pointing):*    And over there?

Reader 1:    (Granny *glances in the direction that* Hatoyama *is pointing)*

Hatoyama *(with a menacing smile):*
 That's the gate to paradise, where your son will [ascend] to heaven.

 (Granny *shivers.)*

Hatoyama:    When a man has committed a crime, madam, and his mother refuses to save his life, don't you think she is rather cruel?

Granny:    What do you mean, Mr. Hatoyama? You've arrested my son for no reason and thrown him into prison. Now you want to kill him. You are the ones that are committing a crime, you are the ones that are cruel. How can you shift the blame for his murder on to me?

Hatoyama:    Have you thought what will come of talking like that, old lady?

Granny:    The lives of our family are in your hands. You can do whatever you like.

Hatoyama *(controlling himself):*
 All right, go and see your son.

 This is his last chance, old lady. I hope you will all decide to steer clear of trouble and be reunited as one family.

Granny:    I know what's right.

Hatoyama:    Take her away.

Reader 1:    (Hou Hsien-pu, Hatoyama's *Chinese lieutenant, takes* Granny *away.)*

Hatoyama:    Take Li to the execution grounds.

Sergeant:    Bring Li Yu-Ho.

Reader 1:    (The scene changes. On the left is the path to the prison. In the rear on the left a slope leading to the execution grounds is backed by a high wall covered with barbed wire. It is dark. Offstage the Japanese gendarmes yell: "Fetch Li Yu-ho!" Chains clank.)

 (Li *enters)*

Li:    At the jailers' blood-thirsty cry I leave my cell;
 Though my hands and feet are manacled and fettered
 They cannot chain my soaring spirit.
 Hatoyama has tortured me to get the code;
 My bones are broken, my flesh torn, but firm my will.
 Walking boldly to the execution grounds
 I look up and see the red flag of revolution,

         The flames of the resistance.
         Not for long will these invaders lord it over us,
         And once the storm is past fresh flowers will bloom;
         New China will shine like the morning sun,
         Red flags will flutter over all the country—
         I smile through tears of joy at the thought of it.
         I have done very little for the Party,
         Worst of all, I failed to send the code to the hills;
         That renegade Wang's only contact was with me,
         The wretch can betray no one else;
         And my mother and daughter are as staunch as steel,
         So Hatoyama may search heaven and earth,
         But he will never find the secret code.

**Reader 1:**     (Granny *enters and looks round.*)

**Granny** (*seeing* Li, *cries*):

         Yu-Ho!

**Li** (*startled*):     Mother!

**Granny:**     My son.

**Li:**     Mother.

**Reader 1:**     (Granny *runs over to put her arms around him.*)

**Granny:**     Again I live through that day seventeen years ago,
         And burn with hate for the foe of my class and country.
         The cruel Japanese devils
         Have beaten and tortured you, my son, my son!

**Li:**     Don't grieve for me, mother.

**Granny:**     I shouldn't grieve to have such a fine son.

**Li:**     Brought up in a hard school
         I'll fight and never give ground;
         Though they break every bone in my body,
         Though they lock me up until I wear through my chains.
         As long as our country is ravaged my heart must bleed;
         As long as the war lasts my family is in danger;
         However hard the road to revolution,
         We must press on in the steps of the glorious dead.
         My one regret if I die today
         Is the debt I have left unpaid.
         I long to soar like an eagle through the sky,
         Borne on the wind above the mountain passes
         To rescue our millions of suffering countrymen—
            Then how gladly would I die for the revolution!

Granny:    That unpaid debt is in good hands,
    Cost what it may, we shall pay it.

Reader 1:    *(Hou enters with the guards.)*

Hou:    I'll say this for you: You certainly know how to keep your mouths shut and not give anything away. Come on, old woman. Captain Hatoyama wants you.

Li:    Mother . . .

Granny:    Don't worry, son. I know what he wants.

Reader 1:    *(Granny goes out fearlessly, followed by the guards.)*

Hou:    Bring Tieh-mei here! *(Exit.)*

Li *(calling):*    Tieh-mei!

Reader 1:    *(Tieh-mei comes running in)*

Tieh-mei:    Dad!

Li:    Tieh-mei.

Tieh-mei:    Dad.
    I hoped day and night to see my dad again,
    Yet I hardly know you, so battered and drenched with blood
    I wish I could break your chains,
    Dear father . . .

Li *(smiling):*    Silly child.

Tieh-mei *(sobbing):*    If you have anything to say to me, Dad, tell me quickly.

Li:    Child,
    One thing I have wanted many times to tell you,
    It's been hidden in my heart for seventeen years . . .

Tieh-mei *(quickly stopping him):*

    Don't say it. You are my own true father.
    Don't say it, Father,
    I know the bitter tale of these seventeen years.
    You are so good, our country needs you;
    Why can't I die in your stead?
    Ah, Dad. *(She kneels and clasps Li's knees, sobbing.)*

Li:    Nurse your hatred in your heart.
    Men say that family love outweighs all else,
    But class love is greater yet.
    Listen, child, your dad is a poor man,
    With no money at home to leave you;

All I have is a red lantern,
I entrust it to your safe keeping.

Tieh-mei:    You have left me a priceless treasure,
How can you speak of money?
You have left me your integrity
To help me stand firm as a rock;
You have left me your wisdom
To help me see clearly through the enemy's wiles;
You have left me your courage
To help me fight those brutes;
This red lantern is our heirloom,
A treasure so great
That a thousand carts and boats
Could not hold it all.
I give you my word I shall keep the lantern safe.

Li:    As wave follows wave in the great Yangtse River,
Our red lantern will be passed from hand to hand.
If they let you go home,
Find friends to help settle that debt and I'll be content.

Tieh-mei    I will, father.

Li:    Good child.

Hou *(to* Tieh-mei*):*    What about the secret code, girl?
(*She ignores him.*)

Hou:    Why don't you speak?

Tieh-mei:    My dad and my grandmother have said all there is to say. I've nothing to add.

Hou:    Why don't you speak?

Even this child is so pig-headed, confound her! Bring that old woman back.

Reader 1:    (*Two guards bring in* Granny.)

Hou:    Why don't you speak?

Now your whole family is here. Think well. If you don't give us the code, not one of you will leave this place alive.

Li:    They've tortured you, mother. The swine!

Granny:    It doesn't matter if my old bones ache a little, my heart is still sound.

Reader 1:    (Tieh-mei *sobs with her head on* Granny's *lap.*)
(*The* Sergeant *enters and* Tieh-mei *looks up.*)

Sergeant:    Captain Hatoyama gives you five more minutes to think it over. If you still won't give up the secret code, you will all be shot.

Granny *(indignantly):* You brutes, won't you even let the child go?

Sergeant: We'll spare no one.

Reader 1: (Li *and* Granny *look at* Tieh-mei, *who meets their eyes and straightens up.)*

(The *Sergeant* begins dragging Tieh-mei *away):*

Sergeant: Only five minutes left, girl. Give up the code and save your whole family. Speak!

Reader 1: (Tieh-mei *shakes off his hand and walks back to stand between* Granny *and* Li)

Sergeant: Where is the code?

Tieh-mei: I don't know.

Sergeant *(looking at his watch):*
Firing squad!

Li: There's no need for such a commotion. This is nothing much.

Granny: That's right, child, let's go together, the three of us.

Li: Tieh-mei, take Granny's other arm.

Tieh-mei: Right.

Li: Tieh-mei, mother, I'll lead the way. *(He holds himself proudly.)*

Reader 1: *(They begin to walk up the slope toward the execution grounds. Enter* Hatoyama.)

Hatoyama: Wait! I want to give you every chance. You can have another minute to think it over.

Li: Hatoyama, you can never kill all the Chinese people or Chinese Communists. I advise you to think that over.

Hatoyama *(frustratedly to himself):*
These Reds are the very devil. Carry out your orders.

Reader 1: *(Hatoyama leaves)*

Sergeant: Shoot them!

Reader 1: *(The three disappear from the slope followed by the sergeant and guards.)*

Li *(off stage):* Down with Japanese imperialism! Long live the Chinese Communist Party!

*(Two shots are heard.)*

Reader 1: (Tieh-mei *reappears on the slope. She is being pushed by two guards.)*

Tieh-mei *(walking down the slope in a daze, turns to call):*
Dad! Granny!

*Undaunted by torture, Li Yu-ho denounces Hatoyama. Courtesy of China Today [China Reconstructs], December, 1965.*

Reader 1:    (Hatoyama *and* Hou *come up behind* Tieh-mei)

Hatoyama:    Where is the code book? Tell me quick.

Reader 1:    (Tieh-mei *says nothing but stares at him with loathing.*)

Hatoyama:    Let her go.

Hou:    What? Let her go? (*He looks at* Hatoyama *in surprise.*)

Hatoyama:    Yes, let her go.

Hou:    Very good, sir.

Hou:    Get out, get out.

Reader 1:    (Tieh-mei *runs off.*)

Hou:    Why are you letting her off, sir?

Hatoyama (*smiling coldly*):
    If I kill them all, how can I find the code? This is called using a long line to catch a big fish.

Reader 2:    **SCENE 9**    *THE NEIGHBORS HELP*

    (*Back at* Li's *house. The door is sealed. The room wears an air of desolation.*)

(Tieh-mei *walks slowly in. She stares at the house, quickens her steps and pushing the door open steps inside. She looks around, crying.*)

Tieh-mei: Dad! Granny!

Reader 1: (*Then she rests her head on the table and sobs. Slowly rising, she sees the red lantern and picks it up.*)

Tieh-mei: Ah, red lantern, I've found you again but I shall never see Granny or Dad again. Granny, Dad, I know what you died for. I shall carry on your work. I've inherited the red lantern. That scoundrel Hatoyama has only let me go in the hope that I will lead them to the code. (*Pause.*) Never mind whether you arrest me or release me, you'll never get the code.

Reader 1: (*She puts down the red lantern and smooths her hair.*)

Tieh-mei: My heart is bursting with anger,
I grind my teeth with rage;
Hatoyama has tried every trick to get the code,
He has killed my granny and dad.
In desperation he threatened me,
But I defy his threats,
Nursing hatred in my heart;
No cry shall escape me,
No tears wet my cheeks,
But the sparks of my smoldering fury
Will blaze up in flames of anger
To consume this black reign of night.
Nothing can daunt me now:
Arrest, release, torture, imprisonment . . .
I shall guard the code with my life.
Wait, Hatoyama! This is Tieh-mei's answer.

Reader 1: (Tieh-mei *polishes the red lantern and rearranges her peddler's basket.*)

Tieh-mei (*sadly*): Granny, Dad, I'm leaving now. This isn't our home any more. Only the red lantern will be ours for ever. I promise to take the code to the north hills. I promise to avenge you. Don't you worry.

Reader 2: A neighbor, Aunt Liu, and a friend, Kuei-lan, hear Tieh-mei sobbing and slip into the room through a hole in the wall. Tieh-mei tells them about granny and Li Yu-ho. Aunt Liu tells Tieh-mei a spy has followed her and is waiting outside. Despite Tieh-mei's pleas, Aunt Liu insists on helping her escape, declaring,

Aunt Liu: No one but the poor will help the poor,
Two bitter gourds grow on a single vine;
We must save you from the tiger's jaws,
And then you can press on.

Tieh-mei changes clothes with Kuei-lan, and with red lantern in hand, slips out the door. The disguise works, and she successfully loses Hatoyama's spy who had been following her.

Reader 1:    **SCENE 10    *THE END OF THE RENEGADE***

Tieh-mei safely makes it to the northern town of Lungtan, where she encounters the Communist guerrillas "Knife-grinder" and Chou. The three set off for the Communist base in the north hills. But Hatoyama has sent agents to stop them. During a ferocious fight, the guerrillas kill the enemy agents and escape as a police siren wails in the distance.

Reader 2:    **SCENE 11    *THE TASK IS ACCOMPLISHED***

*(In the north hills, which rise steep and sheer, the guerrillas have formed a line stretching behind the hills. Halfway up the slope is a big red flag and scouts there are keeping a lookout.)*

*(Guerrilla officers come up the slope. The "Knife-grinder" appears. He salutes the Guerrilla commander and points behind him. Chou comes in with Tieh-mei. A bugle blows. Tieh-mei salutes the commander and gives him the code.)*

**The End**

---

### Activity: Persuasion and Propaganda

Propaganda is a form of persuasion in that it attempts to change our thinking, to influence our behaviors, or to change society. Mao believed that propaganda was necessary for people "to unlearn the bad habits and thoughts acquired from the old society" and to re-educate themselves to think as Communists. If people thought correctly, he reasoned, they would behave correctly. Mao and other government officials relied on propaganda to influence the thoughts and behaviors of the Chinese people. The Central Propaganda Department[1] endeavored to indoctrinate people in Communist ideology and urged them to comply with government policies and directives. Propaganda served to expose and criticize dissent and secure the Communist power base at the same time.

To those in the West the word "propaganda" has negative connotations. We associate propaganda with emotional slogans and half-truths that political leaders use to brainwash and control people.

1. Consider different ways people have tried to persuade others—nationally, statewide, or locally. List at least two examples each of fair and unfair ways of attempting to persuade others. Be as specific as you can.
2. Explain why you think your examples are fair or unfair forms of persuasion. Use the following questions as guides.

   a. What does the message appeal to? Reasoning and intelligence? Common sense? Emotions such as fear, jealousy, pride, compassion? Explain.
   b. Is the language clear? Does it use emotional slogans?
   c. Does the message seem to leave out important information?

3. Does propaganda differ from advertising? If so, how?

[1] The literal translation from the Chinese is the Centralized "Unite and Battle" Department.

## Activity: Persuading Others

In this activity you will attempt to change the thinking and behavior of society as a whole or of one segment of society.

1.  Think of one aspect you would like to change about American society. Or on a smaller scale, think of one thing you would like to change about the way people think and behave in your community, or even in your school. Write it down.
2.  Consider how you might attempt to bring about the change you want. For example, let us say you want people to stop polluting the lake near your town. People currently think that it does not matter if they throw their garbage in the lake. How might you use words, symbols, music, art, or drama to show why polluting the lake is bad and that dumping garbage in the lake should stop? You should also show the benefits of adopting new thinking and behavior. If people think that having a clean and unpolluted lake is important, they will stop throwing their garbage in it.
3.  Decide what medium best suits your message. You may create a work of art (drawing, painting, sculpture, cartoon), write a short story, a short play, a poem, or a song to put your message across.
4.  Avoid unfair forms of persuasion.

## Extension Activities

**Research**. You might want to investigate the way propaganda has been used in the United States. One example is the Voice of America; another is propaganda in film during World War II.

## Further Reading

Gunn, Edward M. *Twentieth-Century Chinese Drama: An Anthology*. Bloomington: Indiana University Press, 1983.

Holm, David. *Art and Ideology in Revolutionary China*. Oxford: Clarendon Press, 1991.

Meserve, Walter J., and Ruth Meserve, eds. *Modern Drama from Communist China*. New York and London: New York University Press and University of London Press, 1970.

Yu, Frederick T. T. *Mass Persuasion in Communist China*. New York: Frederick A. Praeger, 1964.

# 3 "Dare to Act": Restructuring Society and the Economy, from 1949

*A s you learned in Section 1, the Chinese Communists told the landless peasants they would take land from the rich and redistribute it to the poor. The Communists did as they had promised. Millions of peasants supported the Communist Party over the Guomindang, bringing the Communists to power in 1949. In this section we examine further reform efforts of Mao Zedong and Communist Party officials. These efforts aimed to change agricultural and industrial production as well as people's ways of life, with the goal of speedily improving the circumstances of poverty-stricken peasants. Mao used the phrase "dare to act" in pushing through sweeping fundamental changes.*

---

## Reading: *Land and Economic Reforms in the First Decade*

---

Once in power, the Communists continued to redistribute land and to seek other ways to improve the lives of the peasants. The leaders believed that one way was to bring families together in a collective effort to boost production. At first, peasants formed mutual-aid teams while being allowed to work their own land. Later, they formed cooperatives, pooling land and equipment and reaping rewards according to their contribution. Still later, they received an income based on the type of work they did and the size of their families. By the end of 1956, collectivization had spread throughout the country. And despite some resistance and disruption, production and incomes rose considerably.

While farms were being grouped into large collectives, Communist leaders instituted the First Five-Year Plan, modeled after a similar plan in the Soviet Union. Chinese officials designed the plan, which lasted from 1953 to 1957, to develop heavy industries such as production of steel, coal, and electric power. Their thinking was that heavy industry would employ surplus laborers from the countryside and stimulate production in other areas of the economy.

*After the Communists came to power, they rounded up landlords and former Guomindang officials for public denunciation and trials by "people's tribunals." In this picture a landlord in Kwangtung province is on trial for his life. People's tribunals executed many landlords throughout China. Courtesy of UPI/Bettman.*

pig iron fails b/c people don't know how to manefacture and they are making iron in their backyard

5 year plan fails because no enough industrializat in the cities. → great leap forward

groups of people out in graps for manefactur ↓ Don't reach goals so they make down their own stuff ↓ officials rised taxes high so they took more food causing a famine and 40-50 million dead

Communist soldier reading new land reform law to peasants after it was passed on June 28, 1950. Just a few years after the Communists had given poor peasants land, they began to abolish private property and create huge collectives. Courtesy of Shanghai People's Press.

A commune childcare center in Jiangxi province. A slogan on the wall says, ". . . People's commune, superior and happy." Courtesy of Shanghai People's Press.

Party cadres joining work on a reservoir project in Hubei province, circa 1957. During the 1950s the government carried out many large public works projects, such as the construction of dams and reservoirs to control flooding and produce hydroelectric power. Courtesy of Shanghai People's Press.

In general the First Five-Year Plan succeeded, but it failed to absorb the huge surplus of rural labor. Dissatisfied, Mao changed his strategy to push production to greater heights. The next step was the Great Leap Forward, Mao's grand design to mobilize the whole population in an effort to industrialize China quickly. As part of this effort, officials in 1958 abolished the vestiges of private plots and other means of production to create people's communes. Each commune included about thirty cooperatives of about 5,000 households, or 25,000 people each. Thus one commune held about 750,000 people, about as many as a medium-sized city.

Commune officials decided what to farm and manufacture, collected taxes, operated public kitchens and mess halls, and ran childcare centers, banks, and schools. By November 1958, party officials had transformed the entire countryside into communes. Unfortunately, Mao set unrealistic targets; he purged Communist Party leaders who disagreed or pointed out problems. Poor leadership, bad weather, and withdrawal of Soviet aid ended the Great Leap Forward in failure and famine.

## Questions

1. How does collective farming differ from individual farming? Why did the Communists institute collectivized farming?

2. The First Five-Year Plan, the Great Leap Forward, and people's communes were instituted in response to challenges confronting China's rulers. What were these challenges?

---

### Reading: *Experiencing the Great Leap*

In the following excerpt, author Jung Chang describes her experiences during the Great Leap Forward.

In the autumn of 1958, when I was six, I started going to a primary school about twenty minutes' walk from home, mostly along muddy cobbled back alleys. Every day on my way to and from school, I screwed up my eyes to search every inch of ground for broken nails, rusty cogs, and any other metal objects that had been trodden into the mud between the cobbles. These were for feeding into furnaces to produce steel, which was my major occupation. Yes, at the age of six, I was involved in steel production, and had to compete with my schoolmates at handing in the most scrap iron. All around me uplifting music blared from loudspeakers, and there were banners, posters, and huge slogans painted on the walls proclaiming "Long Live the Great Leap Forward!" and "Everybody, Make Steel!" Although I did not fully understand why, I knew that Chairman Mao had ordered the nation to make a lot of steel. In my school, crucible-like vats had replaced some of our cooking woks and were sitting on the giant stoves in the kitchen. All our scrap iron was fed into them, including the old woks, which had now been broken to bits. The stoves were kept permanently lit—until they melted down. Our teachers took turns feeding firewood into them around-the-clock, and stirring the scraps in the vats with a huge spoon. We did not have many lessons, as the teachers were too preoccupied with the vats. . . .

[Inside my family's compound] a huge furnace was erected in the parking lot. . . . My family's woks went into this furnace, together with all our cast-iron cooking utensils. We did not suffer from their loss, as we did not need them anymore. No private cooking was allowed now, and everybody had to eat in the canteen. The furnaces were insatiable. Gone was my parents' bed, a soft, comfortable one with iron springs. Gone also were the iron railings from the city pavements, and anything else that was iron. I hardly saw my parents for months.

*Beijing citizens collecting iron products to melt down during the Great Leap Forward, circa 1958. Courtesy of Shanghai People's Press.*

They often did not come home at all, as they had to make sure the temperature in their office furnaces never dropped.

It was at this time that Mao gave full vent to his half-baked dream of turning China into a first-class modern power. He called steel the "Marshal" of industry, and ordered steel output to be doubled in one year—from 5.35 million tons in 1957 to 10.7 million in 1958. But instead of trying to expand the proper steel industry with skilled workers, he decided to get the whole population to take part. There was a steel quota for every unit, and for months people stopped their normal work in order to meet it. The country's economic development was reduced to the simplistic question of how many tons of steel could be produced, and the entire nation was thrown into this single act. It was officially estimated that nearly 100 million peasants were pulled out of agricultural work and into steel production. They had been the labor force producing much of the country's food. Mountains were stripped bare of trees for fuel. But the output of this mass production amounted only to what people called "cattle droppings" (niu-shi-ge-da), meaning useless turds. . . .

In an effort to please Mao and the Communist Party officials when they visited the People's Communes, peasants made fantastic claims about the amount of grain and food they were producing.

It was a time when telling fantasies to oneself as well as others, and believing them, was practised to an incredible degree. Peasants moved crops from several plots of land to one plot to show Party officials that they had produced a miracle harvest. Similar "Potemkin fields" [fields that seemed impressive but were not real] were shown off to gullible—or self-blinded—agricultural scientists, reporters, visitors from other regions, and foreigners. Although these crops generally died within a few days because of untimely transplantation and harmful density, the visitors did not know that, or did not want to know. A large part of the population was swept into this confused, crazy world. "Self-deception while deceiving others" (zi-qi-qi-ren) gripped the nation. Many people—including agricultural

*Local officials said that the grain on the piece of land pictured here grew so dense and strong that a girl could sit on top of the stalks without bending them. In reality this effect was achieved by packing the area with crops moved over from other fields. These outrageous claims of unprecedented crop production were referred to as "exaggeration wind." From Duan Liancheng, Gu Jin, and Zhang Yuanlei, eds.,* As the Dragon Stirs. *Hong Kong: New Horizon Press, 1990, p. 104.*

scientists and senior Party leaders—said they saw the miracles themselves. Those who failed to match other people's fantastic claims began to doubt and blame themselves. Under a dictatorship like Mao's, where information was withheld and fabricated, it was very difficult for ordinary people to have confidence in their own experience or knowledge. Not to mention that they were now facing a nation-wide tidal wave of fervor which promised to swamp any individual coolheadedness. It was easy to start ignoring reality and simply put one's faith in Mao. To go along with the frenzy was by far the easiest course. To pause and think and be circumspect meant trouble. . . .

In many places, people who refused to boast of massive increases in output were beaten up until they gave in. In Yibin, some leaders of production units were trussed up with their arms behind their backs in the village square while questions were hurled at them:

"How much wheat can you produce per mu?"

"Four hundred jin" (about 450 pounds—a realistic amount).

Then, beating him: "How much wheat can you produce per mu?"

"Eight hundred jin."

Even this impossible figure was not enough. The unfortunate man would be beaten, or simply left hanging, until he finally said: "Ten thousand jin." Sometimes the man died hanging there because he refused to increase the figure, or simply before he could raise the figure high enough. . . .

Agriculture was also neglected because of the priority given to steel. Many of the peasants were exhausted from having to spend long hours finding fuel, scrap iron, and iron ore and keeping the furnaces going. The fields were often left to the women and children, who had to do everything by hand, as the animals were busy making their contribution to steel production. When harvest time came in autumn 1958, few people were in the fields.

The failure to get in the harvest in 1958 flashed a warning that a food shortage was on its way, even though official statistics showed a double-digit increase in agricultural output. It was officially announced that in 1958 China's wheat output had overtaken that of the United States. . . .

From Jung Chang, *Wild Swans: Three Daughters of China*. London: HarperCollins, 1993, pp. 291–93.

## Questions

1. Why did peasants make incredible claims of food production?
2. What was the writer Jung Chang's opinion of the Great Leap Forward? What words and phrases convey her opinion?
3. Create a different title for the reading "Experiencing the Great Leap Forward."

---

**Reading:** *The Great Leap Forward to the Great Proletarian Cultural Revolution*

---

The Great Leap Forward was well intended; it accelerated earlier efforts such as building dams and reservoirs and recruiting women into the work force. Nevertheless, it had devastating consequences. As we saw in the previous reading, Communist Party leaders, led by Mao Zedong, sought to industrialize quickly by diverting peasants from the fields and ordering them to make steel in "backyard furnaces." Other peasants were directed to labor on public works projects such as road building and dam construction. Added to this loss of farm workers, poor weather beginning in 1959 continued for three years. Crop production dropped precipitously.

Officials closed their eyes to this reality. Pretending that harvests were plentiful, they increased the amount of grain they took from the communes to feed city workers. Left with

*A review of Red Guards in Tiananmen Square carrying characters that say "Long Live the Great Cultural Proletarian Revolution," circa 1966. Courtesy of Shanghai People's Press.*

little to eat, tens of thousands of peasants died of starvation.

The disastrous results of the Great Leap Forward aggravated divisions among Communist Party leaders as more and more of them saw that Mao had made grave mistakes. Some, like Deng Xiaoping, promoted individual rather than collective responsibility and urged rewards to motivate peasants to work harder and produce more crops. Mao denounced this course of action as capitalistic and revisionist—revising the fundamental principles of Marxism–Leninism.

Mao believed that certain Communist Party officials were losing sight of the original vision of China as a revolutionary socialist society. Not only did he see them stressing individualism instead of the collective good; he also noted that they gave better opportunities to children of intellectuals and party officials than to working people and peasants. He feared that China would return to the dark days of the past, a path he believed the Soviet Union had taken.

The Great Leap Forward created a deep split among party leaders over the direction and the pace of change. In the ensuing power struggle, a prominent official, Minister of Defense Peng Dehuai, criticized the blunders of the Great Leap Forward. Taking the criticism as a personal attack, Mao flew into a rage, denounced Peng, and removed him from his post. A ground swell

*People's Liberation Army soldiers (left) laugh and jeer as those accused of being counterrevolutionaries are paraded through the streets of Beijing, 1967. The accused wear dunce caps inscribed with their names. Courtesy of UPI/Bettman.*

*As part of destroying the "Four Olds," Red Guards smash statues in the Temple of Confucius at Qufu, Confucius' ancestral home. From Duan Liancheng, Gu Jin, and Zhang Yuanlei, eds.,* As the Dragon Stirs. *Hong Kong: New Horizon Press, 1990, p. 144.*

*Communist official being denounced by Red Guards, 1967. Courtesy of Shanghai People's Press.*

*Red Guards changing a road name to "Anti-Imperialist Road," circa 1966. Courtesy of Shanghai People's Press.*

of Peng's supporters rallied behind him. Some wrote plays and essays in which they recounted as a parable the story of a famous court official of imperial times who had courageously sided with the people against the authorities. Mao's attack on one of these plays launched the Great Proletarian Cultural Revolution.

The Cultural Revolution, which began in 1966, was a nationwide movement led by Mao to mobilize the masses to attack and cleanse the party of revisionists. Key leaders in the party, government, and army were demoted or dismissed. To prevent China from taking "the revisionist road to capitalist restoration," Mao sought to cultivate a new generation of revolutionaries having unquestioned dedication to the revolution. To this end he formed groups of youthful Red Guards, who rampaged through the cities, entering homes and destroying the "Four Olds"—old ideas, old customs, old culture, and old habits. Officials and "intellectuals" (those who had at least an intermediate-level education) were paraded through the streets as criminals. For ten years until Mao's death in 1976, millions of innocent people were harassed and tortured. This decade-long period of anarchy has been called China's "Ten Lost Years."

## Questions

1. Did China "catch up with Great Britain in fifteen years"? Explain what happened.
2. Why did Mao launch the Great Proletarian Cultural Revolution?

## Child of the Revolution

In the following selection, Liang Heng describes how the Communist Revolution affected his family in the years before and during the Cultural Revolution. Liang first recounts his escape from a day-care center, where he lived before he turned four. Like other Chinese dedicated to Communism, his parents believed that the revolution came first, their family second.

Once when I was nearly four, I decided to escape from the child-care center. The idea of waiting through another Saturday afternoon was unbearable. I would stand with the other children in the office doorway, yelling out the names of those whose relatives we spotted coming to rescue them. I would become frantic and miserable as the possibility that I had been forgotten seemed more and more real. Then at last the frail figure of my beloved Waipo, my maternal grandmother, would appear to take me away. But this week I wouldn't have to wait. I had just discovered a doorway leading from the kitchen directly onto the Changsha streets, left ajar, perhaps, by the cooks now that the bitter winter weather had passed. So, during after-lunch nap, I crawled over the green bars of my crib and stole softly out, past the sleeping rows of my fellow inmates, past Nurse Nie dozing in her chair. I crept into the coal-dark kitchen with its silent black woks. Then I exploded out the door into the dazzling light of freedom.

The child-care center was hateful. You couldn't eat sweets when you wanted to, and you had to fold your hands behind your back and sing a song before the nurses would let you eat your meals. Then, if you ate too fast, they hit you over the head with a flyswatter. The songs and dances—like "Sweeping the Floor," "Working in the Factory," and "Planting Trees in the Countryside"—were fun, but I was constantly in trouble for wanting to dance the army dance when it was time for the hoeing dance or for refusing to take the part of the landlord, the wolf, or the lazybones. I also had problems with the interminable rest periods. We weren't allowed to get up even if we weren't tired, so I had nothing to do but stare at a small mole on my leg for hours at a time.

At the time, such early education was a privilege for which only the children of cadres were eligible. Although neither of my parents' ranks was high, my father's position as reporter, editor, and founding member of the Party newspaper the *Hunan Daily*, and my mother's as a promising cadre in the Changsha Public Security Bureau were enough to qualify me. My parents were deeply involved in all the excitement of working to transform China into a great Socialist country, eager to sacrifice themselves for others. They dreamed passionately of the day when they would be deemed pure and devoted enough to be accepted into the Party. It was only natural that the family come second; Father's duties at the newspaper often kept him away for several months at a time, and my mother came home only on Sundays, if at all, for she had a room in her own unit and stayed there to attend evening meetings. So at the age of three I was sent off to the child-care center for early training in Socialist thought through collective living far from the

potentially corrupting influence of family life. My departure may have been harder for my two grandmothers, of course. They had the major responsibility for raising the three of us children; I was the last child to go and they would miss me very much.

I had lived first with my paternal grandmother, my Nai Nai, a tall, stern, bony woman who always wore traditional black. She lived in the apartment the *Hunan Daily* had allotted to Father, two rooms on the second floor of a cadres' dormitory, spacious enough but with a shared kitchen and an outhouse some distance away. She was a pious Buddhist and a vegetarian, strict with herself and everyone else but her own grandchildren. . . .

[Later,] Nai Nai sent me to live with my maternal grandmother, my Waipo, who lived off a winding little alleyway not far away.

It was much more crowded there, since Waipo, my Uncle Yan, and his wife and their small children made three generations in a single dark room. But I liked the place for its liveliness and because I was Waipo's favorite. She gave me candies and took me everywhere with her, even to the free market to buy from the peasants who had carried in their vegetables from the suburbs. Waipo was a tiny woman with big twisted teeth and little wrinkled hands, talkative and lively and very different from Nai Nai. Her husband had died when she was young, after only two children, whereas Nai Nai's husband had given her nine before he slipped and fell on the icy road in front of the old City Gate. In the old society, a woman couldn't remarry and remain respectable, so Waipo had supported herself and her children by making shoe soles at home. She continued to do this even after Mother and Uncle Yan were grown and had jobs, and the cloth patches she used were among my first toys.

Another reason I liked living with Waipo was that Mother often preferred to go there on Sundays rather than to our own home, where Nai Nai was, because she didn't get along well with her mother-in-law. . . .

So it was Waipo's home that was my early emotional center, and it was there that I went on the fresh spring day of my flight. I had to cross a large street, but fortunately I made it from one side to the other without a mishap, and ran the remaining few hundred yards to the narrow room off the little gray alley.

To my utter dismay, Waipo didn't look at all glad to see me, "Little Fatso, what are you doing here?" she cried, and with scarcely a pause grabbed my hand and pulled me the few blocks to Nai Nai's home in the *Hunan Daily* compound. From there the two old ladies half lifted, half dragged me back to my confinement, ignoring my screams and tears. . . .

* * * * * * * * * *

[W]henever I went home to Waipo's, I hoped Mother would be there, for I loved her very much despite our limited time together. But when I was about four, I began to sense there was something wrong. She would come home looking worried and she never played with me, just talked on and on with Uncle Yan in a hushed Liuyang County dialect which I couldn't understand. Finally, one Saturday afternoon it was Nai Nai who came to get me, and I was told Mother had gone away and I shouldn't go to Waipo's house anymore.

Only years later was I old enough to understand what had happened, and more than twenty years passed before anyone, including Mother herself, got the full picture. In early 1957 the "Hundred Flowers Movement" had been launched. Its official purpose was to give the Party a chance to correct its shortcomings by listening to the masses' criticisms. Father was away in the countryside reporting on something, but in the Changsha Public Security Bureau, meetings were held and everyone was urged to express his or her opinions freely.

Mother didn't know what to do. She really loved the Party and didn't have any criticisms to make; the Party had given her a job and saved her from the most abject poverty. Still, her leaders said that everyone should participate actively in the movement, especially those who hoped someday to join the Party. Mother was already in favor; she had been given the important job of validating arrest warrants for the whole city. So, regarding it her duty to come up with something, she finally thought of three points she could make. She said that her Section Head sometimes used crude language and liked to criticize people, that he should give his housekeeper a bed to sleep on instead of

making her sleep on the floor, and that sometimes when it came time to give raises, the leaders didn't listen to the masses' opinions.

But then, with utterly confusing rapidity, the "Hundred Flowers Movement" changed into the "Anti-Rightist Movement." Perhaps the Party was caught off guard by the amount of opposition and felt compelled to crack down. Or maybe, as I've heard said, the "Hundred Flowers Movement" had been a trap designed from the beginning to uncover Rightist elements. Anyway, every unit was given a quota of Rightists, and Mother's name was among those at the Public Security Bureau.

It was disastrous. When she was allowed to see her file in 1978, she found out that she had been given a Rightist's "cap" [that is, she was labeled a Rightist] solely because of those three criticisms she had made. Perhaps her Section Head was angry at her; perhaps her unit was having trouble filling its quota. At the time she had no idea what the verdict was based on, she only knew that a terrible wrong had been done. But there was no court of appeal. Mother was sent away to the suburb of Yuan Jia Ling for labor reform. She lost her cadre's rank and her salary was cut from fifty-five to fifteen yuan a month. (A *yuan* is one hundred Chinese cents. . . .) My naïve and trusting mother went to work as a peasant.

Just as his wife was being declared an enemy of the Party, Father was actively participating in the Anti-Rightist Movement in his own unit. Father believed in the Party with his whole heart, believed that the Party could never make a mistake or hand down a wrong verdict. It was a tortuous dilemma; Father's traditional Confucian sense of family obligation told him to support Mother while his political allegiance told him to condemn her. In the end, his commitment to the Party won out, and he denounced her. He believed that was the only course that could save the family from ruin. . . .

When Mother first came under attack, her older brother had been as outraged as she. He went to the Public Security Bureau to argue in her defense, and spoke for her at his own unit, the No. 1 Hospital, where he worked with the Communist Youth League. He even came to our house to urge Father to try to help her, although Father thought he was crazy to stick out his neck like that. Sure enough, Uncle Yan was punished for his family loy-alties and given a Rightist "cap" of his own to wear, bringing a second black cloud to rest over Waipo's home. His experience proved that Father's sad choice had been a practical one in view of the harsh political realities; when we were old enough to understand, we could hardly blame Father for what he had done. . . .

\* \* \* \* \* \* \* \* \* \* \*

Liang Heng's father understood that with a Rightist mother, the boy and his two older sisters would have difficulty in continuing their school-ing, getting decent jobs, and finding spouses. For this reason the father decided to divorce his wife and break off all ties with her. Because she had been branded a Rightist, the court gave her hus-band custody of the children. Then in 1966, when Liang Heng was twelve years old, the Great Proletarian Cultural Revolution began.

\* \* \* \* \* \* \* \* \* \* \*

[One day] one of our ex-comrades walked by and sneered at us and then spat on the cement at our feet. "You sons of Reactionary Capitalist stink-ing intellectuals. Run and look at your father's big character posters. Then hurry home and criticize *them,* why don't you."

I was simply unable to comprehend his words. My father wasn't a powerful official, had never accepted bribes or used public furniture, had never used power to criticize a worker unfairly. He was just a low-ranking cadre working for a Party news-paper, and no one in the whole world loved Chairman Mao better than he. How could there be posters about him? How could anyone say he had Capitalist thought? . . .

Then [my friend] Gang Di pulled me by the sleeve. He had found my father's posters. I fol-lowed him numbly through the gaily painted paper, still believing there had been a mistake. But then I saw the terrible words, burning characters on bril-liant yellow paper. EXPOSE THE PLOT OF THE REACTIONARY SCHOLAR LIANG SHAN TO THE LIGHT OF DAY!!!!!

There were too many sheets, maybe ten or more, each as tall as a man. And every word engraved itself on my heart with a blazing knife,

every phrase struck me with a blow that was even greater than terror. I would never believe the ground was steady again.

Liang Shan is a thoroughly Capitalist news-man. . . . He has used the knowledge given to him by the Party to attack the Party, writing many Reactionary articles. . . . That Liang Shan opposes the Party and Socialism is only natural. Let's investi-gate his history. His father was a doctor who came from Zhejiang to Hunan through tricking his "pri-vate patients" out of their money. So Liang Shin learned this skill from his family. When he was young, he eagerly entered the KMT's [Kuomintang's] Youth League. His ex-wife is a Rightist, and she certainly became a Rightist under his influence. Then he saw by what happened to her that it won't do to oppose the Party openly, and he used articles and poetry to try to under-mine it secretly. So his injury to the Revolution is even greater than his wife's. Chairman Mao teach-es us, "Sham is sham, and the mask must be stripped off." Now the Great Proletarian Culture Revolution is stripping off Liang Shan's skin to reveal his true appearance!!!!!

There was more, but the words wouldn't stay still. I was trembling all over. . . . Everything was backwards, distorted, corrupted, insane. I didn't know if I was dreaming or if my life at home was a dream. I hugged myself, pinching my arms, but I didn't wake up. I closed my eyes and opened them but the words were still there. My Revolutionary father was an enemy. My father whose dream it was to join the Party was a Capitalist. How had things been ruined? Why had he ruined things? I didn't know where to put my misery and my hatred. I would never trust my perception of reality again.

When the signal for dinner sounded, there was nothing to do but walk slowly home. . . .

Our home presented a peculiar, sad, unfriend-ly appearance, which only deepened my misery. I pushed my way in and discovered Father sitting in a dense cloud of cigarette smoke, which he was concentrating on making thicker, the butts lying on the wooden floor like wreckage after some dis-aster. He barely moved when I came in. It hurt me to look at him. . . .

My father's hand trembled as he struck anoth-er match. Then in the silence we heard a great

*A "struggle session" in which those accused of counterrevolutionary activities are denounced in front of large crowds and ordered to admit their wrongdoing. Harbin, 1967. Courtesy of Shanghai People's Press.*

clattering on the stairs, and Liang Fang and Liang Wei-ping [Liang Heng's two sisters] burst into the room. They were both crying, and they ran directly to their bed and threw themselves onto it, hugging the pillows. Their sobs were terrible in the silence.

Soon Liang Fang started accusing Father. "I'm so miserable being born into a family like this. First I had a mother who prevented me from joining the League. Now that I'm finally accepted as a Revolutionary, you have to ruin everything. Look," she cried, taking out a piece of paper. "Tonight I was supposed to be a marshal at the parades. This was the plan for the march. Do you think I can possibly face anyone now?" With a wail, she ripped her map into little pieces.

Father sat by the table with his head in his hands, passively accepting Liang Fang's fury as if he deserved it. He reached automatically for his pack of cigarettes, but it was empty. Liang Wei-ping, always the gentlest of us, nudged Liang Fang as if asking her to control herself and went into the other room and got another pack. As she handed it to Father I asked him, "Do you know what they called us today? 'Sons of Capitalist Reactionary stinking intellectuals'." . . .

Father raised his head and repeated, "You should believe the Party. Believe Chairman Mao." His words sounded like a prayer, a principle kept in his heart to invoke in times of trouble. They had been the key to his spirit for the past twenty years.

But Liang Fang raged. "Others don't believe

*you!* They say you're a Capitalist, a bloodsucker, a foreigner's dog!"

Then my father stood up, his face white, his words tumbling out in one breath. "It's because I'm none of those things that I believe the Party and Chairman Mao. I've done nothing to wrong you. You can continue to participate in the Revolution. If you want to, you can break off with me. Go live at school if you like. But I'll tell you one thing. No matter how you hate me, I've always been loyal to Chairman Mao. And I've always supported the Party and Socialism." . . .

\* \* \* \* \* \* \* \* \* \* \* \* \* \*

At eleven one night the knocks finally came, loud, sharp, and impatient. We sat up in bed automatically. Father emerged from the inside room and turned on the light. He motioned with his head for Liang Wei-ping to get the door.

There were seven or eight of them, all men or boys, and the small room seemed very crowded. Despite the heat they were all wearing white cloths over their mouths and noses, and dark clothes. The one who seemed to be the leader carried a long metal spring with a rubber tip. He struck it against the table top with a loud crack.

"Liang Shan!" he said. "Is there anything Feudalist-Capitalist-Revisionist in your house?"

Father stammered, "No, no. I had pictures of Liu Shao-qi [former chairman of the People's Republic, later accused of being a Revisionist and purged from the Party] but I turned them in to the Work Team. Nothing else."

"Worthless scum!" The man sliced at the table again.

Liang Wei-ping started to cry.

"What are you blubbering about? Cut it out. You and the boy, get over there in the corner."

We cowered there, trying to keep our sobs silent.

"What you must understand is that this is a Revolutionary action," the man announced. "Right?"

"Yes, yes, a Revolutionary action." I had never seen my father plead with anyone before. I had never seen him without his dignity.

"You welcome it, don't you! Say it!"

Something stuck in my father's throat.

"Cursed liar! You've always been a liar!" Two Red Guards took him by each arm and grabbed his head, pushing it down so he was forced to kneel on the floor. They shook him by the hair so his glasses fell off, and when he groped for them they kicked his hands away. "Liar!"

The others were already starting to go through our things, some going into the other rooms for the books, others to the boxes. For several minutes there was silence except for the rustling of paper and the opening of boxes and drawers. Then one of them cried out.

"Quite a fox, isn't he? We said he was a liar!" The Red Guard had two Western ties and a Western-style jacket. "What's the meaning of this?"

"Ties," my father mumbled.

They kicked him. "Ties! Do you think we're children? Everyone knows these are ties. Capitalist ties. Or hadn't you heard?"

Father was pointing excitedly. "They were ordered through the newspaper. For some jobs. It wasn't my idea. For receptions and—" The spring slammed down on his hand and he cringed in pain.

"Who told you to point your finger? Think you can order people around still, don't you? Stinking intellectual!"

Liang Wei-ping cried, "How can you go hitting people that way? He can't even see properly."

"Shut up, little crossbreed, or we'll be hitting you next," snapped the Red Guard standing by the bureau. "Look at this! Fancy pants and sleeves with three buttons!"

From the other room came two Red Guards with armfuls of books. They dumped them unceremoniously on the floor near where Father was kneeling and went back for more. Tang poetry fell on top of histories, foreign novels on the Chinese Classics. Our house had always looked very neat and spare; I had never realized we had so many books.

After an hour they had finished going through everything. . . . Everything we owned was in disorder on the floor, and even our pillows had been slit open with a knife. Father had been on his knees for a long time, and was trembling all over. The Red Guards were stuffing things into a large cloth bag when one of them got an idea for another game.

He put our large metal washbasin on the floor and built a little mound in it out of some of the finest books. He lit a match underneath and fanned it until the whole thing was aflame. Then he fed the fire, ripping the books in two one at a time and tossing them on. Father turned his head away. He didn't need his glasses to know what was on the pyre.

"What's the matter, Liang Shan? Light hurt your eyes?" The leading Red Guard held the metal spring out in front of him like a snake. " 'A Revolutionary action.' Say it. 'It's a good fire.' "

Father was silent. I prayed he would speak.

"You !*#*! liar. Say it!" The man grabbed Father by the hair and twisted his head to make him look at the flames. " 'It's a good fire!' "

My father's face looked very naked without his glasses, and the light from the fire shone on it and glistened in the tear lines on his cheeks. I could hardly hear him.

"A Revolutionary action," he whispered. "It's a good fire!"

They let him go; it was over. They shouldered the bag and filed out, the last putting our transistor radio into his pocket as he passed the table. We three couldn't find a word of comfort for each other; we just put things back in order in silence. The next day we discovered they had also helped themselves to Father's salary for that month. . . .

That summer, things got even worse in Changsha: The Rebels began fighting among themselves. Those who had once been comrades became mortal enemies, and the streets of Changsha ran with blood in the hundred-degree heat of August. The Cultural Revolution lost all connection with its original crackdown on anti-Socialist elements, now long forgotten. A civil war was going on, with each side claiming to love Chairman Mao better than the other, to be protecting his Revolutionary line against the policies that threatened it. Both sides were willing to die for the right to wield power under Chairman Mao's name.

The Rebels had guns now, and more. They had grenades and bayonets and machine guns and cannon and tanks and anti-aircraft missiles, all the weapons that China's military arsenals had to offer. Jiang Qing [Mao's wife] and the Cultural Revolution Directorate's slogan "Attack with Words, Defend with Guns" had been interpreted throughout the country to mean that all questions should be settled through armed struggle, and since Chairman Mao himself had said that the Rebels should have arms, they felt they were entitled to all the weapons they could get. . . . Then they started shooting at each other in order to decide arguments about who was going to be in charge. . . . It was during this gory climax that people began to realize that the Cultural Revolution would never make sense.

It was absolutely terrifying. Bullets whistled in the streets, and the roar of a motorcycle or the wail of a siren meant violence and tragedy. The gateways of many units had broad white lines drawn across them, and armed guards waited on the other side to shoot anyone who stepped across without permission. There was a 9 p.m. curfew, and no one wanted to go out during the day unless he had to; there were many reports of the deaths of innocent vegetable-buyers by stray bullets. People crisscrossed their windows with tape to prevent their shattering as the city shook with explosions and gunfire, and at night the sky flashed light and then dark with the passing of rockets.

Every evening Father pushed a heavy bureau up against the door and sat down in his old bamboo chair with a volume of *Chairman Mao's Selected Works* open on his lap, his broad brow knitted in concentration. But he never read anything, for the sounds of war in the city beyond disturbed him. Then some alarm would sound, warning us to turn off all the lights, and we would wait in darkness wondering. . . .

From *Son of the Revolution* by Liang Heng and Judith Shapiro. Copyright © 1983 by Liang Heng and Judith Shapiro. Reprinted by permission of Alfred A. Knopf, Inc., pp. 3–11, 51–59, 72–74, 132–33.

## Questions

1. Why was Liang Heng sent to live at the child-care center when he was three? Why didn't he live with either of his grandmothers?
2. Why was the Communist victory in China referred to as a revolution? Relate the concept of revolution to what was happening in this story.
3. What "crimes" were Liang Heng's mother and father accused of committing? In your judgment, why did his father keep to his faith in the Party and Chairman Mao despite the treatment he received?
4. What did the Red Guard search raids do to the earlier Chinese value of respect for elders?

*Marchers in Tiananmen Square carry pictures of Mao and copies of* Quotations from Chairman Mao Zedong. *From* Ten-Thousand-Year Spring of the People's Country, *cover photo.*

## The Cult of Mao

The words, thoughts, and deeds of the Great Helmsman were the focal point of every Chinese person's life during the Cultural Revolution. Education consisted of readings from his work; billboards carried his sayings; the entire canon of entertainment was, for a time, confined to songs, plays, and operas praising his greatness. His image hung in every house, in every school, and in every restaurant. All good was attributed to the person of the great leader, and even casual remarks had to be carefully gauged, lest they contain any hint of disrespect to Mao's person.

The personality cult around Mao was not unique in Chinese history. The Chinese had long believed that, in a distant past, great leaders had ruled with a heaven-sent combination of wisdom, ingenuity, and discretion. The great philosopher Mencius spoke of the "mandate of heaven" given to the emperor, who had the right and duty to rule because it was heaven's will. The dictates of the ruler could not be disputed, for the emperor's word was also the word of heaven.

Mao Zedong was a Communist; he did not believe in heaven, so he and his followers could hardly sanction a claim that his wisdom was heaven-sent. Instead, they argued that applying "Mao Zedong thought" allowed them to perform miracles; they said that "reading the words of the Great Helmsman" gave them the strength to perform extraordinary acts of heroism and courage; they believed that "a critical examination of one's own behavior in the light of the words of Chairman Mao" allowed them to put aside their petty concern for their own health and welfare and to work tirelessly for their country. A story told of doctors who removed a 45-pound tumor from the stomach of a woman, saying that it was the application of Mao Zedong thought that allowed them to perform the operation successfully. Another story told of untrained peasants using acupuncture to cure blindness, inspired by passages from the Little

Red Book (a collection of Mao's sayings). Yet another told of a miner sacrificing his own life to save others from a mine collapse. As he was about to be crushed to death, the miner called out, "Long live Chairman Mao!" When his body was uncovered later, he was clutching a copy of the Little Red Book opened to a passage advocating personal sacrifice for the sake of the group. (The idea of such sacrifice was hardly new in Chinese thought, but during the Cultural Revolution all Chinese pretended that Mao possessed the charisma to induce the Chinese to make sacrifices.)

The irony is that the atheistic People's Republic was dominated, at the height of the Mao cult, with ideas and ideals that mimicked a religion. Mao was a godlike figure, all-knowing, all-caring, and infallible. There were saints and martyrs, like Norman Bethune, a Canadian doctor who had died heroically for the cause. The Little Red Book was a holy book, the inspired words of the great leader. Hymns of praise were written for Mao. (For a while the only music allowed was praises to Mao.) The Chinese sent missionaries abroad to sell the vision of peasant and proletariat revolution to the poor and oppressed throughout the third world. There were heretics who were demonized, like Liu Shaoqi, who had strayed from reverence for every word of Mao Zedong and hence had scorn heaped on him. (He had said, among other heresies, that for anyone to claim to be infallible was "like pushing leeks up a pig's snout to make it look like an elephant.")

The cult of Mao did not survive him; it was carefully engineered by the Great Helmsman himself, and his closest followers lacked the political skills to keep it going after his death. When in the early 1980s the leaders of China began to refer to Chairman Mao as "a great man, but fallible," official sanction for the cult of Mao worship was over.

## Keeping Control

To create a socialist society, Chinese Communists have used a variety of measures to stifle dissent, enforce their policies, and keep people under tight control. Rights that Americans take for granted, such as freedom of speech, freedom of the press, and habeas corpus, have been severely curtailed or do not exist in the People's Republic. Chinese leaders simply have not tolerated opposition to their policies.

While the Ministry of Propaganda has attempted to persuade citizens to support government directives, the Ministry of Public Security has ferreted out people suspected of "counterrevolutionary activity." Organized by Mao Zedong, this powerful agency still carries out surveillance of Chinese citizens, controls all media, censors mail, thwarts labor unrest, and operates forced-labor camps.

One means the Ministry of Public Security uses to keep tabs on the population has been Residents' Committees, a network of neighborhood households that keep watch over each other and report to a police substation. Through these committees the government closely monitors political dissension and compliance with family-planning programs. During Mao's regime, in times of intense political fervor such as the Cultural Revolution, many families lived in fear that neighbors might report them as "enemies of the people."

Despite recent attempts to reform the legal system, loopholes still permit arbitrary arrest and sentencing of accused criminals and political dissidents. Since the early days of the People's Republic, those accused of being counterrevolutionary have been rounded up and sent to "re-education through labor" camps. Here they are forced to work under harsh conditions and submit to systematic brainwashing to make them see the error of their ways. For those accused of committing specific crimes, the legal system offers little hope of acquittal. Defendants are presumed guilty until proven innocent. With limited access to legal representation, many are sentenced to terms in forced-labor camps. Capital punishment is common; it can be prescribed even for nonviolent crimes such as fraud or embezzlement.

Under Mao, the government clamped down on travel by requiring anyone leaving home for more than two days to get an official pass and to check in with the police at their destination. This system ensured that peasants return home after visiting a city, and it helped police keep track of visiting strangers. After Mao's death, when Deng Xiaoping's economic reforms boosted commercial activity, restrictions on travel were eased. The government then issued national identification cards to make it easier for police to track the movement of citizens.

The household registration system is yet another way of controlling people. Local police substations keep a file on each family in their jurisdictions. Besides other information, these files state the official residence of every family and tell whether households have been designated as agricultural or nonagricultural. To change residences or household designations, families must get permission from Communist officials. A family that moves without permission forfeits all access to government benefits and social services. With this system, Mao's government controlled internal migration and prevented large numbers of peasants from moving to the cities. But since Deng's reforms brought dramatic economic growth in the 1980s, the household registration system has lost some of its effectiveness. By the mid-1990s millions of peasants, willing to risk their government benefits, had illegally moved to cities and near special economic zones in hopes of finding jobs at good pay.

## Activity: Slogans, Speeches, and Posters

### Part 1.

The Chinese government used posters and slogans to convey messages to the people. What follow are slogans popular during the Great Leap Forward and the Cultural Revolution. With a partner, answer these questions.

1. What are slogans? Why are they effective?
2. Choose three slogans popular during the Great Leap Forward and three slogans used during the Cultural Revolution. Explain the message that each slogan tries to convey.
3. What might be the government's purpose in spreading these sayings?

**Slogans of the Great Leap Forward**

Three years of effort, a thousand years of happiness!
Dare to think, dare to act!
Women hold up half of heaven!
Man is the decisive factor!
Concentrate twenty years in a single day!
Do everything better, faster, more economically!
Everybody make steel!
Catch up with Great Britain in 15 years.
Under the leadership of the Communist Party, as long as there are people, every kind of miracle can be performed.
Chairman Mao is the Red Sun inside our hearts!

**Slogans of the Cultural Revolution**

Never forget class struggle.
Serve the people!
To rebel is justified.
Destroy the four olds.
Destroy those who follow the capitalist road!
Bombard the Headquarters.
Uphold the banner of Mao Zedong's Thought.
Mao Zedong Thought is our lifeline.
We will smash whoever opposes Chairman Mao.
We vow to launch a bloody war against anyone who dares to resist the Cultural Revolution, who dares to oppose Chairman Mao.

高举毛泽东思想伟大红旗
把无产阶级文化大革命进行到底

*Workers and peasants carry copies of* Quotations from Chairman Mao Zedong *in this propaganda poster. The caption reads, "Raise high the great red flag of Mao Zedong Thought. Carry out thoroughly the Great Proletarian Cultural Revolution." From* Ten-Thousand-Year Spring of the People's Country, *p. 32.*

Destroy the old world so a new one can be born.
We can soar to heaven, and pierce the earth, because our Great Leader Chairman Mao is our supreme commander.

### Part 2.

Your teacher will divide the class. Half will support and the other half will oppose the Great Leap Forward and the Cultural Revolution. Use your imagination and be creative, but be historically realistic in what you say.

**For those in favor.** You are a Red Guard during the Cultural Revolution. Your task is to write a speech that supports Mao's policies during the Great Leap Forward and the Cultural Revolution. You may create an imaginary person to denounce. Include one or more slogans you have read or ones you make up yourself.

**For those opposed.** You believe in Communism but are bothered by the direction it has taken. You are afraid to speak out, for you have seen what happened to those who did. You are to write a speech that expresses your thoughts, raising questions and criticizing the Great Leap Forward and the ongoing Cultural Revolution. This is a speech you could safely deliver in public only outside China. Create slogans to support your viewpoint.

1. To get started, review all the activities and readings in this section. Take notes on information and ideas that will help you write your speech, and record phrases that you can use as slogans. For example, if you support the Great Leap Forward, you might choose to write "Twenty Years in a Day!" or "Double Our Steel Production in One Year!" Slogans against the Great Leap Forward might be "A Half-Baked Dream!" "Our Steel is but Cattle Droppings!" Use your imagination to create other slogans. Then compose your speech, which should be about 250 words long.

   You might want to write your speech in the style used by the Chinese government in justifying its actions. To get an idea of this style of writing, see the reading "The Chinese and the Soviets: The Era of Hostility" in Section 5 of this chapter.

2. Pairing up. Share your first draft with a classmate having the same viewpoint. Together decide which speech to revise and deliver before the class, or write another one together, incorporating ideas from both. Discuss ways to improve the speech.

3. While one of you works on the speech, the other makes a poster and chooses or creates five slogans that support the speech.

4. While one of you gives the speech for the class, your partner will hold up a poster supporting the speech. During the speech, the

person holding the poster must raise a fist and shout out the five slogans. Both partners must decide which slogan to shout at what points during the speech. Those in favor of the Great Leap Forward and Cultural Revolution should make a red poster and those against should produce a green one. Use poster-size paper and large felt-tipped pens.

5. On the appointed day, supporters and opponents will take turns presenting their posters and speaking before the class. Those in favor should sit on one side of the room, those opposed on the other. While listening to the speeches of members of your side, show your support by loudly repeating, in unison, the slogans the person holding the poster shouts.

## Activity: Producing Circles

This activity illustrates the role of incentives on production levels. Your teacher will divide the class in half and distribute handouts. Read your directions carefully, do not show them to anyone, and begin only after your teacher gives you the signal to do so.

When time is up, count the circles you drew and write the total in the top right-hand corner of the sheet. Then turn in your paper and respond to the following questions in a class discussion.

### For those who were *X*'s

1. How many of you who were *X*'s drew the required 200 circles? How many of you drew more than 200 circles? Why?

2. What reason did you have to work harder and produce more than 200 circles?

3. Who received the most and fewest pieces of candy?

4. How many of you drew more than 350 circles? 400 circles? For those of you who did so: if you had to work that hard every day but received the same amount of goodies as those who drew 200 circles, for how many

days would you feel like doing so much more work than you had to?

## For those who were *Y*'s

1. How many of you who were *Y*'s drew more than 200 circles? Why?
2. How did the *Y*'s compare among themselves? What will be the results of their differences?
3. Why were some able to produce more circles than others?

## For both *X*'s and *Y*'s

The *X*'s were producing under rules similar to those of socialism and communism. The *Y*'s were producing under rules similar to those of capitalism.

1. What are the rules of communism? Of capitalism?
2. What are the advantages and disadvantages of each system?

## Reading: *Mao to Deng*

After twenty-seven years at the helm of the People's Republic of China, Mao Zedong succumbed to illness and old age in 1976 at eighty-three. A power struggle ensued, and those responsible for the excesses of the Great Proletarian Cultural Revolution—Mao's wife, Jiang Qing, and three others, known as the Gang of Four—were put on public trial. Jiang Qing and another of the gang were sentenced to death (later commuted to life imprisonment); the other two received long prison terms. In 1978, after much political maneuvering, Deng Xiaoping emerged as victor.

Under Deng's leadership, government officials revised their interpretation of Mao's legacy. They adopted a resolution stating that Mao had made "great contributions" but had erred repeatedly, beginning with the Great Leap Forward. The resolution concluded that Mao's policies were 70 percent good and 30 percent bad for the country.

In this frame of mind, Deng began an "Open Door" policy that encouraged foreign contact. Although there had been some contact with the United States after President Richard Nixon's historic visit to China in 1972, it had been minimal. Deng set out to improve relations with a visit to the United States in January 1979. Soon after, thousands of Chinese were permitted to study in the United States, and thousands of American tourists streamed into China. The Chinese government welcomed the infusion of

outside knowledge and foreign investment—a radical change from Mao's policy.

*The first experiments in dismantling the communes and reestablishing family farms started in Fengyang County, Anhui province, an area known for its extreme poverty. Land reform allowed farmers working on family plots to decide what crops they would grow and to sell their excess for profit, leading to increased production and rapid rise in the standard of living. Pictured here, a Fengyang family pose in front of their old shack and their new house, built only a few years after Deng Xiaoping instituted reforms. From Duan Liancheng, Gu Jin, and Zhang Yuanlei, eds., As the Dragon Stirs. Hong Kong: New Horizon Press, 1990, p. 187.*

Seeking to stimulate the economy and increase production, Deng Xiaoping gradually relaxed central control over much of the economy in favor of competition and the free market. Government officials dismantled the communes and encouraged family farms, allowing families to decide what crops to grow and to keep whatever they produced beyond what they owed to the government. They let farmers earn extra income by selling other crops and products. Food production surged. In the cities the government let people open small stores, restaurants, and repair shops. People responded with enthusiasm, initiative, and hard work, increasing their incomes and becoming more prosperous.

*Helping economy*

In 1979 the Chinese government established four "special economic zones" on the coast, near Macao, Hong Kong, and Taiwan. Improved transportation networks, lower taxes, and other incentives attracted investments from foreigners and overseas Chinese. Greater exposure to foreign ideas stimulated innovation.

Since Deng's reforms, China's economic growth has been spectacular. By the early nineties its economy was the fastest-growing in the world, increasing at 13 percent a year. Deng's mix of private enterprise and socialism, which he called "Chinese-style socialism," dramatically raised the living standard of many Chinese in a relatively brief time. The World Bank has estimated that since the reform era began, over 170 million Chinese have risen from subsistence living. Many peasants can now afford simple luxuries such as cassette stereos and even televisions. With greater prosperity, disparities in wealth widened as some families became rich. In the cities, an elite group of technocrats, managers, professionals, and intellectuals emerged. It is no wonder then that some call the economic reforms of the late seventies "the second Communist revolution."

*The city of Shenzhen, 1994. Located on the border of Hong Kong, this city has grown impressively since it was chosen to be China's first special economic zone. Courtesy of China Pictorial.*

## Deng Xiaoping

Many people have found it strange that from the late 1970s to the middle 1990s the most powerful man in China was merely the vice-chairman of the Communist Party. Deng Xiaoping controlled the country without giving himself the usual power title. His rise to power had been checkered; retaining the title that was given to him as a slap in the face reminded everyone of his ability to overcome adversity at notable times in his career.

Although Deng was not a peasant, like Mao, his party credentials ran deep. He came from a middle-class family and converted to Communism while studying in Paris. By 1927 he was commanding an army in the Jiangxi mountains; he was on the Long March; he was vitally important in the fight against the Guomindang that led to the Communist takeover in 1949. By 1953 he was secretary-general of the Communist Party. By 1956 he was clearly identified with the moderate wing of the government; that is, he opposed the rapid, wholesale changes in China that Mao was so fond of. When Mao went briefly into eclipse in 1957 after the failure of the Hundred Flowers Movement, Deng took over the day-to-day running of the party. He maintained a position of authority until the Cultural Revolution, when he became the second most vilified man in China (after Liu Shaoqi). He was upbraided for his lack of revolutionary fervor, his pragmatism, and especially for his belief that positions of authority should be filled by experts, not by people of revolutionary zeal. He was able to retain some status in China, although Mao clearly despised him, because he always had the support of Zhou Enlai. By 1973 Deng was back in the public eye. In January 1976 he read the eulogy at Zhou Enlai's funeral but was passed over for the post of prime minister in favor of Hua Guofeng, a relatively minor political figure loyal to Mao. Mao tried to destroy Deng but ran into difficulties. In April 1976, rioting broke out in Tiananmen Square between the police and those who supported Deng and opposed the ascendan-

*Deng Xiaoping, 1986. Courtesy of* China Pictorial.

cy of Mao's wife, Jiang Qing. The rebellion was brutally suppressed. (Ironically, Deng himself callously suppressed protests in Tiananmen Square thirteen years later.) Deng was shorn of all official titles except vice-chairman of the Communist Party. But when Mao died in September 1976 and the Gang of Four were arrested three weeks later, Deng began his last maneuver to return to power, gaining the support of powerful allies in the government and the party. By 1979 he was widely perceived to be in charge, and Hua Guofeng, Mao's chosen heir, gradually lost power. Until physical weakness impaired Deng's abilities in the early 1990s, he was firmly in control in China. He died in 1997 at the age of ninety-three.

Deng's pragmatism helped him weather the reversals of fortune that he suffered. He never confronted Mao head on, nor did he scheme behind his back. Although Deng made his positions clear, he backed off rather than risk tearing the country apart. It was as if he always knew his time would come.

As China's leader, Deng permitted almost no political freedom. He crushed criticism and killed as many people as necessary to keep his hold on the country. On the other hand, he advanced economic freedom, allowing people to open stores and restaurants and to sell things they made and crops they grew. Under his leadership, living conditions improved for many people, but crime and corruption grew.

## Slaughter in Tiananmen Square

The spring of 1989 was a time of enormous change in the Communist world. Communist governments in Czechoslovakia, Poland, and East Germany collapsed—so easily that the world was caught by surprise. Liberalization continued in the Soviet Union, and other east European states moved away from the old status quo.

When protesters gathered in Tiananmen (Gate of Heavenly Peace) Square in Beijing to demonstrate for freedom of the press and an end to the corruption that had seeped into Chinese business and bureaucracy during the 1980s, the world watched closely. Would China join the "liberated" countries? Would this event presage the collapse of the largest Communist state of them all? In the atmosphere of euphoria, some people did not notice signs that the authorities were not embracing the protesters. On June 4 and 5, officials acted the way we expect murderous dictators to act. Armed troops fired indiscriminately into crowds of unarmed civilians, killing over seven hundred.

What confused some is that the government was slow to react to the protesters. Signs and banners criticizing the government had hung for weeks. More people gathered in the square each day, but the official reaction was muted. Party secretary Zhao Ziyang let it be known that he thought the protesters had some valid points. But then the countersigns began to show. Martial law was imposed. Zhao Ziyang was not seen in public with other prominent officials. A large and conspicuous military force assembled in the streets of Beijing, gathering ominously around Tiananmen.

For two weeks the military presence failed to intimidate the protesters. Finally the government ordered the slaughter. It worked: the protests stopped.

Over the next few years, only mild and rather ineffective opposition to the government was occasionally heard, while the government continued to behave as it always had. Political prisoners were routinely tortured and killed. The press had no freedom. Corruption persisted. Amnesty International in 1995 declared that China had the worst human rights record in the world.

In the general elation over the freeing up of eastern Europe, people were surprised when the Chinese government acted so harshly. The state of internal politics in China was unclear. Chinese had more economic freedom in 1989 than at the time of Mao's death. In 1989, they could listen to Beethoven or read Confucius, both serious crimes during the Cultural Revolution. But economic freedom is not political freedom, and reading Confucius is not the same as criticizing the government. What in fact happened was that repression in the 1980s reverted to the pattern in dictatorships, where people are rarely in danger unless they directly oppose the government or insist on the right to oppose the government.

The Chinese government simply acted like a typical brutal dictatorship in this situation. Its reaction to Tiananmen was relatively slow. Because the protests were both well attended and widespread, not only in Beijing but also in some other cities, the officials may have been wary of their ability to control the situation. They waited until they could muster an overwhelming show of strength that would stifle further acts of dissent. If that was their intent, they did a good job.

*A man stands before a convoy of tanks during the Tiananmen Square incident of 1989. Courtesy of Reuters/Bettman.*

## Activity: Which Came First?

Your teacher will assign each student one of the events listed below. Write the name of your event on looseleaf paper.

1. When your teacher gives the signal, find six people assigned the other events and line yourselves up in chronological order. The first group to do so wins.
2. After sitting down, volunteer to give your teacher the first event and its significance. The teacher will call on others to continue with the other six events in chronological order.

Deng Xiaoping becomes leader
Great Leap Forward
Tiananmen Square incident
Mao Zedong dies
First Five-Year Plan
Cultural Revolution and Red Guards
Special Economic Zones

## Extension Activities

1. **Book Review.** Write a review and give an oral report on one of these books about the Cultural Revolution: *Wild Swans, Life and Death in Shanghai, Born Red, Son of the Revolution, Turbulent Decade.* See "Further Reading" below.
2. **Dramatization.** With some classmates, dramatize parts of "Child of the Revolution." Create props and costumes to enhance the presentation.
3. **Speaker.** If someone in your community lived in China during the Cultural Revolution, invite that person to tell your class about it.
4. **Videos.** Suggested videos on the period covered by this section are *The Mao Years,* produced by Ambrica Production and WGBH Educational Foundation; *The Last Emperor,* produced by Hanmade Film Corporation; *To Live,* produced by ERA International, Ltd.; *The Blue Kite,* produced by Longwick Production, Ltd.; and *Raise the Red Lantern,* produced by ERA International, Ltd.

## Further Reading

Bloodworth, Dennis. *The Messiah and the Mandarins: Mao Tse-tung and the Ironies of Power.* New York: Atheneum, 1982.

Chang, Jung. *Wild Swans: Three Daughters of China.* London: HarperCollins, 1992.

Cheng, Nien. *Life and Death in Shanghai.* New York: Grove Press, 1987.

Gao, Yuan. *Born Red: A Chronicle of the Cultural Revolution.* Stanford: Stanford University Press, 1987.

Kau, Michael Ying-Mao, and Susan H. Marsh, eds. *China in the Era of Deng Xiaoping: A Decade of Reform.* Armok, NY: M. E. Sharpe, 1993.

Liang, Heng, and Judith Shapiro. *Son of the Revolution.* New York: Alfred A. Knopf, 1983.

Liu, Alan P. L. *How China is Ruled.* Englewood Cliffs, N.J.: Prentice-Hall, Inc., 1986.

Meisner, Maurice J. *Mao's China and After: A History of the People's Republic.* New York: Free Press, 1986.

Shambaugh, David, and Thomas W. Robinson, eds. *China's Foreign Policy: Theory and Practice.* Clarendon: Oxford University Press, 1994.

Solomon, Richard, with Talbott W. Huey. *A Revolution is Not a Dinner Party: A Feast of Images of the Maoist Transformation of China.* New York: Anchor Press, 1975.

Uhalley, Stephen, Jr. *A History of the Chinese Communist Party.* Stanford: Hoover Institution Press, 1988.

Urban, George, ed. *The Miracles of Chairman Mao: A Compendium of Devotional Literature, 1966–1970.* London: Tom Stacey, Ltd., 1971.

Yan, Jiaqi and Gao Gao. *Turbulent Decade.* Translated by Daniel W. Y. Kwok. Honolulu: University of Hawai'i Press, 1996.

Yang, Xiushi. "Household Registration, Economic Reform and Migration." *International Migration Review,* Vol. 27 (Winter 1993). New York: Center for Migration Studies of New York, Inc., 1993.

Zhang, Xinxin and Sang Ye. *Chinese Lives: An Oral History of Contemporary China.* New York: Pantheon, 1987.

# 4 Marriage, Women, and the Family

*Communist mass movements designed to transform Chinese society from feudal to socialist produced not only sweeping economic and political changes but also changes in the very foundation of society—the family. In this section we examine the impact that social legislation, political movements, and economic policies have had on family life in the People's Republic of China.*

---

## Reading: *Changes in Marriage*

### Marriage Before Communism

Do you expect your parents to choose a spouse for you? If they chose, what qualities would they look for in that person? How would their choice differ from yours?

Unlike parents in modern societies, Chinese parents traditionally chose mates for their children. These arranged marriages were often decided years in advance with little or no thought for the desires of the future bride or groom, who often met for the first time on their wedding day. For families that enjoyed financial security, a marriage was mostly a business transaction with a family of similar economic status. Go-betweens often acted as negotiators who decided on appropriate betrothal presents: a "bride price" from the bridegroom's family and a dowry from the bride's family. The costs could be staggering. For many of the poor, this system meant years of debt, or even no marriage at all.

An arranged marriage was not a partnership between equals; it was the pairing of a man obliged to provide economic security for his family with a woman obliged to serve and obey her husband and to produce a son.

For a woman, an arranged marriage often meant a life of hardship, submission, and child-bearing with a man she did not love but could not divorce. Upon marrying, a woman became part of her husband's family and had limited contact with her own parents. She did the housework and attended to the needs of her husband and children and, if she were married to an oldest son, his parents. She was expected to obey her husband, his parents, and his brothers without question. A young wife's life was often made miserable by a demanding mother-in-law who seemed impossible to please. A woman's standing improved when she bore her first son. For then she had fulfilled her wifely duty—to provide a male heir to continue the family line.

An arranged marriage disrupted a man's life less than a woman's. A new wife often meant a new servant for him and his family. If a husband who was well-off did not learn to love his wife or if she did not bear him sons, he was free to take a second wife, or concubine, to fulfill his emotional and familial needs.

### Marriage During Communism

In China's large coastal cities, family roles began to change as early as the turn of the twentieth century. Foreign trade through port cities created a demand for labor that brought women and young men into the work force. During the first few decades of the century, these bustling industrial and commercial centers provided ever-increasing job opportunities for residents. Fathers found they had less and less say in choosing a son's employment, and women began working outside the home in factories. New educational opportu-

*The national Marriage Law adopted in May 1950 was a major step in social reform and particularly important in improving women's rights. This picture shows a simple wedding ceremony of a young Beijing-area couple (first and second left) who chose to marry despite opposition from their families and village neighbors, circa 1950. From Duan Liancheng, Gu Jin, and Zhang Yuanlei, eds.,* As the Dragon Stirs. *Hong Kong: New Horizon Press, 1990, pp. 84 and 85.*

nities became available to both boys and girls. Footbinding, formally outlawed in 1902, gradually died out. (See Chapter 1 on footbinding.) And the number of arranged marriages decreased. But for the 90 percent of Chinese in the countryside, the family system changed little until after the Communist takeover.

During the Mao Zedong years, the role of women changed. Mao considered women the most oppressed segment in feudal society, oppressed by their husbands, fathers-in-law, sons, and other male relatives.

To achieve the socialist society he envisioned, Mao believed, men and women had to work as equal partners in building a new China. But the rigid hierarchical and patriarchal structures of feudal society and the family had to be dismantled first. One of the first steps Communists took toward this end was promulgating the Marriage Law of 1950.

At first most Chinese, especially those in rural areas, thought the ideas and ideals put forth in the Marriage Law of 1950 too radical. In fact, male cadres in the countryside often postponed implementing the Marriage Law in their districts, fearing it would undermine peasant support for complying with other Communist directives.

Read these excerpts from the 1950 Marriage Law and answer the questions that follow.

### ARTICLE 1

The feudal system, which was based on arbitrary and compulsory arrangements and the supe-

riority of man over woman, and ignores the children's interests, shall be abolished. The New-democratic marriage system, which is based on free choice of partners, on monogamy, on equal rights for both sexes, and on the protection of the lawful interests of women and children, shall be put into effect.

### ARTICLE 2

Bigamy, concubinage, child betrothal, interference in the remarriage of widows, and the exaction of money or gifts in connection with marriages, shall be prohibited.

### ARTICLE 3

Marriage shall be based upon the complete willingness of the two parties. Neither party shall use compulsion and no third party shall be allowed to interfere.

### ARTICLE 4

A marriage can be contracted only after the man has reached twenty years of age and the woman eighteen years of age.

### ARTICLE 7

Husband and wife are companions living together and shall enjoy equal status in the home.

### ARTICLE 8

Husband and wife are in duty bound to love, respect, assist and look after each other, to live in harmony, to engage in productive work, to care for

*Following local custom, a procession of farmers fetch a bride and her dowry items from another village. As the standard of living improved for many Chinese during the post-Mao era, traditional practices, such as paying a dowry, became popular again. From Duan Liancheng, Gu Jin, and Zhang Yuanlei, eds.,* As the Dragon Stirs. *Hong Kong: New Horizon Press, 1990, p. 264.*

their children and to strive jointly for the welfare of the family and for building up a new society.

### Article 10

Both husband and wife shall have equal rights in the possession and management of family property.

### Article 11

Both husband and wife shall have the right to use his or her own family name.

### Article 12

Both husband and wife shall have the right to inherit each other's property.

### Article 13

Parents have the duty to rear and educate their children; the children have the duty to support and to assist their parents. Neither the parents nor the children shall maltreat or desert one another.

The foregoing provision also applies to foster-parents and foster-children.

Infanticide by drowning and similar criminal acts are strictly prohibited.

### Article 17

Divorce shall be granted when husband and wife both desire it. In the event of either the husband or the wife alone insisting upon divorce, it may be granted only when mediation by the district people's government and the judicial organ has failed to bring about a reconciliation.

From M. J. Meijer, *Marriage Law and Policy in the Chinese People's Republic.* Hong Kong: Hong Kong University Press, 1971, pp. 300–301.

## Questions

1. From the excerpts of the 1950 Marriage Law, what can you deduce about marriage and the rights of women in feudal China? What practices were the Communists trying to eliminate, and what were they trying to promote by enacting this law?
2. How might free choice of marriage partners affect relationships between family members: husband and wife, parent and child, mother-in-law and daughter-in-law?
3. What portion of the Marriage Law of 1950 do you think would be the hardest for most Chinese to accept? Explain your answer.

New laws do not eliminate ingrained social customs and practices overnight. Such was the case with the 1950 Marriage Law. Yet of all the law's provisions, Article 3 gained relatively quick acceptance in urban areas. A survey of women in Chengdu, a large city in Sichuan province, yielded these findings.

## Choosing Mates in Chengdu, 1922–1987

| | Year First Married | | | | |
|---|---|---|---|---|---|
| | 1933–48 (N = 71) | 1949–57 (N = 107) | 1958–65 (N = 82) | 1966–76 (N = 116) | 1977–87 (N = 210) |
| | % | % | % | % | % |
| **Type of marriage** | | | | | |
| Arranged | 68 | 27 | 0 | 1 | 2 |
| Intermediate | 15 | 33 | 45 | 40 | 41 |
| Individual choice | 17 | 40 | 55 | 59 | 57 |
| **Dominant role in mate choice** | | | | | |
| Parents | 56 | 30 | 7 | 8 | 5 |
| Mixed | 15 | 11 | 6 | 3 | 6 |
| Respondent | 28 | 59 | 87 | 89 | 89 |
| **Who provided the introduction?** | | | | | |
| Own generation | 38 | 43 | 75 | 75 | 74 |
| Other | 8 | 17 | 7 | 6 | 9 |
| Parents' generation | 53 | 40 | 18 | 19 | 17 |
| **How much in love when married?[a]** | | | | | |
| 1. Completely | 17 | 38 | 63 | 61 | 67 |
| 2. | 26 | 29 | 22 | 26 | 19 |
| 3. | 35 | 20 | 9 | 11 | 10 |
| 4. | 9 | 4 | 4 | 1 | 3 |
| 5. Not at all | 13 | 9 | 2 | 1 | 0 |

[a] Respondents were shown a five-point scale with only the end points labeled.
From Martin King Whyte, "Wedding Behavior and Family Strategies in Chengdu,"
in Deborah Davis and Harrell Stevan, eds., *Chinese Families in the Post-Mao Era.* © 1993,
Regents of the University of California Press, p. 194.

## Questions

1. Between 1933 and 1987, what happened to the percentages of arranged marriages among the women surveyed?
2. Who played the dominant role in mate choice during each of the five periods in the survey?
3. Members of what generation first introduced husband and wife for each period in the survey?
4. What conclusions can you draw about the role love played in the choice of marriage partners between 1933 and 1987?

### Reading: *Women in the Work Force*

The Little Red Book of quotations from Mao Zedong carries this thought from the Chairman:

> In order to build a great socialist society, it is of the utmost importance to arouse the broad masses of women to join in productive activity. . . . Genuine equality between the sexes can only be realized in the process of the socialist transformation of society as a whole.

During the Great Leap Forward and the collectivization movement, family life changed

*(top) Woman lathe operators discussing how to improve the quality of their work, 1956. (bottom) Woman stevedores on the Shanghai waterfront, 1956. To achieve public acceptance for women working outside the home, especially in occupations considered suitable only for men, the Communist government carried out propaganda campaigns featuring women "model workers" doing their part and contributing to the socialist revolution. Courtesy of Foreign Language Press.*

dramatically in the countryside. In feudal society the patriarch saw to the economic well-being of his family. He managed his family's property and decided what work his sons would do and what rewards they would receive. But when the government eliminated private property and com-

bined family farms into communes, the commune leaders decided what work would be done, who would do it, and what rewards they would get.

Not only did the state supplant some of the patriarch's authority; it also changed the status of women by recruiting them for the work force. By 1958 women made up half of the agricultural laborers, and in urban communes many worked in factories and service industries. With widespread participation in the work force, women began to take on management responsibilities and to participate in public life. Yet resistance to equality between the sexes persisted, especially in the countryside. Although women held leadership positions in communes, production teams, and work brigades, most women were assigned to sex-segregated work teams or to "women's jobs," where they earned fewer work credits than men.

In farming communities daughters traditionally received less formal schooling than sons did. Even under the Communists, peasant parents still considered higher education more important for boys than for girls. As a result, during the Great Leap Forward, rural women were commonly shut out from jobs that called for technical training or a certain level of education. In contrast, urban women fared better in jobs and careers because more city girls attended school than did country girls. They also had more years of schooling and attended better schools than their rural counterparts. Whereas rural women were often seen as helpers to men, urban women had real career opportunities.

## Questions

1. List five adjectives that describe the women in the photos.
2. What is the message in the photos and captions?
3. How might working outside the home affect a woman's status within her family?
4. Who do you suppose took care of young children when mothers were away at work?

## Reading: *Class and the Family*

Because of the centrality of class and class struggle in Mao's thinking, soon after liberation, cadres throughout China set about assigning all families a class designation. Most fell into either the exploiting classes (landlords, rich peasants, capitalists) or the exploited classes (factory workers, poor peasants.) Cadres based these designations on a family's economic condition before liberation, after which all exploiting classes had supposedly been eliminated.

Mao turned traditional social status on its head. Under the Communists, a history of poverty before 1949 provided security and opportunity for families. The government favored members of the exploited classes in land redistribution, employment, and education. The importance of class in Mao's China peaked during the Cultural Revolution when some Communists went so far as to promote the "bloodline theory" —that descendants of the exploiting class could never be trusted because they were genetically predisposed to exploit others.

The following is a letter to the editor of the *People's Daily*, China's leading newspaper and the official voice of the Communist Party. This letter, which reflects the realities of the Cultural Revolution, was published in 1978, the year Deng Xiaoping's government abolished official class designations.

Comrade Editor:

My birth has brought me endless sufferings. Last September, I left home in anger. I am a political pariah: my spirit tortured, my body ill, my life doomed. Today, with tears in my eyes, I write this letter as does a man with a grave illness seek medical help.

By the time that I was born, most of the country had come under the warming rays of the new dawn, liberation. My infancy was spent in innocence under the red flag. As a child, I watched with fascination films showing the heroic deeds of Huang Jiguang, Dong Cunrei, Liu Hulan and Lei Feng.[1] From an early age, I wanted to be a soldier in the People's Liberation Army so that I, like Huang

Jiguang, could block the enemy's guns' advance and, like Lei Feng, could wholeheartedly serve the people.

Whenever I went into town and saw trains, trucks, boats, bustling crowds, wide streets, high buildings and thriving factories, my world would expand a bit and, returning, I would talk endlessly with my little friends about my experiences. I would imagine that, when I grew up, I would be a steel worker, braving the flying sparks before an open hearth furnace. Or maybe I would be a new-style peasant, racing through the fields on a tractor. Or maybe I would keep on going to school, acquiring the knowledge to become a philosopher or a creative writer.

I approached my teens just as Lin Biao and the "Gang of Four" were gaining control. They promoted the reactionary bloodlines theory, and my hopes and ideals, now at odds with my birth, popped one by one, like so many soap bubbles. After completing primary school, I was not allowed to attend a regular middle school because of my background. When my little brother finished primary school, an education cadre said, "We can't allow children from that kind of family to go to school." His comment cut me to the quick.

When I was seventeen, the peasants asked me to become a primary school teacher in the brigade's school. I threw myself into my work with relish but, two years later, I was thrown out by an education cadre. The reason given was that one with a bad class background should himself be receiving instruction from the poor and lower middle peasants.

One year, during army recruitment, I asked at the county's and commune's recruiting offices for permission to join, but I was wasting my breath!

Since infancy, I have received the party's class education. I understood the oppression and exploitation of the working people by the evil imperialists, Kuomintang reactionaries, landlords and rich

[1] Dong Cunrei (Tung Tsun-jei) and Huang Jiguang (Huang Ji-kuang) were soldiers martyred during the War of Liberation and the Korean War, respectively. Liu Hulan was martyred during the Anti-Japanese War when, as a fifteen-year-old party member, she refused to reveal the whereabouts of her comrades. Lei Feng was a People's Liberation Army soldier in the early 1960s, famous for his selflessness.

peasants. When I thought of the rich peasant origin of my family, I realized that my ancestors could not have been good people. I became very angry with my family. I remember one year at Qing Ming Festival,[2] I refused to go up to our ancestral tomb, participating instead in the tomb sweeping ceremony held by our school in commemoration of revolutionary heroes. I was beaten at home for that. From that time on, I have never practiced ancestor veneration, but I received no understanding for my change in attitude. Once I ran afoul of a young cadre over a small incident. Not bothering to scold anyone else, he spat out at me, "Landlords and rich peasants are liars." Then he added, "How dare you! To the last generation, you'll be a landlord-rich peasant!" I couldn't tell what was right or wrong. I mutely took his abuse, the tears streaming down my cheeks.

I started to read the works of Chairman Mao as well as Marx, Engels, Lenin and Stalin. I read some literature, newspapers, and magazines. I came to love and be greatly influenced by the works of Lu Xun.[3] Mr. Lu Xun had not been born a proletarian, but he became a great proletarian revolutionary. I began to believe in communism and longed to be able to join the youth league and the Communist Party. I wished to spend my life striving for communism. From the point of view of some lower level leaders, however, I was the offspring of a parasite seeking to worm my way into power. It was as if our bodies were alive with contagion so that none even approached us, let alone taught us, helped us or encouraged us.

For many years now, my revolutionary ideals and energy of youth have lain shattered by unyielding reality. I, who used to have so many beautiful dreams, the romantic revolutionary of yesterday, have become a ruined, wasted man.

My mother would look at me with tears in her eyes and say, "Your mother has hurt you so." You see, she had been born into a poor peasant home. Just after liberation she made the mistake of marrying into my father's family.

I am the eldest, and now I am grown up. Mother always has hoped that I could marry and raise a family. I have loved several times, but the plays are all tragedies. One girl, understanding, said, "I like you but not your family. Not only could they bring disaster on me, but also on my own family. When my brothers and sisters grow up and want to join the youth league, the party or the army, when they want to start work or go to school, any investigation will show the bad connection and then they will blame me." She was right. Others were not alone in disliking my family. I, too, was disgusted by them. I wanted to leave them, to go to a worker's family having only a daughter so that I might become their son-in-law. Another girl said to me, "I would like you to join our family, but your family background could tarnish ours, so that we wouldn't be as good as other people." Naturally that would happen. I didn't want to harm others.

Having written this far, I cannot stop the tears from falling. Once more, I remember those tragic days after Chairman Mao died. The brigade party branch issued black armbands to all others, but they would not give them to the landlords' and rich peasants' children. That experience is deeply etched on my soul.

So many times, I resolved to leave my despicable family. Last September, I gave my notice to the brigade party branch that I had left them.

Now I have no family. But under the leadership of the Central Party Committee led by Chairman Hua, I neither can nor do I wish to wander aimlessly as did Jia Baoyu;[4] I neither can nor should escape to Yan'an to look for the revolutionary road as they did in the period of the democratic revolution.[5] And so, in anguish, my hopes are extinguished. I ask that the party and the government might carry out policies more effectively in our village and release me from my sufferings. Whatever hard work they ask of me, I would willingly do. Even more so, I hope that others like me will no longer suffer as I have. I hope that, in going to school, finding work, enlisting in the army, in all

---

[2] Qing Ming: an old Chinese spring festival when people would clean the tombs of their ancestors, and make offerings to pay their respects. Now the day is used to commemorate martyrs to the revolution.

[3] Lu Xun (Lu Hsun): a famous left-wing social critic and novelist active in China during the 1920s and 1930s. Today in China he is considered the most important writer of the period.

[4] Jia Baoyu (Chia Pao-yu): the central character in the Chinese classic novel *The Dream of the Red Chamber*.

[5] In the late 1930s and the 1940s, many leftist intellectuals left the cities to join Mao Zedong and the People's Liberation Army in the liberated zone around Yan'an in Shaanxi Province.

these things and more, they will not meet obstructions. Let them work to the best of their abilities. It is better to unite with a few more people in pursuing the work of the revolution.

He Benxian Jianyang Region General Farm, Fujian Province, December 15, 1978 From *Comrade Editor: Letters to the People's Daily.* Hong Kong: Joint Co., Hong Kong Branch, 1980. pp. 129–133.

## Questions

1. What was the class background of the writer?
2. What kinds of discrimination did he suffer because of his class background?
3. Why did he feel that the discrimination against him was unfair?
4. Why did his mother blame herself for her son's fate?
5. How did the writer's class background affect his marriage prospects?
6. How important are a person's political convictions to you? Will you take them into account when selecting a spouse?
7. How important is a person's class to you? Will it influence you in selecting a spouse?

## Reading: *The Family and the Population Crisis*

The growth of the population must be put under control. We must practice family planning; that is simply a fundamental national policy for our country. The reason we carry out such a policy is predicated on China's national conditions. We are a developing country with a huge population, a weak background, relatively backward forces of production and an extremely unbalanced economic development; we are still in the primary stage of socialism. Our arable land is merely 7 percent of that of the world, but we have to feed and keep alive a population that is 21 percent of the world's total population. . . . Our country's population has a large base figure; if we do not practice the control and limitation of the population, the increased wealth we generate each year will be canceled out by the growth of the population. Not only will it then be impossible for our country's national strength to be increased, and not only will there not be any sustaining force behind the development of production, but it will be difficult to improve people's lives.

Li Peng, "Speech While Receiving the Report of the National Conference of Director of Family Planning Commissions," 20 January 1988. In *Chinese Sociology and Anthropology* 24: 3 (Spring 1992), p. 65.

Although it was 1988 when Premier Li gave the speech from which this excerpt is taken, you could have heard a similar sense of urgency expressed by Chinese leaders twenty years earlier. And you will probably hear the same message from leaders for some time to come.

### China's Population

| | | | |
|---|---|---|---|
| 1950 | 551,960,000 | 1971 | 852,290,000 |
| 1951 | 563,000,000 | 1972 | 871,770,000 |
| 1952 | 574,820,000 | 1973 | 892,110,000 |
| 1953 | 587,960,000 | 1974 | 908,590,000 |
| 1954 | 602,660,000 | 1975 | 924,200,000 |
| 1955 | 614,650,000 | 1976 | 937,170,000 |
| 1956 | 628,280,000 | 1977 | 949,740,000 |
| 1957 | 646,530,000 | 1978 | 962,590,000 |
| 1958 | 659,940,000 | 1979 | 975,420,000 |
| 1959 | 672,070,000 | 1980 | 987,050,000 |
| 1960 | 662,070,000 | 1981 | 1,000,720,000 |
| 1961 | 658,590,000 | 1982 | 1,015,410,000 |
| 1962 | 672,950,000 | 1983 | 1,024,950.000 |
| 1963 | 691,720,000 | 1984 | 1,034,750,000 |
| 1964 | 704,990,000 | 1985 | 1,045,320,000 |
| 1965 | 725,380,000 | 1986 | 1,057,210,000 |
| 1966 | 745,420,000 | 1987 | 1,080,730,000 |
| 1967 | 763,680,000 | 1988 | 1,089,780,000 |
| 1968 | 785,340,000 | 1989 | 1,106,760,000 |
| 1969 | 806,710,000 | 1990 | 1,133,680,000 |
| 1970 | 829,920,000 | | |

From *Almanac of China's Population*, edited by Population Research Institute. Beijing: Chinese Academy of Social Sciences, 1991, p. 425. [In Chinese]

# China's Population, 1950–1990

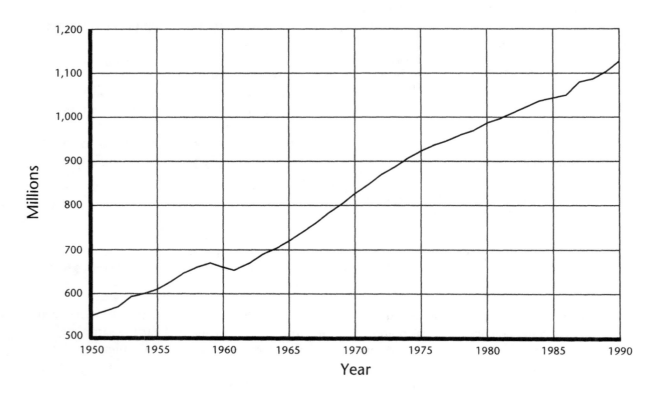

## Questions

1. About how much has the population of the People's Republic increased since 1950?
2. According to the table, by how many people did the population increase from 1989 to 1990? Is this number larger than the population of your state? If so, how many times larger?

### Activity: China Today: How Big is Big?

Create a display comparing the populations of the world's six largest countries.

1. Select a unit of measurement to represent a given number of people. You may use any object or material—for example, a toothpick, a grain of rice, an empty can, a centiliter of water. Use the same unit for all six countries.

2. Decide how many people your unit will represent. Each unit may represent no more than 10 million people.

3. Calculate how many units you will need for each country. Just divide the population of each country by the number of people that your unit represents. For example, if a toothpick represents 10 million people, you will need 15.5 toothpicks to represent Brazil's population.

| | |
|---|---|
| Russia | 147,800,000 |
| Canada | 29,100,000 |
| People's Republic of China | 1,192,000,000 |
| United States | 260,800,000 |
| Brazil | 155,300,000 |
| Australia | 17,800,000 |

Estimates from 1994 World Population Data Sheet, Population Reference Bureau, Inc., Washington, DC.

4. Create a visually effective and informative three-dimensional display. Indicate the number of people your unit represents.

## Reading: *Family Planning*

Throughout its long and turbulent history, China's population was held in check by wars, famines, disease, and natural disasters. But by the 1950s overcrowding in many cities prompted the new Communist government to begin family planning campaigns in urban areas. Planned-birth education soon spread to the countryside, where a largely illiterate and skeptical peasant population began to understand the importance of population control.

By the early seventies Chinese leaders knew they were facing a huge demographic crisis. Following liberation, progress in health care, child care, and food production (except for the lean years during the Great Leap Forward) lowered death rates and encouraged higher birth rates. The population exploded. The Chinese government, worried that food production would not keep pace with population growth, launched more organized, widespread, and coercive birth control campaigns.

In the countryside during the seventies, many health-clinic workers along with local leadership groups decided how many children could be born in their commune, when they could be born, and who could bear them. A woman who chose to defy her commune's directives or became pregnant without permission was likely to be visited by party cadres and forced to attend group criticism sessions until she agreed to an abortion.

The government also launched a barrage of propaganda to support its family-planning policies. Chinese citizens listened to radio broadcasts, read newspaper and magazine articles, and attended rallies, cultural performances, and group discussion meetings telling them to wait until they were older to marry, to wait longer to have children, and to have fewer children. "One is good, two is all right, three is too many."

During the late 1970s major eastern cities started experimenting with a new strategy: the one-child family. City governments began rewarding parents of just one child with monthly subsidies for health care, along with priority in housing assignments, kindergarten enrollment, and job allocations. Family-planning workers in large cities met little resistance to the one-child policy because city families tended to be smaller than country families.

In 1979 the government called on the entire nation to adopt the single-child policy. Rural governments took up the cause, promising tax breaks and educational and health-care benefits to couples who took the one-child pledge. The government also assessed extra fees and taxes to punish couples who chose to have more than one child. But it was more difficult to control behavior in the countryside, especially after the government dismantled the commune system.

Moreover, not long after Deng's economic reforms took root, many peasants found they could afford the penalties for having additional children. In fact, more male children could help to boost farm production and profits once they reached adolescence. Sympathetic cadres in charge of local planned-birth committees sometimes also excused peasant parents, especially those with only a daughter or daughters, and allowed them to have a second and in rare cases a third child without penalty. Since 1985, enforcement of the one-child policy in rural China has been alternately relaxed and tightened, depending on the resistance of local populations.

## Activity: China's Population Policies

Answer the following questions from the information in the graph "Urban and Rural Fertility Rates."

1. According to the graph, have Chinese family-planning policies reduced the size of families? Explain your answer.
2. How do rural and urban fertility rates compare? What might be reasons for this?
3. What fertility rate would eventually lower the population?

## Urban and Rural Fertility Rates

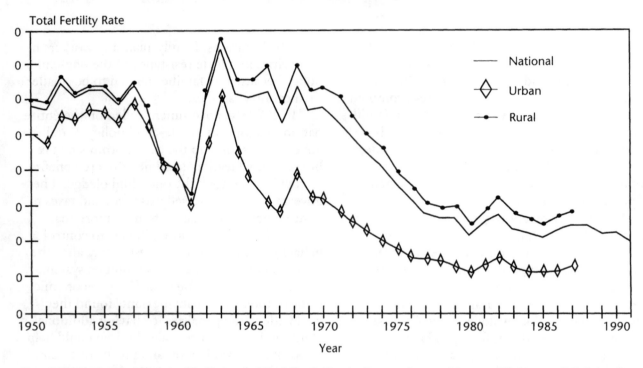

Total Fertility Rate

Legend:
— National
◇ Urban
● Rural

Year axis: 1950, 1955, 1960, 1965, 1970, 1975, 1980, 1985, 1990

From Judith Banister and Christina Wu Harbaugh, *China's Family Planning Program: Inputs and Outcomes.* Washington, DC: Center for International Research, Bureau of the Census, 1994, p. 18.

*A happy one-child family at the Grand Garden in Shanghai, 1989. Courtesy of Xu Ping.*

4. What would account for the decline in population and the huge drop in the fertility rate between 1957 and 1962?

5. If all, or even most, families had only one child, what might happen to relationships among cousins, aunts, uncles, and other relatives?

6. Since China has no social security system, the government relies on adult children, usually a son, to live with and take care of elderly parents. (This is probably why there were no rewards for couples who chose not to have children.) How might this cause problems in the future if there were only one child per family?

---

### Activity: Write an Essay

Write a short essay expressing your views on family planning in China. Do you agree with the government's family-planning policies, do you

## China's Minority Peoples

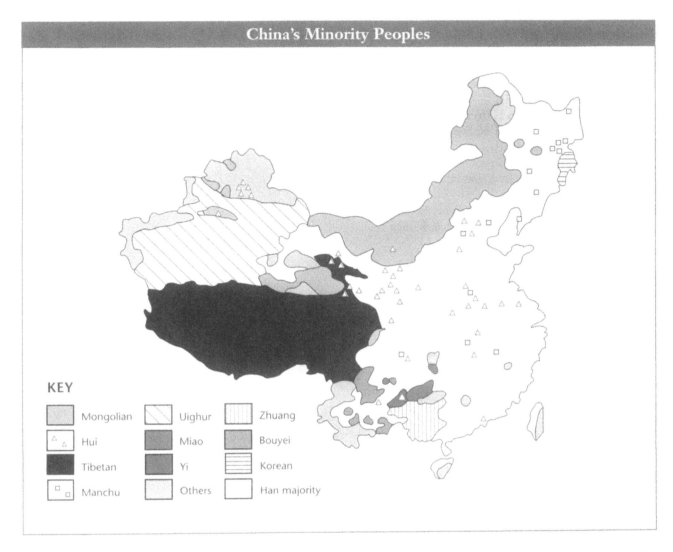

**KEY**

- Mongolian
- Hui
- Tibetan
- Manchu
- Uighur
- Miao
- Yi
- Others
- Zhuang
- Bouyei
- Korean
- Han majority

believe they go too far, or do you think they don't go far enough? Support your views with information in this section. At what point, if any, do people's desires for children outweigh the needs of a society? Can you think of any instance when the American government would be justified in controlling family planning for its citizens?

## Extension Activities

1. **Book review and presentation.** You may be interested in reading *China Wakes: The Struggle for the Soul of a Rising Power,* by Nicholas D. Kristof and Sheryl WuDunn. New York: Times Books, 1994. The authors state that China's one-child policy and the market economy have lowered the status of women since the days of Mao Zedong. According to the authors, the 1980s have seen an increase in wife selling and female infanticide. Turn in a written review of this book and make an oral presentation to the class.

2. **Videos.** Suggested videos on topics covered by this section: "Marrying," Episode 8 of the series *The Heart of the Dragon* (New York: Ambrose Video Publications, 1988) examines the changing status of women and reactions to the government's birth-control policy. "Mediating," Episode 10 of the same series, shows the importance of the family. A couple wanting a divorce are pressured into continuing their marriage.

# Further Reading

Andors, Phyllis. *The Unfinished Liberation of Chinese Women, 1949–1980.* Bloomington: Indiana University Press, 1983.

Davis, Deborah, and Stevan Harrell, eds. *Chinese Families in the Post-Mao Era.* Berkeley: University of California Press, 1993.

Kane, Penny. *The Second Billion: Population and Family Planning in China.* New York: Penguin Books, 1987.

Meijer, M. J. *Marriage Law and Policy in the Chinese People's Republic.* Hong Kong: Hong Kong University Press, 1971.

*New Trends in the Chinese Marriage and Family.* Beijing: Women of China, 1987.

Poston, Dudley L., Jr., and David Yaukey, eds. *The Population of Modern China.* New York: Plenum Press, 1992.

Xizhe, Peng. *Demographic Transition in China: Fertility Trends Since the 1950s.* Oxford: Clarendon Press, 1991.

# 5 China and Other Countries, from 1949

*Having examined China's internal situation in the previous sections, we now turn to China's relationships with other countries during the five decades after World War II. Political cartoons, background essays, and writings from the Chinese press illustrate the state of these relationships and give us insight into the feelings of government leaders.*

## Activity: Political Cartoons

Political cartoons are among the most effective means of presenting a political point of view. As the saying goes, "A picture is worth a thousand words."

1. In your local newspaper or a current news magazine such as *Time*, *U.S. News and World Report*, or *Newsweek*, find a political cartoon you understand. Bring the cartoon to class.
2. Your teacher will make photocopies and overhead transparencies of about a half-dozen cartoons for the class to analyze. With a partner, see if you can "read" the cartoons, keeping in mind the following questions. Then each person (not each pair) should write responses to the questions.

   a. What political issue does this cartoon present?
   b. What do you think each figure and object in the cartoon represents?
   c. Effective political cartoons express a point of view. What is the point of view of this cartoon?

3. Your teacher will call on pairs to share their analyses with the rest of the class.

As you read the following selections, consider the viewpoints presented and think about how the incidents might be depicted in political cartoons. Later you will be asked to draw political cartoons about China's foreign relations.

## Reading: *China and the United States, from 1949*

### China and the United States, from 1949

Relations between the People's Republic of China and the United States over the last fifty years have, at times, been quite tense. China has been a communist country; the United States has been vehemently anti-communist. While the Chinese government has believed that the communist revolution should spread around the world, American officials have generally held that every effort must be made to stop its spread, even to the extent of propping up brutal but anti-communist dictators. Thus from a purely ideological standpoint, one would expect the two nations to be at each other's throats.

This natural antipathy was made worse during Mao's lifetime because he was the inspiration for revolutionary Communism. During the Korean war (1950–1953), American and Chinese troops fought each other; during the war in Vietnam, the Chinese sent guns, money, and other military aid to the Vietnamese but stopped short of sending troops. During this period, the anti-American rhetoric of the Chinese reached an extraordinary pitch.

*Chinese troops crossing the Han River in Korea during the Korean war. China's entry into the war saved communist North Korea from defeat at the hands of American and South Korean forces. The Korean War also began a period of "cold war" between the United States and China. Following the war, the United States became much more adamant in its support for the Nationalist government led by Chiang Kai-shek on Taiwan. Courtesy of the Military Museum, Beijing.*

Ironically, during the last years of the Vietnam war, with the American pullout assured, relations between the United States and China achieved, if not warmth, at least civility. The American president Richard Nixon visited China in 1972. Diplomatic relations were established seven years later, when the United States withdrew its recognition of the Guomindang on Taiwan as the legitimate government of all China. Since then the two sides have often been at odds on issues of international importance, but no one has actually feared that war would break out between them, as some did in the 1960s.

*Chairman Mao meeting President Nixon in February 1972. The meeting of these two leaders helped speed the process of normalizing relations between the United States and China. Courtesy of the Military Museum, Beijing.*

## China and the United States in the 1960s

The following excerpt illustrates the tenor of anti-American sentiment in China during the mid to late 1960s. The title of this part of the article was "Defeat U.S. Imperialism and its lackeys by a People's War." It may be hard to take this rhetoric seriously today, but many Communist revolutionaries then believed that the United States was "the most rabid aggressor in human history." Chinese Communists used the word "imperialism" in a different sense from the nineteenth-century meaning, empire-building through conquest. To the Communists, imperialism meant control of one country by another through political and economic exploitation. In this view, the United States was imperialist in

propping up corrupt Third World dictators who let American companies use their people as cheap labor to produce goods consumed by Americans.

While you read this selection, keep in mind that it is political propaganda, designed to inflame the passions of its readers. It is at the opposite extreme from the ways of diplomacy. Diplomacy is a game of great subtlety: The smallest change in language can signal an enormous change in position; the omission of a single key phrase can signal a great concession. Political propaganda is painted in great brush strokes, and even the most aggressive words may have little factual meaning.

While the aim of diplomacy is to keep options open, the aim of propaganda is to arouse an audience.

Since World War II, US imperialism has stepped into the shoes of German, Japanese, and Italian fascism and has been trying to build a great American empire by dominating and enslaving the whole world. It is actively fostering Japanese and West German militarism as its chief accomplices in unleashing a world war. Like a vicious wolf, it is bullying and enslaving various peoples, plundering their wealth, encroaching upon their countries' sovereignty and interfering in their internal affairs. It is the most rabid aggressor in human history and the most ferocious common enemy of the people of the world. Every people or country in the world that wants revolution, independence, and peace cannot but direct the spearhead of its struggle against US imperialism. . . .

History has proved and will go on proving that people's war is the most effective weapon against US imperialism and its lackeys. All revolutionary people will learn to wage people's war against US imperialism and its lackeys. They will take up arms, learn to fight battles, and become skilled in waging people's war, though they have not done so before. US imperialism, like a mad bull dashing from place to place, will finally be burned to ashes in the blazing fires of the people's war it has provoked by its own actions.

From Lin Biao, "Long Live the Victory of People's War," in *Peking Review* 8: 36 (Sept. 3, 1965), pp. 9–30.

## Question

What major struggle was going on between nations in 1965 that the Chinese could have considered evidence of American aggression? Be ready to do research to answer this question.

---

## Reading: *China and the Soviet Union, from 1949*

On the surface, one would expect China and the Soviet Union to get along together better than the United States and China. But between the establishment of the People's Republic of China and the fall of Soviet Communism, the two largest Communist countries on earth went through a remarkable series of spasms in their relationship.

At times they seemed the best of friends; at other times they fought border wars. By the late 1960s relations between the two Communist countries were just as bad as relations between the Americans and the Chinese. What happened?

China and Russia share a border of 1,300 miles, about 2,100 kilometers; three other republics that were part of the Soviet Union also border China. During the Soviet years, the length of the border between the two countries was some 2,500 miles, or 4,032 kilometers. Only Canada and the United States share a longer border.

During the mid-nineteenth century, border disputes between the Chinese and Russian empires had strained their relations. After Russia became the first Communist country in 1917, it joined with other parts of the old Russian empire

*Mao Zedong at Joseph Stalin's seventieth birthday party in Moscow, December 21, 1949. Courtesy of Shanghai People's Press.*

in 1922 to form the Union of Soviet Socialist Republics (U.S.S.R.). When China joined the family of Communist nations in 1950, a natural alliance formed between China and the U.S.S.R. But there was potential for trouble. For China was a large country with ambitions of its own. Would the Chinese agree with every change of policy the Soviet Union proposed, as most Communist parties elsewhere did? What would happen to relations between the U.S.S.R. and China if the Chinese disagreed with Soviet policy?

For the first few years after the Communist victory in China, the Chinese and the Soviets spoke with one voice. Then, in 1956, the Communist world was shaken to its foundations. The leader of the U.S.S.R., Nikita Khrushchev, stated before a meeting of the Congress of the Communist Party of the Soviet Union that his predecessor, Josef Stalin, was not the saint that official Communist policy had pretended. He was, instead, a brutal and vindictive mass murderer. Khrushchev criticized the "cult of personality" that had raised Stalin to the position of a demigod.

Mao Zedong was not amused. Khrushchev's speech contradicted a crucial Communist belief: that each stage of Communist history would be better than the one before. If Stalin was a monster and his predecessor, Lenin, was a saint (as Khrushchev maintained), then during the course of Communist history things got worse, not better. Furthermore, because Khrushchev had made this speech without alerting anyone, Mao felt obliged to go along with a major shift in the Communist belief system that he had never agreed to. Mao was also building his own cult of personality, and it probably made him nervous to hear that such cults were not acceptable for living Communists. Moreover, there was a key disagreement in policy. While the Soviet Union focused on rapid development of urban heavy industry, China was mobilizing peasants to transform the economy and the society. (Recall the Great Leap Forward.)

For the next few years the dispute simmered, in spite of attempts to patch it up. The "Mao Tse-tung–Khrushchev communiqué" of 1958 was one such attempt to convince the world that life was still good in the Communist household. But by 1960, criticism of the Soviet Union was appearing in the Chinese press.

Things got worse in 1964, when border disputes erupted between the Soviet Union and China. During the Cultural Revolution, particularly from 1966 to 1969, it was hard to tell whom the Chinese hated more—Soviets or Americans. During the years 1973–1976, it often seemed as

if relations between the United States and China were better than relations between the Soviet Union and China.

Mao died in 1976. By the 1980s China had re-established at least civil relations with the Soviet Union. During the 1980s the Chinese voted with the Soviets 90 percent of the time on Security Council resolutions at the United Nations but with the United States less that 50 percent of the time. However, the press in both China and the Soviet Union generally criticized the other country. The two sides were reluctant to present a united front even when they agreed.

Although the fall of Communism in the Soviet Union in 1991 made the Chinese nervous, they have stopped short of denouncing the new government in Russia. In the summer of 1994, the two countries took steps to end their border dispute, achieving some progress toward re-establishing friendly relations.

### A Period of Friendship

The following selection is from the period of warm friendship between China and the Soviet Union. Notice the specific kinds of help the Soviets proffered and what the Chinese thought they would gain from this help.

Our country's being able so speedily to carry out the first Five-Year Plan for the development of national economy is inseparable from the assistance of the Soviet Union and the people's democracies, particularly the assistance of the Soviet Union. The 156 industrial construction projects which the Soviet Union is helping our country to design constitute the nucleus of industrial construction in our first Five-Year Plan. . . .

In the midst of her own bustling Communist construction, the Soviet Union has sent large numbers of experts to our country to help us. They supply us with advanced experience from the Socialist construction of the Soviet Union and give concrete help to us in all kinds of economic work. All the experts sent to our country from the Soviet Union possess not only profound scientific and technical knowledge and rich experience in practical work, but also a lofty spirit of internationalism and selfless working attitude. In industry, agriculture, forestry, water conservancy, geology, transport, posts and telecommunications, building construction, geology, education, public health and other departments, in scientific, technical and cultural cooperation, the Soviet experts faithfully and unreservedly contribute their experience, knowledge and skill. They regard the great cause of Socialist construction of our country as their own cause. The Communist working attitude of the Soviet experts has set an example for the people of our own country. It must be said that the great achievements of our economic construction are inseparable from the help of the Soviet experts.

Tremendous efforts have been made by the Soviet Union in helping our country to train technical personnel. The Soviet Union has accepted a large number of students and trainees from our country and provided them with every convenience in their studies and practical training. This is highly important for us in mastering modern industrial technique, guaranteeing the putting into operation of our new enterprises and raising our scientific level. The Soviet experts who have come to our country have also made great contributions to the training of technical personnel of our country.

The Soviet Union has extended great financial aid to our country by granting us successive loans on the most favorable terms and selling us technical equipment and materials at low prices in trade relations. Such benefits in loans and trade also help in the speedy restoration and development of our country's economy, particularly our country's industrial construction.

It is clear from the above that Soviet assistance plays an extremely important role in enabling us to carry on our present construction work on such a large scale, at such high speed, on such a high technical level, and at the same time, avoiding many mistakes. . . .

The Chinese Government and people give heartfelt thanks for the assistance of the Soviet Union and the people's democracies, especially the great, long-term, all-round and unselfish assistance of the Soviet Union. To consolidate and develop the Socialist industrialization of our country, we should further consolidate and develop our economic alliance and friendly cooperation with the Soviet Union and the people's democracies, so as

to promote a common economic upsurge of the Socialist camp and strengthen the world forces of peace and democracy.

From Li Fun-Chun, "Report on China's First Five-Year Plan to the National People's Congress, 5–6 July 1955," *Current Background*, No. 335, pp. 52–54.

## *A Period of Hostility*

The next excerpt comes from a propaganda publication put out by the Chinese government to explain and justify its anti-Soviet position. Notice the enormous difference between this article and the previous one. In fourteen years the "friends of socialism" had become the "Soviet modern revisionist renegade clique." Even if you don't understand the precise meaning of each cliché in this article, you will get the general picture. It is written in a style that immediately identifies it as late 1960s Chinese Communist propaganda. The title of the article is "Soviet Revisionist Renegade Clique Directs Soviet Frontier Guards to Intrude Flagrantly into China's Territory on Chenpao Island."

On March 2 the Soviet modern revisionist renegade clique directed Soviet frontier guards to intrude flagrantly into the area of Chenpao Island, Heilungkiang [Heilongjiang] Province, China, and outrageously open cannon and gun fire, killing and wounding many Chinese frontier guards. The Chinese frontier guards were compelled to fight back in self-defence. This extremely grave incident of armed provocations deliberately created by the Soviet revisionist renegade clique is another grave crime perpetrated by it against the Chinese people and once again reveals its fiendish features as social-imperialism.

At about 09:00 hours on March 2, large numbers of fully armed soldiers, together with armored vehicles, a lorry [a truck] and a command car, sent by the Soviet frontier authorities, flagrantly intruded into the area of Chenpao Island which is indisputable Chinese territory, and carried out provocations against the Chinese frontier guards who were on normal patrol duty on the island. At that time, the Chinese frontier guards, showing very great restraint, repeatedly warned the intruding Soviet soldiers and ordered them to stop their provocations and withdraw from the Chinese territory. However, the intruding Soviet soldiers refused to heed these warnings and became even more truculent. At 09:17 hours, the intruding Soviet soldiers outrageously opened up with cannon and gun fire on the Chinese frontier guards. Having reached the end of their forbearance, the Chinese frontier guards were compelled to fight back in self-defence, giving the intruders, who were committing provocations, their deserved punishment and triumphantly safeguarding our country's sacred territory.

This extremely grave armed conflict single-handedly created by the Soviet revisionist renegade clique is by no means an isolated incident. For a long time, the Soviet revisionist renegade clique, ignoring the repeated warnings of the Chinese Government, has time and again encroached upon China's territory and her air space and created incidents involving bloodshed on many occasions. During the ice-bound season in the more than two years between January 23, 1967, and March 2 this year [1969], Soviet frontier guards intruded into the area of Chenpao Island on sixteen occasions, and on several occasions wounded Chinese frontier guards who were on normal patrol duty, and looted arms and ammunition. Between the end of November 1967 and January 5, 1968, the Soviet revisionist renegade clique sent Soviet frontier guards on eighteen occasions to intrude into the area of Chilichin Island, north of Chenpao Island, Heilungkiang Province, China, disrupting Chinese people's production and on many occasions killing and wounding Chinese people engaged in productive labor. Soviet frontier guards also intruded into the area of Kapotzu Island, south of Chenpao Island, Heilungkiang Province, China, on many occasions. And, on a still greater number of occasions, Soviet military planes intruded into China's air space over Heilungkiang Province.

The criminal activities of the Soviet revisionist renegade clique in deliberately encroaching upon China's territory and creating incidents involving bloodshed one after another have glaringly exposed the vicious features of the clique, which for a long time has collaborated with US imperialism, frenziedly opposed China and practised social-imperialism and social-fascism. These grave crimes of the clique have aroused the utmost indignation of the Chinese armymen and civilians. The Chinese people sternly warn the Soviet revisionist renegade clique: The 700 million Chinese people, tempered in the great proletarian cultural revolution, are not to be trifled with. China's sacred territory brooks no violation. If you should willfully cling to your reckless course and continue to provoke armed conflicts along the Sino–Soviet border, you will certainly receive resolute counter-blows from the 700 million Chinese people who are armed with Marxism–Leninism–Mao Tse-tung Thought!

From "Down With The New Tsars," Peking: Foreign Languages Press, 1969, pp. 9–11.

## Questions

1. What kinds of assistance did the Soviet Union provide to China? Be specific. According to the article, how would China gain from this assistance?

2. According to the section "A Period of Friendship," why did the Soviets assist the Chinese?

3. What did the Soviets do that was so bad, according to the Chinese? Was it an isolated incident?

4. According to the article, what do this and similar incidents reveal about the Soviet Union?

5. What do you think the article means when it says that the Soviets will "receive resolute counter-blows from the 700 million Chinese people who are armed with Marxism – Leninism–Mao Tse-tung Thought"?

## Overseas Chinese

Over the past several hundred years, many enterprising Chinese have lived and worked overseas—in Southeast Asia, the Americas, Europe, and the Pacific Islands. Among the earliest to leave were people from southeast China, where land is poor but where good natural harbors and plentiful timber made it possible to sail to other places to trade and live. Between 1405 and 1433, the Ming Dynasty's Zheng He led grand fleets of over three hundred ships and more than 27,000 men on expeditions that traveled as far as East Africa (see Chapter 1, Section 5). Later, other Chinese traded extensively with Thailand, Indochina, the Malay Peninsula, the islands of Indonesia, and the Philippines, establishing settlements in all these locales. By 1603, for instance, more than 20,000 Chinese traders, artisans, workers, and their families lived in Manila.

From the 1500s to the 1700s, traders and artisans formed the bulk of the emigrants. In most cases they intermarried, and their descendants gradually assimilated into the local environment. With the advent of cheap steamship passage in the 1800s, zealous middlemen recruited poverty-stricken, unskilled laborers in China for work in Latin America and the Caribbean. Many of those who survived the horrendous conditions on the ships died working the mines and plantations of places like Peru and Cuba. The discovery of gold in California in 1848 drew other Chinese to North America, but hostilities toward them led the U.S. government to enact Chinese exclusion laws, beginning in 1882. (It was not until World War II, when China and the United States became allies, that the American government again opened its doors to Chinese.) Since the 1920s many educated professionals and political refugees from China have emigrated to all parts of the world.

Like other groups who emigrated, overseas Chinese sought the support of those who shared their heritage. Chinatowns sprang up in cities all over the world. In their adopted lands the Chinese also established kinship and district organizations and joined with like-minded associates for entertainment, mutual aid, and protection.

Although far from China, many overseas Chinese maintained an active interest in events there. For example, during the turbulent period that eventually ended the Qing Dynasty in 1911, overseas Chinese sheltered exiled reformers and revolutionaries and donated huge sums of money to the movement for nationalism and democracy. After the Communist victory in 1949, multitudes of patriotic overseas Chinese, particularly in Southeast Asia, gave up their wealth and livelihood to go home and help build a new China. Forty years later, when soldiers shot and killed hundreds of demonstrators and bystanders in Tiananmen Square, Chinese all over the world marched in protest.

The Chinese have participated in the growing economies of overseas countries. In the mid-1970s, for example, Chinese constituted 8 to 10 percent of the population in Thailand but owned 90 percent of the commercial and manufacturing assets and half the capital of the banks.

Since the 1980s the Chinese government has loosened its control over the economy. New opportunities have opened up for overseas Chinese to do business inside China, and increasingly they have done so.

*Laborers from China on board a ship bound for Honolulu in the late 1800s. Courtesy of Hawaii State Archives.*

## Hong Kong, Macao, and Taiwan

### Hong Kong

After Britain's victory in the Opium War in 1842 (see Chapter 2, Section 2), the British took Hong Kong Island and made it a crown colony. Later, in 1860, Britain also took Kowloon, the peninsula across the harbor, and made it part of the colony. Then in 1898 Britain leased from China a small area beyond the Kowloon peninsula, known as the New Territories, for a period of ninety-nine years.

As the end of this period approached, the Chinese made it clear they would not renew the lease on the New Territories. Furthermore, China wanted Hong Kong Island and Kowloon back. Because the island and the peninsula could not survive without China's cooperation (for example, their water is piped in from mainland China), Britain decided to return the crown colony to China at the same time that the lease on the New Territories expired.

In December 1984, Britain and China announced a Joint Declaration (curiously, Hong Kong was not represented in the negotiations). The agreement stipulated that Hong Kong would retain capitalism as its economic system, along with a great deal of judicial autonomy. But China later wrote a constitution for Hong Kong, called Basic Law, which, according to some Hong Kong people, deviated in some ways from the Joint Declaration. Only time will reveal how well the concept "one country, two systems" will work.

### Macao

Macao, a small island near Hong Kong, has been administered by the Portuguese since 1557, but China has always been looking over its shoulder, collecting taxes from the territory revenues until the middle of the nineteenth century. Shortly after Britain and China completed negotiations on the status of Hong Kong, the Chinese began negotiating with Portugal on the status of Macao. The talks, between 1984 and 1987, ended with an agreement to turn Macao over to China in 1999. Macao lacked the economic importance of Hong Kong, but the Chinese felt that because the population was 99 percent Chinese and the island depended on China for much of its food and water, they could make a legitimate claim on it. The Portuguese, following the precedent established by the British, agreed to go along.

### Taiwan

With the takeover of Hong Kong, China has become even more interested in reunification with Taiwan, historically a part of China. In 1949 the Communists defeated Chiang Kai-shek, who along with Guomindang troops and supporters fled to the island to set up an exile government, which they continued to call the Republic of China. Chiang declared his government on Taiwan the rightful government of China—an idea the United States endorsed until the 1970s—and dreamed of one day recapturing the mainland from the Communists.

United States support for Chiang began during the War of Resistance when it supplied the Guomindang with financial aid and military supplies to use against the Japanese. Again, during the Chinese Civil War the U.S. provided the Guomindang with financial aid. Following the Guomindang defeat and Chiang's retreat to Taiwan, the United States became the primary protector of the island from Communist invasion. Although, since the 1970s the United States and Western European powers have officially recognized the Beijing government as the true government of China, they continue to supply weapons to Taiwan and to warn the Communists against forcing reunification through military means.

Even though the Communist and Guomindang governments remain officially hostile, by the 1980s neither side could resist the economic appeal of the other. China coveted

*(Hong Kong, Macao, and Taiwan—continued)*

Taiwan's advanced technology and investment capital (under the Guomindang, Taiwan's capitalist economy has grown rapidly, raising living standards far above those on the mainland), while Taiwan desired access to the huge mainland market. With ideology taking a back seat to pragmatism in Taipei and Beijing, each side began allowing increased contact with the other. As a result, business ties between the two thrived, and relations improved.

Despite improving economic relations, major political differences between Taiwan and China remain. During the 1990s, Taiwan, ruled for decades by an authoritarian Guomindang government, made strides toward becoming a democratic society. On the other hand, leaders of the People's Republic showed their disdain for democratic movements with the brutal massacre in Tiananmen Square. (See Chapter 3, "Massacre at Tiananmen.") Peaceful reunification may ulti-

mately depend on whether these two governments can reconcile their political disparities.

*A family reunion after fifty years of separation. China-born Yang Meng-zhong (top right) returned to Yunnan province from Taiwan in 1993 to visit his siblings and his father's grave. Improved relations between China and Taiwan have made it possible for residents of Taiwan to travel to the People's Republic. Many make the trip to see the sights and to visit relatives. Courtesy of Yang Meng-zhong.*

## Hong Kong, Macao, and Taiwan

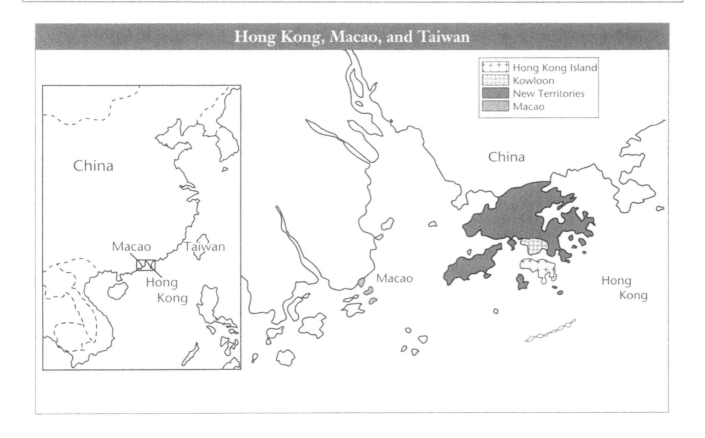

## Reading: *The Middle Kingdom*

### China and the Rest of the World

During the 1950s, China's relations with both Japan and Western Europe, both solidly capitalist and staunch U.S. allies, were unabashedly hostile. Chinese leaders felt particularly threatened by American military bases in Japan and by troops in Korea after the war there, repeatedly calling for American troops to withdraw from both these neighboring countries. Chinese Communists also attacked European imperialism in Africa and backed national independence movements in European colonies throughout the continent.

The fanaticism of the Cultural Revolution further strained relations with Japan and Western Europe in the 1960s. Demonstrations against European capitalist nations, which recognized the Guomindang government on Taiwan as the legitimate government of China, peaked when Red Guards attacked European legations and roughed up European diplomats in Beijing. Chinese Communists also accused Japan of scheming to remilitarize so as to dominate Asia once again, and Chinese support of Communist revolutionaries in the Third World became even more relentless during this period of ideological fervor.

### *Pragmatism Replaces Ideology*

After the Sino–Soviet split and the ensuing border clashes between the two Communist giants in the late sixties, anti-West and anti-Japan rhetoric began to cool. China now considered the Soviet Union its most immediate threat. In line with the maxim "The enemy of my enemy is my friend," Mao began trying to improve relations with the West and Japan to counteract China's deteriorating relations with the Soviet Union. In the 1970s Western nations and Japan finally withdrew their recognition of the Taiwan government and established formal diplomatic ties with the People's Republic.

Following Mao's death, Deng Xiaoping's ambitious economic policies opened China to foreign investment and joint ventures between Chinese and foreign companies. Economic

interests and flexibility replaced hard-nosed ideological radicalism as the basis for China's international relations. Relations with capitalist and developing countries around the world began to center on trade rather than personalities or political ideologies. As an example of this new pragmatism, Japan, reviled by Chinese leaders for much of the twentieth century as China's foremost enemy, has become China's closest and most important economic partner since the late 1970s.

Then, in June of 1989, China's more pragmatic image suffered a serious blow with the slaughter of hundreds of unarmed people demonstrating for democracy in Tiananmen Square. Chinese leaders were clearly unwilling to let their country go the way of Russia and Eastern Europe, where pro-democracy demonstrators had brought down Communist governments. China's officials tolerated some economic freedom, yet rejected political freedom. Some American officials tried to tie human rights to trade, but they failed to force the Chinese government to improve its treatment of political dissidents.

China's last fifty years have been a time of enormous upheaval. As a result of the seismic shifts in their country, the Chinese have maintained an uncertain relationship with the rest of the world. Because China is an important country for its size alone, other countries have worried about the Chinese attitude toward them. China's interpretation of its place in the Communist world especially interested Soviets and Americans. With the collapse of Communism in the Soviet Union and Eastern Europe, the world has been waiting to see how the Chinese respond to the new international reality.

During Mao's lifetime, China claimed leadership in the "vanguard of world revolution." In recent years it has been regarded as an independent and powerful, pragmatic international power. Wary of new developments in Russia and other parts of the old Soviet Union, the Chinese have refrained from taking a strong position on events there.

## Activity: Cartoons

The following cartoons reflect official Chinese attitudes toward the United States and the former Soviet Union when the cartoons were published in the 1950s. With a partner, or as a class, discuss the cartoons for about five minutes. Then answer these questions.

1. In "Position of Strength" what are the Chinese suggesting that Americans are doing by having bases all over the world? Is the caption intended seriously or ironically? Explain.
2. In "Crocodile Tears" what do you notice about the "tears"? What does the phrase "to shed crocodile tears" mean? Why are American "tears" over Chinese aggression "crocodile tears"?
3. The "Mao Tse-tung–Khrushchev communiqué" was an agreement between China and the Soviet Union asserting their common interest in world peace and their cooperative support for the development of poorer nations. What does the cartoon "Stemming the Tide of War" suggest that the communiqué can achieve? How does it illustrate its point?

*Stemming the Tide of War*
Peking Review *1:24 (Aug. 12, 1958), p. 21.*

*Crocodile Tears*
Peking Review *9: 9 (Feb. 25, 1958), p. 9.*

## Activity: Drawing Your Own Cartoon

This activity asks you to create a cartoon that illustrates an aspect of China's relationship with either the United States or the Soviet Union. You do not need artistic talent to do this exer-

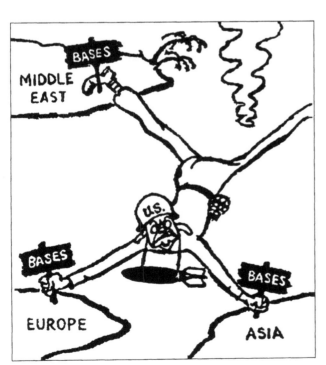

*Position of Strength*
Peking Review *1:33 (Oct. 14, 1958), p. 17.*

cise. You can draw stick figures and symbols or cut pictures from magazines and newspapers. Your teacher will put you into pairs. Follow these steps with your partner to produce your cartoons.

1. Review all the readings in this section. List possible subjects for your cartoon. Then decide on one.
2. Brainstorm ways you might depict your idea. Choose one.
3. Using chart paper or construction paper, felt-tip pens, paste, and cutouts from magazines and newspapers, create a cartoon. Make each object in the cartoon symbolize something. For example, a bear sometimes symbolizes the Soviet Union, Uncle Sam sometimes symbolizes the United States, and a dragon sometimes symbolizes China.
4. Make sure your cartoon presents a point of view.
5. Write a caption for your cartoon to help explain your message. Or write a metaphor like the following.

   China saw _____ as _____.
   China's relationship with _____ was like a _____.

6. When all the cartoons are finished, exchange cartoons with another pair. Then see if you can interpret the other pair's cartoon. On paper, answer these questions.

   a. What is the subject of this cartoon?
   b. What do objects in the cartoon represent?
   c. What point of view does the cartoon present?
   d. Is the cartoon easy or difficult to understand? Explain.

7. Discuss your interpretation with the cartoon's creators. How accurately did you interpret the cartoon? If you read it incorrectly, was it due to your ignorance, to an unclear caption, or to an unclear cartoon?
8. Share your results with the class.

## Extension Activities

**Videos.** Suggested videos on the period covered by this section: *China: The Cold Red War* (Oak Forest, IL: MPI Home Video, 1990) demonstrates the power of propaganda in film. Given from the Soviet Union's perspective, this video shows the fierce battles between the U.S.S.R. and China, portrays Mao Zedong as an imperialist dictator brainwashing his people, and depicts China as a country constantly preparing to fight for world domination. *Dateline 1972, China* (Northbrook, IL: MTI Film and Video, 1989) describes the gradual warming of relations between China and the United States and the concurrent deteriorating of relations between China and the Soviet Union.

## Further Reading

Hsüeh, Chün-tu, *China's Foreign Relations*. New York: Praeger, 1982.

Jones, Peter, and Sian Kevill, *China and the Soviet Union 1949–1984*. New York: Facts on File, 1985.

The best way to monitor the changes in the official Chinese positions from 1959 to 1979 is to read *Peking Review* for those years.

# Glossary

## A

**acculturate:** to take on behaviors of another culture as a result of contact with it.

**alum:** a powdery substance that shrinks tissues and checks bleeding.

**Anti-Rightist Movement:** a campaign led by Chinese Communist Party officials to punish many so-called rightists, mostly intellectuals, who had responded to the call during the *Hundred Flowers Movement* to criticize the party. Many who criticized were exiled or imprisoned. After 1978, most were "rehabilitated." See also *Rightist*.

**aristocracy:** a privileged hereditary upper class in society.

## B

**ballast:** something added to make a load stable.

**benevolent despotism:** rule by a fair or kindly despot (a ruler having absolute power).

**bourgeoisie:** according to Marx, wealthy business owners who employ wage earners; wealthy capitalists.

**bureaucrat:** a nonelected government official.

## C

**cadre:** in Communist China, a civil servant or bureaucrat; someone who works for the government; also, an enthusiastic activist dedicated to furthering the cause of the Chinese Communist Party.

**cangue** (pronounced kang): a wooden framework or yoke enclosing the neck and hands of an offender. It weighed twenty or thirty pounds, and once it was in place wearers could not feed themselves or lie down. It was used as a punishment well into the twentieth century.

**capitalism:** an economic system in which factories, land, and other means of production are privately owned by individuals and corporations. Market competition and the profit motive drive the economy. Capitalism can be better understood when it is compared with the ideas of communal ownership and socialism.

**capitalists:** according to Marx, those who own businesses and employ wage earners; those who promote or practice capitalism. In Communist China, to be called a capitalist was to be denounced.

**Changsha:** the capital city of Hunan province, where Mao Zedong was born.

**Chinese Communist Party (CCP):** a political party that has governed China since 1949. The CCP organized its first meeting in 1921. In 1949, led by Mao Zedong, the CCP was victorious in a civil war against the Guomindang. During the 1950s, 1960s, and 1970s, the CCP emphasized Marxist, Leninist, and Maoist thinking. Since the late 1970s it has allowed increasing capitalistic practices in the country.

**chinoiserie** (pronounced sheen wah zah ree): an eighteenth-century European style of decoration in which supposedly Chinese motifs were used.

**circa:** about; used to indicate approximate date. Sometimes abbreviated as *ca.*

**civil service:** nonmilitary government work.

**civil war:** a war between regions or political factions in the same country.

**class:** a group of people who share a common economic situation.

**collective:** a group of farms managed as a unit, in which farmers work cooperatively under government supervision.

**collectivization:** the bringing together of farms into collectives. See *collective*.

**communes:** See *people's communes*.

**communism:** an economic and social system in which classes are eliminated and the means of production are owned in common. (See "From Marxism to Marxism–Leninism to Maoism" in Chapter 3, Section 1.)

**compound:** one or more buildings enclosed by a wall or fence.

**comprador:** Chinese middleman who worked for foreign companies in China in the late nineteenth and early twentieth centuries.

**concessions:** special privileges. Certain areas in Shanghai where foreigners lived free of Chinese control were sometimes called concessions.

**Confucius:** China's great philosopher and teacher, who lived from 551 B.C.E. to 479 B.C.E. Confucius articulated ideas that became the foundation of Chinese thinking about the family, state, and society.

**Confucianism:** a system of principles and a code of ethics based on the teachings of Confucius.

**cultural clash:** See *cultural conflict*.

**cultural conflict:** Culture is the sum of ways of living built up by a group of people and passed on from one generation to the next. Culture includes values, attitudes, knowledge, ideas, and learned behavior, as well as material objects. When people from different cultures meet, they may misunderstand each other and come into conflict..

**Cultural Revolution:** See *Great Proletarian Cultural Revolution*.

# D

**domestic:** in this usage, a country's internal affairs, as opposed to foreign affairs.

**dowager:** in this context, the widow of a king or emperor. The title Empress (or Queen) Dowager differentiates her from the wife of the reigning king or emperor.

**dynastic cycle:** traditional Chinese interpretation of China's history as a series of cycles with one dynasty replacing another. Each dynasty began with a heroic leader who unseated a corrupt or weak emperor, opening an extended period of stability and prosperity. After several hundred years internal decay set in and the dynasty became corrupt. People suffered from famine and natural disasters while peasant revolts along with external threats destroyed the power of the central government. Eventually the old ruler would be unseated, and a new leader would take the Dragon Throne. Then the dynastic cycle would start again.

**dynasty:** a succession of rulers who come from the same family line.

# E

**economy:** a system by which wealth in a region is produced, developed, and managed; a system for meeting the wants and needs of the people with limited resources.

**ethnocentrism:** the belief that one's own ethnic group or culture is superior to others'.

**eunuch:** a castrated man. Since the Zhou dynasty, eunuchs served the Chinese emperor by guarding and administering the imperial harem of wives and concubines. Uncastrated men who were not part of the emperor's immediate family were not allowed the enter the inner palace. Because of their closeness to the emperor, eunuchs had unequaled opportunities to win his favor and attain powerful positions.

**extraterritoriality:** the right of foreign citizens to be judged by the laws of their country of citizenship rather than the country in which they live.

# F

**fertility rate:** the average number of children that women within a certain age group can expect to bear during their lifetimes if the birthrate remains steady. For example, if the fertility rate were 2.8, then 100 women in the group can expect to bear 280 babies in all, averaging out to 2.8 children each.

**feudal:** characteristic of feudalism, a political and economic system in Europe during the Middle Ages. In the feudal system, a monarch gave nobles land and the power to govern the serfs who farmed and lived on the land. In turn, the nobles swore loyalty to the monarch and gave him military aid. In return for their labor, the serfs were protected by their nobles. When Mao Zedong used the term *feudal*, he was criticizing practices common during the time of imperial China, when emperors ruled through local government officials, who were of the gentry (upper) class. Chapter 1 focuses on imperial China.

**feudalist-capitalist-revisionist:** three words that marked a person as an enemy of Chinese Communism. See also *feudal*, *capitalist*, and *revisionist*.

**filial piety:** the absolute obedience and devotion of children to their parents or those who have taken the place of their parents, including a woman's parents-in-law.

**First Five-Year Plan:** an economic plan instituted in China from 1953 to 1957 to develop steel and coal production, electric power, and other heavy industries.

**Five Cardinal Relationships:** relationships taught by Confucius that became the foundation of Chinese society—emperor and official, father and son, husband and wife, elder brother and younger brother, male friend and male friend. Each person in the relationship has a responsibility to the other.

# G

**Gang of Four:** Jiang Qing and three others who were said to be responsible for the excesses of the Great Proletarian Cultural Revolution. After Mao's death, they were put on public trial for their deeds. Jiang and another of the gang were sentenced to death, later reduced to life imprisonment. Jiang committed suicide in 1991.

**Great Leap Forward:** Mao Zedong's grand design of 1957–58 to mobilize the country's massive population so as to industrialize China overnight. Mao set unrealistic targets; he purged Communist Party leaders who disagreed or pointed out problems. Poor leadership, bad weather, and withdrawal of Soviet aid brought failure and famine.

**Great Proletarian Cultural Revolution:** Mao Zedong's nationwide movement begun in 1966 to mobilize the masses to cleanse the party of revisionists. Key leaders in the party, government, and army were demoted or dismissed. Cadres of youthful Red Guards rampaged through the cities, entered homes, and destroyed old ideas, old customs, old culture, and old habits. Officials and "intellectuals" (those who had at least an intermediate-school education) were paraded through the streets as criminals. For ten years until Mao's death in 1976, China was in anarchy and chaos as millions of innocent people were harassed and tortured.

**guerrilla warfare:** fighting by small mobile groups of irregular soldiers using hit-and-run tactics.

*Guomindang* **(GMD):** political party, also called the Nationalist Party, organized in 1912 by Sun Yat-sen and led by him until his death in 1925. His successor, Chiang Kai-shek, reunified China under Guomindang rule in 1928 but was driven out by the Communists in 1949. He fled to Taiwan with the Guomindang and established an opposing regime there.

# H

**Han Chinese:** the ethnic group considered to be the original group of people who resided in China proper.

**Heavenly Way:** the term used to describe the emperor's wishes and orders, and by extension, China's entire Confucian worldview. Thus the term really meant China itself and its entire way of life.

**heterodox:** departing from accepted beliefs; heretical.

**Hundred Flowers Movement:** a call by Chinese Communist leaders to the people in 1957 to criticize the Communist Party so that it could correct its errors. A flood of criticisms surprised party officials, and they reacted with the Anti-Rightist Movement, in which many people were jailed or exiled.

# I

**ideology:** a systematic set of ideas, with moral overtones, about human beings and society that direct the choices people make in their social and political worlds. Those believing in a particular ideology follow its dictates faithfully.

**imperialism:** the domination and extension of a nation's authority over another nation; one country's dominance over the economic and political affairs of a weaker country. Traditionally, imperialism has referred to nations like Great Britain, which during the nineteenth century turned weaker places into protectorates, spheres of influence, or colonies. In the first half of the twentieth century, Japan was the imperialist power that posed the greatest threat to China. The Chinese Communists claimed that in the twentieth century, countries like the United States were also imperialists because they exploited poorer countries and controlled them.

**imperialists:** those who extend their nation's control over a weaker nation through economic or military means. When Mao talked about imperialists, he was referring to foreign countries that had dominated China since the 1850s.

**indoctrinate:** to teach people to believe in a system of thought. Communists used propaganda as one means of indoctrinating people.

**infanticide:** the practice of killing unwanted infants.

**ingot:** a mass of metal shaped for easy carrying.

## K

*kang* (pronounced kahng): a platform, usually made of brick, heated from beneath and used as a bed and a sitting area.

*koutou:* to touch the forehead to the ground while kneeling as an act of reverence or apology.

## L

**lackey:** one who does the bidding of another in the hope of getting personal favors.

**Long March:** the legendary march of 6,000 miles taken by Chinese Communists from 1934 to 1935, which saved the Communist forces. (See the map and legend "Long March, 1934–1935" in Chapter 3, Section 1.)

## M

**mandarin:** a high government scholar-official in imperial China.

**mandate:** authorization or decree.

**Maoism:** an ideology developed by Mao Zedong in which peasants would play a major revolutionary role in overthrowing a capitalist society. Mao believed that widespread peasant support of and participation in guerrilla warfare—a "people's war"—against the Guomindang was essential for the success of the Communist revolution.

**Marriage Law of 1950:** legislation designed to do away with feudal marriage practices and to fundamentally change the nature of familial relationships to comply with Communist ethics.

**Marxism:** a theory of economics and society by Karl Marx and Friedrich Engels in which the struggle between an exploiter class and an exploited class culminates in violent revolution

and the establishment of a classless society. (See "From Marxism to Marxism–Leninism to Maoism" in Chapter 3, Section 1.)

**Marxism–Leninism:** Whereas Marxism dealt with social and economic theories, Marxism–Leninism offered practical strategies for revolution. Developed by V. I. Lenin, Marxism–Leninism aimed to overthrow a capitalist society and replace it with a Marxist one. (See "From Marxism to Marxism–Leninism to Maoism." in Chapter 3, Section 1.)

**metaphysical:** beyond ordinary experience or material existence.

**monogamous:** having only one spouse at time.

**most-favored-nation clause:** a clause written into a commercial treaty saying that if certain rights and privileges are later granted to a third country, they will automatically be given to the country making the treaty as well. For example, in the Treaty of the Bogue, Britain was the most-favored nation, meaning that Britain automatically got any privileges or immunities that China would grant by treaty to other countries in the future.

*mou:* about one sixth of an acre.

## N

**nationalism:** a desire for national advancement or independence; a desire for one's country to be free from foreign domination. Both the Guomindang and the Communist Party were nationalist in wanting to end foreign imperialism in China.

**Nationalist Party (KMT):** See *Guomindang*.

**nomads:** people who move from place to place seeking better grazing lands for their flocks or herds.

**Northern Expedition:** the Guomindang-led military campaign against warlords (1926–1928) that unified China after thirteen years of civil disorder.

## P

**patriarch:** the male ruler of a family or clan. The patriarchal family system dominated European and Asian societies of long ago.

**people's communes:** In 1958 the Chinese government abolished the vestiges of private plots and other means of production to create people's communes, in which all land belonged to the government. Each commune included about thirty cooperatives of about 5,000 households, or 25,000 people each. Thus one commune held about 750,000 people, about as many as a medium-sized city. By November 1958, practically all peasants lived in communes. Officials of a commune decided what to farm and manufacture, collected taxes, operated public kitchens and mess halls, and ran child care centers, banks, and schools.

**People's Republic of China (PRC):** the name Chinese Communists gave to China after their victory over the Guomindang in 1949.

**people's war:** according to the Chinese, a Communist uprising inspired and led by peasants and proletariat to overthrow the landlords and capitalist bosses.

**physiognomy:** the art of judging a person's character from facial features.

**proletariat:** according to Marx, factory workers and other working people who sell their labor in return for wages.

**propaganda:** the intentional use of words, symbols, music, art, drama, or other forms of communication to influence people's thinking and behavior. Mao believed that thought determined action. If people thought correctly, he reasoned, they would behave correctly. According to Mao, propaganda was necessary for people "to unlearn the bad habits and thoughts acquired from the old society" and to re-educate themselves to think as Communists. Westerners have had a dim view of propaganda because they have associated it with attempts to play on people's emotions, to misrepresent facts, and to manipulate people's thinking.

**province:** a section of a country governed by a distinct unit.

# Q

**queue:** a braid or pigtail worn hanging down from the back of the head. During the Qing dynasty the Manchus made Chinese men wear the queue as a sign of submission to Manchu rule. Chinese men had to shave their foreheads and braid their hair to demonstrate loyalty to the emperor or face execution. During the waning years of the Qing dynasty (1900–1911), men cut off their queues in defiance of Manchu rule.

# R

**Red Guards:** students who during the Cultural Revolution entered homes to destroy objects that represented old ideas and old customs and punish those who followed the old ways. With Mao's encouragement, Red Guard organizations spread throughout China.

**regent:** one who rules when the ruler is absent or too young to rule.

**republic:** a country in which the head of state is not a monarch but an elected or appointed official, often called a president. Although most republics hold elections, a republic is not necessarily a democratic state.

**Republic of China (ROC):** the name for China from 1912 to 1949; also the government that Chiang Kai-shek established on Taiwan when he fled there in 1949 after being defeated by the Communists in China's civil war.

**revisionist:** advocating or causing changes in an accepted doctrine or way of thinking. According to Mao Zedong, revisionists were those who claimed to be Communists but were not because they actually revised the true principles of Marxism–Leninism. *Revisionist* may also be used as an adjective, as in "revisionist capitalist roader" or "revisionist renegade clique."

**revolution:** a drastic change, most often a violent overthrow of a political and/or social system, leading to a fundamental break with the past. The Chinese Communist revolution that began in 1949 was both political and social. The Cultural Revolution was a violent transformation of society without a change of state power.

**rightist:** according to Chinese Communism, someone, often an intellectual, who was accused of rejecting Chinese Communism.

# S

**seal:** a stone or metal stamp used to make an imprint on a document.

**self-strengthening movement:** a movement from the 1860s to the 1890s by Chinese officials to improve the military and technological efficiency of China.

*sini* and *sino:* combining forms referring to China and the Chinese. For example, *sinicize* means to transform into the manner of the Chinese; *sinology* is the study of China; *sinocentric* means China-centered; and the *Sino*-Japanese war is the war between China and Japan.

**social fascism:** according to the Chinese, the Soviet version of fascism. In this view the Soviets were fascists for their disregard of the interests of other nations and their willingness to exploit their own people for military purposes.

**social imperialism:** according to the Chinese, imperialism disguised as socialism. In this view the Soviets, although Communists, were practicing imperialism in trying to control and exploit other nations.

**socialism:** a theory of government that advocates government intervention to effect a more equitable distribution of resources and jobs over the society as a whole. In its more common use, socialism requires that factories, land, and other means of production be owned by the government and used to benefit all. As Communists use the word, *socialism* refers to a stage in their society's evolution—between capitalism and full Communism—which they claim to have achieved but in which economic classes remain. Their ultimate goal is pure Communism.

**socialist:** promoting or practicing socialism or a person who practices or promotes socialism.

**spheres of influence:** large geographical areas within China where certain foreign nations exercised control over natural resources, trade, and transportation.

**steppe:** treeless, semi-arid, grass-covered plains characterized by cold winters and hot summers.

# T

**tael** (pronounced tail): one and a third ounces of silver, a Chinese monetary unit.

**tenth century:** the 900s, the century leading up to the 1000s. In the same way, the nineteenth century refers to the 1800s, just as your fifteenth year is the year before you turn fifteen. On your fifteenth birthday you start your sixteenth year.

**Third World:** poorer countries of the world. Before 1990, the phrase was applied only to poorer non-Communist countries. The First World referred to industrialized non-Communist countries and the Second World to Communist countries.

**tributary states:** regions that acknowledged China's superiority and paid tribute to China by sending missions there laden with gifts.

**tsar:** also spelled *tzar* and *czar*. A male emperor who ruled Russia before the Bolshevik Revolution of 1917, which brought the Marxist–Leninists to power.

# V

**vanguard:** the leading position in a movement; one who occupies such a foremost position.

# W

**warlord:** a military commander who controls a region. In China, warlords controlled parts of the country from 1916 to 1928.

**windlass:** a hauling or lifting machine consisting of a drum wound with rope and turned by a crank.

**worldview:** a collection of beliefs about life and the universe held by a person or group.

# X

**Xiongnu:** a nomadic tribe that became a menace to the northern Chinese border for several centuries beginning in the second century B.C.

# Y

*yamen:* the office or home of a Chinese official.

# Index

# *Acknowledgments*

Grateful acknowledgment is made to the following authors, publishers, agents, and individuals for permission to reprint excerpts from copyrighted materials.

*Ancestors: 900 Years in the Life of A Chinese Family*, by Frank Ching. Copyright 1988 by Frank Ching. Reprinted with permission of William Morrow & Company.

*Almanac of China's Population*, edited by the Institute of Population Studies, 1991. Reprinted with permission of the Chinese Academy of Social Sciences, Beijing.

*The Analects of Confucius*, translated and annotated by Arthur Waley. Copyright 1938 by George Allen & Unwin, Ltd. Reprinted with permission of Simon and Schuster.

*The Awakening of China, 1793–1949*, by Roger Pellisier, translated by Martin Kieffer. English translation copyright 1967 by Martin Secker and Warburg, Ltd. Reprinted by permission of Reed International Books, Ltd.

*China and the West: Cultural Collision*, edited by Richard L. Walker. Reprinted by permission of Far Eastern Publications, Yale University Press.

*China's Examination Hell: The Civil Service Examinations of Imperial China*, by Ichisada Miyazaki, translated by Conrad Schirokauser. Copyright 1976 by John Weatherhill, Inc. Reprinted by permission of John Weatherhill, Inc.

*China's Foreign Relations since 1949*, by Alan Lawrance. Copyright 1975 by Alan Lawrance. Reprinted by permission of Routledge, Ltd.

*China's Response to the West: A Documentary Survey, 1839–1923*, by Ssü-yu Teng and John K. Fairbank. Copyright 1954, 1979 by the President and Fellows of Harvard College. Copyright 1982 by Ssü-yu Teng and John K. Fairbank. Reprinted by permission of Harvard University Press.

*Chinese Civilization: A Sourcebook*, by Patricia Buckley Ebrey; second edition revised and expanded. Copyright 1993 by Patricia Buckley Ebrey and 1981 by The Free Press. Reprinted with permission of The Free Press, a division of Simon and Schuster.

*Chinese Families in the Post-Mao Era*, edited by Deborah Davis and Stevan Harrell. Copyright 1993 by the Regents of the University of California. Reprinted by permission of the University of California Press.

*Chinese Footbinding: The History of a Curious Erotic Custom*, by Howard S. Levy. Copyright by Walton H. Rawls. Courtesy of Howard S. Levy and Walton H. Rawls.

*Chinese Lives: An Oral History of Contemporary China*, by Zhang Xinxin and Sang Ye. Translated and edited by W. J. F. Jenner and Delia Davin. Copyright 1987 by W. J. F. Jenner and Delia Davin. Reprinted by permission of Pantheon Books, a division of Random House.

*Comrade Editor: Letters to the People's Daily*. Selected and translated by Hugh Thomas. Copyright 1980 by Joint Publishing Co. Reprinted by permission of Joint Publishing Co.

*A Daughter of Han: The Autobiography of a Chinese Working Womaan*, by Ida Pruitt. Copyright 1945 by Yale University Press. Reprinted by permission of Yale University Press.

*The Death of Woman Wang*, by Jonathan D. Spence. Copyright 1978 by Jonathan D. Spence. Reprinted by permission of Viking Penguin, a division of Penguin Books USA, Inc.

*Fanshen: A Documentary of Revolution in a Chinese Village*, by William Hinton. Copyright 1966 by William Hinton. Reprinted by permission of the University of California Press.

*Fifty-Five Days of Terror: The Story of the Boxer Rebellion*, by Burt Hirschfeld. Copyright 1964 by Burt Hirschfeld. Reprinted by permission of Pinder Lane & Garon-Brooke Associates, Ltd.

*Folktales of China*, edited by Wolfram Eberhard. Copyright 1965 by Wolfram Eberhard. Reprinted by permission of the University of Chicago Press.

*Marriage Law and Policy in the Chinese People's Republic*, by M. J. Meijer, 1971. Reprinted by permission of Hong Kong University Press.

*Modern Drama from Communist China*, by Walter J. Meserve and Ruth I. Meserve. Copyright 1970 New York University Press. Reprinted by permission of Walter J. Meserve.

*The Opium War Through Chinese Eyes*, by Arthur Waley. Copyright 1958 by George Allen & Unwin, Ltd. Reprinted by permission of HarperCollins Publishers.

*Sources of Chinese Tradition*, Vol. 2, edited by William Theodore de Bary. Copyright 1964 by Columbia University Press. Reprinted by permission of Columbia University Press.

*Wild Swans*, by Jung Chang. Copyright 1991 by Globalflair, Ltd. Reprinted by permission of Simon & Schuster and HarperCollins Publishers.

Every effort has been made to contact the copyright holders of excerpts and photographs that appear in this book; where it has not been possible to do so, the authors apologize and ask you to contact the Curriculum Research & Development Group, University of Hawaii, 1776 University Avenue, Honolulu, Hawaii 96822.

CPSIA information can be obtained
at www.ICGtesting.com
Printed in the USA
BVHW070036271020
591757BV00006B/19